DEFEND
THE FAITH!

ROBERT M. HADDAD

Nihil Obstat: Rev. Peter Joseph, STD

Imprimatur: + Cardinal George Pell
Archbishop of Sydney

Date: 13th September, 2011

The *Nihil Obstat* and *Imprimatur* are a declaration that a book or pamphlet is considered to be free from doctrinal or moral error. It is not necessarily implied that those who have granted them agree with the contents, opinions or statements expressed.

Scripture quotes taken from the ***Revised Standard Version of the Bible (Second Catholic Edition)***, copyright © 2006 (Ignatius Press).

Extracts from ***The Faith of the Early Fathers,*** Rev. William A. Jurgens, copyright © 1970 by The Order of St Benedict, Inc., The Liturgical Press, Collegeville, Minnesota. Used with permission.

Extracts from ***The Roman Catechism***, issued by order of Pope St Pius V, 1566, reprinted by TAN Books and Publishers Inc., Rockford, Illinois 61105.

Extracts from English translation of ***Catechism of the Catholic Church*** for Australia copyright © June 1994 St Pauls/Libreria Editrice Vaticana. Used with permission.

Cover design: Parousia Media Pty Ltd, PO Box 59, Galston, NSW, 2159. (02) 8776-8778; www.parousiamedia.com

Published by: Parousia

© **Robert M. Haddad 2011.** All rights reserved. Extracts and copies of various parts or chapters of the series may be made in cases of 'fair dealing', viz., for the purpose of teaching, promoting and defending the Catholic Faith. All acknowledgments given to Robert M. Haddad.

ISBN: 978-0-9751571-6-9

Contents

Foreword	vii
Introduction	1
The Blessed Trinity	5
The Divinity of Jesus Christ	12
Original Sin	22
Justification and Salvation	30
The Meritorious Value of Works	41
Is there an Assurance of Salvation?	55
The Necessity of Baptism	70
Infant Baptism	82
Canon of the Bible	89
Sola Scriptura?	104
Bible Truth	115
The One True Church	130
Infallibility of the Church	139
St Peter and Papal Primacy	146
The Pope is Infallible	157
Was St Peter Ever in Rome?	165
Apostolic Succession	174
The Priesthood	186
The Real Presence	195
The Holy Sacrifice of the Mass	207
Your Sins Are Forgiven	218
Veneration of the BVM as "Mother of God"	228
Mary – The Immaculate Conception	242
Mary – Her Assumption and Coronation	252
The Perpetual Virginity of Mary	260
The Holy Rosary of the Blessed Virgin Mary	272
Guardian Angels	285
The Immortality of the Soul	291
The Invocation of Saints	302
Purgatory and Praying for the Dead	312
Indulgences	322
Hell is Eternal	330

Sunday Worship	338
Statues and Images	343
Relics	351
Celibacy of the Clergy	359
Call No Man Your Father	367
Fasting	372
The Sign of the Cross	378
The Rapture	383
The Antichrist	396
Crucifiction?	412
Answering Islam – Basic Objections	423
The Crusades	443
The Inquisition	453
Persecution	463
Jesuits!	472
The Index of Forbidden Books	482
Dawkins' Delusions	490

Appendices:

A. Ecumenical Councils	504
B. Doctors of the Church	504
C. Fathers of the Church	505
D. Popes	506
Further Reading	509
About the Author	512
Other Works by the Author	513

Dedication

To all those who strive to proclaim and defend the Catholic Faith in the face of an indifferent and hostile world.

Foreword

Apologetics is the art of providing a reasoned defense for one's beliefs. For Catholics, it is the 'business' of defending their faith against the many attacks launched against it today. All faithful Catholics should be both willing and able to defend their faith.

From the earliest days of Christianity, the Church as a whole and individual Christians have continuously been called upon to defend their claims regarding Jesus Christ, particularly his divinity and resurrection from the dead. Over the past two thousand years, there have never lacked enemies of the humble carpenter from Nazareth. Nor has there been a lack of defenders.

Unfortunately, apologetics fell upon hard times after the mid-1960s. This drop-off coincided with the collapse in effective catechesis, Mass attendance and vocations to priestly and religious life. Australia was not immune to this decline. Though renowned for producing some of the most effective apologists, in particular Frank Sheed, Australia likewise saw apologetics virtually disappear from the scene. If it continued to exist it was only in the hearts and minds of a few enthusiasts who continued to read 'old books.'

Providentially, apologetics in recent times has made a remarkable comeback in the English-speaking world. This revival has come out of the United States and is characterized by an explosion of new literature, dynamic speakers and exciting converts. This phenomenon is being closely watched and replicated in Australia.

Defend the Faith! is a prime example of some of the exciting things happening in Catholic apologetics in Australia. There are few introductory books that cover so many topics so thoroughly and persuasively, based strongly on Scripture, along with Church Fathers and formal Church documents. It is a must for those who wish to lay a solid foundation for defending their Catholic Faith. I could not recommend a better book to those beginning their adventure in apologetics.

Fr Peter Joseph STD
September 2011

Introduction

The word *apologetics* is derived from the Greek, *apologia*, which means to provide a "reasoned explanation." Apologetics as a branch of Catholic theology is therefore aimed at establishing and defending the reasonableness of the Catholic Faith. Specifically, it has a threefold aim: (i) to strengthen the faith of believers by illustrating that the articles of the Catholic Faith are in full harmony with reason; (ii) to persuade unbelievers, inquirers and those in good faith that the articles of the Catholic Faith are in full harmony with reason; (iii) to refute the arguments and objections of those who reject the Catholic Faith.

An apologist is strictly speaking a theologian. In defending the Catholic Faith, he draws his arguments principally from Sacred Scripture and Apostolic Tradition. Nevertheless, the apologist is free to utilize and develop arguments from philosophy and history. Divine revelation and natural reason are consequently combined to prove that God exists, that he has revealed himself in Jesus Christ, that Jesus established a visible Church on earth to teach truths infallibly, and that this Church is the Holy, Catholic, Apostolic and Roman Church.

Apologetics has been an integral part of the life of the Church since Apostolic times. Jesus himself was the first apologist, when after his resurrection, he instructed the two disciples on the way to Emmaus: "And beginning with Moses and all the prophets, he interpreted to them in all the Scriptures the things concerning himself" (Lk 24:27). St Luke in writing his Gospel did so with an apologetical purpose: "it seemed good to me also, having followed all things closely for some time past, to write an orderly account for you, most excellent Theophilus, that you may know the truth concerning the things of which you have been informed" (Lk 1:3-4). In fact, it can be argued that all four Gospels are apologetical in nature, having been written to show the faithful that their belief in Jesus Christ was well grounded, and to lead Jews and pagans to belief in Jesus.

St Paul was no less of an apologist. St Luke records that when in Rome "they came to him at his lodging in great numbers. And he expounded the matter to them from morning till evening, testifying to the kingdom of God and trying to convince them about Jesus both from the law of Moses and from the prophets" (Acts 28:23).

During the first centuries of the Church's history, the Christian religion was outlawed by the civil authorities of Rome and attacked by pagan apologists as atheistic, cannibalistic and sexually promiscuous. Christian apologists such as Aristides, St Justin Martyr and Athenagoras responded by showing that these accusations were no more than calumnies and that Rome had nothing to fear from toleration of the Christian religion.

The apologetical struggle against paganism was taken up in the late second and early third centuries AD by St Irenaeus of Lyons, Clement of Alexandria and Tertullian. They aimed their energies at exposing and refuting the plethora of mystery cults, Greek mythology and Gnostic heresies prevalent at the time. The first half of the third century was dominated by the character and works of Origen, who produced a monumental work against the teachings of Celsus, a pagan philosopher who attacked the supernatural nature of Christianity, the miracles of Jesus and the reliability of the Gospels.

The central figures that stood out as defenders of Christianity after its toleration by Constantine in AD 313 were Lactantius, Eusebius of Caesarea, St Augustine of Hippo and St Cyril of Alexandria. St Augustine, in particular, was continually engaged in apologetical contest against pagans and heretics, including the trenchant anti-Christian scholar and philosopher Porphyry of Tyre. His greatest work, *The City of God Against the Pagans*, took thirteen years to complete and was aimed at refuting allegations that the calamities befalling the Roman Empire at the time, such as the sack of Rome in AD 410, were due to the abandonment of the pagan gods. Breaking new ground, St Augustine went on to provide a Christian understanding of human history, as well as an outline of authentic civilization based on the teachings of Jesus. A few decades later St Cyril of Alexandria would provide a long refutation of Julian the Apostate's *Contra Galilaeos* written during a brief interlude of pagan resurgence.

With the rise of Islam, a new apologetical opponent entered the arena. Its challenge was met early on by St John Damascene in the eighth century and systematically dealt with by St Thomas Aquinas in the thirteenth century in his *Summa Contra Gentiles*, where the errors of

Introduction

the Muslim philosopher Averroës were given particular treatment. St Thomas was also active apologetically in meeting the resurgent challenge of Gnosticism as manifested in the Albigensian heresy.

The outbreak of the Protestant revolt in the sixteenth century gave rise to a new dimension in Catholic apologetics. St John Fisher and St Thomas More engaged themselves early in dispute against the Lutherans and other English heretics. The newly formed Jesuits became active in apologetical work throughout most of Europe, led by the example of St Peter Canisius. By the end of the sixteenth century, another Jesuit, St Robert Bellarmine, provided the Church with an arsenal to combat all the main Protestant heresies with his *Controversies of the Christian Faith against the Heretics of Our Time*. St Francis de Sales, through great courage and charity, would challenge the Calvinists in their very heartland of Switzerland and convert tens of thousands of them through his apologetical pamphlets and writings.

The rising tide of rationalism soon came to dominate intellectual life in the eighteenth and nineteenth centuries. Led by anti-Christian philosophers such as Rousseau and Voltaire, it asserted that there was no divine revelation, and that all that we know or need to know can be gauged from human reason rightly used. Hence, the teaching and sanctifying mission of Jesus and the Church has no relevance. In opposition to such, the First Vatican Council declared that the learning of all religious and moral truths necessary for the right ordering of human life is derived both from natural reason and divine revelation, and that in the present condition of humanity even naturally known truths cannot be known readily by all with firm certitude and complete accuracy.

The history of Catholic apologetics in the twentieth century was a chequered one. The first half of the century witnessed the creation and work of the Catholic Evidence Guild. Begun in England by Frank Sheed and Maisie Ward, it was to bear fruit on behalf of the Catholic Church throughout the English-speaking world for many decades. Unfortunately, after the Second Vatican Council, the word and idea of apologetics went the way of the dinosaurs for many, particularly those imbued with modernist notions of ecclesiology and universal salvation. Nevertheless, calls for its revival were heard, including one from a 1981 edition of *L'Osservatore Romano* under the headline *"Apologia for Apologetics."* Furthermore, since the mid-1980's a series of astonishing conversions of Protestant ministers and clergy to the Catholic Church in the United States has led to a dramatic revival of interest in apologetics, leading to the establishment of several strong and committed new organizations specializing in countering the aggressive work of the modern-day anti-Catholic.

Finally, the relentless rise of atheism within an increasingly secular Western world has given added urgency for apologetics in defense of the existence of God. The 'new atheism' has entered the popular mainstream through the works of notorious and aggressive atheists led by the likes of Richard Dawkins and Christopher Hitchens, to name the two most popular. These men and their respective works receive enormous publicity in the media and have sold in the millions, while theistic responses receive almost no media attention and are purchased mostly by the already converted. Characterized by a scorn and ridicule of all things religious, the 'new atheism' threatens to dismantle all traditional institutions previously identified with Western Christian civilization. The family, in particular, is becoming an endangered species. At its worst, the 'new atheism' is intolerant, dictatorial and radically fundamentalist in its determination to rid the world of religion. There is much to fear from this rising specter, but much to gain from opposing it. The very survival of Christianity and the future for our children is ultimately at stake.

The Blessed Trinity

Objection: *"The doctrine of the Trinity is not found in the Bible. It is really a disguised form of pagan polytheism — the worship of three gods in one!"*

The Blessed Trinity is God, one and undivided, in three distinct divine Persons. It is the most fundamental doctrine of Christianity. Unaided human reason could never have known of the Blessed Trinity. It is a strict supernatural mystery only revealed by Jesus Christ himself.

Early Christian Fathers of the West grappled with trying to understand the Blessed Trinity through the notion of the "mental word" in God. The argument runs as follows: as humans, we know and love ourselves according to the idea we have of ourselves in our minds, but this idea is limited and imperfect. God also knows and loves himself in the idea he has of himself. But God's idea of himself is utterly unlike any human idea. His knowledge of himself is infinite and perfect. Furthermore, as there are no parts in God, this idea, or "mental word," is not separate from God and, therefore, is divine in essence.

Being divine, it follows that the mental word is eternal, and therefore uncreated. This mental word St John calls "the Word," or the Second Person of the Blessed Trinity. God the Father knows himself in the Word and the Word knows God the Father. This mutual knowledge brings forth mutual love. This mutual love the New Testament calls the Holy Spirit, or the Third Person of the Blessed Trinity.

Those who claim to be Christian yet attack the doctrine of the Blessed Trinity initially base their objections on the fact that the word "Trinity" is not found in the Scriptures, and conclude that it is therefore an unscriptural invention. According to groups such as the Jehovah's Witnesses, early Christian theologians slowly incorporated the doctrine of the Trinity from paganism, and being unable to adequately explain it cloaked it in the term "mystery":

Jehovah God is one, and Jesus Christ is his creature Son, and the holy spirit is Jehovah's active force, and therefore the doctrine of a trinity is unchristian and really of pagan origin.[1]

In the view of the Witnesses, the Council of Nicaea formally accepted the doctrine of the Trinity in AD 325. Of course, the Jehovah's Witnesses claim that the originator of the 'pagan' doctrine of the Trinity is Satan himself:

> The plain truth is that this is another of Satan's attempts to keep God-fearing persons from learning the truth of Jehovah and his Son, Christ Jesus. No, there is no trinity.[2]

The fact that the doctrine of the Trinity is a mystery does not of itself render it unchristian or an absurdity. We can in this life know many things about the Trinity through the lights of faith and reason, yet we can never hope to fully understand it as it touches upon the very nature of God himself: "For now we see in a mirror dimly, but then face to face" (1 Cor. 13:12). The opponents of the Trinity themselves create absurdity and confuse the debate by often misrepresenting its meaning, for example, by stating that it is "three gods in one person" or "three persons in one."

As for the word "Trinity," it simply means "threefold." "Trinity" does not appear in the Scriptures, nevertheless, the doctrine of the Trinity certainly does. The first recorded use of the word "Trinity" in relation to God was by St Theophilus of Antioch (c. AD 180). He speaks of "the Trinity (*Trias* – τριας): God, his Word, and his Wisdom." Most probably, the word Trinity was in use even before this time, and soon after it appears in the West in the Latin form *Trinitas*.

The doctrine of the Trinity was unknown to the Jews during Old Testament times, and so the clearest scriptural evidence for it is found in the New Testament. However, there are several Old Testament verses where the Trinity looms implicitly as a mystery that

---

[1] *Let Your Name be Sanctified*, p. 300. Taken from John Francis Coffey, *The Gospel According to the Jehovah's Witnesses*, The Polding Press, Melbourne, 1979, p. 18.

[2] *The Word – Who is He? According to John*, p. 7, quoted by J. F. Coffey, p. 18.

retrospectively becomes apparent in the light of Jesus' subsequent revelation. For example, the use of the word "us" in the following verses implies the plurality of Persons in the Godhead:

"*Then God said, 'Let us make man in our image, after our likeness' ... So God created man in his own image, in the image of God he created him ...*" (Gen. 1:26-27).

"*Then the Lord God said, 'Behold, the man has become like one of us, knowing good and evil'*" (Gen. 3:22).

"*Come, let us go down, and confuse their language ...*" (Gen.11:7).

From the very beginning of Christianity, this plurality of Persons in God has been evident:

"*And the angel said to her, 'The Holy Spirit will come upon you, and the power of the Most High will overshadow you; therefore the child to be born will be called holy, the Son of God'*" (Lk 1:34-35).

The New Testament supplies the specific names of the trinity of Persons in God in Jesus' great commission to his disciples at the end of Matthew's Gospel:

"*Go therefore and make disciples of all nations, baptizing them in the name of the Father and of the Son and of the Holy Spirit, teaching them to observe all that I have commanded you; and behold, I am with you always, to the close of the age*" (Mt 28:19-20).

In this verse the Father, Son and Holy Spirit are mentioned distinctly but under the singular term "name" (ὄνομα). They are therefore distinct Persons but not separate beings or gods. Their grouping together also denotes their equality.

The commencement of Jesus' public ministry provided another reference to the Trinity:

"And when he came up out of the water, immediately he saw the heavens opened and the Spirit descending upon him like a dove; and a voice came from heaven, 'You are my beloved Son; with you I am well pleased'" (Mk 1:10-11).

This verse clearly reveals the First and Second Persons of the Trinity, Jesus coming out of the water and his Father's voice from heaven. The Holy Spirit, the Third Person, is revealed as a dove, descending from heaven upon Jesus.

Jesus as the Second Person of the Trinity is equal to the Father:

"Behold, a virgin shall conceive and bear a son, and his name shall be called Emmanuel, which means, God with us ..." (Mt 1:23).

"In the beginning was the Word, and the Word was with God, and the Word was God" (Jn 1:1).

"I and the Father are one" (Jn 10:30).

"... the Father is in me and I am in the Father" (Jn 10:38).

"He who has seen me has seen the Father" (Jn 14:9).

The Jews, when hearing these words of Jesus, understood their significance and for this reason sought to stone him to death, "because you, being a man, make yourself God" (Jn 10:33).

The Holy Spirit, who proceeds from the Father and the Son as the Third Person of the Trinity, will be a living teacher of truth:

"And I will ask the Father, and he will give you another Counselor" (Jn 14:16).

"... the Holy Spirit, whom the Father will send in my name, he will teach you all things" (Jn 14:26).

"When the Spirit of truth comes, he will guide you into all the truth; for he will not speak on his own authority, but whatever he hears he will speak, and he will declare to you the things that are to come" (Jn 16:13).

Rather than being simply an impersonal "active force," the Holy Spirit is a personal guide, directing the Church in its decisions:

"For it has seemed good to the Holy Spirit and to us to lay upon you no greater burden than these necessary things" (Acts 15:28).

To sin against the Holy Spirit is to sin against God:

"... why has Satan filled your heart to lie to the Holy Spirit and to keep back part of the proceeds of the land? ... You have not lied to men but to God" (Acts 5:3-4).

Further evidence of the Holy Spirit's distinct personality is found in the following verses:

"Likewise the Spirit helps us in our weakness; for we do not know how to pray as we ought, but the Spirit himself intercedes for us with sighs too deep for words" (Rom. 8:26).

"And do not grieve the Holy Spirit of God, in whom you were sealed for the day of redemption" (Eph. 4:30).

"How much worse punishment do you think will be deserved by the man who has spurned the Son of God, and profaned the blood of the covenant by which he was sanctified, and outraged the Spirit of grace?" (Heb. 10:29).

"He who has an ear, let him hear what the Spirit says to the churches" (Rev. 2:7).

The *Athanasian Creed* (so-called after St Athanasius, the great fourth century opponent of Arianism) encapsulates perfectly the Catholic expression of the doctrine of the Trinity:

> The Christian faith is this: That we worship one God in Trinity, and the Trinity in unity; neither confounding the Persons, nor dividing the substance; for there is one Person of the Father, another of the Son, and another of the Holy Spirit. But the Godhead of the Father, and of the Son, and of the Holy Spirit, is all one; the glory equal; and the majesty co-eternal.

The Fathers

Pope St Clement of Rome, *Letter to the Corinthians* **46, 6 (c. AD 98)**
"Do we not have one God, one Christ, and one Spirit of Grace poured out upon us? And is there not one calling in Christ?"

***The Martyrdom of St Polycarp* 14, 3 (c. AD 155-157)**
"In this way and for all things I do praise you, I do bless you, I do glorify you through the eternal and heavenly High Priest Jesus Christ, your beloved child: through whom be glory to you with him and with the Holy Spirit, both now and through ages yet to come. Amen."

St Theophilus of Antioch, *To Autolycus* **2, 15 (AD 181)**
"The three days before the luminaries were created are types of the Trinity: God, his Word, and his Wisdom."

St Irenaeus of Lyons, *Against Heresies* **2, 28, 6 (c. AD 180)**
"If any one, therefore says to us, 'How then was the Son produced by the Father?' we reply to him, that no man understands that production, or generation, or calling, or revelation, or by whatever name one may describe his generation, which is in fact altogether indescribable. Neither Valentinus, nor Marcion, nor Saturninus, nor Basilides, nor angels, nor archangels, nor principalities, nor powers (possess this knowledge), but the Father only who begat, and the Son who was begotten."

St Ambrose of Milan, *Hexameron* **6, 7, 40 (post AD 389)**
"But let us consider the course of our own creation. He says: 'Let Us make man to our image and to our likeness.' Who says this? Is it not God, who made you? ... To whom does he say it? Certainly not to himself, for he does not say 'Let Me make' but 'Let Us make.' Nor to the Angels, for they are ministers; and servants can have no partnership in the operation of the master, nor works with their author. It is the Son to whom he speaks, even if the Jews will not have it and the Arians fight against it ..."

St Augustine of Hippo, *The Trinity* Bk 7, Ch. 4 (inter AD 400-416)
"For that which must be understood of persons according to our usage, this is to be understood of hypostases according to the Greek usage; for they say three hypostases, one essence, in the same way as we say three persons, one essence or substance."

The Roman Catechism (1566)

Pt. I, Ch. II: Since nowhere is a too curious inquiry more dangerous, or error more fatal, than in the knowledge and exposition of this, the most profound and difficult of mysteries ...
... We should be satisfied with the assurance and certitude which faith gives us that we have been taught these truths by God himself, to doubt whose word is the extreme of folly and misery. He has said: *Teach ye all nations, baptizing them in the name of the Father, and of the Son, and of the Holy Ghost*; and again, *there are three who give testimony in heaven, the Father, the Word, and the Holy Ghost; and these three are one.*

Catechism of the Catholic Church (1992)

No. 237: The Trinity is a mystery of faith in the strict sense, one of the mysteries that are hidden in God, which can never be known unless they are revealed by God. To be sure, God has left traces of his Trinitarian being in his work of creation and in his Revelation throughout the Old Testament. But his inmost Being as Holy Trinity is a mystery that is inaccessible to reason alone or even to Israel's faith before the Incarnation of God's Son and the sending of the Holy Spirit.

The Divinity of Jesus Christ

Objection: *"Jesus Christ was no doubt the Son of God, but not God the Son!"*

The modern-day denial of Jesus' divinity has its roots in the Christological controversies of the fourth and fifth centuries AD. Of the many heresies that have beset the Church, one of the most devastating was *Arianism*. During the mid-third century, Lucian of Antioch began teaching the inferiority and subordination of the Son to the Father. Decades later, this teaching was picked up and developed by Arius of Alexandria. Focusing, firstly, on human fatherhood, Arius taught that as a father always pre-dates his son there is a time when the son was not. Applying this to the Father and the Word, Arius coined the phrase, "There was a time once when the Word was not." Therefore, Jesus was not co-eternal and not the same substance as the Father. Rather, he was only a creature and son of God by virtue of being "like in substance" to the Father.

Arianism was to sweep across the Christian world at a time when the Church had just been freed from official Roman persecution. The Arian whirlwind caught all virtually by surprise. As St Jerome declared, "The world awoke and found itself Arian." The number of bishops who resisted was only a handful. One of them was St Athanasius of Alexandria.

With Arianism causing contention and strife throughout the Empire, the Emperor Constantine agreed to resolve the crisis by summoning a general council of bishops to meet at Nicaea commencing 20 May, AD 325. At this Council, the bishops condemned Arianism and proclaimed Jesus as *homo-ousios* (consubstantial), that is, "as the same substance" as the Father.

Though condemned, Arianism lingered on for centuries afterwards. Arius himself died an impious death in AD 336 and St Athanasius continued the struggle in the face of multiple exiles and excommunications until his death in AD 373. Nevertheless, the Church and the world had been preserved from a gross heresy and recovered to meet the challenge of another and more aggressive threat to Jesus' divinity – Islam.

Modern-day deniers of Jesus' divinity such as the Jehovah's Witnesses claim an affinity with Arius. They assert that he was one example of the earlier Witnesses who have been "on earth in every period of human history." Such a claim, however, is scarcely accurate and borders on the fanciful. Arius taught that Jesus was a semi-divinized man, while the Jehovah's Witnesses hold that he is actually the Archangel Michael in human form. This is a teaching they rarely reveal early on to prospective converts. Before coming into the world clothed in human flesh, they say Jesus had the singular privilege of sharing in the creation of all other creatures with Jehovah. In fact, Jesus is the only creature directly created by Jehovah.

Numerous passages in Scripture provide evidence of Jesus' divinity:

"... For to us a child is born, to us a son is given; and the government will be upon his shoulder, and his name will be called 'Wonderful Counselor, Mighty God, Everlasting Father, Prince of Peace'" (Is. 9:6).

The term "mighty God" in this passage is derived from the Hebrew *El Gibbor* which literally means "God the mighty." The Witnesses try to get around this verse by claiming that it speaks of Jesus only as "mighty God" and not as "Almighty God," which is the term usually given to Jehovah. Jesus is not God in the supreme sense, but only a god in the same sense the angels were called gods for their superhuman powers (Job 1:6). However, the alleged distinction between "mighty God" and "Almighty God" does not always hold, for God himself is called mighty on many occasions (Gen. 49:24; Ps. 50:1; Ps. 132:2, 5; Is. 10:21; Jer. 32:18).

"In the beginning was the Word, and the Word was with God, and the Word was God ... And the Word was made flesh and dwelt amongst us" (Jn 1:1-14).

The Divinity of Jesus Christ

The Witnesses have a great preoccupation with this passage, devoting four pages of footnotes in their *New World Translation* of the Bible to explain it away. They render the last part of John 1:1 to read "and the Word was *a god*." Again, the Witnesses try to argue that Jesus was only "*a god*" in the same sense mentioned above. However, as the original Greek has the definite article (*ho* – ὁ – the) preceding the word Word (*Logos*) and no article preceding God (*Theos*), one would naturally translate the verse as "and the Word was God." The Gospel of John is devoted to the divinity of Jesus. If the Apostle meant to say in the prologue that Jesus is only "a god" – one god among many – he would destroy the purpose of the entire Gospel that follows.

"*Truly, truly, I say to you, before Abraham was, I am*" (Jn 8:58).

Scholars have always understood Jesus' use of "*I am*" (ἐγώ εἰμί) as a claim to divinity, identifying himself with the God of Moses: "*I am who am.*" The implication is obvious – Jesus pre-exists all the Patriarchs and the Prophets, even all humanity itself. He belongs to a different order of being, the eternal self-existence of God. For the Witnesses, as Jesus simply said in John 8:58 "*I am*" and not "*I am who am,*" he was only intending to say "I existed before Abraham was born." They accept Jesus' pre-existence but as the "first-born of all creatures" only, not as God. However, "*I am*" by itself is often used in the Old Testament to refer to God, for example, in Is. 43:25, 45:18 & 48:12. This is how the Jews understood him, which is why they "took up stones to throw at him" (8:59).

"*I and the Father are one*" (Jn 10:30).

Christianity has always understood these words of Jesus to refer to the unity of being that exists between the Father and the Son. For the Witnesses, these words simply indicate the "moral unity of will, purpose and activity" existing between Jehovah God and his first-born creature. Such an assertion, however, does not hold weight in light of the Greek word used for "one," namely *hen* (ἕν), which is neuter and means "one thing" or "one being" – "I and the Father are *one being.*" Again, this is how the Jews understood him, taking up stones once more to stone him ... "because you, being a man, make yourself God" (10:33).

In this same chapter, we read the following passage:

"Jesus answered them, 'Is it not written in your law, I said, you are gods? If he called them gods to whom the word of God came (and scripture cannot be nullified), do you say of him whom the Father consecrated and sent into the world, You are blaspheming, because I said, I am the Son of God?'" (Jn 10:34-36).

The Witnesses often seize upon this verse and claim that Jesus is comparing himself to the judges of the Old Testament in the following sense: If they could be given the title of "gods" (Ps. 82:1-6, 8) despite their injustice, then how much more did he deserve to be called "Son of God" due to his righteousness. There is an argument here from the lesser to the greater, but it runs more like this: if the judges were called "gods" because they were vehicles of the word of God, how much more permissible is it then to call him who is the actual Word of God, "Son of God"?

"My Lord and my God" (Jn 20:28).

These clear and unequivocal words of St Thomas the Apostle pose the greatest difficulty for the Witnesses. One argument of theirs is that St Thomas was directing his words as an exclamation of astonishment to God rather than to Jesus. Furthermore, they state that even if they were directed to Jesus, St Thomas' words have to be "harmonized with the rest of the Scriptures," meaning re-interpreted according to the Witnesses' pre-conceived doctrines.

The following passages also speak of Jesus' divinity:

"Therefore the Lord himself will give you a sign. 'Behold, a young woman shall conceive and bear a son, and shall call his name Immanuel'" (Is. 7:14).

"... to them belong the patriarchs, and of their race, according to the flesh, is the Christ, who is God over all, blessed for ever. Amen" (Rom. 9:5).

"Have this mind among yourselves, which was in Christ Jesus, who, though he was in the form of God, did not regard equality with God a thing to be grasped" (Phil. 2:5-6).

"For in him the whole fullness of deity dwells bodily" (Col. 2:9).

"But of the Son he says, 'Your throne, O God, is for ever and ever, and the righteous scepter is the scepter of your kingdom'" (Heb. 1:8).

Jehovah's Witnesses accept the term "Son of God" for Jesus but alter its meaning to suit their theology. Son of God becomes "Son by adoption"; "Only Son" becomes "only created Son." No such qualifiers are actually used in reference to Jesus' Sonship in the New Testament. On the contrary, Christians are urged to acknowledge the true Sonship of Jesus: "Whoever confesses that Jesus is the Son of God, God abides in him, and he in God" (1 Jn 4:15). Jesus constantly applied to himself the supreme title of "Son of God," and accepted it from his followers without question:

St Peter: *"You are the Christ, the Son of the living God"* (Mt 16:16).

The High Priest: *"'I adjure you by the living God, tell us if you are the Christ, the Son of God.' Jesus said to him, 'You have said so'"* (Mt 26:63-64).

John the Baptist: *"Behold, the Lamb of God, who takes away the sin of the world! ... And I have seen and have born witness that this is the Son of God"* (Jn 1:29-34).

St Martha: *"Yes, Lord, I believe that you are the Christ, the Son of God, he who is coming into the world"* (Jn 11:27).

Not only did Jesus take the title of Son of God, but also he assumed all the functions, acts, and the necessary and supreme attributes of God:

"... the Father loves the Son, and has given all things in his hands" (Jn 3:35).

"... whatever the Father does, the Son does likewise" (Jn 5:19).

"If I am not doing the works of my Father, then do not believe me; but if I do them, even though you do not believe me, believe the works, that you may know and understand that the Father is in me and I am in the Father" (Jn 10:37-38).

"Let not your hearts be troubled; believe in God, believe also in me" (Jn 14:1).

"'I am the way, and the truth, and the life; no one comes to the Father but by me. If you had known me, you would have known my Father also; henceforth you know him and have seen him.' Philip said to him, 'Lord, show us the Father, and we shall be satisfied.' Jesus said to him, 'Have I been with you so long, and you do not know me, Philip? He who has seen me has seen the Father ... Do you not believe that I am in the Father and the Father is in me?'" (Jn 14:6-10).

"Whatever you ask in my name, I will do it, that the Father may be glorified in the Son; if you ask anything in my name, I will do it" (Jn 14:13-14).

"If a man loves me, he will keep my word, and my Father will love him, and we will come to him and make our home with him" (Jn 14:23).

"All that the Father has is mine" (Jn 16:15).

The following points shed more light on the divine attributes of Jesus:

- Yahweh was called "the God of glory" (Ps. 29:3); the resurrected Jesus is "Lord of glory" (1 Cor. 2:8).
- God is "Lord of Lords" (Deut. 10:17); Jesus is "Lord of Lords" (Rev. 17:14).
- God is the "only savior" (Is. 43:11); Jesus is "savior" (Lk 2:11).
- God is the "fountain of living water" (Jer. 17:13); Jesus is the "spring of water welling up to eternal life" (Jn 4:14).

- The Lord's thoughts cannot be directed (Is. 40:13); so too, no one can instruct the mind of Jesus (1 Cor. 2:16).
- The Lord God owns earth and all its fullness (Ps. 24:1); likewise does the Lord Jesus (1 Cor. 10:26).
- God never changes (Ps. 102:26-27); Jesus is the "same yesterday and today and for ever" (Heb. 13:8).
- God is "the light" (Ps. 27:1); Jesus is "the light of the world" (Jn 8:12).
- God is the searcher of hearts and minds (Jer. 17:10); Jesus is he who searches mind and heart (Rev. 2:23).
- God will come with all the holy ones (Zech. 14:5); Jesus will come with all the saints (1 Thess. 3:13).

Furthermore, Jesus is Lord of the Sabbath (Mt 12:8), is eternal (Heb. 1:10), is omniscient (Lk 6:8), and is the Alpha and Omega (Rev. 1:17).

While others worked miracles in the name of God, Jesus performed miracles as Supreme Master:

"Little girl, I say to you, arise" (Mk 5:41).

"Young man, I say to you, arise" (Lk 7:14).

"Lazarus, come out" (Jn 11:43).

As God, he forgives sins:

"But that you may know that the Son of man has authority on earth to forgive sins ... Rise, take up your bed and go home" (Mt 9:6).

And in the case of St Mary Magdalene, he forgives all her sins against God as a debt contracted towards himself.

Jesus also declared that he would rise again by his own power:

"Destroy this temple, and in three days I will raise it up" (Jn 2:19).

"No one takes it from me, but I lay it down of my own accord. I have power to lay it down, and I have power to take it up again" (Jn 10:18).

Final objections against the divinity of Jesus are based on John 14:28 and Col. 1:15-16. These two verses respectively say, "the Father is greater than I"; "the first-born of all creation." Together, they imply that Jesus is only a creature and inferior to the Father. With respect to John 14:28, some early Christian writers understood the text in the sense that as man, but not as God, Jesus is inferior to the Father. It could also mean that the Father is greater than the Son simply for having sent the Son into the world. This is gathered from the fact that the Greek word used here for "greater" – *meizon* (μείζων) – is a term normally used to denote comparisons of position rather than quality or nature. So, some other early Fathers said the phrase "greater than I" means "my origin" – since the Son has his origin in the Father. Reading John 13:1-3 together with John 14:28, it becomes evident that this is a reasonable interpretation in the context.

As for "the first-born of all creation," St Paul was only meaning to point out the pre-eminence of Jesus over all creation. St Paul tells us in the same verse that in Jesus *"all things* were created through him and for him" (v.16) – he does not say "all *other things."* Furthermore, by calling Jesus the "image of the invisible God" in the sentence immediately previous (v.15), St Paul is calling to mind Jesus' essential likeness to God and hence his divine nature.

The Fathers

St Ignatius of Antioch, *Letter to the Romans* Address (c. AD 110)
"Ignatius, also called Theophorus, to the Church that has found mercy in the greatness of the Most High Father and in Jesus Christ, his only Son: to the Church beloved and enlightened after the love of Jesus Christ, our God, by the will of him that has willed everything which is: to the Church also which holds the presidency in the place of the country of the Romans ... To those who are united in flesh and in spirit by every commandment of his, who are filled with the grace of God

without wavering, and who are filtered clear of every foreign stain, I wish an unalloyed joy in Jesus Christ, our God."

St Melito of Sardes, *Fragment in Anastasius of Sinai* 13 (c. AD 177)
"The activities of Christ after his Baptism, and especially his miracles, gave indication and assurance to the world of the Deity hidden in his flesh. Being God and likewise perfect man, he gave positive indications of his two natures: of his Deity, by the miracles during the three years following after his Baptism; of his humanity, in the thirty years which came before his Baptism, during which, by reason of his condition according to the flesh, he concealed the signs of his Deity, although he was the true God existing before the ages."

St Irenaeus of Lyons, *Against Heresies* 3, 19, 1 (c. AD 180)
"Nevertheless, what cannot be said of anyone else who ever lived, that he is himself in his own right God and Lord and Eternal King and Only-begotten and Incarnate Word, proclaimed as such by all the Prophets and by the Apostles and by the Spirit himself, may be seen by all who have attained to even a small portion of the truth. The Scriptures would not have borne witness to these things concerning him, if, like everyone else, he were mere man."

Clement of Alexandria, *Exhortation to the Greeks* 1, 7, 1 (ante AD 200)
"This Word, then, the Christ, the cause of both our being at first (for he was in God) and of our well-being, this very Word has now appeared as man, he alone being both, both God and man – the Author of all blessings to us; by whom we, being taught to live well, are sent on our way to life eternal."

St Athanasius, *Letter Concerning the Decrees of the Council of Nicaea* 20 (c. AD 350-351)
"The generation of the Son from the Father is otherwise than that which accords with the nature of men; and he is not only like, but is in fact inseparable from the substance of the Father. He and the Father are indeed one, as he did say himself; and the Word is ever in the Father and the Father in the Word, as is the way of radiance in relation

to light. The term itself indicates this; and the Council, so understanding the matter, did well, therefore, when it wrote *homoousios* [consubstantial], so that it might defeat the perverseness of the heretics, while proclaiming that the Word is other than created things."

The Roman Catechism (1566)

Pt. I, Ch. III: "Our Lord" ... this name applies to both natures, rightly is he to be called our Lord. For as he, as well as the Father, is the eternal God, so is he Lord of all things equally with the Father; and as he and the Father are not the one, one God, and the other, another God, but one and the same God, so likewise he and the Father are not the one, one Lord, and the other, another Lord.

Catechism of the Catholic Church (1992)

No. 461: Taking up St John's expression, "The Word became flesh," the Church calls "Incarnation" the fact that the Son of God assumed a human nature in order to accomplish our salvation in it. In a hymn cited by St Paul, the Church sings the mystery of the Incarnation:

> Have this mind among yourselves, which is yours in Christ Jesus, who, though he was in the form of God, did not count equality with God a thing to be grasped, but emptied himself, taking the form of a servant, being born in the likeness of men. And being found in human form he humbled himself and became obedient unto death, even death on a cross.

Original Sin

Objection: *"How can any reasonable person accept the Catholic doctrine of original sin? Why should we be punished for the alleged sins of others committed so long ago?"*

The state of original sin is the consequence of the sin of our first parents, Adam and Eve. This sin involved their disobedience, through pride, in eating of the fruit of the Tree of Knowledge of Good and Evil located in the Garden of Eden (Gen. 3:6).

Adam and Eve were endowed with various supernatural and preternatural gifts. By definition, a gift is something freely given that is not owed. The supernatural gifts were given by God to raise man above his nature to share in the divine life, to know and serve God far beyond his natural capacities, and to behold God in the Beatific Vision in the next world. They included sanctifying grace, the supernatural theological virtues of faith, hope and charity, the supernatural infused moral virtues of prudence, justice, fortitude and temperance, and the seven gifts of the Holy Spirit. Concomitant with sanctifying grace is Uncreated Grace, or the indwelling of the Blessed Trinity (Jn 14:23). The preternatural gifts were given by God to perfect man as man, not to elevate him above his nature. These gifts included immortality, impassibility (freedom from suffering), integrity (freedom from disordered passions), and infused knowledge. Through natural generation, all these gifts were to be transmitted to the whole human race. By their disobedience, Adam and Eve lost them for themselves and for all future generations.

The loss of sanctifying grace is the greatest consequence of Adam's sin. It carried with it the privation of the supernatural destiny God willed for humanity, namely, heaven. Man was also expelled from the Garden of Eden and became subject to pain, sickness, suffering and death. In addition, our natural powers were 'wounded' – ignorance in the intellect, malice in the will, concupiscence in the concupiscible appetite, and debility in the irascible appetite. Pain and sorrow in childbirth, together with subjection to the lust of men, were to be the specific lot of women. The natural elements, plants and animals, were no longer subject to man and a curse came upon the earth, necessitating sweat and hard labor (Gen. 3:16-24).

Many passages of Scripture testify to the reality of original sin:

"Behold, I was brought forth in iniquity, and in sin did my mother conceive me" (Ps. 51:5).

"Therefore as sin came into the world through one man and death through sin, and so death spread to all men because all men sinned – sin indeed was in the world before the law was given, but sin is not counted where there is no law. Yet death reigned from Adam to Moses, even over those whose sins were not like the transgression of Adam, who was a type of the one who was to come. But the free gift is not like the trespass. For if many died through one man's trespass, much more have the grace of God and the free gift in the grace of that one man Jesus Christ abounded for many. And the free gift is not like the effect of that one man's sin. For the judgment following one trespass brought condemnation, but the free gift following many trespasses brings justification. If, because of one man's trespass, death reigned through that one man, much more will those who receive the abundance of grace and the free gift of righteousness reign in life through the one man Jesus Christ. Then as one man's trespass led to condemnation for all men, so one man's act of righteousness leads to acquittal and life for all men. For as by one man's disobedience many were made sinners, so by one man's obedience many will be made righteous" (Rom. 5:12-19).

"For as by a man came death, and by a man has come also the resurrection of the dead. For as in Adam all die, so also in Christ shall all be made alive" (1 Cor. 15:21-22).

"Among these we all once lived in the passions of our flesh, following the desires of body and mind, and so we were by nature children of wrath, like the rest of mankind" (Eph. 2:3).

Throughout history there have been several significant heresies that have either denied the existence or distorted the consequences of original sin. The first of these was Pelagianism. Founded by a British monk named Pelagius (+AD 418), Pelagianism denied the supernatural elevation of humanity by asserting that Adam and Eve were created only in a natural state without sanctifying grace. Consequently, the Fall had no effect on them and their children by way of loss of grace, the only effect of original sin on others was by way of setting bad example. Hence, sin was not contracted through natural generation but was learnt from the bad example of others. It followed, further, that the children of Adam were born naturally good and were in no need of a Redeemer. Jesus' act of redemption was thus reduced to providing lofty teaching and virtuous example, while forgiveness of sin through faith meant forgiveness from punishment, not renewal in grace. If the children of Adam kept good company and directed their wills and ordinary powers to live sinless and holy lives, they could achieve eternal beatitude through their own natural efforts. This many had done, not only since Jesus, but also before. Pelagianism thus descended to pure naturalism, and was an unmistakable reproduction of the Stoic ideal of virtue.

Pelagius' errors found a partial vacuum in which to disseminate, as the Church, absorbed by the controversies concerning the Incarnation, had not developed in detail the doctrines concerning humanity's fall, renewal, grace and freewill. Though meeting sporadic opposition in Rome, Carthage and in the East, it was St Augustine of Hippo as the 'Doctor of Grace' who rose to combat Pelagianism with his powerful pen: "They (Pelagians) contend that in this life there are or have been righteous men having no sin at all. By this presumption they most clearly contradict the Lord's Prayer, in which all the members of Christ cry aloud with true heart these words to be said each day: 'Forgive us our debts.'"[1] For the self-confident Pelagian, the Lord's Prayer served only as a profession of humility, not a statement of fact.

St Augustine drew on the parable of the vine and the branches (Jn 15:1) to strike at Pelagianism and expose it as a novelty contrary to the teachings of Jesus. Only when the vital union between Jesus (the vine) and his members (the branches) is established is it possible to bring forth supernatural fruit, for "apart from me you can do nothing" (Jn 15:5). St Augustine also presented this particular thought: "Could we bring together here in living form all the saints of both sexes and question them whether they were without sin, would they not exclaim

---

[1] *Against Two Letters of the Pelagians* 4, 10, 27 (AD 420).

unanimously, 'If we say that we have no sin, we deceive ourselves, and the truth is not in us'?"[2] Before all the world St Augustine attested that "Such is the Pelagian heresy, not ancient, but having sprung up a short time ago."[3]

Appealing to Pope Zosimus, Pelagius received an opportunity to defend his teachings before a Council. On 1 May 418 the Council of Carthage formally condemned Pelagius and defined these doctrines against his errors:

(i) That death, in Adam, is the result of sin.
(ii) That infants require baptism due to their contracting original sin as children of Adam.
(iii) That grace is needed both to know and obey God's commandments.
(iv) That without grace it is impossible to perform good works.

The Council of Trent more than a thousand years later would answer the proud assertions of Pelagianism in more precise language:

> If any one shall say that a man once justified ... can throughout his life, avoid all sins, even venial, except by a special privilege of God, as the Church believes of the Blessed Virgin Mary, let him be anathema.[4]

While Pelagius denied the supernatural elevation of man, Martin Luther and John Calvin in the sixteenth century went to the opposite extreme by asserting that grace was an essential part of human nature, not super-added to it by way of gratuitous elevation. Hence, the loss of grace caused by the Fall had the effect of depriving man of an essential, not a gratuitous part, of his nature, leaving it *totally depraved*. Luther's and Calvin's total depravity consists of more than simply the 'wounding' of man, and entails the following more far-reaching effects:

---

[2] *On Nature and Grace* 36 (AD 415); cf. 1 John 1:8.
[3] *Grace and Free Choice* 6 (AD 426).
[4] *Decree on Justification*, Canon 23, 13 January, 1547.

(i) The destruction of the human intellect to the point of rendering man by himself incapable of achieving knowledge of religious truth.
(ii) The enslavement of the will, reducing it to merely a passive agent, incapable of actively cooperating with grace, rejecting the inspirations of God or the temptations of the devil.
(iii) The total vitiation of the life of grace, leaving humanity incapable of performing any morally good actions (in fact, all human actions are at least venially sinful).
(iv) The inability of grace to intrinsically regenerate the human soul, grace being not a reality infused by God into the soul but simply God's good will towards it. Justification is reduced to a juridical act of God whereby he mystically "cloaks" the Christian in the merits of Christ (*Justitia Christi extra nos* – the Justice of Christ outside us).

In response to Luther and Calvin, the Council of Trent asserted that in justification an actual and real regeneration of the soul takes place, removing both original and actual sin through the infusion of sanctifying grace by the sacraments of Baptism and Penance:

> If anyone denies that, by the grace of our Lord Jesus Christ, which is conferred in baptism, the guilt of original sin is remitted; or even asserts that the whole of that which has the true and proper nature of sin is not taken away; but says that it is only canceled, or not imputed; let him be anathema.[5]

The Council of Trent also restated the Church's traditional teaching on original sin:

> If anyone does not confess that the first man, Adam, when he had transgressed the commandment of God in Paradise, immediately lost the holiness and justice wherein he had been constituted; and that he incurred, through the offense of that prevarication, the wrath and indignation of God, and consequently death, with which God had previously threatened him, and together with death captivity under his

---

[5] *Decree on Original Sin*, Canon 5, 17 June, 1546.

power who thenceforth had the empire of death, that is to say the devil, and that the entire Adam, through that offense of prevarication, was changed in body and soul for the worse: let him be anathema.[6]

If anyone asserts that the sin of Adam – which in its origin is one, and being transfused into all by propagation, not by imitation, is in each one as his own – is taken away either by the powers of human nature, or by any other remedy than the merit of the one mediator, Our Lord Jesus Christ, who has reconciled us to God in his own blood, made unto us justice, sanctification, and redemption; or if he denies that the said merit of Jesus Christ is applied, both to adults and to infants, by the sacrament of Baptism rightly administered in the form of the Church: let him be anathema.[7]

Today, the main opponents of the doctrine of original sin are those who propagate atheistic evolution theory. For these people, humanity has its beginnings not in Adam and Eve as our original parents but in a multitude descended from lower life forms. Pope Pius XII formally condemned this belief, known otherwise as Polygenism, in his encyclical *Humani Generis*:

> For the faithful cannot embrace that opinion which maintains that either after Adam there existed on this earth true men who did not take their origin through natural generation from him as from the first parent of all, or that Adam represents a certain number of first parents. Now it is in no way apparent how such an opinion can be reconciled with that which the sources of revealed truth and the documents of the Teaching Authority of the Church propose with regard to original sin.[8]

---

[6] *Decree on Original Sin*, Session V, 1.
[7] *Ibid.* 3.
[8] *Humani Generis*, #37, 12 August, 1950.

The Fathers

St Theophilus of Antioch, *To Autolycus* 2, 25 (c. AD 181)
"For the first man, disobedience resulted in his expulsion from Paradise. It was not as if there were any evil in the tree of knowledge; but from disobedience man drew labor, pain, grief, and, in the end, he fell prostrate in death."

Tertullian, *The Testimony of the Soul* 3, 2 (inter AD 197-200)
"Finally, in every instance of vexation, contempt, and abhorrence, you pronounce the name of Satan. He it is whom we call the angel of wickedness, the author of every error, the corrupter of the whole world, through whom man was deceived in the very beginning so that he transgressed the command of God. On account of his transgression man was given over to death; and the whole human race, which was infected by his seed, was made the transmitter of condemnation."

St Cyprian of Carthage, *The Advantage of Patience* 19 (AD 256)
"The devil bore impatiently the fact that man was made in the image of God; and that is why he was the first to perish and the first to bring others to perdition. Adam, contrary to the heavenly command, was impatient in regard to the deadly food, and fell into death; nor did he preserve, under the guardianship of patience, the grace received from God."

St Ambrose of Milan, *Explanation of David the Prophet* 1, 11, 56 (inter AD 383-389)
"No conception is without iniquity, since there are no parents who have not fallen. And if there is no infant who is even one day without sin, much less can the conceptions of a mother's womb be without sin. We are conceived, therefore, in the sin of our parents, and it is in their sins that we are born."

St Augustine of Hippo, *Against the Pelagians* 1, 2, 5 (AD 420)
"Who of us would say that by the sin of the first man free will perished from the human race? Certainly freedom perished through sin, but it was that freedom which was had in paradise, of having full

righteousness with immortality; and it is on that account that human nature has need of divine grace."

The Roman Catechism (1566)

Pt. IV, Ch. XIII: Our condition, therefore, is entirely different from what his and that of his posterity would have been, had Adam listened to the voice of God. All things have been thrown into disorder, and have been changed sadly for the worse ... The dreadful sentence pronounced against us in the beginning remains.

Catechism of the Catholic Church (1992)

No. 403: Following St Paul, the Church has always taught that the overwhelming misery which oppresses men and their inclination toward evil and death cannot be understood apart from their connection with Adam's sin and the fact that he has transmitted to us a sin with which we are all born and afflicted, a sin which is the "death of a soul."

No. 404: How did the sin of Adam become the sin of his descendants? It is a sin which will be transmitted by propagation to all mankind, that is, by the transmission of a human nature deprived of original holiness and justice. And that is why original sin is called "sin" only in an analogical sense: it is a sin "contracted" and not "committed" – a state and not an act.

Justification and Salvation

Questions: *"Are you born-again?" "Are you saved?" "Do you have assurance of salvation?" "Do you know you will go to heaven if you die today?"*

These are all questions Catholics are confronted with from time to time by 'Born-again' Christians. In the face of these questions many Catholics are often left dumbfounded, confused, bemused, or are led even to renounce their faith.

What do 'Born-again' Christians usually mean by these questions? How should Catholics respond? Are they even valid questions?

"Are you born-again?"

'Born-again' Christians believe they are "born again" by simply accepting Jesus Christ as their "personal Lord and Savior." Once Jesus is accepted in this way one is saved, or "born again" (Jn 3:3). However, Jesus specifically tells us that we are "born again" through Baptism:

"Truly, truly, I say to you, unless one is born of water and the Spirit, he cannot enter the kingdom of God" (Jn 3:5).

'Born-again' Christians regard Baptism as only an ordinance and not necessary for salvation. Contrary to this, the Catholic Church, basing herself on the following texts, teaches that Baptism is necessary for salvation:

"Truly, truly, I say to you, unless one is born of water and the Spirit, he cannot enter the kingdom of God" (Jn 3:5).

"Baptism, which corresponds to this, now saves you ..." (1 Pet. 3:21).

"He who believes and is baptized will be saved ..." (Mk 16:16).

Defend the Faith!

'Born-again' Christians assert that upon accepting Jesus as personal Lord and Savior one's sinful soul is "covered up" by his *imputed* merits. However, Scripture tells us that our sins are not simply "covered up" but washed away, and this by Baptism:

"Peter said to them, 'Repent, and be baptized every one of you in the name of Jesus Christ for the forgiveness of your sins; and you will receive the gift of the Holy Spirit'" (Acts 2:38).

"Rise and be baptized, and wash away your sins, calling on his name" (Acts 22:16).

"... he saved us, not because of deeds done by us in righteousness, but in virtue of his own mercy, by the washing of regeneration and renewal in the Holy Spirit, which he poured out upon us richly through Jesus Christ our Savior, so that we might be justified by his grace and become heirs in hope of eternal life" (Tit. 3:5-7).

Furthermore, Scripture throughout conceives the forgiveness of sins as a real and total removal: "wash," "cleanse" (Ps. 51:2; 1 Jn 1:7); "removes" (Ps. 103:12); "takes away" (Jn 1:29; 1 Jn 3:5); "renewed" (Eph. 4:23); "washed," "sanctified" (1 Cor. 6:11).

Even the sixteenth century Protestant leader John Calvin wrote the following:

> Paul proves his previous assertion that Christ destroys sin in his people from the effect of baptism, by which we are initiated into faith in him.[1]

'Born-again' Christians teach that even after one is justified, the soul remains "totally depraved,"[2] covered only by Jesus' imputed merits. However, Scripture tells us that the Christian becomes a "temple of the Holy Spirit" and that the soul is filled with the life of the

---

[1] *Calvin's New Testament Commentaries*, 1540, 8:122.
[2] Calvin taught total depravity in his *Institutes of the Christian Religion*, 1559 ed., Bk 2, ch. 2, sect. 26-27; ch. 3, sect. 1-7; ch. 4, sect. 1-5.

Blessed Trinity:

"Jesus said to her, 'Every one who drinks of this water will thirst again, but whoever drinks of the water that I shall give him will never thirst; the water that I shall give him will become in him a spring of water welling up to eternal life'" (Jn 4:13-14).

"He who believes in me, as the scripture has said, 'Out of his heart shall flow rivers of living water.' Now this he said about the Spirit, which those who believed in him were to receive; for as yet the Spirit had not been given, because Jesus was not yet glorified" (Jn 7:38).

"If a man loves me, he will keep my word, and my Father will love him, and we will come to him and make our home with him" (Jn 14:23).

"... through these you may escape from the corruption that is in the world because of passion, and become partakers of the divine nature" (2 Pet. 1:4).

Many 'Born-again' Christians hold that all the saved in heaven are equal because the justified all receive the same mystical covering of Jesus' imputed merits. However, Scripture tells us that each of the saved will receive a different reward and shine with a greater or lesser glory depending on their respective meritorious works done in faith:

"Other seeds fell on good soil and brought forth grain, some a hundredfold, some sixty, some thirty. He who has ears, let him hear" (Mt 13:8).

"He who plants and he who waters are equal, and each shall receive his wages according to his labor" (1 Cor. 3:8).

"There is one glory of the sun, and another glory of the moon, and another glory of the stars; for star differs from star in glory" (1 Cor. 15:41).

"Behold, I am coming soon, bringing my recompense, to repay every one for what he has done" (Rev. 22:12).

Jesus spoke of those who are greater and lesser in the Kingdom of Heaven:

"Whoever then relaxes one of the least of these commandments and teaches men so, shall be called least in the kingdom of heaven; but he who does them and teaches them shall be called great in the kingdom of heaven" (Mt 5:19).

In the Parable of the Talents (Mt 25:14ff.) the three servants who had received varying talents received similarly varying rewards.

Ever since the beginning of the Reformation, Protestants have stridently claimed that we are justified by faith alone and that good works are not necessary for salvation. This is based on Martin Luther's interpretation and insertion of the word "alone" in Rom. 3:28 and 5:1. At most, they say, good works are only the results of imputed justification, not necessities in their own right. John Calvin was of the view that the whole Reformation stood or fell on the issue of "faith alone." For both Luther and Calvin, Catholics taught a gospel of justification by "good works."

In response to the Protestant challenge the Council of Trent formally declared as follows:

> If anyone says man can be justified before God by his own works, whether done by his own natural powers or through the teaching of the law without divine grace through Jesus Christ, let him be anathema.[3]

St Paul uses the word "faith" more than two hundred times in his writings but he never qualifies it with the words "alone" or "only." In fact, the only time the words "faith alone" (*pisteos monon* – πιστεως μόνον) appear is when St James declares that, "a man is justified by works and *not by faith alone.*" The reality is that Scripture repeatedly tells us of the need for good works to be saved:

---

[3] Canon 1 on Justification, 13 January, 1545.

Justification and Salvation

"Not every one who says to me, 'Lord, Lord', shall enter the kingdom of heaven, but he who does the will of my Father who is in heaven" (Mt 7:21).

"If you would enter life, keep the commandments" (Mt 19:17).

"And behold, a lawyer stood up to put him to the test, saying, 'Teacher, what shall I do to inherit eternal life?' He said to him, 'What is written in the law? What do you read there?' And he answered, 'You shall love the Lord your God with all your heart, and with all your soul, and with all your strength, and with all your mind; and your neighbor as yourself'" (Lk 10:25-27).

"And a ruler asked him, 'Good Teacher, what shall I do to inherit eternal life?' And Jesus said to him, 'Why do you call me good? No one is good but God alone. You know the commandments: Do not commit adultery, Do not kill, Do not steal, Do not bear false witness, Honor your father and mother'" (Lk 18:18-20).

(God) "will render to every man according to his works" (Rom. 2:6).

"For it is not the hearers of the law who are righteous before God, but the doers of the law who will be justified" (Rom. 2:13).

"And if I have prophetic powers, and understand all mysteries and all knowledge, and if I have all faith, so as to remove mountains, but do not have love, I am nothing" (1 Cor. 13:2).

"For we must all appear before the judgment seat of Christ, so that each may receive good or evil, according to what he has done in the body" (2 Cor. 5:10).

"For in Christ Jesus neither circumcision nor uncircumcision is of any avail, but faith working through love" (Gal. 5:6).

"What does it profit, my brethren, if a man says he has faith but has not works? Can his faith save him? ... So faith by itself, if it has no works, is dead ... Do you want to be shown, you shallow fellow, that faith apart from works is barren? ... You see that a man is justified by works and not by faith alone ... For *as the body apart from the spirit is dead, so faith apart from works is dead*" (Js 2:14, 17, 20-26).

There are numerous other verses in Scripture that concur with the above, speaking both of the meritorious value of good works as well as their necessity to enter eternal life: Mt 6:3-5; 6:19; 13:23; 25:31; Lk 3:8; 21:1; Jn 5:29; 1 Cor. 3:13; 1 Cor. 4:5; Gal. 6:7-9; Col. 3:23-25; 1 Jn 2:4; 1 Jn 3:18; 1 Jn 5:3. Faith in Jesus enables one to enter the covenant of grace and initiates justification, but works must be added for one to remain justified. The works required are not the "works of law" (*ergon nomou* – ἔργων νόμου [Rom. 3:28; Gal. 2:16]) such as circumcision but works of obedience, repentance and love flowing naturally from believers through conscious decisions. Faith and works are distinct entities, yet must operate together for one to achieve salvation.

"Are you saved?"

Salvation has a three-dimensional element:

(i) We have been saved. The objective salvation, or redemption, by Jesus' death on the Cross on our behalf. This is an unmerited free gift from God: "For by grace you have been saved through faith; and this is not your own doing, it is the gift of God – not because of works, lest any man should boast" (Eph. 2:8-9).[4]

(ii) We are being saved by working out our salvation "*with fear and trembling*" (Phil. 2:12).

(iii) We will be saved if we persevere through God's grace: "*... he who endures to the end will be saved*" (Mt 10:22).

'Born-again' Christians believe that upon performing the one-

---

[4] Eph. 2:8-9 is one of the most frequently used verses to support "faith alone" doctrine. Yet the very next verse (v. 10) illustrates St Paul's belief that good works proceeding from grace are necessary for salvation: "*For we are his workmanship, created in Christ Jesus for good works, which God prepared beforehand, that we should walk in them.*"

off act of accepting Jesus as 'personal Lord and Savior' they are 'saved,' and that essentially nothing further needs to be done except wait for death. However, Scripture tells us that Christians should be working constantly to earn their salvation:

> "Therefore, my beloved, as you have always obeyed, so now, not only as in my presence but much more in my absence, work out your own salvation with fear and trembling" (Phil. 2:12).

If Christians are saved by a one-off acceptance of Jesus as 'personal Lord and Savior' then what is the point of Jesus' continued intercession for us in heaven as High Priest, which is to "save those who draw near to God through him" (Heb. 7:25)?

"Do you have assurance of salvation?"

'Born-again' Christians believe that once they are 'saved' they cannot lose their salvation, not even by serious sin. This was the teaching of Luther:

> Even if you sin greatly, believe even more greatly, and be a sinner and sin boldly but believe and rejoice in Christ even more boldly. No sin will separate us from the Lamb even though we commit fornication and murder a thousand times a day (Epistle #99 to Melanchthon, *Let Your Sins Be Strong*, 1 August, 1521).

In contrast, Jesus taught, "Whoever then relaxes one of the least of these commandments and teaches men so, shall be called least in the kingdom of heaven" (Mt 5:19). Therefore, the Catholic Church relying on these words of Jesus and the following verses, teaches that disobeying the Ten Commandments can cause us to lose our salvation:

"Note then the kindness and the severity of God: severity toward those who have fallen, but God's kindness toward you, provided you continue in his kindness; otherwise you too will be cut off" (Rom. 11:22).

"... but I pommel my body and subdue it, lest after preaching to others I myself should be disqualified" (1 Cor. 9:27).

"Therefore let any one who thinks that he stands take heed lest he fall" (1 Cor. 10:12).

"You are severed from Christ, you who would be justified by the law; you have fallen away from grace" (Gal. 5:4).

"For if we sin deliberately after receiving the knowledge of the truth, there no longer remains a sacrifice for sins, but a fearful prospect of judgment, and a fury of fire which will consume the adversaries" (Heb. 10:26-27).

"For if, after they have escaped the defilements of the world through the knowledge of our Lord and Savior Jesus Christ, they are again entangled in them and overpowered, the last state has become worse for them than the first. For it would have been better for them never to have known the way of righteousness than after knowing it to turn back from the holy commandment delivered to them" (2 Pet. 2:20-21).

King David, the Prodigal Son and St Peter were all justified but then lost their justification in the eyes of God through sin. Later, all three were "restored to life" through repentance and sorrow.

"Do you know you will go to heaven if you die today?"

'Born-again' Christians believe if they die today, that they are certain of entering heaven. However, Scripture tells us that St Paul himself had no such belief:

"I am not aware of anything against myself, but I am not thereby acquitted. It is the Lord who judges me" (1 Cor. 4:4).

"Not that I have already obtained this or am already perfect; but I press on to make it my own, because Christ Jesus has made me his own" (Phil. 3:12).

In conclusion, one receives new birth, justification, salvation and eternal life by:

- Grace (Eph. 2:8).
- Jesus' Blood (Rom. 5:9; Heb. 9:22).
- Jesus' Cross (Eph. 2:16; Col. 2:14).
- Faith in Jesus (Jn 3:16; Acts 16:31).
- Repentance (Acts 2:38; 2 Pet. 3:9).
- Baptism (Jn 3:5; 1 Pet. 3:21).
- Confessing publicly with our mouths (Rom. 10:9).
- Knowing and adhering to the truth (1 Tim. 2:4).
- Obeying the Commandments (Mt 5:19 & 19:17).
- Doing good works in faith (Js 2:24).

We could add others to the list, but the point has been made. The first three express what God has done to save us; all the others express our required response in co-operation with God. All of the latter are non-negotiable.

"Are you born-again?" "Yes", answers the Catholic, "by baptism (Jn 3:5), faith in Jesus and in the word of God (1 Pet. 1:23) and obeying the Ten Commandments" (Mt 19:17).

"Are you saved?" "We are redeemed," is our answer, "and like St Paul we are working out our salvation in *'fear and trembling'* (Phil. 2:12), doing good and avoiding evil, waiting for judgment day with hope when we will be judged according to all our works" (2 Cor. 5:10).

"Do you have assurance of salvation?" Like St Paul, the Catholic answers, "*I pommel my body and subdue it, lest after preaching to others I myself should be disqualified*" (1 Cor. 9:27).

"Do you know you will go to heaven if you die today?" Again, with St Paul we answer, "*I am not aware of anything against myself, but I am not thereby acquitted. It is the Lord who judges me*" (1 Cor. 4:4).

The Fathers

St Justin Martyr, *First Apology* 61 (c. AD 155)
"Then they are led by us to a place where there is water; and there they are reborn in the same kind of rebirth in which we ourselves were reborn: in the name of God, the Lord and Father of all and of our Savior, Jesus Christ, and of the Holy Spirit, they receive the washing with water. For Christ said, 'unless you be reborn, you shall not enter into the Kingdom of Heaven.' The reason for doing this, we have learned from the Apostles."

St Theophilus of Antioch, *To Autolycus* 2, 16 (c. AD 181)
"Moreover, those things which were created from the waters were blessed by God, so that this might also be a sign that men would at a future time receive repentance and remission of sins through water and the bath of regeneration – all who proceed to the truth and are born again and receive a blessing from God."

Clement of Alexandria, *Miscellanies* 6, 14, 108, 4 (ante AD 217)
"When we hear, 'Your faith has saved you,' we do not understand (the Lord) to say simply that they will be saved who have believed in whatever manner, even if works have not followed. To begin with, it was to the Jews alone that he spoke this phrase, who had lived in accord with the law and blamelessly, and who had lacked only faith in the Lord."

Origen, *Commentaries on John* 19, 6 (inter AD 226-232)
"Whoever dies in his sins, even if he profess to believe in Christ, does not truly believe in him; and even if that which exists without works be called faith, such faith is dead in itself, as we read in the epistle bearing the name of James."

St Jerome, *Commentaries on the Epistle to the Galatians* 2, 3, 11 (c. AD 386)
"'But since in the Law no one is justified before God, it is evident that the just man lives by faith' ... It should be noted that he does not say that a man, a person, lives by faith, lest it be thought that he is

condemning good works. Rather, he says the just man lives by faith. He implies thereby that whoever would be faithful and would conduct his life according to the faith can in no other way arrive at the faith or live in it except first he be a just man of pure life, coming up to the faith as it were by certain degrees."

The Roman Catechism (1566)

Pt. III, Ch. I: ... in these our days there are not wanting those who, to their own serious injury, have the impious hardihood to assert that the observance of the law, whether easy or difficult, is by no means necessary for salvation ... A man, it is true, may be justified, and from wicked may become righteous, before he has fulfilled, by external acts, each of the Commandments; but no one who has arrived at the use of reason can be justified, unless he is resolved to keep all of God's Commandments.

Catechism of the Catholic Church (1992)

No. 1989: The first work of the grace of the Holy Spirit is conversion, effecting justification in accordance with Jesus' proclamation at the beginning of the Gospel: "Repent, for the kingdom of heaven is at hand." Moved by grace, man turns toward God and away from sin, thus accepting forgiveness and righteousness from on high. "Justification is not only the remission of sins, but also the sanctification and renewal of the interior man."

The Meritorious Value of Works

Objection: *"Works have no role in the final judgment of Christians — they are irrelevant."*

The above objection has its basis in the Protestant teaching of 'justification by faith alone.' Salvation for most Protestants is viewed solely as a free gift given by God and not earned by human works. All that we must do to be saved is to respond with faith. Works are only *evidence* of saving faith; they have no intrinsic salvific value in themselves. If works are not relevant for justification, then it follows they are equally not relevant when Christians come before Jesus in judgment — all that Jesus will be looking for will be whether we had faith in him as personal Lord and Savior. One formulation of this belief is as follows:

> Our good works play no part in our being acceptable to God — that is, justified and saved. But they do play a big part in our lives, because the very reason God has resurrected us to new life in Christ is so that we might do all the holy and good things he has already prepared for us to do![1]

The Biblical data, however, presents a different picture. Every judgment scene mentioned in Scripture indicates that evidence of good works will be a decisive factor in the personal judgment of everyone:

"For the Son of Man is to come with his angels in the glory of his Father, and then he will repay every man for what he has done" (Mt 16:27).

"Then he will say to those at his left hand, 'Depart from me, you cursed, into the eternal fire prepared for the devil and his angels; for I was hungry and you gave me no food, I was thirsty and you gave me no drink, I was a stranger and

---

[1] Ray Galea, *Nothing In My Hand I Bring*, Matthias Media, Sydney, 2007, p. 68.

you did not welcome me, naked and you did not clothe me, sick and in prison and you did not visit me.' Then they also will answer, 'Lord, when did we see thee hungry or thirsty or a stranger or naked or sick or in prison, and did not minister to thee?' Then he will answer them, 'Truly, I say to you, as you did it not to one of the least of these, you did it not to me.' And they will go away into eternal punishment, but the righteous into eternal life" (Mt 25:41-46).

"Do not marvel at this; for the hour is coming when all who are in the tombs will hear his voice and come forth, those who have done good, to the resurrection of life, and those who have done evil, to the resurrection of judgment" (Jn 5:28-29).

"For he will render to every man according to his works: to those who by patience in well-doing seek for glory and honor and immortality, he will give eternal life; but for those who are factious and do not obey the truth, but obey wickedness, there will be wrath and fury" (Rom. 2:6-8).

"Now if any one builds on the foundation with gold, silver, precious stones, wood, hay, straw - each man's work will become manifest; for the Day will disclose it, because it will be revealed with fire, and the fire will test what sort of work each one has done. If the work which any man has built on the foundation survives, he will receive a reward. If any man's work is burned up, he will suffer loss, though he himself will be saved, but only as through fire. Do you not know that you are God's temple and that God's Spirit dwells in you? If any one destroys God's temple, God will destroy him. For God's temple is holy, and that temple you are" (1 Cor. 3:12-17).

"So whether we are at home or away, we make it our aim to please him. For we must all appear before the judgment seat of Christ, so that each one may receive good or evil, according to what he has done in the body" (2 Cor. 5:9-10).

"For I am already on the point of being sacrificed; the time of my departure has come. I have fought the good fight, I have finished the race, I have kept the faith. Henceforth there is laid up for me the crown of righteousness, which the Lord, the righteous judge, will award to me on that Day, and not only to me but also to all who have loved his appearing" (2 Tim. 4:6-8).

"And I saw the dead, great and small, standing before the throne, and books were opened. Also another book was opened, which is the book of life. And the dead were judged by what was written in the books, by what they had done" (Rev. 20:12).

"Behold, I am coming soon, bringing my recompense, to repay every one for what he has done" (Rev. 22:12).

Though Catholics also view salvation as an unmerited gift from God, all the above make it absolutely clear that faith alone on our part is not sufficient for final justification and salvation; good works are also essential, not because we are justified by works but because Christians must live fruitful lives of faith, hope and love – and the love element manifests itself through our well-intentioned works performed in faith in response to God's grace.

Second objection: *"Since all our actions are sinful they are worthless in the eyes of God."*

This view of works is traced back to the writings of Luther and Calvin, who, because of their belief in the exaggerated notion of *total depravity* advocated that humans were no more than wild beasts incapable of any good works. For them, all human actions are sinful; they are hence worthless and play no role in our final judgment and reward from God. However, the following Scripture verses indicate otherwise:

"But when you give alms, do not let your left hand know what your right hand is doing, so that your alms may be in secret; and your Father who sees in secret will reward you" (Mt 6:3-4).

"Do not lay up for yourselves treasures on earth, where moth and rust consume and where thieves break in and steal, but lay up for yourselves treasures in heaven, where neither moth nor rust consumes and where thieves do not break in and steal" (Mt 6:19-20).

"He who receives a prophet because he is a prophet shall receive a prophet's reward, and he who receives a righteous man because he is a righteous man shall receive a righteous man's reward. And whoever gives to one of these little ones even a cup of cold water because he is a disciple, truly, I say to you, he shall not lose his reward" (Mt 10:41-42).

"And every one who has left houses or brothers or sisters or father or mother or children or lands, for my name's sake, will receive a hundredfold, and inherit eternal life" (Mt 19:29).

"And a poor widow came, and put in two copper coins, which make a penny. And he called his disciples to him, and said to them, 'Truly, I say to you, this poor widow has put in more than all those who are contributing to the treasury. For they all contributed out of their abundance; but she out of her poverty has put in everything she had, her whole living'" (Mk 12:42-44).

"But when you give a feast, invite the poor, the maimed, the lame, the blind, and you will be blessed, because they cannot repay you. You will be repaid at the resurrection of the just" (Lk 14:13-14).

"About the ninth hour of the day he saw clearly in a vision an angel of God coming in and saying to him, 'Cornelius.' And he stared at him in terror, and said, 'What is it, Lord?' And he said to him, 'Your prayers and your alms have ascended as a memorial before God'" (Acts 10:3-4).

"He who plants and he who waters are equal, and each shall receive his wages according to his labor" (1 Cor. 3:8).

"Do not be deceived; God is not mocked, for whatever a man sows, that he will also reap. For he who sows to his own flesh will from the flesh reap corruption; but he who sows to the Spirit will from the Spirit reap eternal life. And let us not grow weary in well-doing, for in due season we shall reap, if we do not lose heart. So then, as we have opportunity, let us do good to all men, and especially to those who are of the household of faith" (Gal. 6:7-10).

"... knowing that whatever good any one does, he will receive the same again from the Lord, whether he is a slave or free" (Eph. 6:8).

"I have received full payment, and more; I am filled, having received from Epaphroditus the gifts you sent, a fragrant offering, a sacrifice acceptable and pleasing to God" (Phil. 4:18).

"And so, from the day we heard of it, we have not ceased to pray for you, asking that you may be filled with the knowledge of his will in all spiritual wisdom and understanding, to lead a life worthy of the Lord, fully pleasing to him, bearing fruit in every good work and increasing in the knowledge of God" (Col. 1:9-10).

"Finally, brethren, we beseech and exhort you in the Lord Jesus, that as you learned from us how you ought to live and to please God, just as you are doing, you do so more and more" (1 Thess. 4:1).

"For God is not so unjust as to overlook your work and the love which you showed for his sake in serving the saints, as you still do" (Heb. 6:10).

"Do not neglect to do good and to share what you have, for such sacrifices are pleasing to God" (Heb. 13:16).

Yes, Christians should not be deceived. The true Gospel of Jesus indicates that those in friendship with God (i.e., in a state of grace) can perform works that are pleasing to God, not because Christians are sinless beings capable of doing perfect acts, but because God is a gracious and loving Father who generously rewards his children for trying to do their utmost in living out a life of charity.

Third objection: *"The Ten Commandments belong to the Old Law, a Law that advocated justification through works. Faith replaces works of the Law."*

Are the Ten Commandments still relevant for Christians? According to the minds of Jesus, St John and St Paul the answer is an unequivocal, "Yes!":

"Whoever then relaxes one of the least of these commandments and teaches men so, shall be called least in the kingdom of heaven; but he who does them and teaches them shall be called great in the kingdom of heaven" (Mt 5:19).

"If you would enter life, keep the commandments" (Mt 19:17).

"And as he was setting out on his journey, a man ran up and knelt before him, and asked him, 'Good Teacher, what must I do to inherit eternal life?' And Jesus said to him, 'Why do you call me good? No one is good but God alone. You know the commandments: Do not kill, Do not commit adultery, Do not steal, Do not bear false witness, Do not defraud, Honor your father and mother.' And he said to him, 'Teacher, all these I have observed from my youth.' And Jesus looking upon him loved him, and said to him, 'You lack one thing; go, sell what you have, and give to the poor, and you will have treasure in heaven; and come, follow me.' At that saying his countenance fell, and he went away sorrowful; for he had great possessions" (Mk 10:17-22).

"And whenever you stand praying, forgive, if you have anything against any one; so that your Father also who is in heaven may forgive you your trespasses" (Mk 11:25).

"And behold, a lawyer stood up to put him to the test, saying, 'Teacher, what shall I do to inherit eternal life?' He said to him, 'What is written in the law? How do you read?' And he answered, 'You shall love the Lord your God with all your heart, and with all your soul, and with all your strength, and with all your mind; and your neighbor as yourself.' And he said to him, 'You have answered right; do this, and you will live'" (Lk 10:25-28).

"Every branch of mine that bears no fruit, he takes away, and every branch that does bear fruit he prunes, that it may bear more fruit ... If you keep my commandments, you will abide in my love, just as I have kept my Father's commandments and abide in his love. These things I have spoken to you, that my joy may be in you, and that your joy may be full. This is my commandment, that you love one another as I have loved you" (Jn 15:2 & 10-12).

"For neither circumcision counts for anything nor uncircumcision, but keeping the commandments of God" (1 Cor. 7:19).

"He who says 'I know him' but disobeys his commandments is a liar, and the truth is not in him; but whoever keeps his word, in him truly love for God is perfected. By this we may be sure that we are in him: he who says he abides in him ought to walk in the same way in which he walked" (1 Jn 2:4-6).

"And this is his commandment, that we should believe in the name of his Son Jesus Christ and love one another, just as he has commanded us. All who keep his commandments abide in him, and he in them. And by this we know that he abides in us, by the Spirit which he has given us" (1 Jn 3:23-24).

Christians obey the Ten Commandments not because they must pile up a certain amount of good works in order to please God but because they are required to *love their neighbor as themselves*. Love is the necessary *fruit* of a genuine selfless life of faith. Christians show such love through obeying the Commandments and God in his graciousness is ever ready to reward such love.

Fourth objection: *"Salvation is a free gift from God. However, Catholics think they can buy their way into heaven through good works!"*

This objection has its remote basis in the extreme Protestant denial of free will. According to Luther and Calvin, original sin left humans *totally depraved*, one consequence being that humans no longer have the free use of their wills – instead we have *bonded wills* which perform only those acts (whether good or bad) predestined by God. As humans have no free will, they are incapable of making any decision that determines their eternal destiny. It is God alone who chooses who are the saved (the elect) and who are the damned (the reprobate). The decision by God to elect someone for salvation is an unmerited free grace that cannot be resisted. God does everything; we do nothing (*monergism*). Least of all, humans cannot do any works to merit or earn heaven. Catholics who believe that we can or have to do good works to be saved make God a debtor, deny the total efficacy of Jesus' Cross and subscribe to a false gospel of works salvation. They are no different than the Semi-Pelagians of the sixth century.

Catholics respond by denying that original sin destroyed the human will; rather, it was only wounded by a proneness to excessive self-love, a wound that can be healed by God's grace. God calls all to salvation through unmerited grace but not all are saved, as everyone is free to respond positively or negatively to his invitation. Our response must be one embodying a lifetime of faith, hope and love. In other words, our lives must be fruitful in faith. Our acts of faith, hope and love are how we cooperate with God's grace to merit. Though it is we who perform such acts, they are meritorious because they are done in response to God's prevenient (prompting) grace and with the right intentions (*synergism*). In other words, they are not strictly our own actions but God's because he is the one who initially inspires them. This is the opposite of Semi-Pelagianism. It is, therefore, clear that Catholics are not trying to work their way into heaven through their own efforts. Nor are Catholics making God a debtor because it is God himself who freely promises to reward his children for the good works he inspires. All of this is attested to by Scripture.

The following official statements provide clear evidence that the Catholic Church condemns the notion that anyone can earn their way into heaven through their own works apart from Jesus and the help of grace:

> If anyone affirms that we can form any right opinion or make any right choice which relates to the salvation of eternal life ... or that we can be saved, that is, assent to the preaching of the gospel through our natural powers without the illumination and inspiration of the Holy Spirit ... he is led astray by a heretical spirit, and does not understand the voice of God who says in the Gospel, 'For apart from me you can do nothing' (Jn 15:5).[2]

> If anyone says man can be justified before God by his own works, whether done by his own natural powers or through the teaching of the law without divine grace through Jesus Christ, let him be anathema.[3]

---

[2] Second Council of Orange, Canon 7, 3 July, AD 529.
[3] Council of Trent, Canon 1 on Justification, 13 January, 1545.

The Meritorious Value of Works

These statements reflect the famous words of St Augustine of Hippo, who centuries earlier wrote:

> What merit, then, does a man have before grace, by which he might receive grace, when our every good merit is produced in us only by grace and when God, crowning our merits, crowns nothing else but his own gifts to us?[4]

We have already outlined many quotes from Scripture that testify to the meritorious value of works and their importance in our final judgment and reward. The following can be added testifying to the eternal reward or punishment Christians receive depending on whether they cooperated or not with God's grace to do good works:

"Watch therefore, for you know neither the day nor the hour. For it will be as when a man going on a journey called his servants and entrusted to them his property; to one he gave five talents, to another two, to another one, to each according to his ability. Then he went away. He who had received the five talents went at once and traded with them; and he made five talents more. So also, he who had the two talents made two talents more. But he who had received the one talent went and dug in the ground and hid his master's money. Now after a long time the master of those servants came and settled accounts with them. And he who had received the five talents came forward, bringing five talents more, saying, 'Master, you delivered to me five talents; here I have made five talents more.' His master said to him, 'Well done, good and faithful servant; you have been faithful over a little, I will set you over much; enter into the joy of your master.' And he also who had the two talents came forward, saying, 'Master, you delivered to me two talents; here I have made two talents more.' His master said to him, 'Well done, good and faithful servant; you have been faithful over a little, I will set you over much; enter into the joy of your master.' He also who had received the one talent came forward, saying, 'Master, I knew you to be a hard man, reaping where you did not sow, and gathering where you did not winnow; so I was afraid, and I went and hid your talent in the ground. Here you have what is yours.' But his master answered him, 'You wicked and slothful servant! You knew that I reap where I have not sowed, and gather where I have not winnowed? Then you ought to have invested my money

---

[4] St Augustine of Hippo, *Letters* 194, 5, 19 (AD 418).

with the bankers, and at my coming I should have received what was my own with interest. So take the talent from him, and give it to him who has the ten talents. For to every one who has will more be given, and he will have abundance; but from him who has not, even what he has will be taken away.' And cast the worthless servant into the outer darkness; there men will weep and gnash their teeth" (Mt 25:13-30).

"And as he was setting out on his journey, a man ran up and knelt before him, and asked him, 'Good Teacher, what must I do to inherit eternal life?' And Jesus said to him, 'Why do you call me good? No one is good but God alone. You know the commandments: Do not kill, Do not commit adultery, Do not steal, Do not bear false witness, Do not defraud, Honor your father and mother.' And he said to him, 'Teacher, all these I have observed from my youth.' And Jesus looking upon him loved him, and said to him, 'You lack one thing; go, sell what you have, and give to the poor, and you will have treasure in heaven; and come, follow me.' At that saying his countenance fell, and he went away sorrowful; for he had great possessions. And Jesus looked around and said to his disciples, 'How hard it will be for those who have riches to enter the kingdom of God!'" (Mk 10:17-23).

"I am the vine, you are the branches. He who abides in me, and I in him, he it is that bears much fruit, for apart from me you can do nothing. If a man does not abide in me, he is cast forth as a branch and withers; and the branches are gathered, thrown into the fire and burned" (Jn 15:5-6).

"For if I preach the gospel, that gives me no ground for boasting. For necessity is laid upon me. Woe to me if I do not preach the gospel! For if I do this of my own will, I have a reward; but if not of my own will, I am entrusted with a commission" (1 Cor. 9:16-17).

"Whatever your task, work heartily, as serving the Lord and not men, knowing that from the Lord you will receive the inheritance as your reward; you are serving the Lord Christ. For the wrongdoer will be paid back for the wrong he has done, and there is no partiality" (Col. 3:23-25).

In summary, the Catholic Church believes that without faith one cannot be saved, however, it must be a faith that is fruitful in hope and love. Grace precedes all, inspiring all faith, hope and love. Unless one first has faith, his/her works are not meritorious in the eyes of God. Done in faith and in response to grace, those who practise hope and love receive an eternal reward from God. Those who have faith but are not fruitful in hope and love cannot be saved. God rewards the just for their good works not because he is obliged to (strict merit) but because he freely and graciously chooses to do so as a Father and friend (condign merit). Let us then heed the words of St Paul, who in writing to the Philippians said:

"Therefore, my beloved, as you have always obeyed, so now, not only as in my presence but much more in my absence, work out your own salvation with fear and trembling; for God is at work in you, both to will and to work for his good pleasure" (Phil. 2:12-13).

Fifth objection: *"In heaven we are all the same. No one is higher because they 'earned' more merit."*

This objection likewise has its remote roots in the teachings of Luther and Calvin and their *forensic* model of justification. For them, justification is nothing more than a juridical act of God whereby he mystically 'cloaks' the Christian in the merits of Christ (*Justitia Christi extra nos* – the Justice of Christ outside us). As the merits of Jesus are the same for each Christian, there can be no hierarchy in heaven based on individual merits. However, the following Scripture passages tell us that individual Christians can merit and that God bestows varying levels of rewards depending on varying levels of merit:

"As for what was sown on good soil, this is he who hears the word and understands it; he indeed bears fruit, and yields, in one case a hundredfold, in another sixty, and in another thirty" (Mt 13:23).

"Judge not, and you will not be judged; condemn not, and you will not be condemned; forgive, and you will be forgiven; give, and it will be given to you; good measure, pressed down, shaken together, running over, will be put into your lap. For the measure you give will be the measure you get back" (Lk 6:37-38).

"When he returned, having received the kingdom, he commanded these servants, to whom he had given the money, to be called to him, that he might know what they had gained by trading. The first came before him, saying, 'Lord, your pound has made ten pounds more.' And he said to him, 'Well done, good servant! Because you have been faithful in a very little, you shall have authority over ten cities.' And the second came, saying, 'Lord, your pound has made five pounds.' And he said to him, 'And you are to be over five cities'" (Lk 19:15-19).

"He who plants and he who waters are equal, and each shall receive his wages according to his labor" (1 Cor. 3:8).

"There are celestial bodies and there are terrestrial bodies; but the glory of the celestial is one, and the glory of the terrestrial is another. There is one glory of the sun, and another glory of the moon, and another glory of the stars; for star differs from star in glory. So is it with the resurrection of the dead. What is sown is perishable, what is raised is imperishable" (1 Cor. 15:40-42).

The Fathers

St Justin Martyr, *First Apology* 43 (AD 155)
"We have learned from the prophets and we hold it as true that punishments and chastisements and good rewards are distributed according to the merit of each man's actions. Were this not the case, and were all things to happen according to the decree of fate, there would be nothing at all in our power. If fate decrees that this man is to be good and that one wicked, then neither is the former to be praised nor the latter to be blamed."

St Theophilus of Antioch, *To Autolycus* 1, 14 (c. AD 180)
"He who gave the mouth for speech and formed the ears for hearing and made eyes for seeing will examine everything and will judge justly, granting recompense to each according to merit. To those who seek immortality by the patient exercise of good works (Rom. 2:7), he will give everlasting life, joy, peace, rest, and all good things, which neither eye has seen nor ear has heard, nor has it entered into the heart of man (1 Cor. 2:9). For the unbelievers and the contemptuous and for those

who do not submit to the truth but assent to iniquity ... there will be wrath and indignation (Rom. 2:8)."

St Irenaeus of Lyons, *Against Heresies* 4, 37, 7 (c. AD 180)
"(Paul), an able wrestler, urges us on in the struggle for immortality, so that we may receive a crown and so that we may regard as a precious crown that which we acquire by our own struggle and which does not grow upon us spontaneously ... Those things which come to us spontaneously are not loved as much as those which are obtained by anxious care."

St Cyprian of Carthage, *Works and Almsgivings* 14 (AD 253)
"... you who are a matron rich and wealthy, anoint not your eyes with the antimony of the devil, but with the collyrium of Christ, so that you may at last come to see God, when you have merited before God both by your works and by your manner of living."

St Cyril of Jerusalem, *Catechetical Lectures* 18, 1 (AD 350)
"The root of every good work is the hope of the resurrection, for the expectation of a reward nerves the soul to good work. Every laborer is prepared to endure the toils if he looks forward to the reward of these toils."

St Jerome, *Against Jovinian* 2, 32 (AD 393)
"It is our task, according to our different virtues, to prepare for ourselves different rewards ... If we were all going to be equal in heaven it would be useless for us to humble ourselves here in order to have a greater place there ... Why should virgins persevere? Why should widows toil? Why should married women be content? Let us all sin, and after we repent we shall be the same as the apostles are!"

The Roman Catechism (1566)

Pt. II, Ch. V: It is his Passion that imparts to our good actions two greatest advantages: the first, that we may merit the rewards of eternal glory, so that a cup of cold water given in his name shall not be without its reward; the second, that we may be able to satisfy for our sins.

Nor does this lessen the most perfect and superabundant satisfaction of Christ our Lord, but, on the contrary, renders it still more conspicuous and illustrious. For the grace of Christ is seen to abound more, inasmuch as it communicates to us not only what he merited and paid of himself alone but also what, as Head, he merited and paid in his members, that is, in holy and just men. Hence it can be seen how much great weight and dignity belong to the good actions of the pious. For Christ our Lord continually infuses his grace into the devout soul united to him by charity, as the head to the members, or as the vine through the branches. This grace always precedes, accompanies and follows our good works, and without it we can have no merit, nor can we at all satisfy God.

Catechism of the Catholic Church (1992)

No. 2008: The merit of man before God in the Christian life arises from the fact that *God has freely chosen to associate man with the work of his grace*. The fatherly action of God is first on his own initiative, and then follows man's free acting through his collaboration, so that the merit of good works is to be attributed in the first place to the grace of God, then to the faithful. Man's merit, moreover, itself is due to God, for his good actions proceed in Christ, from the predispositions and assistance given by the Holy Spirit.

Is There An Assurance of Salvation?

Objection: *"True Christians know that if they die tonight they are going to go straight to heaven."*

Many Protestants exhibit a confidence about their ultimate salvation that appears surprising to most Catholics. It is not uncommon to meet certain Protestants who believe with absolute certainty that if they were to suddenly die they would go straight to heaven. These same Protestants see this 'assurance of salvation' as a sign of authentic faith, while many Catholics see the same as no more than brazen presumption.

The Protestant belief in assurance of salvation has its basis in another belief, namely, that once one is 'saved' by a one-off act of faith in Jesus as personal Lord and Savior all of one's sins past, present and future are forgiven and salvation cannot be lost, not even by subsequent serious sin. This belief is expressed in the maxim *once saved, always saved* (OSAS) and has *prima facie* support in verses of Scripture such as 1 John 5:13 which reads, *"I write this to you who believe in the name of the Son of God, that you may know that you have eternal life."*

No one denies that St Paul was a true Christian. Yet it is evident from Scripture that he did not exhibit assurance of salvation in the Protestant sense. Writing to the Corinthians he stated:

"But with me it is a very small thing that I should be judged by you or by any human court. I do not even judge myself. I am not aware of anything against myself, but I am not thereby acquitted. It is the Lord who judges me. Therefore do not pronounce judgment before the time, before the Lord comes, who will bring to light the things now hidden in darkness and will disclose the purposes of the heart. Then every man will receive his commendation from God" (1 Cor. 4:3-5).

Nor did St Paul have any certainty about the fate of his Christian friend Onesiphorus:

> "May the Lord grant mercy to the household of Onesiphorus, for he often refreshed me; he was not ashamed of my chains, but when he arrived in Rome he searched for me eagerly and found me – may the Lord grant him to find mercy from the Lord on that Day – and you well know all the service he rendered at Ephesus" (2 Tim. 1:16-18).

In these two verses St Paul exhibits what should be the mindset and practice of all Christians. From time to time Christians should examine themselves to determine whether they are in good standing with God or not. Informed Christians can make a judgment about themselves with a good degree of *moral certainty* and upon such can possess a *confident hope* of salvation. However, St Paul is clear that any positive self-assessment is no guarantee of justification let alone salvation as it is only the Lord who can judge us with *absolute certainty*. As that judgment lies in the future and is presently unknown to us it should not be pre-empted or presumed by any Christian. This is why St Paul prays that the dead Onesiphorus may *"find mercy from the Lord on that day!"*

Consequently, the Council of Trent was correct to declare the following:

> For even as no pious person ought to doubt of the mercy of God, of the merit of Christ, and of the virtue and efficacy of the sacraments, even so each one, when he regards himself, and his own weakness and indisposition, may have fear and apprehension touching his own grace; seeing that no one can know with a certainty of faith, which cannot be subject to error, that he has obtained the grace of God.[1]

As a final point, there have been rare occasions when Jesus, the Virgin Mary, etc., have appeared and told certain individuals that they would end up in heaven. This was the case, for example, with St Bernadette of Lourdes and the three children of Fatima, to whom the

---

[1] *Decree on Justification*, Chapter IX, Session VI, 13 January, 1547.

Virgin Mary appeared respectively in 1858 and 1917. These chosen souls were each given an authentic assurance of salvation through a specific private revelation by God. 'Ordinary' Christians, however, cannot expect or rely upon private revelations of their own and instead should always practise lives of faith and love and live in confident hope of salvation.

Second objection: *"Catholics do not have assurance of salvation because theirs is a faith of doubts and fear."*

It is sometimes the case that people go to extremes when arguing the finer points of the justification and salvation debate. Hence, many who advocate assurance of salvation tend to accuse their opponents of substituting the peace of mind that assurance allegedly gives with doubt and fear. But are doubts and fear the only alternatives to assurance?

Doubts and fear certainly have no place in the lives of mature Christians. As stated above, someone who has come to have faith in God and Jesus ought to live a joyful life of hope and love. Hope is the virtue of specific relevance here. Hope is not just an expectation of acquiring or achieving something in the future but a trust in God's infinite power to assist us in everything we need to attain heaven. Hope is the root of Christian confidence.

St Paul emphasises the virtue of hope in the following passage:

"Therefore, since we are justified by faith, we have peace with God through our Lord Jesus Christ. Through him we have obtained access to this grace in which we stand, and we rejoice in our hope of sharing the glory of God. More than that, we rejoice in our sufferings, knowing that suffering produces endurance, and endurance produces character, and character produces hope, and hope does not disappoint us, because God's love has been poured into our hearts through the Holy Spirit which has been given to us" (Rom. 5:1-5).

Even though Catholics deny that one can have an absolute assurance of salvation, this does not mean that we cannot have a confident moral assurance of salvation based upon an examination of our consciences. St Paul himself urged Christians in Corinth to "Examine yourselves, to see whether you are holding to your faith. Test yourselves. Do you not realize that Jesus Christ is in you? – unless indeed you fail to meet the test?" (2 Cor. 13:5). It is after his own self-examination that St Paul confidently exclaimed the following:

"I have fought the good fight, I have finished the race, I have kept the faith. Henceforth there is laid up for me the crown of righteousness, which the Lord, the righteous judge, will award to me on that Day, and not only to me but also to all who have loved his appearing" (2 Tim. 4:7-8).

St John also provides certain criteria for Christians to assess whether they are in good standing with God or not. According to him, those loving both God and brother could be justifiably confident of their salvation. On the other hand, those who claim to love God without loving brother were little more than wallowing under a false assurance of salvation:

"By this it may be seen who are the children of God, and who are the children of the devil: whoever does not do right is not of God, nor he who does not love his brother" (1 Jn 3:10).

"If any one says, 'I love God,' and hates his brother, he is a liar; for he who does not love his brother whom he has seen, cannot love God whom he has not seen" (1 Jn 4:20).

It is also grossly unfair to accuse Catholics of living in perpetual fear of losing their salvation through sin. Informed Catholics know that salvation is lost only through *mortal sin*, which only occurs when an individual wilfully and fully consents to commit an act or omission they know to be gravely wrong. Committed Catholics are not the type of people who simply fall or slip into mortal sins. The same struggle daily against temptation and do so with a level of deep spiritual joy and peace. They also know that they are constantly assisted by the sacraments, visible assurances of God's grace. Those who persevere in this struggle until death can confidently look forward to an eternal rest in heaven.

Third objection: *"True Christians are guaranteed to persevere. If any so-called Christian falls that means they were never truly saved in the first place."*

Many Protestants (especially of the Reformed persuasion) believe that a person with a genuine saving faith will certainly persevere until the end of his/her life. Where, however, a person does not persevere the same Protestants conclude that he/she never had a genuine saving faith in the first place. It was John Calvin who first developed this belief, known popularly as the "perseverance of the saints." However, is this belief in accord with the teaching and experiences of the early Church community recorded in the New Testament? The answer is an unequivocal, "No!" Note the following verses:

"The ones along the path are those who have heard; then the devil comes and takes away the word from their hearts, that they may not believe and be saved. And the ones on the rock are those who, when they hear the word, receive it with joy; but these have no root, they believe for a while and in time of temptation fall away" (Lk 8:12-13).

This verse tells us that there are Christians who joyfully believe "for a while" but when temptation comes they "fall away."

"I am the vine, you are the branches. He who abides in me, and I in him, he it is that bears much fruit, for apart from me you can do nothing. If a man does not abide in me, he is cast forth as a branch and withers; and the branches are gathered, thrown into the fire and burned. If you abide in me, and my words abide in you, ask whatever you will, and it shall be done for you. By this my Father is glorified, that you bear much fruit, and so prove to be my disciples. As the Father has loved me, so have I loved you; abide in my love. If you keep my commandments, you will abide in my love, just as I have kept my Father's commandments and abide in his love" (Jn 15:5-10).

In this verse, Jesus says that Christians are like "branches" that belong to the "vine" (Jesus). Those Christians, however, who do "not abide" in Jesus are "cast forth" and "thrown into the fire" (i.e., hell).

"They were broken off because of their unbelief, but you stand fast only through faith. So do not become proud, but stand in awe. For if God did not spare the natural branches, neither will he spare you. Note then the kindness and the severity of God: severity toward those who have fallen, but God's kindness to you, provided you continue in his kindness; otherwise you too will be cut off" (Rom. 11:20-22).

According to this verse a Christian can be in God's "kindness" through faith in Jesus, then quit believing with the severe consequence of being "cut off."

"Do you not know that in a race all the runners compete, but only one receives the prize? So run that you may obtain it. Every athlete exercises self-control in all things. They do it to receive a perishable wreath, but we an imperishable. Well, I do not run aimlessly, I do not box as one beating the air; but I pommel my body and subdue it, lest after preaching to others I myself should be disqualified" (1 Cor. 9:24-27).

In this verse, it is clear that St Paul did not even consider his own perseverance certain, but recognized that he too could fall away if he did not discipline himself in holiness.

"For freedom Christ has set us free; stand fast therefore, and do not submit again to a yoke of slavery. Now I, Paul, say to you that if you receive circumcision, Christ will be of no advantage to you. I testify again to every man who receives circumcision that he is bound to keep the whole law. You are severed from Christ, you who would be justified by the law; you have fallen away from grace" (Gal. 5:1-4).

St Paul makes it clear that Christians who wish to accept the slavery of circumcision fall "away from grace" and "are severed from Christ."

"Therefore, my beloved, as you have always obeyed, so now, not only as in my presence but much more in my absence, work out your own salvation with fear and trembling" (Phil. 2:12).

Christians need to work out their salvation "with fear and trembling" because salvation is not achieved or guaranteed by a one-off act of faith but is "worked out" through a daily struggle against the world, the flesh and the devil. The word "fear" implies that the consequences for those who do not persevere in this struggle will be severe, namely the loss of salvation.

"By rejecting conscience, certain persons have made shipwreck of their faith, among them Hymenaeus and Alexander, whom I have delivered to Satan that they may learn not to blaspheme" (1 Tim. 1:19-20).

Hymenaeus and Alexander could only suffer shipwreck in the faith if they had first been in the ship – that is, they were Christians. The consequence of being shipwrecked is subjection to the devil.

"For it is impossible to restore again to repentance those who have once been enlightened, who have tasted the heavenly gift, and have become partakers of the Holy Spirit, and have tasted the goodness of the word of God and the powers of the age to come, if they then commit apostasy, since they crucify the Son of God on their own account and hold him up to contempt" (Heb. 6:4-6).

This verse is clear proof that one can be enlightened with Jesus' message and share in the gifts of the Holy Spirit yet still fall away through one's own rebellion and sin.

"Let us hold fast the confession of our hope without wavering, for he who promised is faithful; and let us consider how to stir up one another to love and good works, not neglecting to meet together, as is the habit of some, but encouraging one another, and all the more as you see the Day drawing near. For if we sin deliberately after receiving the knowledge of the truth, there no longer remains a sacrifice for sins, but a fearful prospect of judgment, and a fury of fire which will consume the adversaries" (Heb. 10:23-27).

This verse is a clear warning to Christians not to persist in sin after receiving the truth. Why? Because sin will lead the unfaithful Christian to the "fury of fire"!

"For if, after they have escaped the defilements of the world through the knowledge of our Lord and Savior Jesus Christ, they are again entangled in them and overpowered, the last state has become worse for them than the first. For it would have been better for them never to have known the way of righteousness than after knowing it to turn back from the holy commandment delivered to them. It has happened to them according to the true proverb, 'The dog turns back to his own vomit, and the sow is washed only to wallow in the mire'" (2 Pet. 2:20-22).

According to this verse someone can come to know Jesus and then become "overpowered" again. What is the consequence? They are worse than they were before their conversion!

To sum up, these verses (and many more) prove that not even a spiritual giant like St Paul can be infallibly certain of persevering in grace until death. However morally confident we may be of our spiritual health and ultimate destiny, we must still continually work with God's grace if we wish to persevere. There are no guarantees.

Fourth objection: *"There are many verses in the Bible that support the belief that 'once saved always saved.'"*

"Once saved always saved" is espoused by many Evangelical Christians today. One formulation of this belief is as follows:

> We constantly remain justified or 'right with God' throughout our Christian walk, regardless of how we happen to be going at the time. It's a bit like being married – some days I'm a great husband, and some days I'm not, but I am not more 'married' on some days than on others. I am always married because of the complete change in relationship and status that happened at the beginning, at the wedding.[2]

Therefore, according to OSAS no sin subsequent to justification has any impact on our standing with God and our prospects of future eternal life. What does Scripture have to say?

---

[2] Ray Galea, *Nothing In My Hand I Bring*, Matthias Media, Sydney, 2007, p. 62.

St Paul, the author of Hebrews, and St John together tell us that sin certainly can have the most serious consequences for any Christian. To the Romans (11:20-33) St Paul states that those Christians who do not continue in God's kindness "will be cut of," that is, cut off from the Body of Christ and eternal life. Later, St Paul reminds himself (1 Cor. 9:27) to continue his struggle against his own bodily passions lest he "should be disqualified," that is, forfeit eternal life. To the Corinthians (1 Cor. 15:1-2) St Paul exhorts the Christian community to remain faithful to his preaching lest they "have believed in vain," that is, have forfeited the salvific fruits of faith. To the Galatians (5:4), St Paul characterizes their adoption of circumcision as an act of alienation from Jesus, resulting in their falling "away from grace." The author to the Hebrews (10:23-29) warns those who continue to sin after receiving "the knowledge of the truth" of "a fearful prospect of judgment, and a fury of fire which will consume the adversaries," that is, hell-fire. Finally, St John (Rev. 22:19) warns his Christian readers that "if any one takes away from the words of the book of this prophecy" will lose "his share in the tree of life and in the holy city," that is, forfeit their entry into heaven.

OSAS is the ultimate in presumption, a dangerous trap that ensnares Christians into believing that there are no consequences for sin. This is why the Council of Trent in the sixteenth century declared:

> In opposition also to the subtle wits of certain men, who, by pleasing speeches and good words, seduce the hearts of the innocent, it is to be maintained, that the received grace of Justification is lost, not only by infidelity whereby even faith itself is lost, but also by any other mortal sin whatever, though faith be not lost; thus defending the doctrine of the divine law, which excludes from the kingdom of God not only the unbelieving, but also those with faith who are fornicators, adulterers, effeminate, sodomites, thieves, covetous, drunkards, railers, extortioners, and all others who commit deadly sins; from which, with the help of divine grace, they can refrain, and on account of which they are separated from the grace of Christ.[3]

---

[3] *Decree on Justification*, Chapter XV, Session VI.

In response to the above verses, proponents of OSAS usually respond with the following quotes, among others, in support of their position:

"*All that the Father gives me will come to me; and him who comes to me I will not cast out*" (Jn 6:37).

"*For I have come down from heaven, not to do my own will, but the will of him who sent me; and this is the will of him who sent me, that I should lose nothing of all that he has given me, but raise it up at the last day*" (Jn 6:38-39).

"*For this is the will of my Father, that every one who sees the Son and believes in him should have eternal life; and I will raise him up at the last day*" (Jn 6:40).

"*My sheep hear my voice, and I know them, and they follow me; and I give them eternal life, and they shall never perish, and no one shall snatch them out of my hand*" (Jn 10:27-28).

All that John 6:37 is trying to say is that anyone who genuinely comes to Jesus *will not be rejected by him*. However, that does not mean that there will never be Christians who will turn their backs on Jesus and walk out on him. In fact, *many have*. He/she who is not cast out by Jesus is he/she who comes to Jesus and *continuously comes to Jesus* each day until their final breath.

John 6:38-39 tells us that it is the Father's will that none who choose to follow Jesus are ever lost. However, it is also the Father's will that nobody commit sin, but we know that each day "a righteous man falls seven times" (Prov. 24:16). One must distinguish here between the divine will that *desires something to happen* and the divine will that *decrees what will happen*. The divine will in this case is the former rather than the latter. God certainly desires that everyone who comes to Jesus persevere but that desire does not prevent some who so wish to freely renounce their allegiance to him.

John 6:40 is like John 6:37. Again, the key verbs are in the present tense, so that the promise of resurrection on the last day is only

Is There An Assurance of Salvation?

for those who *continue to see the Son* and who *continue to believe in him*, not those who fail to persevere until the end.

Finally, as regards John 10:27-28, while it is true that no-one can snatch a Christian out of Jesus' hand, it is equally true that any Christian can still willingly leave the sheep-fold of Christ. This verse gives the Christian assurance that *no-one can make him/her sin*, but the final choice remains with each individual. Furthermore, the great Baptist theologian Dale Moody in his systematic theology, *The Word of Truth* (p. 357), provides the following interesting explanation:

> John 10:28 is frequently used as a security blanket by those who ignore many of the New Testament warnings about going back or falling away, but a literal translation of John 10:27-28 ... hardly needs explanation ... 'My sheep keep on hearing my voice, and I keep on knowing them, and they keep on following me: and I *keep on giving* them eternal life, and they shall never perish, and no one shall snatch them out of my hand.' Some read the passage as if it says: 'My sheep *heard* my voice, and I *knew* them, and they *followed* me, and I *gave* to them eternal life.' [But] The verbs are present linear, indicating continuous action by the sheep and by the Shepherd, not the punctiliar fallacy of the past tense.

Fifth objection: *"Salvation is a one-off event, not a continuous process."*

For those who ascribe either to the Reformed position of 'perseverance of the saints' or the Evangelical position of OSAS one's assurance of salvation is normally viewed as having been acquired through a one-off act of faith in Jesus as personal Lord and Savior. After this one-off act the Christian is either guaranteed perseverance and salvation or guaranteed salvation irrespective of what may follow.

However, is salvation really achieved through a one-off event or is it the end result of a continuous life-long struggle? Scripture sees salvation as being three-dimensional, namely, we have been saved (a past event), we are being saved (a present event), we will be saved (a future event). Put more fully, we have been saved by the Cross of Jesus, we are being saved by continuously working with God's grace to remain faithful as Christians, we will be saved if we persevere in faithfulness to Jesus until the end. The following verses testify to this three-fold dimension of salvation:

We have been saved

"For in this hope we were saved" (Rom. 8:24).

"Do not be ashamed then of testifying to our Lord, nor of me his prisoner, but share in suffering for the gospel in the power of God, who saved us and called us with a holy calling, not in virtue of our works but in virtue of his own purpose and the grace which he gave us in Christ Jesus ages ago" (2 Tim. 1:8-9).

"... but when the goodness and loving kindness of God our Savior appeared, he saved us, not because of deeds done by us in righteousness, but in virtue of his own mercy, by the washing of regeneration and renewal in the Holy Spirit" (Tit. 3:4-5).

We are being saved

"For the word of the cross is folly to those who are perishing, but to us who are being saved it is the power of God" (1 Cor. 1:18).

"For we are the aroma of Christ to God among those who are being saved and among those who are perishing" (2 Cor. 2:15).

"Therefore, my beloved, as you have always obeyed, so now, not only as in my presence but much more in my absence, work out your own salvation with fear and trembling" (Phil. 2:12).

We will be saved

"He who believes and is baptized will be saved" (Mk 16:16).

"But we believe that we shall be saved through the grace of the Lord Jesus, just as they will" (Acts 15:11).

"Besides this you know what hour it is, how it is full time now for you to wake from sleep. For salvation is nearer to us now than when we first believed" (Rom. 13:11).

"If any man's work is burned up, he will suffer loss, though he himself will be saved, but only as through fire" (1 Cor. 3:15).

"... you are to deliver this man to Satan for the destruction of the flesh, that his spirit may be saved in the day of the Lord Jesus" (1 Cor. 5:5).

"The saying is sure: If we have died with him, we shall also live with him" (2 Tim. 2:11).

In this last quote, St Paul makes it clear that only those who die in Jesus will reign with him. Furthermore, St Paul's "if" makes it clear that perseverance is not guaranteed, especially by any one-off act. We only persevere if we will to work with God's grace every moment of our lives. As Jesus himself warned, only *"he who endures to the end will be saved"* (Mt 10:22).

The Fathers

The Didache 16 (inter AD 90-150)
"Watch for your life's sake. Let not your lamps be quenched, nor your loins unloosed; but be ready, for you know not the hour in which our Lord comes. But often shall you come together, seeking the things which are befitting to your souls: for the whole time of your faith will not profit you, if you are not made perfect in the last time."

The Shepherd of Hermas 3, 8, 7 (AD 155)
"And as many of them, he added, as have repented, shall have their dwelling in the tower. And those of them who have been slower in repenting shall dwell within the walls. And as many as do not repent at all, but abide in their deeds, shall utterly perish ... Yet they also, being naturally good, on hearing my commandments, purified themselves, and soon repented. Their dwelling, accordingly, was in the tower. But if

any one relapse into strife, he will be cast out of the tower, and will lose his life."

St Irenaeus of Lyons, *Against Heresies* 4, 27, 2 (AD 180)
"We ought not, therefore, as that presbyter remarks, to be puffed up, nor be severe upon those of old time, but ought ourselves to fear, lest perhaps, after [we have come to] the knowledge of Christ, if we do things displeasing to God, we obtain no further forgiveness of sins, but be shut out from his kingdom. And therefore it was that Paul said, 'For if [God] spared not the natural branches, [take heed] lest he also spare not thee, who, when you were a wild olive tree, were grafted into the fatness of the olive tree, and were made a partaker of its fatness.'"

St Cyprian of Carthage, *The Unity of the Church* 21 (AD 251)
"Confession is the beginning of glory, not the full desert of the crown; nor does it perfect our praise, but it initiates our dignity; and since it is written, 'He that endures to the end, the same shall be saved,' whatever has been before the end is a step by which we ascend to the summit of salvation, not a terminus wherein the full result of the ascent is already gained."

St Cyril of Jerusalem, *Catechetical Lectures* 1, 4 (AD 350)
"You are made partaker of the Holy Vine. Well then, if you abide in the Vine, you grow as a fruitful branch; but if you abide not, you will be consumed by the fire. Let us therefore bear fruit worthily. God forbid that in us should be done what befell that barren fig-tree, that Jesus come not even now and curse us for our barrenness."

St Athanasius, *Discourse Against the Arians* 3, 25 (AD 362)
"When then a man falls from the Spirit for any wickedness, if he repent upon his fall, the grace remains irrevocably to such as are willing; otherwise he who has fallen is no longer in God (because that Holy Spirit and Paraclete which is in God has deserted him), but the sinner shall be in him to whom he has subjected himself, as took place in Saul's instance; for the Spirit of God departed from him and an evil spirit was afflicting him."

St John Chrysostom, *Concerning Statues* 21 (AD 387)
"Let us admonish each other. Let us correct each other, that we may not go to the other world as debtors, and then, needing to borrow of others, suffer the fate of the foolish virgins, and fall from immortal salvation."

St Augustine of Hippo, *On Nature and Grace* 18 (AD 427)
"It is, indeed, to be wondered at, and greatly to be wondered at, that to some of his own children – whom he has regenerated in Christ – to whom he has given faith, hope, and love, God does not give perseverance also."

The Roman Catechism (1566)

Pt. IV, Ch. XIII: Distrusting our own strength, we thus throw ourselves unreservedly upon the goodness of God, not doubting that he, who cherishes us in the bosom of his paternal wondrous love, will afford us in abundance whatever is necessary for life and salvation.

Catechism of the Catholic Church (1992)

No. 1821: We can therefore hope in the glory of heaven promised by God to those who love him and do his will. In every circumstance, each one of us should hope, with the grace of God, to persevere "to the end" and to obtain the joy of heaven, as God's eternal reward for the good works accomplished with the grace of Christ. In hope, the Church prays for "all men to be saved." She longs to be united with Christ, her Bridegroom, in the glory of heaven:

> Hope, O my soul, hope. You know neither the day nor the hour. Watch carefully, for everything passes quickly, even though your impatience makes doubtful what is certain, and turns a very short time into a long one. Dream that the more you struggle, the more you prove the love that you bear your God, and the more you will rejoice one day with your Beloved, in a happiness and rapture that can never end.

The Necessity of Baptism

Objection: *"Baptism is not necessary for salvation. It is only an optional ceremony."*

Unlike many Protestant churches, the Catholic Church teaches that for both adults and infants baptism is necessary for salvation. In the words of the Council of Trent:

> If anyone says that baptism is free, that is, not necessary for salvation; let him be anathema.[1]

The following quotes from Scripture clearly support the notion that baptism is mandatory and necessary for salvation:

"Go therefore and make disciples of all nations, baptizing them in the name of the Father and of the Son and of the Holy Spirit" (Mt 28:19).

"All nations" according to this verse are to be baptized. Jesus makes no mention of exceptions.

"He who believes and is baptized will be saved ..." (Mk 16:16).

Faith alone is not sufficient for salvation. It is clear from this verse that baptism is also required out of obedience to Jesus.

"... unless one is born of water and the Spirit, he cannot enter the Kingdom of God" (Jn 3:5).

"Water and the Spirit" refer to baptism. Baptism is therefore an essential part of the "born again" experience and hence necessary for the Kingdom of God.

Faith is necessary for salvation; however, for those with the use of reason faith is only the beginning of the Christian journey. Faith

---

[1] *Canons on the Sacrament of Baptism*, Canon 5, 3 March, 1547.

allows the new convert to enter the "new covenant" with the Lord Jesus Christ. What follows from accepting Jesus' Lordship is obedience. It is plainly clear from the above verses that Jesus both desires and commands everyone to be baptized. Willingly to refuse baptism after coming to know that Jesus commands it is to place one's salvation in grave danger.

It is through baptism that one becomes a child of God and is supernaturally "born again." In addition to bestowing the right to inherit God's Kingdom, baptism pours the Holy Spirit together with sanctifying grace into our souls to remove all stain of sin, original and actual (mortal and venial), as well as extinguishing all debt of temporal punishment due for sin. With sanctifying grace, we also receive the supernatural theological virtues (faith, hope and charity) and moral virtues (prudence, temperance, fortitude and justice), the seven gifts of the Holy Spirit (fear of the Lord, piety, counsel, fortitude, knowledge, understanding, wisdom) and sacramental grace, that is, the right to actual graces of union, light and fruitfulness to enable us to live the Christian life.

Second objection: *"Baptism is no more than the washing of the skin with water. It cannot forgive sins."*

Many Protestants (for example, Baptists and Presbyterians) hold firmly to the view that baptism, while enjoined by Jesus, is only a symbolic ceremony that signifies the 'washing' that has already occurred upon the Christian accepting Jesus as personal Lord and Savior; baptism itself neither forgives sins nor regenerates the soul of the new believer. For these same Protestants, Christians ought to be baptized out of respect for Jesus' command, but baptism itself is not required for the believer's sanctification or salvation.

Is there any warrant in Scripture for the belief that baptism itself effects a spiritual change in Christians? The following verses suggest so:

"Jesus answered him, 'Truly, truly, I say to you, unless one is born anew, he cannot see the kingdom of God ... Truly, truly, I say to you, unless one is born of water and the Spirit, he cannot enter the kingdom of God'" (Jn 3:3-5).

Jesus connects being "born anew" directly with "water and the Spirit," undoubtedly a reference to how water baptism and the Holy Spirit work together to bring about a profound change in the Christian. The 'new birth' is spiritual in nature as it is a pre-condition to "see" and "enter" the "Kingdom of God."

"And Peter said to them, 'Repent, and be baptized every one of you in the name of Jesus Christ for the forgiveness of your sins; and you shall receive the gift of the Holy Spirit'" (Acts 2:38).

St Peter makes it clear that repentance and baptism working together will forgive sins through the "gift of the Holy Spirit." Repentance is necessary for adults and precedes baptism; baptism is the visible instrument used by the Holy Spirit to affect the invisible washing of the neophyte's soul from sin.

"... let us draw near with a true heart in full assurance of faith, with our hearts sprinkled clean from an evil conscience and our bodies washed with pure water" (Heb. 10:22).

The "pure water" here is undoubtedly baptismal water, which is sprinkled upon those with faith in Jesus to cleanse them of "an evil conscience," that is, wash them of sin and the guilt associated with it. These words recall the words of the Prophet Ezekiel, who foretold that the Lord will one day "sprinkle clean water upon you, and you shall be clean from all your uncleannesses" (Ezek. 36:25-26).

"Baptism, which corresponds to this, now saves you, not as a removal of dirt from the body but as an appeal to God for a clear conscience, through the resurrection of Jesus Christ ..." (1 Pet. 3:21).

Again, this is another verse that evidences the salvific effect of baptism. It resembles closely Heb. 10:22, emphasizing that there is more to baptism than the external washing; there is the purifying of the conscience. Baptism "saves," not apart from Jesus, but as an instrument applying his re-generative grace to souls.

As a final point, it should be reiterated that not all Protestants reject baptismal regeneration. The Lutheran, Anglican and Wesleyan traditions certainly accept it, as is evident in the following statements:

Martin Luther:

> Through the prayer of the believing church which presents it, ... the infant is changed, cleansed, and renewed by inpoured faith. Nor should I doubt that even a godless adult could be changed, in any of the sacraments, if the same church prayed for and presented him, as we read of the paralytic in the Gospel, who was healed through the faith of others.[2]

The Anglican *Thirty-Nine Articles of Religion*, No. 27:

> Baptism is not only a sign of profession, and a mark of difference, whereby Christian men are discerned from others that are not christened, but it is also a sign of regeneration or new-birth, whereby, as by an instrument, they that receive baptism rightly are grafted into the Church; the promises of the forgiveness of sin, and of our adoption to be the sons of God by the Holy Ghost, are visibly signed and sealed.[3]

John Wesley in his *Articles of Religion* (1784), No. 17, referred to baptism as "a sign of regeneration, or the new birth."

Third objection: *"Baptism was not important for St Paul. Rather, he emphasized faith for salvation. The same goes for other converts."*

The very contrary is the case. St Paul was baptized himself and later wrote regularly concerning the sacrament:

"So Ananias departed and entered the house. And laying his hands on him he said, 'Brother Saul, the Lord Jesus who appeared to you on the road by which you came, has sent me that you may regain your sight and be filled with the

---

[2] *The Babylonian Captivity of the Church*, 1520, trans. by A.T.W. Steinhauser, Philadelphia: Fortress Press, rev. ed. 1970, p. 197.
[3] *The Book of Common Prayer*, NY: The Seabury Press, 1979, p. 873.

Holy Spirit.' And immediately something like scales fell from his eyes and he regained his sight. Then he rose and was baptized ..." (Acts 9:17-18).

Ananias baptized Saul (Paul) so he could be "filled with the Holy Spirit."

"And now why do you wait? Rise and be baptized, and wash away your sins, calling on his name" (Acts 22:16).

It is plain from this verse that it was not enough for St Paul to simply "accept Jesus as his personal Lord and Savior" to have his sins forgiven; St Paul also needed to be baptized. Furthermore, the Greek word for "wash away" is *apolousai* (ἀπόλουσαι), which means an actual washing that removes sin, not just a symbolic covering up of sin.

"Do you not know that all of us who have been baptized into Christ Jesus were baptized into his death? We were buried therefore with him by baptism into death, so that as Christ was raised from the dead by the glory of the Father, we too might walk in newness of life" (Rom. 6:3-4).

Through baptism we die to sin; arising out of the waters of baptism we walk in newness of life.

"And such were some of you. But you were washed, you were sanctified, you were justified in the name of the Lord Jesus Christ and in the Spirit of our God" (1 Cor. 6:11).

St Paul speaks of "washed," "sanctified" and "justified" in the same sentence, implying that the first (baptism) is the cause of the latter two.

"For as many of you as were baptized into Christ have put on Christ" (Gal. 3:27).

It is through baptism that we "put on Christ," namely Christ comes to live in our souls.

"*... and you were buried with him in baptism, in which you were also raised with him through faith in the working of God, who raised him from the dead*" (Col. 2:12).

Baptism and faith work together to cause the adult to die to sin and to rise in new life in and with Jesus.

"*... he saved us, not because of deeds done by us in righteousness, but in virtue of his own mercy, by the washing of regeneration and renewal in the Holy Spirit, which he poured out upon us richly through Jesus Christ our Savior*" (Tit. 3:5-6).

There is a great deal of theology packed into this single verse, all consistent with Catholic doctrine. Firstly, St Paul restates his consistent teaching that no amount of good deeds done before baptism can save us. Salvation is an unmerited gift that is made available through God's mercy in the person and sacrifice of Jesus on Mt Calvary. Once a person under the influence of grace comes to believe in Jesus he/she then receives "the washing" (baptism) that regenerates (*palingenesia* – παλιγγενεσία) and renews (*anakainosis* – ἀνακαινώσις) the soul of the new Christian. The words "he saved us" indicates that this washing is salvific in nature; hence it is not an optional extra. Baptism is "poured out upon us" from (the side of) Jesus and effects the washing of the Christian as an instrument of and "in the Holy Spirit."

As for "other converts," each one of them mentioned in the Acts of the Apostles is instantly baptized, emphasizing again the absolute necessity of baptism in the mind of the Apostolic Church:

Simon Magus and his followers:

"*But when they believed Philip as he preached good news about the kingdom of God and the name of Jesus Christ, they were baptized, both men and women. Even Simon himself believed, and after being baptized he continued with Philip. And seeing signs and great miracles performed, he was amazed*" (Acts 8:12-13).

The Ethiopian Eunuch:

"Then Philip opened his mouth, and beginning with this scripture he told him the good news of Jesus. And as they went along the road they came to some water, and the eunuch said, 'See, here is water! What is to prevent my being baptized?' And he commanded the chariot to stop, and they both went down into the water, Philip and the eunuch, and he baptized him" (Acts 8:35-38).

The household of Cornelius:

"For they heard them speaking in tongues and extolling God. Then Peter declared, 'Can any one forbid water for baptizing these people who have received the Holy Spirit just as we have?' And he commanded them to be baptized in the name of Jesus Christ. Then they asked him to remain for some days" (Acts 10:46-48).

Lydia and her household:

"One who heard us was a woman named Lydia, from the city of Thyatira, a seller of purple goods, who was a worshiper of God. The Lord opened her heart to give heed to what was said by Paul. And when she was baptized, with her household, she besought us, saying, 'If you have judged me to be faithful to the Lord, come to my house and stay.' And she prevailed upon us" (Acts 16:14-15).

The jailer and all his family:

"And they said, 'Believe in the Lord Jesus, and you will be saved, you and your household.' And they spoke the word of the Lord to him and to all that were in his house. And he took them the same hour of the night, and washed their wounds, and he was baptized at once, with all his family" (Acts 16:31-33).

Crispus and his entire household:

"Crispus, the ruler of the synagogue, believed in the Lord, together with all his household; and many of the Corinthians hearing Paul believed and were baptized" (Acts 18:8).

The believers in Ephesus:

"And he said to them, 'Did you receive the Holy Spirit when you believed?' And they said, 'No, we have never even heard that there is a Holy Spirit.' And he said, 'Into what then were you baptized?' They said, 'Into John's baptism.' And Paul said, 'John baptized with the baptism of repentance, telling the people to believe in the one who was to come after him, that is, Jesus.' On hearing this, they were baptized in the name of the Lord Jesus" (Acts 19:2-5).

The objection is often raised that the 'Good Thief' was never baptized; yet he was promised "paradise" by Jesus himself (Lk 23:43). The answer to this is twofold: firstly, Jesus' promise was made during his crucifixion; the command to baptize "all nations" came afterwards, immediately before Jesus' ascension into heaven. So, there was no obligation on the part of the 'Good Thief' to be baptized. Secondly, baptism is a normative, not an absolute necessity. There are exceptions to the rule in cases where it is impossible for the convert to receive water baptism (e.g., where he/she converts immediately before an execution). As the maxim goes, "God binds himself by the sacraments but is not bound by the sacraments." God is not prevented from bestowing grace upon a convert in circumstances where water baptism is impossible. This is the case with all *baptisms of desire*.

Fourth objection: *"Even if baptism is necessary for salvation, it must be by full immersion in water, not the false practices of pouring or sprinkling!"*

The Catholic Church accepts the validity of baptism, whether by immersion, pouring, or sprinkling. Why does she do so given that the Greek word baptizo (βαπτίζω) and its related tenses (e.g., ἐβαπτίσατο [2 Kgs 5:14]) usually mean immersion?
Before analyzing the meaning of baptizo, etc., let us have a brief look at a prophecy relating to water baptism in Ezek. 36:25. There, Ezekiel foretells that one day God "will sprinkle clean water upon you, and you shall be clean" (36:25). The relevant word in this sentence is ranō (ρανω), which translates as 'sprinkle.' Ranō never means immersion.

The Necessity of Baptism

In the New Testament, the word baptizo and its related tenses are used regularly, but not always with the intention of denoting immersion. For example, in Matt. 3:11, Mark 1:8 and Luke 3:16 we read of John the Baptist's prophecy that Jesus will 'baptize' (βαπτίζω) his followers with the Holy Spirit and fire. This occurred on Pentecost Day, when the Holy Spirit descended upon the heads of Mary and the Apostles as tongues of fire (Acts 2:3-4). The Holy Spirit on that day baptized ('baptizo') the followers of Jesus, not by immersing them, but with a pouring upon their heads.

In Mark 10:38-39 and Luke 12:50 Jesus speaks about his upcoming baptism (βάπτισμα). In hindsight, we understand that Jesus was not intending to refer to water baptism but to his passion and death on the Cross. This did not involve Jesus being immersed in his own blood; rather, it saw Jesus' blood being shed and sprinkled over his body.

In Heb. 10:22 mentioned above, the author uses the word *tismenoi* (τισμένοι) to describe baptism and its cleansing effects. *Tismenoi* likewise means "sprinkled" and so can only refer to aspersion, not immersion.

In Acts 2:41 we read of the three thousand who "were baptized" (ἐβαπτίσθησαν) after listening to St Peter's first sermon. This event occurred "in Jerusalem" (Acts 2:5) where there is no proximate river or large body of water to cater for a mass immersion. To complete the baptism of all three thousand in a single day the Apostles would necessarily have poured or sprinkled water upon them.

Finally, in Acts 9:18 (and 22:16) St Paul is baptized after "he rose" in the house of Ananias. In Acts 10:47-48, St Peter baptizes Cornelius and his household after the Holy Spirit had fallen upon them. In both cases, those baptized received the sacrament while inside a home. As large bathtubs and swimming pools were not the norm in homes during this time in history it is most likely that baptism was administered by pouring or sprinkling, not full immersion.

Fifth objection: *"Christian baptism is in the name of the Lord Jesus, not the Trinity."*

Those who advocate a 'Jesus only' formula for baptism come from both Trinitarian and anti-Trinitarian denominations and usually cite Acts 2:38-39 (as well as Acts 8:16, 10:48, 19:1-5, 22:16) in support:

"And Peter said to them, 'Repent, and be baptized every one of you in the name of Jesus Christ for the forgiveness of your sins; and you shall receive the gift of the Holy Spirit.'"

In contrast, those who advocate baptism in the name of the Trinity cite Matt. 28:19:

"Go therefore and make disciples of all nations, baptizing them in the name of the Father and of the Son and of the Holy Spirit."

Are Acts 2:38 and Matt. 28:19 irreconcilable? Not at all. The phrase "in the name of Jesus Christ" is not a liturgical formula; rather, it was an idiomatic phrase to distinguish the baptism of Jesus Christ (which bestows the Holy Spirit) from the baptism of John the Baptist (which did not). St Peter in Acts 2:38 is not actually performing a baptism or reciting a baptismal formula; he is simply exhorting people to receive Jesus' baptism. It is inconceivable that St Peter, who was present when the command recorded in Matt. 28:19 was given, would have administered baptism in words other than those prescribed by Jesus himself, that is *"in the name of the Father and of the Son, and of the Holy Spirit."* The same goes for all the other Apostles as well.

The Fathers

The Didache 7, 1 (inter AD 90-150)
"Baptize thus: After the foregoing instructions, baptize in the name of the Father and of the Son, and of the Holy Spirit, in living water. If you have no living water, then baptize in other water; and if you are not able in cold, then in warm. If you have neither, pour water three times

on the head, in the name of the Father, and of the Son, and of the Holy Spirit. Before the Baptism, let the one baptizing and the one to be baptized fast, as also any others who are able."

St Justin Martyr, *Dialogue with Trypho the Jew* **44 (c. AD 155)**
"It is necessary to hasten to learn in what way forgiveness of sins and a hope of the inheritance of the promised good things may be yours. There is no other way than this: acknowledge this Christ, be washed in the washing announced by Isaiah for the forgiveness of sins; and henceforth live sinlessly."

Tertullian, *Baptism* **12, 1 (inter AD 200-206)**
"Since it is in fact prescribed that no one can attain to salvation without baptism, especially in view of that declaration of the Lord, who says: 'Unless a man shall be born of water, he shall not have life,' there immediately arise scrupulous, or rather, audacious doubts on the part of some, as to how, in accord with that precept, salvation may be attained to by the Apostles, who, except for Paul, we do not find baptized in the Lord ... I have heard – the Lord is my witness – doubts of that kind."

Origen, *Commentaries on Romans* **5, 8 (post AD 244)**
"Why, when the Lord himself told his disciples that they should baptize all peoples in the name of the Father and of the Son and of the Holy Spirit, does this Apostle employ the name of Christ alone in Baptism, saying, 'we who have been baptized in Christ'; for indeed, legitimate Baptism is had only in the name of the Trinity."

St Cyril of Jerusalem, *Catechetical Lectures* **3, 4 (c. AD 350)**
"And he says, 'Unless a man be born again' – and he adds the words of water and of the Spirit, – 'he cannot enter into the kingdom of God.' He that is baptized with water, but is not found worthy of the Spirit, does not receive the grace in perfection. Nor, if a man be virtuous in his deeds, but does not receive the seal by means of the water, shall he enter into the kingdom of heaven. A bold saying, but not mine; for it is Jesus who has declared it."

The Roman Catechism (1566)

Pt. II, Ch. II: If the knowledge of what has been hitherto explained be, as it is, of highest importance to the faithful, it is no less important to them to learn that the law of Baptism, as established by our Lord, extends to all, so that unless they are regenerated to God through the grace of Baptism, be their parents Christians or infidels, they are born to eternal misery and destruction. Pastors, therefore, should often explain these words of the Gospel: *Unless a man be born again of water and the Holy Ghost, he cannot enter into the Kingdom of God.*

Catechism of the Catholic Church (1992)

No. 1257: The Lord himself affirms that Baptism is necessary for salvation. He also commands his disciples to proclaim the Gospel to all nations and to baptize them. Baptism is necessary for salvation for those to whom the Gospel has been proclaimed and who have had the possibility of asking for this sacrament. The Church does not know of any means other than Baptism that assures entry into eternal beatitude; this is why she takes care not to neglect the mission she has received from the Lord to see that all who can be baptized are "reborn of water and the Spirit." *God has bound salvation to the sacrament of Baptism, but he himself is not bound by his sacraments.*

Infant Baptism

Objection: *"'He who believes and is baptized shall be saved.' Therefore, only people who have faith can be baptized. So why baptize infants? It is also unfair as infants have no say in the matter."*

Those who believe that we should baptize only adults usually quote Mark 16:16 for support: "He who believes and is baptized will be saved." They also point out that Jesus himself was not baptized until the age of thirty. Therefore, only those who are capable of consciously accepting Jesus as their 'personal Lord and Savior' and have undergone a "born again" experience should be baptized.

Catholics and 'Born-again' Christians differ radically as to the meaning and effect of Baptism. 'Born-again' Christians hold that Baptism is only an ordinance whereby the "born-again" adult makes a public manifestation of his/her conversion. It is not necessary for salvation, as the person has already been saved through accepting Jesus as personal Lord and Savior. Baptism does not infuse any grace to regenerate the soul; rather, the candidate's sins are 'covered up' upon accepting Jesus. Infants without reason who die unbaptized go straight to heaven, as they only need to accept Jesus as Savior after they have committed sin. Therefore, baptizing infants is pointless.

Catholics on the other hand assert that Baptism is an obligatory sacrament instituted by Jesus which when validly administered makes us born-again: "Truly, truly I say to you, unless one is born of water and the Spirit, he cannot enter into the Kingdom of God" (Jn 3:5). Furthermore, Baptism imprints a *character*, which is the seal of the Christian, and bestows the grace it signifies into the soul of the recipient. This includes sanctifying grace, the seven gifts of the Holy Spirit, the infused theological virtues of faith, hope, and charity, the infused moral virtues of prudence, justice, fortitude and temperance, as well as the uncreated grace of the indwelling of the Blessed Trinity: "If a man loves me, he will keep my word, and my Father will love him, and we will come to him and make our home with him" (Jn 14:23). Lastly, the candidate receives a right to actual graces to assist him in carrying out his baptismal promises.

Consequent upon infusion of grace, all sin, original and actual, is forgiven and all temporal punishment due to sin is remitted. Scripture speaks clearly about the power Baptism has to forgive sins, as well as the role it has in bestowing the Holy Spirit:

"And Peter said to them, 'Repent, and be baptized every one of you in the name of Jesus Christ for the forgiveness of your sins; and you shall receive the gift of the Holy Spirit'" (Acts 2:38).

"Rise and be baptized, and wash away your sins, calling on his name" (Acts 22:16).

Without this infusion of grace, the soul cannot be in a fit state to behold the Beatific Vision upon death. Baptism has all these effects, irrespective of the age of the candidate, because the sacraments operate *ex opere operato*, that is, by their very usage. Provided the recipient places no obstacle of actual sin in the way, every sacrament properly administered bestows the grace intended.

On this basis, Catholics see no reason to withhold the wonderful effects of Baptism from infants until they reach the age of reason. By baptizing infants, the Catholic Church frees them as soon as possible from the dominion of Satan and admits them into the company of children of God: "Let the children come to me, and do not hinder them; for to such belongs the kingdom of heaven" (Mt 19:14). Nowhere is it stated in Scripture that Baptism should be administered to adults only.

According to St Paul, Baptism in the Christian religion replaces the Jewish rite of circumcision (Col. 2:11-12). This Jewish rite was normally given to infants and made them 'religiously clean' and a member of God's Chosen People. The Jews always regarded infants and children as members of God's covenant family. With the coming of Christianity, it is appropriate that infants should be accorded a similar yet greater spiritual privilege – namely, incorporation into Christ's Mystical Body through Baptism. If St Paul believed that infants were ineligible for Baptism it would have been strange for him to make the above parallel with circumcision. It would also make the New Covenant narrower and inferior to the Old Covenant.

Infant Baptism

We can also respond to the argument that infants have no choice with another parallel. According to God's original plan, Adam and Eve were to be fruitful and multiply and fill the earth with their descendants. These children, by simply being offspring of Adam, were to be born in grace and hence friends of God. In this they had no choice. With the fall of Adam from grace, disastrous consequences were to befall his children as well. Having a father who was now spiritually bankrupt, Adam's children were no longer going to be born in grace and friends of God, but disgraced and "children of wrath" (Eph. 2:3). Again, in this, Adam's children had no choice. With the coming of Jesus all things were restored. After his redemption and the subsequent abundant flow of grace Christian parents would again have the privilege Adam and Eve had for their children, that is, to place them in grace and make them friends of God – and this through infant Baptism. As we are all born in original sin through no choice of our own, it seems inappropriate to argue about being made a child of God without our consent. Rather, we should be grateful for the grace!

In addition, the Scriptures are replete with numerous examples of how grace is bestowed upon people because of the faith of others. Firstly, Jesus heals the centurion's servant in response to the centurion's faith and prayer (Mt 8:5-13). Secondly, Jesus forgives the sins of the bed-ridden paralytic based on the faith of his friends who lowered him into the crowded room (Mt 9:2). Thirdly, Jesus exorcizes the unclean spirit from the child based on the father's faith (Mk 9:22-25). If Jesus willed to bestow such graces in response to the faith of others, then it is not surprising that he is even more willing to bestow the grace of Baptism to children of faithful parents who request it.

With the enormous growth of the Church after Pentecost, large numbers of adult Jews and pagans were being converted (Acts 2:41). This is why the New Testament speaks explicitly of adult baptisms only. Obviously, these new Christians first had to also express belief in Jesus before being baptized. However, in the case of some of these adults their entire families were baptized with them. Probably some of these families would have had infant children:

The family of Cornelius: *"Can any one forbid water for baptizing these people who have received the Holy Spirit just as we have?"* (Acts 10:47).

"One who heard us was a woman named Lydia, from the city of Thyatira ... And when she was baptized, with her household, she besought us, saying, 'If you have judged me to be faithful to the Lord, come to my house and stay" (Acts 16:14-15).

"And he took them the same hour of the night, and washed their wounds, and he was baptized at once, with all his family" (Acts 16:33).

"I did baptize also the household of Stephanas" (1 Cor. 1:16).

The Greek word "household" is *oikos* (οἶκος). It included infants and children.

Furthermore, in Acts 2:38-39 St Peter's exhortation to Baptism and the benefits thereof are extended to his hearer's children:

"And Peter said to them, 'Repent, and be baptized every one of you in the name of Jesus Christ for the forgiveness of your sins; and you shall receive the gift of the Holy Spirit. For the promise is to you and to your children and to all that are far off, every one whom the Lord our God calls to him' ..."

St Peter's word for children in the above quote is *teknois* (τέκνοις). It includes small infants. A very similar word (*tekna* – τέκνα) is used in Acts 21:21 to describe circumcised infants only eight days old.

Even Martin Luther and John Calvin upheld the legitimacy of infant Baptism and defended it stridently:

> Who is to be baptized? All nations, that is, all human beings, young and old, are to be baptized ... Infants, too, are to be baptized because they are included in the words 'all nations;' (and) because holy Baptism is the only means whereby infants, who, too, must be born again, can ordinarily be regenerated and brought to faith.[1]

> Doubtless the design of Satan in assaulting infant Baptism with all his forces is to keep out of view, and gradually efface,

---

[1] *Luther's Small Catechism*, 1529, Rev. ed.

Infant Baptism

the attestation of divine grace which the promise itself presents to our eyes ... Wherefore, if we would not maliciously obscure the kindness of God, let us present to him our infants, to whom he has assigned a place among his friends and family, that is, the members of the Church.[2]

As for the claim that Jesus was baptized only as an adult, it should be remembered that he did not receive Christian Baptism in the name of the Trinity, but the baptism of John the Baptist, which was only symbolic washing and did not infuse grace.

Finally, it is entirely false that infant Baptism began late in the Church's history. The early Church practised it without any evidence of opposition condemning it in principle or as a novelty. However, it is true that after three centuries of evangelization, generations were now Christian by family tradition and this led to a decrease in the percentage of adult catechumens and baptisms.

Second objection: *"Baptism of infants is also wrong because the child is not fully immersed in water. Simply pouring or sprinkling water on the child is not Baptism at all!"*

It is true that the usual meaning of baptism (Greek: *baptizein*) is immersion, and for centuries immersion was the common form of Christian Baptism. However, simply because immersion was the common practice does not mean that other methods are unlawful or invalid.

The Acts of the Apostles relates how St Paul was baptized in a house (9:17-18), while St Peter baptized numerous people in the house of Cornelius (10:47-48). Now, archaeologists would testify that bathing tubs were not usual fixtures in the homes of the ancients. It is also highly doubtful that there was sufficient open water to baptize by immersion the three thousand who converted to the Lord after St Peter's first sermon (2:41). All these were probably baptized by pouring or sprinkling, just as were thousands of others according to the earliest Christian mosaics, paintings and engravings in the Catacombs and ancient churches.

---

[2] John Calvin, *Institutes of the Christian Religion*, Bk 2, ch. 16, sect. 554.

Besides this, to insist on full immersion leads to situations in which people are denied Baptism. Those living in climactic extremes such as deserts would find it difficult to always procure enough water to fully immerse an adult, while it would be impossible for those rendered bed-ridden by illness to be baptized. Eusebius relates that the heretic Novation "received Baptism in the bed where he lay, by pouring."[3] After all, water poured on the body retains the symbolism of washing. (See again pp. 77-78).

The Fathers

St Hippolytus of Rome, *The Apostolic Tradition* 21 (c. AD 215)
"Baptize first the children; and if they can speak for themselves, let them do so. Otherwise, let their parents or other relatives speak for them."

Origen, *Commentaries on Romans* 5, 9 (inter AD 244-254)
"The Church received from the Apostles the tradition of giving Baptism even to infants. For the Apostles, to whom were committed the secrets of divine mysteries, knew that there is in everyone the innate stains of sin, which must be washed away through water and the Spirit."

St Cyprian of Carthage, *Letters to Fidus* 64 (59), 5 (c. AD 251-252)
"As to what pertains to the case of infants: you said that they ought not to be baptized within the second or third day after their birth ... and that you did not think that one should be baptized and sanctified within the eighth day after his birth. In our council it seemed to us far otherwise."

St Gregory Nazianzus, *Oration on Holy Baptism* 40, 17 (AD 381)
"Do you have an infant child? Allow sin no opportunity; rather, let the infant be sanctified from childhood. From the most tender age let him be consecrated by the Spirit. Do you fear the seal because of the

---

[3] *Ecclesiastical History* 6, 43, 11.

weakness of nature? O what a pusillanimous mother, and of how little faith! ... Give your child the Trinity, that great and noble protector."

St Augustine of Hippo, *The Interpretation of Genesis* **10, 23, 39 (inter AD 401-415)**
"The custom of Mother Church in baptizing infants is certainly not to be scorned, nor is it to be regarded in any way as superfluous, nor is it to be believed that its tradition is anything except Apostolic. The age of infancy also has a great weight of witness; for it was the infant age that first merited to pour out its blood for Christ."

The Roman Catechism (1566)

Pt. II, Ch. II: If, then, through the transgression of Adam, children can inherit original sin, with still stronger reason can they attain through Christ our Lord grace and justice that they may reign in life. This, however, cannot be effected otherwise than by Baptism.

Pastors, therefore, should inculcate the absolute necessity of administering Baptism to infants, and gradually forming their tender minds to piety by education in the Christian religion. For according to these admirable words of the wise man: A *young man according to his way, even when he is old, he will not depart from it.*

Catechism of the Catholic Church (1992)

No. 1250: Born with a fallen human nature and tainted by original sin, children also have need of the new birth in Baptism to be freed from the power of darkness and brought into the realm of the freedom of the children of God, to which all men are called. The sheer gratuitousness of the grace of salvation is particularly manifest in infant Baptism. The Church and the parents would deny a child the priceless grace of becoming a child of God were they not to confer Baptism shortly after birth.

Canon of the Bible

Objection: *"The Catholic Church has added extra corrupt books to the Bible which were never part of the Hebrew canon!"*

This is a serious accusation for Catholics to contend with, because we need to be certain that it is to the word of God and not the word of man that the Church refers to when teaching and preaching and determining vital questions of faith and morals. At the same time, it is a difficult question because the Bible by itself does not tell us the full list of which books belong to it. Jesus himself referred to "the Law and the Prophets." This shows that he recognized, as the word of God, the Law or *Torah*, which is specifically in the Pentateuch, the first five books of the Bible; along with "the Prophets." In his ministry, Jesus more specifically quoted the Prophet Isaiah, the Book of Psalms, and other books of the Old Testament – but nowhere does he outline the full list of divinely inspired books.

The word 'canon' may be defined as the catalogue or collection of books which the Church has declared to be divinely inspired, and which she regards as a rule of faith. The Old Testament books accepted widely from the very beginning of the Church, whose inspiration was never in doubt, are sometimes called *protocanonical* (*protos* = first). Books officially recognized some time later, and about the inspiration of which there was some uncertainty here and there, are called *deuterocanonical* (*deuteros* = second). The Church herself has never officially used the terminology of 'protocanonical' and 'deuterocanonical.' But we will use the terms here for convenience only. A book is simply inspired (and therefore in the canon) or not. For the Church, all the Biblical books are canonical; there is no 'first' or 'second' rank. (An *apocryphal* book is one that some have thought to be inspired by God, but which in fact is not inspired and the Church has rejected it as such, regardless of how historical or orthodox it may be. The word *apocryphal* literally means to 'hide from,' to withhold from the public).

The Church accepts as inspired forty-six books in the Old Testament and twenty-seven books in the New. (The O.T. has forty-five books if *Jeremiah* and *Lamentations* count as one). The complete list is given in the *Catechism of the Catholic Church* #120, and can be found at the front of any Catholic Bible. The Protestant rejection of certain books of the Bible moved the Catholic Church to define the contents of the entire canon for the first time in 1546, in the first months of the Council of Trent. The list of books given was the same as that recognized by the Council of Florence in 1442 and other earlier lists.

At the time of Jesus, there existed two collections of the Old Testament – the *Hebrew* of the Palestinian Jews and the *Greek Septuagint* of the Alexandrian Jews. The latter was a translation of the Hebrew Old Testament into Greek, begun about 250 BC. According to a tradition, seventy Greek-speaking Jewish scholars performed the work. Thus, the name *Septuagint* – Greek for 'seventy.' Due to the Hellenization of the eastern Mediterranean world after the conquests of Alexander the Great, Greek became the popular and common language of that part of the world. The large Jewish communities outside of Palestine no longer spoke Hebrew or Aramaic as their first language. Therefore, it was felt necessary to produce a vernacular version of the Scriptures for them in Greek.

Dispute arises over the canon of Scripture because the Greek Septuagint contains forty-six books while the Hebrew version only thirty-nine. The additional books are *Tobit, Judith, Wisdom, Sirach (Ecclesiasticus), Baruch,* and *1 & 2 Maccabees*. In addition, there are extra fragments and chapters in the Septuagint versions of Esther and Daniel, namely, the seven last chapters of Esther (10:4 to 16:24), the prayer of Azarias and the canticle of the three children in the fiery furnace (Dan. 3:24-90), the history of Susanna (Dan. 13), and the history of Bel and the Dragon (Dan. 14). Together, these additional books and paragraphs constitute the deuterocanonical books. The oldest texts listing all the Old Testament books date back only to the fourth century AD.

An occasional dispute has also arisen over the canon of the New Testament. Some early Christians had doubts as to the genuineness of Hebrews, 2 Peter, 2 & 3 John, James, Jude and Revelation. These doubts were resurrected by some of the early Protestant Reformers, notably Martin Luther. Added to this confusion, some in the early Church regarded letters such as the Epistles of Barnabas and Clement, among others, as part of Scripture.

The initial objection against the deuterocanonical books is that they were not part of the Hebrew Old Testament used by Jesus and the Apostles. Such a theory, however, relies on the incorrect notion that there was a fixed Old Testament canon accepted by all the Jews at this time. From Moses until the coming of Jesus, divine revelation was communicated to the Jewish people through one of three channels: (i) the High Priests; (ii) Prophets; or (iii) special men chosen by God to decide important matters in his name. Of these three, the most common were the Prophets. Their extraordinary vocation, sanctity of life, and miraculous interventions in their favor testified to the divine origin of their public missions. Their testimony that a certain book was inspired was therefore a sure certification that it should be accepted as coming from God.

There are various theories as to when the Jews closed their Old Testament canon. One is that the Old Testament was closed once and for all by Ezra (c. 400 BC). This is a view that was held by some of the Fathers and many Protestants. Such a view, however, runs into several difficulties. For example, the second book of Ezra contains genealogies of the High Priests continuing one hundred and fifty years after the death of Ezra. In the same book is a list of the descendants of King David traced down to the sixth generation after Zerubbabel that is, down to about 300 BC. The existence of these genealogies is proof enough that the Old Testament canon remained open at least one hundred and fifty years after Ezra's death.

In fact, the Old Testament canon was still in a state of flux in the time of Jesus. Both the Sadducees and Samaritans, for example, accepted only the first five books of Moses as inspired and canonical. The great Jewish historian, Josephus Flavius, provides one important hint as to why uncertainty still surrounded the Old Testament canon so late in its history:

> From the time of Artaxerxes to our own time, our history has been written down very particularly (accurately and in detail), but these books have not been considered worthy of the same

credit as the books of earlier date, *because there has not been an exact succession of prophets.*[1]

From these last words, it is evident that Josephus required a Prophet to appear and canonize the deuterocanonical books in the same way other Prophets in the past had done for the protocanonical books. The question at the time of his writing was still open. Unbeknowns to Josephus, this Prophet was to be Jesus speaking through his Church.

Nevertheless, Josephus makes it clear that the deuterocanonical writings enjoyed great credit among the Jews as sacred literature:

> But what credence we have given to all those books of our own nation is evident from our conduct; for, though so long a time has passed, no one has ever been so bold as to add anything to them whatsoever. *But all Jews are instinctively led, from the moment of their birth, to believe that these books contain divine oracles and to abide by them and, if need be, gladly to die for them.*[2]

To emphasize this point, Josephus says that in the composition of his *Jewish Antiquities* he used exclusively "sacred writings," yet he frequently quotes 1 Maccabees and the deutero fragments of Esther. Furthermore, the Talmud refers to Baruch as a "prophetic book", to Wisdom as a book "written by Solomon", and to the book of Sirach in quotation.

In addition – except for Wisdom, 2 Maccabees and possibly Tobit – all the other parts of the deuterocanon were previously written in Hebrew. This points to Palestine as the place, not only whence the texts originated, but whence the Alexandrian Jews received their belief in their inspiration and divine character. This is why there are no records of any schism or controversy on the subject between the Palestinian and Alexandrian Jews.

For Jews today, no final determination of the Old Testament was allegedly made until the so-called *Council of Jamnia (Javnah)* in AD

---

[1] *Contra Apion.*, I, 8.
[2] *Ibid.*

90. The Jews in this gathering (and again in AD 118), seeking to build a new focal point for their religious beliefs after the Roman destruction of the Temple in AD 70, and to counter the early Christians who quoted the Septuagint in support of the messianic claims of Jesus, only accepted those Old Testament books which (i) were written in Hebrew; (ii) conformed to the Torah; (iii) pre-dated the time of Ezra; and (iv) written in Palestine. The Jewish authorities now xenophobically considered the Septuagint "too gentile." Only the Ethiopian Jews retained the Septuagint version and still do so today (*Encyclopaedia Judaica*, vol. 6, p. 1147).

As to what happened at Jamnia, first, it is questionable how a small gathering of Jews could determine anything for Jews worldwide and forever, with no Prophet, no Temple and no recognizable authority when the nation had ceased to exist as a unit. Second, in any case, for Christians, Jamnia is not authoritative, as all legitimate authority had passed to the Catholic Church sixty years earlier at Pentecost. By rejecting the seven additional books of the Septuagint, Protestants therefore effectively follow the canon of the Old Testament as determined by the Jews at Jamnia. If Protestants accord Jews the authority to decide on such a matter, then why not consult Jews on whether Jesus is the Messiah? Third, digging deeper into history, we find that the *Oxford Dictionary of the Christian Church* says, "The suggestion that a particular synod of Jamnia, held c. AD 100, finally settled the limits of the OT Canon, was made by H. E. Ryle[3]; though it has had a wide currency, there is no evidence to substantiate it."[4]

Second objection: *"The Deuterocanonical books and the Septuagint were never cited by Jesus and the Apostles!"*

This objection against the deuterocanonicals is derived from the unfounded principle, 'quotation equals canonicity.' It assumes that if a book was not quoted by Jesus or the Apostles it is not canonical and vice versa. This argument is faulty for three reasons. First, "Jesus

---

[3] *The Canon of the Old Testament*, 1892, p. 171 ff.
[4] *Oxford Dictionary of the Christian Church*, 3rd ed., Oxford University Press, 1997, "Jamnia," p. 861.

did many other signs ... which are not written in this book" (Jn 20:30). Not every action, miracle or statement made by Jesus was recorded in writing. Second, the New Testament authors quote several works not in any Old Testament canon. St Jude quotes the Book of Enoch and the Assumption of Moses, while the author of Hebrews quotes the Ascension of Isaiah (Heb. 11:37) and St Paul quotes pagan authors such as Epimenides, Aratus and Menander (Acts, 1 Cor. and Titus). If quotation means canonicity, then why do Protestants include none of these works in the canon today? Third, there are protocanonical Old Testament books accepted by Protestants that are not referred to in the New Testament either, including the Song of Songs, Ecclesiastes, Esther, Obadiah, Zephaniah, Judges, 1 Chronicles, Ezra, Nehemiah, Lamentations and Nahum. Should these books therefore be excluded from the Old Testament canon? No!

The reality, however, is that there are many hundreds of quotations from, and allusions to, the Septuagint and deuterocanonical books found in the New Testament. For example, when Jesus quoted Isaiah to condemn those whose "heart is far from me; in vain do they worship me" (Mk 7:6-7), he used that version of Isaiah found only in the Septuagint. Jesus also alluded to Sir. 27:6, which reads, "The fruit discloses the cultivation of a tree." In John 10:22-36 Jesus and the Apostles observed the key Feast of the Dedication, or *Hanukkah*, which celebrates events recorded only in 1 & 2 Maccabees. Likewise, St Paul draws from Wisdom chapters 12 & 13 in Rom. 1:19-25. Again, in Heb. 11:35 we read of women who "received their dead by resurrection. Some were tortured, refusing to accept release, that they might rise again to a better life." The ex-Protestant convert James Akin in his tract *Defending the Deuterocanonicals*[5] states:

> There are a couple of examples of women receiving back their dead by resurrection in the Protestant Old Testament. You can find Elijah raising the son of the widow of Zarepheth in 1 Kings 17, and you can find his successor Elisha raising the son of the Shunammite woman in 2 Kings 4, but one thing you can never find – anywhere in the Protestant Old Testament, from front to back, from Genesis to Malachi – is someone

---

[5] http://thecatholicconvert.webs.com/deuterocanonicals.html

being tortured and refusing to accept release for the sake of a better resurrection. If you want to find that, you have to look in the Catholic Old Testament – in the deuterocanonical books Martin Luther cut out of his Bible.

Altogether, there are over twenty allusions to the deuterocanonicals in the New Testament. Furthermore, out of the three hundred and fifty verses cited in the New Testament from the Old Testament, three hundred are taken from the Septuagint. This extensive use of the Septuagint is an informal and practical ratification of its contents by Jesus and the Apostles. In doing so they embedded the Septuagint in the New Testament and made it a lasting inheritance for all Christians. Finally, the Dead Sea Scrolls of the Jewish Essene community also extensively cite passages from the Septuagint, including the deuterocanonical books of Tobit and Sirach – another sign that Palestinian Jews knew these books.

To appeal to Jewish authorities before or after Jesus to settle the canon definitively for Christians is to ascribe to the custodians of a provisional covenant a final and definitive authority for all time – which is a contradiction in terms. The Old Testament, a preparation for Jesus, the fullness of Revelation, is closed upon the arrival of the Messiah – whether the Jews knew this or not. The Protestant appeal to Jewish practice or belief at the time of Jesus attributes an exaggerated, over-arching authority to those who could not be given such authority, something which would have to wait for the commissioning of St Peter and the Apostles by Jesus.

Third objection: *"Many Fathers of the Church and even Catholic popes and saints did not accept the Deuterocanon!"*

Certainly, a number of the early Fathers, especially St Jerome, expressly rejected the deuterocanonical books as canonical Scripture. The same may be said for Pope St Gregory I the Great. This is what they said respectively:

> Just as the Church reads Judith and Tobias and the Books of Maccabees, but does not accept them as belonging among the canonical Scriptures, so too let her read these two volumes for

the edification of the people but not for the purpose of confirming the authority of the Church's teachings.[6]

... we are not acting irregularly, if from the books, though not canonical, yet brought out for the edification of the Church, we bring forth testimony. Thus Eleazar in the battle smote and brought down an elephant, but fell under the very beast that he killed.[7]

First, it must be recognized that no Father *is* the Church or infallible in all he says. Pope St Gregory I the Great did not promulgate the above quotation as Church teaching, but in a private work, which he had begun before being elected Pope. For many centuries, it remained open to all and sundry to express private opinions about the deuterocanonicals. The overwhelming majority of early Christian writers quoted from them as inspired Scripture without question, as, for example: the author of the *Didache*; St Clement I; the author of the *Epistle of Barnabas*; the author of *The Shepherd of Hermas*; St Polycarp of Smyrna; Athenagoras of Athens; St Irenaeus of Lyons; Clement of Alexandria; Tertullian; St Hippolytus of Rome; Origen; St Cyprian of Carthage; Dionysius of Alexandria and St Augustine of Hippo. Other Fathers did not accept the deuterocanonicals as canonical but considered them ecclesiastical, and useful for edification and instruction in doctrine. These included Sts Athanasius, Cyril of Jerusalem, Basil, Gregory Nazianzus and Epiphanius of Salamis. Sts Jerome and Pope St Gregory I the Great fall into this latter category. St Jerome calls Judith and deutero-Esther "holy books." Later Doctors and Saints also questioned the canonicity of the deuterocanon. Those who favored their inclusion included Gratian, St Stephen Harding, Stephen Langton, St Bonaventure, St Albert the Great, St Thomas Aquinas; those against included Hugh of St Victor, Nicholas of Lyra, Cardinal Ximenes and Cardinal Cajetan.

There is a distinction between *inspiration* and *canonization*, although the two are directly related. Inspiration precedes canonization

---

[6] St Jerome, *On the Three Solomonic Books*, Preface (c. AD 398).
[7] Pope St Gregory I the Great, *Moral Teachings Drawn from Job*, Bk 19, 34 (inter AD 578-595).

in order of time and causality. It is only God who inspires, and this occurs simultaneously with the book's composition. Canonization (being put into the canon) takes place after the book's composition and presupposes inspiration. Therefore, all canonical books are known to be inspired; and now – since the final judgment of the Church – all inspired books are canonical. The canon is closed; there are no inspired books that we do not know of.

Who then determines with certainty which books should form part of canonical Scripture, and by what criteria? This question applies to both the Old and New Testament canons. The Holy Spirit did not promise a revelation to any individual Christian concerning the authentic canon. Anglican Church historian J.N.D. Kelly offers one possible solution:

> Unless a book could be shown to come from the pen of an apostle, or at least to have the authority of an apostle behind it, it was peremptorily rejected, however edifying or popular with the faithful it might be.[8]

But how could early Christians know whether a book was Apostolic? Certainly, not simply by a book's claim to be so, since the Gospels were anonymous and there were numerous spurious gospels and epistles in circulation.[9] Protestant Scripture scholar F. F. Bruce writes that:

> [The early Fathers] had recourse to the criterion of orthodoxy ... This appeal to the testimony of the churches of apostolic foundation was developed especially by Irenaeus ... When previously unknown Gospels or Acts began to circulate ... the most important question to ask about any one of them was: What does it teach about the person and work of Christ? Does it maintain the apostolic witness to him ...?[10]

---

[8] *Early Christian Doctrines*, 5th ed. rev., Harper & Row, New York, 1978, p. 60.
[9] For example, the Gospel of Thomas, the Secret Gospel of Mark, the Gospel of the Hebrews, the Acts of Peter, the Acts of John, etc.
[10] *The Canon of Scripture*, Inter-Varsity Press, Leicester, 1954, p. 260.

In other words, a book was reckoned as Apostolic only if its contents were consistent with the teachings of the Apostles (Apostolic paradosis, or tradition) as handed on *by the Church*. Who, however, was to make such a determination? To assert that this was the Holy Spirit alone without men who determined such is neither historical nor honest. The Holy Spirit did do all the work of inspiration and collection but it was through men who were leaders and pillars of the Church divinely founded, that is, the infallible voice of the successors to St Peter and the Apostles. Thus, came about the decrees of Popes St Damasus (AD 382) and St Innocent I (AD 405), and the Councils of Rome (AD 382), Hippo (AD 393) and Carthage (AD 397), which accepted as canonical the Greek Septuagint and all the books of the New Testament. In these pronouncements, the Catholic has the way to certainty. Without such a voice the Protestant has a fallible collection of infallible books.

Fourth objection: *"These councils and popes made no final decision. The Council of Trent added the Deuterocanon to have Scriptural backup for its many false teachings, and in doing so contradicted the universal practice of Christianity up to that time."*

The Council of Trent added nothing to the Old Testament. Rather, it re-affirmed the ancient practice of the Apostles and the decisions of the early Church through a universal dogmatic definition.

The Council of Rome in AD 382 and the Councils of Carthage AD 393, 397 and 419 all published canons entirely identical with that of the Council of Trent. So did Pope Innocent I in AD 405, Pope Gelasius I in AD 495, Pope Hormisdas in AD 520, the Second Council of Nicaea in AD 787 and the Council of Florence in 1442. Likewise, the canon of the separated Oriental Churches has always included the Deuterocanon — which confirms that in severing parts of the Bible, Protestants are out on an unhistorical limb.

However, all these Papal decrees and Council decisions lacked one or other important factor relating to its universal acceptance. Either they were decisions that acted only at a local level or, if they were universal, dealt with the sacredness or usefulness of the deuterocanonicals without necessarily declaring their canonicity. The

Protestant revolt, with its denials of the inspiration (and therefore canonicity) of the deuterocanonicals, provided the occasion for a universal dogmatic definition relating to their canonicity that would end all discussion. The Council of Trent's *Decree Concerning the Canonical Scriptures*[11] solemnly canonized the lists of sacred books promulgated by all the above-mentioned Councils and Popes going back to Rome AD 382.

This Decree is fully justified, for neither the Jews before Jesus, nor any Church Father, Saint, Pope or Council placed the deuterocanonicals on the same level as profane or simply human literature. At the very least they were hanging, as it were, between heaven and earth for that "Prophet" Josephus spoke about who would elevate them to the level of the canon. That Prophet was Jesus and the Apostles and their successors in the Council of Trent.

Protestants may have their own reasons for rejecting the extra seven books of the Septuagint. These additional books contain certain doctrines contrary to their teachings. For example, 2 Maccabees speaks of prayers for the dead in chapter 12 and the communion and intercession of saints in chapter 15. No longer constrained by the authority of the Catholic Church, Martin Luther rejected the epistle of James as an "epistle full of straw ... for it has nothing of the nature of the gospel about it," simply because it contradicted his own theory of justification by faith alone. He said of Revelation, "I find many things defective in this book, which make me consider it neither Apostolic nor Prophetic." He also placed Hebrews and Jude in the back of his Bible as "suspected books." These judgments proceeded from his general arrogance, which he also exhibited in his reply when challenged for changing the text of Rom. 3:28: "Thus I will have it, thus I order it, my will is reason enough ... Dr Luther will have it so, and he is a Doctor above all Doctors in the whole of Popery."[12] Nevertheless, Luther had to admit that "We concede — as we must — that so much of what they (the Catholic Church) say is true: that the papacy has God's word and the office of the apostles, and that we have received Holy Scriptures,

---

[11] Session IV, 8 April, 1546.
[12] *Letter to Wenceslaus Link*, 1530.

Baptism, the Sacrament, and the pulpit from them. What would we know of these if it were not for them?"[13]

Ultimately, only the Magisterium (teaching authority) of the Church can tell us which books are inspired. There are many beautiful books, free from error, and full of truth, which are not inspired. Conversely, in the inspired books, there are many difficult and strange things that could have misled the limited minds of men into thinking they were not from God. In the final analysis, all purely human criteria are inadequate to resolve the question. Inspiration cannot be detected by investigation of the text alone; an external authority is needed to declare it is inspired. Only the authoritative voice of the Church of God can tell us which books are the word of God. So, at Vatican I the Church declared, "These books of the Old and New Testament, complete with all their parts ... as contained in the ancient Latin Vulgate edition, must be held as sacred and canonical. The Church holds them as sacred and canonical, not as having been composed by merely human labor and afterwards approved by her authority; nor merely because they contain revelation without error; but because, written under the inspiration of the Holy Spirit, they have God for their author, and have been transmitted to the Church as such."[14]

The Fathers

***Exhortation to the Greeks* 13 (inter AD 260-302) Author Unknown**
"Ptolemy, the king of Egypt, when he had constructed a library in Alexandria, and had filled it by collecting books from everywhere, afterwards learned that ancient histories written in Hebrew letters had been carefully preserved. Desiring to know these writings, he sent for seventy wise men from Jerusalem who knew both the Greek and the Hebrew languages, and appointed them to translate the books ... He supplied attendants to care for their every need, and also to prevent their communicating with each other, so that it might be possible to know the accuracy of the translation, by their agreement one with

---

[13] *Luther's Works: Sermons on the Gospel of John*, 1537, Vol. 24, chaps. 14-16, p. 304.
[14] *Dogmatic Constitution on the Catholic Faith*, 1870, chapter 2.

another. When he found that the seventy men had given not only the same meaning, but even the same words, and had failed to agree with each other by not so much as a single word, but had written the same things about the same things, he was struck with amazement, and believed that the translation had been written with divine authority." (*This is the Aristean account, third century BC, of the translating of the Septuagint accepted by many of the Fathers, e.g., St Justin Martyr, St Irenaeus of Lyons, Clement of Alexandria, Tertullian, St Cyril of Jerusalem and St Augustine*).

Pope Damasus, *Decree on the Canon of Sacred Scripture* 2 (AD 382)
"Likewise it has been said: now indeed we must treat of the divine Scriptures, what the universal Catholic Church accepts and what she ought to shun ... Likewise Wisdom one book, Ecclesiasticus one book ... Likewise the order of the histories. Job one book, Tobias one book, Esdras two books, Esther one book, Judith one book, Maccabees two books."

St Augustine of Hippo, *Against the Letter of Mani* 5, 6 (AD 397)
"If you should find someone who does not yet believe in the Gospel, what would you answer him when he says: 'I do not believe?' Indeed, I would not believe in the Gospel myself if the authority of the Catholic Church did not influence me to do so."

St Jerome, *On the Three Solomonic Books* Preface (c. AD 398)
"There is also the book of Jesus, son of Sirach ... and another book, Wisdom, attributed to Solomon ... the second was never known in Hebrew, for its very style bespeaks Greek eloquence; and some of the older authors affirm that it is a work of Philo the Jew. Just as the Church reads Judith and Tobias and the Books of Maccabees, but does not accept them as belonging among the canonical Scriptures, so too let her read these two volumes for the edification of the people but not for the purpose of confirming the authority of the Church's teachings."

St Jerome, *Against Rufinus* 11, 33 (AD 402)

"What sin have I committed if I followed the judgment of the churches? But he who brings charges against me for relating the objections the Hebrews are wont to raise against the story of Susanna, the Son of the three Children, and the story of Bel and the Dragon, which are not found in the Hebrew volume, proves that he is just a foolish sycophant. For I wasn't relating my own personal views, but rather the remarks that they are wont to make against us."

St Rufinus of Aquileia, *Explanation of the Apostles' Creed* 35 & 36 (AD 404)

"These are the writings which the Fathers included in the canon, and on which they desired the affirmations of our faith to be based. At the same time we should appreciate that there are certain books which our predecessors designated 'ecclesiastical' rather than 'canonical.' Thus, there is the Wisdom of Solomon, as we call it; and another Wisdom, ascribed to the son of Sirach ... The Book of Tobias belongs to the same class, as do Judith and the books of the Maccabees. In the New Testament we have the little work known as The Book of the Shepherd, or Hermas, and the book which is named The Two Ways, and The Judgment of Peter. They desired that all these should be read in the Churches, but that appeal should not be made to them on points of faith."

Pope Innocent I, *Letter to Exsuperius, Bishop of Toulouse* 6, 7, 13 (AD 405)

"A short annotation shows what books are to be accepted as canonical. As you wished to be informed specifically, they are as follows: The five books of Moses, that is, Genesis, Exodus, Leviticus, Numbers, Deuteronomy; and Jesus Nave, one of Judges, four of Kingdoms, and also Ruth, sixteen books of Prophets, five books of Solomon, the Psalter. Likewise, of histories, one book of Job, one book of Tobias, one of Esther, one of Judith, two of Maccabees, two of Esdras, two books of Paralipomenon. Likewise, of the New Testament: four books of Gospels, fourteen Epistles of Paul, three Epistles of John, two Epistles of Peter, the Epistle of Jude, the Epistle of James, the Acts of the Apostles, the Apocalypse of John. Others, however, which were written under the name of Matthias or of James the Less, or under the name of Peter and of John, by a certain Leucius — or under the name of Andrew, by the philosophers Nexocharis and Leonidas — or under the name of Thomas, and such others as may be, are not only to be repudiated, but, as you know, are also to be condemned."

The Roman Catechism (1566)

No reference was made in the Roman Catechism to the Canon of the Bible; the question was addressed by the Council of Trent in the *Decree Concerning the Canonical Scriptures* in 1546:

> But if anyone receive not, as sacred and canonical, the said books entire with all their parts, as they have been used to be read in the Catholic Church, and as they are contained in the old Latin Vulgate edition; and knowingly and deliberately contemn the traditions aforesaid; let him be anathema.

Catechism of the Catholic Church (1992)

No. 120: It was by the apostolic Tradition that the Church discerned which writings are to be included in the list of the sacred books. This complete list is called the canon of Scripture. It includes 46 books for the Old Testament (45 if we count Jeremiah and Lamentations as one) and 27 for the New ...

Sola Scriptura?

Objection: *"I am not going to believe anything unless it is in the Bible!"*

A Christian who believes that the Bible is the sole rule of faith (*Sola Scriptura*) believes that all questions relating to faith and morals can be answered completely from the written word of God as contained in all the books from Genesis to Revelation. That being the case, there is no need for any other rule of faith to guide the Christian, whether it be tradition, a teaching authority, philosophy, or nature. These only inhibit a Christian's path to salvation.

However, a Bible-only approach, when applied logically, runs into immediate and numerous problems. For example, can a Bible held in the hand of any Christian answer the following questions: "How do I know that my Bible was correctly translated?"; "Does my Bible have the correct number of books in both the Old and New Testaments?"; "Is the interpretation of this or that verse the correct one?" Ordinary Christians lacking an extensive knowledge of the languages, cultures and history of the Holy Land and its surrounds would be hard-pressed to answer with certainty any of these questions, with or without a Bible.

Does the Bible actually teach that it is the sole rule of faith? According to self-described 'Bible Christians' it certainly does. They cite as proof the following verses:

"... but these are written that you may believe that Jesus is the Christ, the Son of God, and that believing you may have life in his name" (Jn 20:31).

"All scripture is inspired by God and profitable for teaching, for reproof, for correction, and for training in righteousness, that the man of God may be complete, equipped for every good work" (2 Tim. 3:16-17).

"Now these Jews were more noble than those in Thessalonica, for they received the word with all eagerness, examining the scriptures daily to see if these things were so" (Acts 17:11).

However, when looking at each of these verses closely it is clear that none say anything in support of *Sola Scriptura*. The verse from St John's Gospel speaks only of the purpose of the book, which is, to convince its readers that Jesus is the Christ. It does not assert that the Bible as it stands today contains all that is needed for salvation, neither does it exclude any other medium, whether written or oral, as a means of passing on the truths of Jesus. In fact, if one were to be consistent, St John's words could be construed as an argument that his Gospel alone, excluding the other three, is necessary for salvation — that is, *Solus Joannes!* (John alone!).

The second verse is the cornerstone for most Protestant arguments in favor of *Sola Scriptura*. Yet, again, there are no words such as "alone" or "only" used with respect to Scripture. No one who claims to be Christian, least of all the Catholic Church, denies that Scripture is "inspired" and "profitable" to perfect a "man of God." But it is certainly different to assert that Scripture is "sufficient." However, "sufficient" is not the word used by St Paul in 2 Tim. 3:16. He uses the Greek word *ophelimos* (ὠφέλιμος), which translates as "useful" or "profitable." Certain Protestants might argue that "profitable" means "sufficient." If so, then they would run into difficulties with Tit. 3:8 which says, "The saying is sure. I desire you to insist on these things, so that those who have believed in God may be careful to apply themselves to good deeds; these are excellent and profitable to men." Would any Protestant assert from this verse that good works are sufficient to get to heaven, thus rendering faith in Jesus unnecessary? Similarly, St Paul in his letter to the Ephesians says, "his gifts were that some should be apostles, some prophets, some evangelists, some pastors and teachers, *to equip the saints* for the work of ministry, for building up the body of Christ" (4:11-12). In others words, is the perfecting of the saints to be done through the leaders of the Church alone without the aid of Scripture?

St John Henry Cardinal Newman certainly saw the Protestant fallacy of employing 2 Tim. 3:16-17 in support of *Sola Scriptura*:

> It is quite evident that this passage furnishes no argument whatever that the Sacred Scripture, without Tradition, is the sole rule of faith; for, although Sacred Scripture is profitable

for these four ends, still it is not said to be sufficient. The Apostle requires the aid of Tradition (2 Thess. 2:14). Moreover, the Apostle here refers to the Scriptures which Timothy was taught in his infancy (i.e., the Old Testament).[1]

The third passage from Acts refers to the Bereans, who received the Gospel enthusiastically and who checked its claims against "the Scriptures." At first glance it could be claimed that as the Bereans were using the written Scriptures as their only 'rule of faith,' they established the precedent for all other Christians. However, what is often overlooked is that the Bereans had "received the word" orally, and that they were checking its claims against the Old Testament Scriptures only. Certainly no one could reasonably suggest that Christians today imitate the Bereans and have only the Old Testament as their rule of faith.

Not only is the doctrine of *Sola Scriptura* not found in the Bible, it is expressly denied by it. In Matt. 28:20 Jesus commands us to "observe *all* that I have commanded you." Yet, the Scriptures we have in hand expressly state that they do not contain everything (Jn 20:30; 21:25), or give us an account of all Jesus said and did (Jn 16:12). In addition, we know that there existed other Apostolic writings now lost, such as an earlier letter of St Paul to the Corinthians mentioned in 1 Cor. 5:9: "I wrote to you in my letter ... But rather I wrote to you ..." Also missing is a Laodicean epistle recommended to the Colossians by St Paul, probably written by himself (Col. 4:16).

Nevertheless, the fact there are certain Apostolic writings missing is of no fatal consequence to Catholics. This is so because the Catholic Church maintains that divine revelation is fully contained in her Deposit of Faith (body of teaching), comprised of both written Scripture and Tradition. Tradition here is Apostolic Tradition, not merely the tradition of men, and ranks equally with the written word to complete divine revelation. Tradition supplements the written word of God, it does not contradict it. Furthermore, it assists the Church to fully understand and appreciate the whole written word. Tradition embraces all those truths which have been passed on from age to age either orally, in the writings of the Church Fathers, in the Acts of the

---

[1] *Inspiration in its Relation to Revelation*, 1884.

Martyrs, in early paintings and inscriptions, in the practices and customs of the Universal Church, and in the definitions of Councils and Popes.

Second objection: *"But 'tradition' is condemned in the Bible as contrary to the Word of God (Mt 15:6)!"*

Contrary to general Protestant opinion, tradition is actually praised in Scripture: "So then, brethren, stand firm and hold *to the traditions which you were taught by us, either by word of mouth* or by letter" (2 Thess. 2:15). Jesus acknowledged the Jewish tradition of the authority of the seat of Moses and commanded his listeners to obey it, even though such a seat is not mentioned in the Old Testament (Mt 23:1-2). Oral preaching was the medium by which the Gospel spread before the New Testament was written: Acts 2:42; Rom. 10:17; 1 Cor. 11:2; 1 Cor. 15:3; 2 Tim. 2:2; 1 Pet. 1:25. St Paul received the following words of Jesus orally, "It is more blessed to give than to receive" (Acts 20:35) for such words are not recorded in the Gospels. Were the early Christians, therefore, victims of false prophets preaching the "commandments of men" simply because they received the Gospel orally? Such an assertion would be ridiculous. Stephen K. Ray, a convert from the Baptist faith, makes the following interesting point:

> As an Evangelical, when I read the phrase 'word of God' I would automatically plug in the word 'Bible'; this, however, is not at all the meaning usually intended in the Bible itself. Roughly nine out of ten times, 'word of God' is referring to the spoken word, not the written word (e.g., 1 Thess. 2:13). The *spoken* words, the oral tradition, were *also* the very 'words of God.'[2]

What was condemned by Jesus in Matt. 15:6 (and by St Paul in Col. 2:8) was not tradition *per se*, but those traditions, whether doctrines or practices, which made God's word and commandments *ineffective*. Jesus himself observed all the noble traditions of the Jews, such as the Pasch and all the liturgical festivals with their

---

[2] *Crossing the Tiber*, Ignatius Press, San Francisco, 1997 Ed., p. 30.

appurtenances, songs and ceremonies. It is the Church, as the indefectible teaching authority established by Jesus (Mt 16:19; 28:18-20), which determines what is or not authentic Tradition.

Other verses that speak laudably of oral Christian tradition include:

"Be imitators of me, as I am of Christ. I commend you because you remember me in everything and maintain the traditions even as I have delivered them to you" (1 Cor. 11:1-2).

"If any one is disposed to be contentious, we recognize no other practice, nor do the churches of God" (1 Cor. 11:16).

"What you have learned and received and heard and seen in me, do; and the God of peace will be with you" (Phil. 4:9).

"Now we command you, brethren, in the name of our Lord Jesus Christ, that you keep away from any brother who is living in idleness and not in accord with the tradition that you received from us" (2 Thess. 3:6).

"... 'but the word of the Lord abides for ever.' That word is the good news which was preached to you" (1 Pet. 1:25).

Interestingly, Jesus himself, as well as some of the Apostles, referred to *unwritten Old Testament tradition*:

(i) St Paul refers to the "rock" that "was Christ" that followed the Hebrews in the desert during the Exodus (1 Cor. 10:4). This Rock is nowhere recorded in the Old Testament.
(ii) St Paul (Gal. 3:19) and St Stephen (Acts 7:52-53) refer to the Law being "ordained by angels." Nowhere is this mentioned in the Old Testament.
(iii) St Paul refers to "Jannes and Jambres" who "opposed Moses" (2 Tim. 3:8-9). Neither of these names are mentioned in the Old Testament.

(iv) St Jude mentions the prophecy of Enoch, saying, "Behold, the Lord came with his holy myriads" (Jude 1:14). This prophecy is nowhere to be found in the Old Testament.

(v) St Jude mentions the struggle between St Michael and the devil for the body of Moses (Jude 1:9). The only prior written account of such a struggle is contained in the apocryphal work, *The Assumption of Moses*.

(vi) The author of *Hebrews* mentions the Prophet Isaiah being "sawn in two" (11:37). Such a death for the Prophet is mentioned only in the apocryphal work, *The Ascension of Isaiah* 5:1-4.

(vii) Jesus says, "The scribes and the Pharisees sit on Moses' seat" (Mt 23:2-3). Nowhere is such a seat mentioned in the Old Testament.

It is, therefore, not a question of Scripture *or* Tradition but rather Scripture *and* Tradition. Ironically, it is the doctrine of *Sola Scriptura* and its condemnation of Tradition *per se* that is the man-made tradition of the sixteenth century Reformers that contradicts the word of God.

Third objection: *"But once the New Testament was finally complete there was no more need for 'tradition.'"*

Such an argument goes back to the very core of the *Sola Scriptura* debate. The short Catholic answer is, "Where does it say that in the Bible?" Nowhere is it recorded that the Apostles or any of their faithful contemporaries gathered all the inspired Gospels and epistles and declared to the Christian world, "this will be the sole rule of faith after we have gone to the Lord." As time passed, the written New Testament would supplement Tradition, but not supplant it. The best response, however, is that Jesus did not intend to leave all his teachings in a single book, but *in the Church*, whether written, oral or otherwise. When Jesus ascended into heaven, he left behind a hierarchical authority to continue his mission in the world. This hierarchy was invested with divine authority to govern in his name (Mt 16:13; 18:18), is to be obeyed by all the faithful (Lk 10:16), and will last until the end of the world (Mt 16:18; 28:20).

Sola Scriptura, by implication, rejects the need for an authoritative body outside of the Bible to determine vital questions of faith and morals. Yet Jesus never promised to give us an authoritative book, but rather an authoritative Church: "on this rock I will build my Church" (Mt 16:18). St Paul attests that "the Church of the living God (is) ... the pillar and bulwark of the truth" (1 Tim. 3:15). It must also be remembered that it was the Catholic Church who assembled and canonized the books of the Old and New Testaments, translated them faithfully, safeguarded them in times of persecution and interpreted them free from error throughout the rise and fall of every heresy under the sun. Without the Church and Tradition, there would have been no Bible to base *Sola Scriptura* on in the first place. As another convert from Protestantism, James Akin, states:

> The Protestant apologist is in a fix. In order to use *Sola Scriptura* he is going to have to identify what the scriptures are, and since he is unable to do this from scripture alone, he is going to have to appeal to things outside of scripture to make his case, meaning that in every act of doing this he undermines this case. There is no way to escape the canon of tradition.[3]

As the Blessed Virgin Mary gave birth to Jesus and then nurtured and protected him as her child and Lord, so the Church gave birth to the New Testament scriptures and now nurtures, protects and adheres to them faithfully.

Fourth objection: *"But the Bible in Revelation 22:18-19 specifically warns that anyone who adds to the written Word of God will be punished with the plagues described in that same book."*

A careful reading of Rev. 22:18-19 indicates that the warning in question is only directed against those who wish to add to the words

---

[3] http://www.catholicfidelity.com/apologetics-topics/bible/the-two-canons-scripture-and-tradition-by-james-akin/

of prophecy "in this book," namely, the Book of Revelation. The Angel was not referring to the whole Bible as such, or even just the New Testament, as the Gospel of St John had not yet been written. If the objection as stated is correct, then St John himself is deserving of the plagues for writing his Gospel two years after the book of Revelation.

Fifth objection: *"But I can understand the Bible through the Holy Spirit without the need for a church or 'tradition'!"*

St Peter himself warned that the "ignorant and unstable" would "twist" the Scriptures "to their own destruction" (2 Pet. 3:16). One fruit of private interpretation of the Bible has been the spawning of over thirty-five thousand different Protestant denominations all claiming to be 'Bible-believing,' yet agreeing on little more than their anti-Catholic tenets. A person who builds his faith on private interpretation is akin to the fool in Matt. 7:24-27 who built his house on the grains of sand. As grains of sand tend to shift to the downfall of the house, so too do individual minds continually change the interpretation of Scripture to the downfall of faith. On the contrary, the wise man built his house on rock (*kepha*); likewise does the faithful Catholic build his faith on St Peter (*Kepha*) and his successors.

The Bible is a compilation of books all written in the ancient past and in languages for the most part dead to the average layman. Scripture itself mentions the difficulty of interpretation: 2 Pet. 3:16; Heb. 5:11-12. If the Holy Spirit gives an infallible explanation of the Bible to every individual reader, why did he not explain it to the Ethiopian minister in Acts 8:30-31?: "So Philip ran to him, and heard him reading Isaiah the prophet, and asked, 'Do you understand what you are reading?' And he said, 'How can I, unless some one guides me?'" It is the Catholic Church that has the true understanding of Scripture, aided by the Holy Spirit who will guide it in all truth until the end of the world (Mt 28:20). It is entirely unreasonable to assert that Jesus would leave behind a written book without a divinely protected living authority to safeguard and interpret it.

The Fathers

Papias (inter AD 125-160) [Fragment in Eusebius, *Ecclesiastical History* **3, 39, 4 (c. AD 303)]**
"And then too, when anyone came along who had been a follower of the presbyters, I would inquire about the presbyters' discourses: what was said by Andrew, or by Peter, or by Philip, or by Thomas or James, or by John or Matthew, or by any other of the Lord's disciples: and what Aristion and the Presbyter John, the disciples of the Lord, say. It did not seem to me that I could get so much profit from the contents of books as from a living and abiding voice."

St Irenaeus of Lyons, *Against Heresies* **3, 4, 1 (c. AD 180)**
"If there should be a dispute over some kind of question, ought we not have recourse to the most ancient Churches in which the Apostles were familiar, and draw from them what is clear and certain in regard to that question? What if the Apostles had not in fact left writings to us? Would it not be necessary to follow the order of tradition, which was handed down to those to whom they entrusted the Churches?"

Tertullian, *The Demurrer Against the Heretics* **19, 3 (AD 200)**
"Wherever it shall be clear that the truth of the Christian discipline and faith are present, there also will be found the truth of the Scriptures and of their explanation, and of all the Christian traditions."

Origen, *Fundamental Doctrines* **1, Preface, 2 (c. AD 220)**
"Although there are many who believe that they themselves hold to the teachings of Christ, there are yet some among them who think differently from their predecessors. The teaching of the Church has indeed been handed down through an order of succession from the Apostles, and remains in the Churches even to the present time. That alone is to be believed as the truth which is in no way at variance with ecclesiastical and apostolic tradition."

St Basil the Great, *The Holy Spirit* **27, 66 (AD 375)**
"Of the dogmas and kerygmas preserved in the Church, some we possess from written teaching and others we receive from the tradition

of the Apostles, handed on to us in mystery. In respect to piety both are of the same force. No one will contradict any of these, no one, at any rate, who is even moderately versed in matters ecclesiastical. Indeed, were we to try to reject unwritten customs as having no great authority, we would unwittingly injure the Gospel in its vitals."

St Epiphanius of Salamis, *Against all Heresies* 61, 6 (AD 377)

"It is not necessary that all the divine words have an allegorical meaning. Consideration and perception is needed in order to know the meaning of the argument of each. It is needful also to make use of Tradition; for not everything can be gotten from Sacred Scripture. The Holy Apostles handed down some things in the Scriptures, other things in Tradition."

St Augustine of Hippo, *Against the Letter of Mani* 5, 6 (AD 397)

"If you should find someone who does not yet believe in the Gospel, what would you answer him when he says: 'I do not believe?' Indeed, I would not believe in the Gospel myself if the authority of the Catholic Church did not influence me to do so."

St Augustine of Hippo, *Letter to Januarius* 54, 1, 1 (c. AD 400)

"But in regard to those observances which we carefully attend and which the whole world keeps, and which derive not from Scripture but from Tradition, we are given to understand that they are recommended and ordained to be kept, either by the Apostles themselves or by plenary councils, the authority of which is quite vital in the Church."

St John Chrysostom, *Homily on 2 Thessalonians* 4, 2 (c. AD 400)

"'Therefore, brethren, stand fast and hold the traditions which you have been taught, whether by word or by our letter.' From this it is clear that they did not hand down everything by letter, but there was much also that was not written. Like that which was written, the unwritten too is worthy of belief. So let us regard the tradition of the Church also as worthy of belief. Is it a tradition? Seek no further."

Sola Scriptura?

The Roman Catechism (1566)

Preface: Now all the doctrines in which the faithful are to be instructed are contained in the Word of God, which is found in Scripture and Tradition. To the study of these, therefore, the pastor should devote his days and nights, keeping in mind the admonition of St Paul to Timothy, which all who have care of souls should consider as addressed to themselves: *Attend to reading, to exhortation, and to doctrine, for all scripture divinely inspired is profitable to teach, to reprove, to correct, to instruct injustice, that the man of God may be perfect, furnished to every good work.*

Catechism of the Catholic Church (1992)

No. 80: Sacred Tradition and Sacred Scripture, then, are bound closely together and communicate one with the other. For both of them, flowing out from the same divine well-spring, come together in some fashion to form one thing and move towards the same goal. Each of them makes present and fruitful in the Church the mystery of Christ, who promised to remain with his own "always, to the close of the age."

No. 82: As a result the Church, to whom the transmission and interpretation of Revelation is entrusted, does not derive her certainty about all revealed truths from the holy Scriptures alone. Both Scripture and Tradition must be accepted and honored with equal sentiments of devotion and reverence.

Bible Truth

Objection: *"The Catholic Church is not a Bible-believing Church. It has no love for the Word of God!"*

The Catholic Church is not only a 'Bible-believing' church but also the Church of the Bible. Only the Catholic Church among the many thousands of others can demonstrate a continued existence from the time of Jesus and the Apostles to the present day. When Jesus ascended into heaven he left behind a living Church endowed with his power and authority to continue his work of salvation in the world. It was only in the decades immediately following that the Holy Spirit inspired certain Apostles and Evangelists to reduce into written form the teachings of Jesus already delivered "once and for all to the saints" (Jude 1:3).

A simple cursory look at the Catholic Church's history suffices to rebut the above objection. The Catholic Church has always extensively used the Scriptures in her public worship, reading out for the spiritual benefit of her children extracts from the Old Testament, the Gospels, the Epistles of St Paul and the Universal Epistles. The Scriptures have always formed the backbone of the Divine Office, the official public prayer of the Church. When heresies arose denying the value of the Old Testament, the Catholic Church responded in its defense. Her apologists and heroes combated all other heresies principally from the Scriptures. The writings of the Church Fathers are replete with tens of thousands of references from every book of the Bible. Catholic philosophers, scholastics, doctors, saints, theologians and writers of all sorts always had the words of Scripture flowing from both their pens and their lips, producing over the centuries the greatest treasury of literature in human history. Not one Council or Papal pronouncement is devoid of references from Scripture; neither does one find the Scriptures absent from one page of any official Church catechism. The Catholic Church gave the world an authoritative list of the canonical books, translated them into every language before the emergence of Protestantism, and has faithfully interpreted them to all generations. Popes have granted plenary indulgences for the faithful reading of the Scriptures. If all this is not enough the following words of the Popes should end all debate:

> ... the Church has never failed in taking due measures to bring the Scriptures within reach of her children, and that she has ever held fast and exercised profitably that guardianship conferred upon her by Almighty God for the protection and glory of his holy Word; so that she has never required, nor does she now require, any stimulation from without.[1]

> ... a whole multitude of Doctors ... have sifted the Sacred Books in every way, and ... have thanked God more and more heartily the more deeply they have gone into them, for his divine bounty in having vouchsafed to speak thus to men.[2]

> Wherefore we exhort all the Church's children, and especially those whose duty it is to teach in seminaries, to follow closely in St Jerome's footsteps. If they will but do so they will learn to prize as he prized the treasure of the Scriptures, and will derive from them most abundant and blessed fruit.[3]

These same Popes simultaneously attacked those who sought to deny the divine inspiration of the Scriptures, who found in them alleged errors and contradictions, who claimed they were forgeries made after the event, or who taught that they were simply collections of myths, stories and exaggerations:

> They deny that there is any such thing as revelation or inspiration, or Holy Scripture at all; they see, instead, only the forgeries and the falsehoods of men; they set down the Scripture narratives as stupid fables and lying stories: the prophecies and the oracles of God are to them either predictions made up after the event or forecasts formed by the light of nature; the miracles and the wonders of God's power are not what they are said to be, but the startling effects of

---

[1] Pope Leo XIII, *Providentissimus Deus*, #8, 1893.
[2] Pope St Pius X, *Pascendi Dominici Gregis*, #34, 1907.
[3] Pope Benedict XV, *Spiritus Paraclitus*, #30, 1920.

natural law, or else mere tricks and myths; and the apostolic Gospels and writings are not the work of the Apostles at all.[4]

What can we say of men who in expounding the very Gospels so whittle away the human trust we should repose in it as to overturn Divine faith in it? They refuse to allow that the things which Christ said or did have come down to us unchanged and entire through witnesses who carefully committed to writing what they themselves had seen or heard. They maintain – and particularly in their treatment of the Fourth Gospel – that much is due of course to the Evangelists – who, however, added much from their own imaginations; but much, too, is due to narratives compiled by the faithful at other periods, the result, of course, being that the twin streams now flowing in the same channel cannot be distinguished from one another.[5]

Second objection: *"The Popes and documents you quote are more than a hundred years old. They do not reflect the position of the Catholic Church today!"*

One current statement that is often heard within Catholic circles is, "Vatican II changed all that." Those who use such a phrase often attribute every authorized or unauthorized change to the Second Vatican Council. The same have usually not even read the Council documents and refer instead to the so-called 'spirit of the Council.' This spirit is really a smoke-screen set up in recent decades by neo-Modernists with the aim of hijacking the Council's agenda and replacing it with their own. When Protestants hear certain Catholic clergy or laity speaking against the authenticity of the Scriptures, without a doubt they have come across a Catholic of modernist persuasion. The Protestant in this case may be excused if he fails to make such a distinction, particularly as Modernism is so widespread today. In such a situation, two things must be pointed out to the Protestant: first, that modernist Biblical criticism actually had its origins in eighteenth and nineteenth century liberal Protestantism (and is

---

[4] Pope Leo XIII, *Providentissimus Deus*, #10, 1893.
[5] Pope Benedict XV, *Spiritus Paraclitus*, #27, 1920.

found more recently in the writings of the German Protestant Rudolf Bultmann); and second, that Modernism is even a greater opponent of authentic Catholic Biblical teaching than Protestantism.

A close study of Church pronouncements immediately before, during and after Vatican II clearly shows that nothing has changed in official Catholic teaching since the time when Vatican I and Pope Leo XIII declared the Scriptures to be "written under the inspiration of the Holy Ghost ... have God for their author, and as such have been delivered to the Church"[6]:

> When, subsequently, some Catholic writers, in spite of this solemn definition of Catholic doctrine, by which such divine authority is claimed for the 'entire books with all their parts' as to secure freedom from any error whatsoever, ventured to restrict the truth of Sacred Scripture solely to matters of faith and morals, and to regard other matters, whether in the domain of physical science or history, as 'obiter dicta' and – as they contended – in no wise connected with faith, Our Predecessor of immortal memory, Leo XIII in the Encyclical Letter *Providentissimus Deus*, published on November 18 in the year 1893, justly and rightly condemned these errors and safe-guarded the studies of the Divine Books by most wise precepts and rules.[7]

> They refuse to admit the existence of a supernatural order and the intervention of a personal God in the world through strict Revelation, and the possibility and existence of miracles and prophecies. Others begin with a false idea of faith, as if it had nothing to do with historical truth – or rather, were incompatible with it. Others deny the historical value and nature of the documents of Revelation *a priori* [as a starting point]. Finally, others make light of the authority of the Apostles as witnesses to Christ, and of their task and influence in the primitive community, extolling rather the creative power of that community. All such views are not only opposed

---

[6] *Providentissimus Deus*, Introductory.
[7] Pope Pius XII, *Divino Afflante Spiritu*, 1943, Preface.

Bible Truth

to Catholic doctrine, but are also devoid of scientific basis and alien to the correct principles of historical method.[8]

Therefore, since everything asserted by the inspired authors or sacred writers must be held to be asserted by the Holy Spirit, it follows that the books of Scripture must be acknowledged as teaching solidly, faithfully and without error that truth which God wanted put into sacred writings for the sake of our salvation. Therefore 'all Scripture is divinely inspired and has its use for teaching the truth and refuting error, for reformation of manners and discipline in right living, so that the man of God may be efficient and equipped for good work of every kind.'[9]

Guided by the Holy Spirit and in the light of the living Tradition which it has received, the Church has discerned the writings which should be regarded as Sacred Scripture in the sense that, 'having been written under the inspiration of the Holy Spirit, they have God as their author and have been handed on as such to the Church' (*Dei Verbum*, 11) and contain 'that truth which God wanted put into the Sacred Writings for the sake of our salvation' (*ibid.*).[10]

The inspired books teach the truth. 'Since therefore all that the inspired authors or sacred writers affirm should be regarded as affirmed by the Holy Spirit, we must acknowledge that the books of Scripture firmly, faithfully, and without error teach that truth which God, for the sake of our salvation, wished to see confided to the Sacred Scriptures.'[11]

---

[8] Pontifical Biblical Commission, *Sancta Mater Ecclesia* (Instruction on the Historical Truth of the Gospels), V, 1964.
[9] Second Vatican Council, *Dei Verbum* (Dogmatic Constitution on Divine Revelation), #11, 1965.
[10] Pontifical Biblical Commission, *The Interpretation of the Bible in the Church*, 1993, III, B, 1.
[11] *Catechism of the Catholic Church* (CCC) #107.

Third objection: *"But virtually all Catholic schools today teach that the book of Genesis, for example, is only a myth. Why is this so?"*

It is true that many Catholic schools and teachers today teach that Genesis is not historical, that chapters 1-11 contain only myths, and that the rest of the book contains numerous errors. This is symptomatic of the widespread surrender to Modernist exegesis and the adoption of dubious evolutionary notions to explain the origins of life and of humanity.

Nevertheless, it is not the role of Catholic schools or teachers to interpret Scripture. Such a role is properly reserved to the Magisterium:

> The task of an authentic interpretation of the Word of God, whether written or handed on, has been entrusted exclusively to the living teaching office [Magisterium] of the Church alone. Its authority in this matter is exercised in the name of Jesus Christ.[12]

It is the Magisterium that has declared consistently from Vatican I to Vatican II that all the books of Scripture were "written under the inspiration of the Holy Spirit ... have God as their author, and have been handed on as such to the Church herself."[13] With regard to the book of Genesis, the *Pontifical Biblical Commission* (PBC) — as an organ of the teaching Magisterium — declared in 1909 that the first three chapters were not legend or mythology, even if the sacred writer did not intend to write with scientific exactitude. Rather, the three chapters are a narrative of events that truly occurred and can be understood in a literal, historical sense, though certain passages are to be understood in a figurative sense. The *Catechism of the Catholic Church* uses similar language in upholding the historicity of Genesis in our days:

> The account of the fall in Genesis 3 uses figurative language, but affirms a primeval event, a deed that took place at the

---

[12] *Dei Verbum, ibid.,* #10.
[13] *Ibid.,* #7; cf. CCC #105.

beginning of the history of man. Revelation gives us the certainty of faith that the whole of human history is marked by the original fault freely committed by our first parents.[14]

Earlier, in 1906 the PBC declared that Moses was the principal and substantial human author of the Pentateuch and hence of Genesis, though he may have been inspired to use and edit earlier manuscripts and/or oral traditions. In 1950, Pope Pius XII stated that the first eleven chapters of Genesis "do nevertheless come under the heading of history." He went on to say, "the same chapters, in simple and metaphorical language adapted to the mentality of a primitive people, both state principal truths which are fundamental for our salvation and also give a popular description of the origin of the human race and the Chosen People."[15]

There is no doubt that Jesus himself accepted the book of Genesis as historical and true. That he came as Redeemer shows that he was aware of the original sin of Adam. His teaching on marriage and divorce reinforces this: "But from the beginning of creation, 'God made them male and female'" (Mk 10:6). Finally, his rebuking of Capharnaum for its faithlessness and his comparison of it with Sodom and Gomorrah illustrates that he believed the latter two were actual cities (Mt 11:23-24).

Fourth objection: *"Many Catholic writers and speakers say that the Gospels were not written by the Apostles and Evangelists. What more proof do I need that the Catholic Church is no longer truly Christian?"*

Unfortunately, many Catholics and non-Catholics have probably read and heard such statements. Again, however, one must listen to the voice of the Magisterium to know the Church's authentic position concerning the Gospels. The following is a list of pronouncements issued by the PBC upholding the traditional belief that all four Gospels were written by Matthew, Mark, Luke and John respectively:

---

[14] CCC #390.
[15] *Humani Generis*, #13, 1950.

(i) *On the Author and the Historical Truth of the Fourth Gospel* (1907).

(ii) *On the Author, Date of Composition, and Historical Truth of the Gospel According to St Matthew* (1911).

(iii) *On the Author, Date of Composition, and Historical Truth of the Gospels According to St Mark and St Luke* (1912).

The PBC likewise ruled that it should be held as certain that St Luke was the author of the Acts of the Apostles (1913) and St Paul of the Pastoral Epistles (1913).

Admittedly, these five pronouncements were handed down over a century ago; nevertheless, *subsequent Church statements have overridden none of them*. Rather, the Second Vatican Council went out of its way to clearly reaffirm the historicity of the Gospels:

> The Church has always and everywhere maintained, and continues to maintain, the apostolic origin of the four Gospels. The apostles preached, as Christ had charged them to do, and then, under the inspiration of the Holy Spirit, they and others of the apostolic age handed on to us in writing the same message they had preached, the foundation of our Faith: the fourfold Gospel, according to Matthew, Mark, Luke and John ... Holy Mother Church has firmly and with absolute constancy held that the four Gospels ... whose historical character the Church unhesitatingly asserts, faithfully hand on what Jesus Christ really did and taught for their eternal salvation.[16]

Of all the Gospels, the one whose authenticity is most challenged is the fourth. Before the end of the eighteenth century no one denied that St John the Apostle was the author. However, sceptical critics emerged at that time, dismissing the fourth Gospel as a work of fiction compiled by unknown Christians in the mid-second century who were disappointed by Jesus' failure to return as promised. These same critics further argued that the historical Jesus had nothing to do with the 'miracle-working divine Son of God,' but rather was simply a

---

[16] *Dei Verbum*, #19.

profound teacher and revolutionary who challenged the corrupt institutions of his day.

The internal evidence in support of the Apostolic authorship of John's Gospel can be briefly summarized as follows[17]:

(i) The author possessed a clear familiarity with Old Testament Jewish thought, as well as social and religious customs. Historical and archaeological research has subsequently revealed that the fourth Gospel depicts exactly the complex social and political orders that existed in the early first century AD, orders destroyed by the Romans in the year AD 70.
(ii) The author had first-hand local knowledge of the topography of Israel and Jerusalem and its surrounds.
(iii) The author expressly claims to be an eyewitness and possess first-hand knowledge of facts, as well as thoughts and conversations of Jesus and the Apostles that no one else was privy to. The author even records the original Aramaic words used by Jesus, such as *Abba*, *Talitha cum*.
(iv) St John the Apostle is never mentioned by name in the Gospel even though the author is meticulous about naming other Apostles and characters. The only explanation for such an omission is that St John was the author, and his devotion and humility led him to write about Jesus and others rather than himself.
(v) Again, the author's humility led him to simply call himself "the disciple whom Jesus loved." Such a reference obviously bespeaks the extraordinary relationship the author had with Jesus, one of beloved disciple and Master.

Fifth objection: *"Why did the Catholic Church condemn the reading of the Scriptures during the Middle Ages? And what about the chaining of Bibles in churches to prevent ordinary people from finding out about Gospel truth?"*

---

[17] From G. H. Duggan SM, *Beyond Reasonable Doubt*, St Paul Books & Media, Boston, MA, 1987, pp. 99-110.

This question insinuates that the Catholic Church is the enemy of the word of God and, as such has strenuously endeavored throughout her history to deprive people from devoutly reading the Scriptures. Nothing could be further from the truth.

Protestant historians such as Dean Maitland[18] show that the Middle Ages was a period of great reverence for the word of God. Numerous monks industriously copied the Scriptures word for word for private and public use. The Scriptures were preached daily by the clergy, quoted by theologians of all ranks in their writings, schools and universities, used in the compilation of popular prayer books, and employed to determine the great deliberations of Popes and Councils. The Scriptures were neither ignored nor disparaged. Maitland admits, "I do not recollect any instance in which it is recorded that the Scriptures, or any part of them, were treated with indignity, or with less than profound respect."[19]

What was condemned during the Middle Ages was not the reading of the Bible but the production, circulation and reading of perverted translations produced by heretical groups or individuals in support of their novel teachings. Such groups included the Albigensians, the Waldensians, and the Lollards (Wycliffites). It was out of zeal for the authentic word of God that the Catholic Church through local and universal laws prohibited the reading of the Scriptures *without the appropriate safeguards* (e.g., Toulouse 1229, Tarragona 1233, Oxford 1408, the Index of Forbidden Books 1574). A close examination of just two of the most well known heretical vernacular translations would reveal the vast number of errors they contained – Tyndale's English Bible contained two thousand errors; Luther's German version three thousand!

In fact, Catholic vernacular translations of the Scriptures were produced abundantly during the Middle Ages and the Renaissance. Non-Latin Scripture versions (in whole or in part) produced before the Protestant Reformation include[20]:

---

[18] *The Dark Ages*, 3rd ed., Leipzig, 1896, pp. 208-241.
[19] *Ibid.*
[20] Cf. *The Oxford Companion to the Bible* (edd. B. Metzger, M. Coogan), Oxford University Press, 1993, pp. 755-758.

(i) Sixty-Two Hebrew editions (twelve of the entire Old Testament, fifty of selected portions)
(ii) Twenty-Two Greek editions (three of the Old Testament, twelve of the New Testament, seven of selected portions)
(iii) Six Italian editions
(iv) Ten French editions
(v) Six Dutch editions
(vi) Four Spanish editions
(vii) Ten German editions

English translations made before the Reformation include[21]:

(i) An Anglo-Saxon translation of portions of the Old and New Testaments by the Northumbrian herdsman, Caedmon, c. AD 600.
(ii) An Anglo-Saxon translation of the Psalms by Guthlac at the end of the seventh century.
(iii) A translation of the Psalms by Aldhelm, Bishop of Scherborne, in the eighth century.
(iv) A translation of the entire Bible by St Bede (+AD 731).
(v) A translation of a portion of the Psalms by King Alfred the Great (+AD 901).
(vi) A translation of the Gospels in the West Saxon dialect, tenth century (the *Wessex Gospels*).
(vii) A translation of the Gospels by Farmer and Owen in the tenth century.
(viii) Interlinear glosses written around AD 950 in the Northumbrian dialect (the *Lindisfarne Gospels*).
(ix) A translation of the first seven books of the Old Testament plus the Book of Job by Archbishop Aelfric of Canterbury in the eleventh century.
(x) A translation of parts of the Old and New Testaments by Orm, an English Benedictine monk, in the thirteenth century.
(xi) A translation of the Psalms by William Shoreham, Vicar of Chart Sutton, in 1320.

---

[21] Cf. *A Companion to Scripture Studies*, Fr. John Steinmuller STD, Joseph Wagner, New York, 1941, p. 208.

Defend the Faith!

(xii) A translation of the Psalms by Richard Rolle, a hermit of Hampole, in the fourteenth century.

All of these appeared before Luther's alleged first German translation of the Bible published in 1534. In addition, there existed another ninety-four vernacular editions of selected portions of the New Testament and the Psalms!

The allegation that the Bible was kept in chains in Catholic churches only affords further proof of the high esteem in which the Catholic Church held the Scriptures. Prior to the invention of the printing press in 1456, the production of new manuscripts was very time-consuming and costly. Many of the Bibles produced manually by monks were also magnificent works of art. Some copies placed for auction in recent times have been sold for many millions of dollars. Bibles were chained simply to prevent them from being stolen and taken away from public use. Only overly imaginative minds laboring under severe anti-Catholic bias could invent and propagate the tale that Bibles were chained to keep them exclusively in the hands of corrupt clergy, etc.

The authentic Catholic attitude towards the Bible and its study remains that of Pope Leo XIII, who said, over a century ago:

> The solicitude of the apostolic office naturally urges and even compels us, not only to desire that this grand source of Catholic revelation should be made safely and abundantly accessible to the flock of Jesus Christ, but also not to suffer any attempt to defile or corrupt it, either on the part of those who impiously and openly assail the Scriptures, or of those who are led astray into fallacious and imprudent novelties.[22]

It is not surprising, therefore, that the Catholic Church presently grants those faithful who devoutly read the Scriptures for up to thirty minutes in any given day a plenary indulgence under the usual conditions.

---

[22] *Providentissimus Deus*, Introductory.

The Fathers

Papias (inter AD 60-130) [Fragment in Eusebius, *Ecclesiastical History* 3, 39, 15 (c. AD 303)]
"And the Presbyter said this also: 'When Mark became the interpreter of Peter, he wrote down accurately whatever he remembered, though not in order, of the words and deeds of the Lord. He was neither hearer nor follower of the Lord; but such he was afterwards, as I say, of Peter, who had no intention of giving a connected account of the sayings of the Lord, but adapted his instructions as was necessary. Mark, then, made no mistake, but wrote things down as he remembered them; and he made it his concern to omit nothing that he had heard nor to falsify anything therein.'"

St Irenaeus of Lyons, *Against Heresies* 3, 11, 7-8 (c. AD 180)
"There is such certainty surrounding the Gospels that the heretics themselves bear witness to them; and starting from the Gospels, each one of them attempts to establish his own doctrine ... Just as there are four regions of the world in which we live, and four universal winds, and since the Church is disseminated over all the earth, and the pillar and mainstay of the Church is the Gospel, the breath of life, it is fitting that she have four pillars ..."

Clement of Alexandria, *Hypotyposeis* (inter AD 190-210) [Fragment in Eusebius, *Ecclesiastical History* 6, 14, 5-6 (c. AD 303)]
"The Gospels containing the genealogies ... were written first. The circumstances which occasioned that of Mark were these: When Peter preached the Word publicly at Rome, and declared the Gospel by the Spirit, many who were present requested that Mark, who had been for a long time his follower and who remembered his sayings, should write down what had been proclaimed. Having composed the Gospel, he gave it to those who had requested it. When Peter learned of this, he did not positively forbid it, but neither did he encourage it. John, last of all, seeing that the plain facts had been clearly set forth in the Gospels, and being urged by his acquaintances, composed a spiritual Gospel under the divine inspiration of the Spirit."

Tertullian, *Against Marcion* 4, 2, 1 (inter AD 207-212)
"First of all, we take the position that the evangelical testament has as its authors Apostles, upon whom the task of promulgating the Gospel was imposed by the Lord himself ... Of the Apostles, then, John and Matthew first introduced the faith to us, and of the apostolic men, Luke and Mark refresh it for us."

St Augustine of Hippo, *Against the Letter of Mani* 5, 6 (AD 397)
"If you should find someone who does not yet believe in the Gospel, what would you answer him when he says: 'I do not believe?' Indeed, I would not believe in the Gospel myself if the authority of the Catholic Church did not influence me to do so."

The Roman Catechism (1566)

Preface: Now all the doctrines in which the faithful are to be instructed are contained in the Word of God, which is found in Scripture and Tradition. To the study of these, therefore, the pastor should devote his days and nights, keeping in mind the admonition of St Paul to Timothy, which all who have care of souls should consider as addressed to themselves: *Attend to reading, to exhortation, and to doctrine, for all scripture divinely inspired is profitable to teach, to reprove, to correct, to instruct in justice, that the man of God may be perfect, furnished to every good work.*

Pt. III, Ch. III: (It is also honored) when we pay a religious attention to the word of God, which announces to us his will; make it the subject of our constant meditation; and strive by reading or hearing it, according to our respective capacities and conditions of life, to become acquainted with it.

Catechism of the Catholic Church (1992)

No. 105: God is the author of Sacred Scripture. "The divinely revealed realities, which are contained and presented in the text of Sacred

Scripture, have been written down under the inspiration of the Holy Spirit."

> For Holy Mother Church, relying on the faith of the apostolic age, accepts as sacred and canonical the books of the Old and the New Testaments, whole and entire, with all their parts, on the grounds that, written under the inspiration of the Holy Spirit, they have God as their author, and have been handed on as such to the Church herself.

The One True Church

Objection: *"All Churches that believe in Jesus and the Bible are the same. In any case, I don't need to attend any church to worship God. All I need is a personal relationship with Jesus which I can have by praying and reading the Bible on my own."*

The Protestant Reformation introduced new and radically different concepts concerning the nature and role of the Church. In contrast to long held doctrines such as the Communion of Saints and the corporate view of the Church as the Body of Christ, Protestantism asserted an individualistic Christianity that focused on one's personal relationship with Jesus to the exclusion of any absolute need for a Church or other visible organization. One modern-day anti-Catholic sums up the Evangelical approach to the Church as follows:

> ... salvation is found, not in a Church and its sacraments, but through a personal relationship with Christ himself. Salvation is given directly by Christ to an individual, without the need for any other mediation.[1]

However, faith in Jesus not only obliges the Christian to trust in and commit to him personally, but to believe in and follow what he taught and established to continue his work of salvation in the world. That Jesus intended to establish an authoritative Church of his own is clear from Scripture: *"and on this rock I will build my Church"* (Mt 16:18).

The Church belongs to Jesus as he founded her while still on earth. Being her founder, he is also her head: "Christ is the head of the church, his body" (Eph. 5:23). Those baptized in the name of the Trinity (Mt 28:19) are incorporated into Christ's Body, that is, the Church. In no way is the Church simply a man-made institution established centuries later bearing the name of the particular individual

---

[1] William Webster, *The Catholic Church at the Bar of History*, Carlisle, Penn.: Banner of Truth Trust, 1995, ch. 9, p. 133.

who spawned its existence. Rather, she is a divine institution which requires the membership of all those who claim the title of Christian.

Denying the absolute necessity of the Church in the economy of salvation, Protestantism also denies the visibility of the Church, insisting instead that it is simply the collection of the 'true believers' or 'saved' whoever and wherever they may be. However, the visibility of the Church is implied in Matt. 5:14: *"A city set on a hill cannot be hidden."* Furthermore, rather than being only a nebulous collection of 'true believers,' Jesus established his Church with a hierarchical authority to govern it (Lk 6:13; Mt 18:17-18), invested it with his own mission (Jn 20:21), the power to sanctify the faithful (Jn 15:16) and to forgive sins (Jn 20:23), as well as the authority to teach (Mt 28:20) and to baptize (Mt 28:19).

As head of this visible and hierarchical Church, Jesus appointed St Peter as his Vicar, or representative:

"You are Peter, and on this rock I will build my church" (Mt 16:18).

As Vicar and head of the Church on earth, St Peter is invested with Jesus' own authority to rule and govern:

"I will give you the keys of the kingdom of heaven, and whatever you bind on earth shall be bound in heaven, and whatever you loose on earth shall be loosed in heaven" (Mt 16:18-19).

St Peter and the Apostles, as rulers of the Church on earth, are to be obeyed:

"Obey your leaders and submit to them; for they are keeping watch over your souls, as men who will have to give account" (Heb. 13:17).

To obey St Peter and the Apostles, and logically their successors, is to obey Jesus:

"Truly, truly, I say to you, he who receives any one whom I send receives me; and he who receives me receives him who sent me" (Jn 13:20).

The Scriptures themselves show that the Apostles handed on their office through the laying of hands to subsequent generations as their successors (Acts 13:2; 1 Tim. 4:14; Tit. 5-10). To believe that the written New Testament replaced the authority of the Apostles after the death of St John is to deny historical reality and believe erroneously that the Church founded by Jesus subsequently changed in her essence.

Those who ignore the legitimate leaders of Jesus' Church through their own disobedience no longer belong to her unity:

"... if he refuses to listen even to the church, let him be to you as a Gentile and a tax collector" (Mt 18:17).

To ignore the leaders of the Church, one effectively ignores Jesus:

"He who hears you hears me, and he who rejects you rejects me" (Lk 10:16).

It is the Church that guarantees that the faithful are taught truth, assisted by the Holy Spirit:

"And I will ask the Father, and he will give you another Counselor, to be with you for ever" (Jn 14:16).

"... if I am delayed, you may know how one ought to behave in the household of God, which is the Church of the living God, the pillar and bulwark of the truth" (1 Tim. 3:15).

The Protestant assertion that Christians need only pray and read the Bible privately in their own homes or in fellowship groups has only resulted in the birth of over thirty-five thousand different Protestant denominations all claiming to be 'Bible-believing,' yet agreeing on little more than their anti-Catholic tenets. They fulfil the very words of St Peter himself who warned of the "ignorant and unstable" who "twist" the Scriptures "to their own destruction" (2 Pet. 3:16).

Despite the disobedience and protestations of so many, Jesus will protect his Church until the end of time:

"... the gates of hades shall not prevail against it" (Mt 16:18).

"... and behold, I am with you always, to the close of the age" (Mt 28:20).

Second objection: *"So Jesus did found a Church. But that Church is definitely not the apostate church of Rome!"*

Not only did Jesus establish a Church, but he also made that Church identifiable according to certain marks. To qualify as a mark the means of identification must possess two aspects: (i) it must be an outwardly visible sign objectively evident to everyone, including non-Christians; and (ii) it must be an essential characteristic without which the Church would not be the Church of Christ.

According to the well-known anti-Catholic Presbyterian minister Loraine Boettner,

> The marks of a true church are:
> 1. The true preaching of the Word of God.
> 2. The right administration of the sacraments. And,
> 3. The faithful exercise of discipline.[2]

One obvious difficulty with Boettner's marks is that they do not include a test to determine whether the church in question was actually founded by Jesus. Furthermore, his criteria (based on Calvin's) do not aim to discover "the true Church" but "a true church." Any man-made institution could therefore claim to be a true church so long as it fulfils the above three criteria. We would soon end up with the absurd situation of having many true churches each considering themselves to be teaching the truth concerning the word of God, the sacraments and discipline, while having no unity of belief, government or discipline between themselves. This absurd situation is what some hope to replace the Catholic Church with.

The real marks of the true Church, which are visible and essential, number four. They are: one, holy, catholic and apostolic.

---

[2] *Roman Catholicism*, Presbyterian and Reformed Publishing Co. (Phillipsburg, NJ), 1962, p. 20.

These marks are found in Scripture, are based on reason and can be defended by it.

One

"I will build my Church" (Mt 16:18).

The true Church is founded and built by Jesus. Jesus founded one Church, not many. Protestantism is not one united body in doctrine and discipline, but a series of disparate organizations antagonistic not only to Catholicism but also often to each other.

"... one flock, one shepherd" (Jn 10:16).

The central authority of the Pope has kept the Catholic Church united in doctrine and discipline since the days of the Roman Empire. Protestantism continues to splinter with the advent of each new self-appointed 'prophet' or minister who claims to hold the true meaning of Scripture.

Holy

"And for their sake I consecrate myself, that they also may be consecrated in truth" (Jn 17:19).

The true Church will be holy in her founder, teachings and worship. There is no guarantee that all its members will practise what she preaches as is gathered from Jesus' images of the wheat and the weeds (Mt 13:24-30), the good and the bad fish (Mt 13:47-52), and the sheep and the goats (Mt 25:31-46). The survival of the Catholic Church — despite the examples of two dozen or so bad Popes (out of 266), and other scandals — only reinforces the fact that the holiness of the Church derives from Jesus and him alone. In any case, Protestantism is far from free when it comes to scandal, and none of its founders can claim to match the holiness of any Catholic saint, let alone Jesus himself.

Catholic

"Go therefore and make disciples of all nations" (Mt 28:19).

The metaphors of the "mustard seed" and "bread" demonstrate that the Church would change in size and appearance over the centuries, but would in essence remain the same. Remaining essentially one and the same, the Church adapts to all times, places and people. No nation or race is excluded from her fold, no language from proclaiming her Gospel. Those who assert that the true believers are only white and Anglo-Saxon limit the redeeming power of Jesus' precious Blood. Jesus opened his arms on the Cross for all peoples and nations, hence the true Church must be universal, not simply a national church based on race, or subject to a particular king or parliament.

Apostolic

"I am with you always" (Mt 28:20).

The true Church will trace its history, episcopal succession and doctrine right back to the Apostles themselves. St Paul refers to this same true Church when he says "to him be glory in the church and in Christ Jesus *to all generations*" (Eph. 3:21). Jesus' Church, therefore, was not established in 1517, 1534, 1540, in the nineteenth century, or last week in California. It must have existed since the Apostles, exist now, and continue to exist until the end of the world.

Only the Catholic Church can show herself to be One, Holy, Catholic and Apostolic.

The Fathers

Pope St Clement of Rome, *Letter to the Corinthians* **42, 1 (c. AD 98)**
"The Apostles received the Gospel for us from the Lord Jesus Christ; and Jesus Christ was sent from God. Christ, therefore, is from God,

and the Apostles are from Christ. Both of these orderly arrangements, then, are by God's will. Receiving their instructions and being full of confidence on account of the resurrection of Our Lord Jesus Christ, and confirmed in faith by the word of God, they went forth in the complete assurance of the Holy Spirit, preaching the good news that the Kingdom of God is coming. Through countryside and city they preached; and they appointed their earliest converts, testing them by the Spirit, to be the bishops and deacons of future believers. Nor was this a novelty: for bishops and deacons had been written about a long time earlier. Indeed, Scripture somewhere says: 'I will set up their bishops in righteousness and their deacons in faith.'"

St Irenaeus of Lyons, *Against Heresies* **3, 4, 1 (c. AD 180)**
"When, therefore, we have such proofs, it is not necessary to seek among others the truth which is easily obtained from the Church. For the Apostles, like a rich man in a bank, deposited with her most copiously everything which pertains to the truth; and everyone who wishes draws from her the drink of life. For she is the entrance to life, while all the rest are thieves and robbers. That is why it is surely necessary to avoid them, while cherishing with the utmost diligence the things pertaining to the Church, and to lay hold of the tradition of truth ... In the Church, God has placed apostles, prophets and doctors, and all the other means through which the Spirit works; in all of which none have any part who do not conform to the Church. On the contrary, they defraud themselves of life by their wicked opinion and most wretched behavior. For where the Church is, there is the Spirit of God; and where the Spirit of God, there is the Church and every grace."

Clement of Alexandria, *Miscellanies* **7, 17, 107, 3 (ante AD 217)**
"From what has been said, then, it seems clear to me that the true Church, that which is really ancient, is one; and in it are enrolled those who, in accord with a design are just ... We say, therefore, that in substance, in concept, in origin and in eminence, the ancient and Catholic Church is alone, gathering as it does into the unity of the one faith which results from the familiar covenants — or rather, from the one covenant in different times, by the will of the one God and

through the one Lord — those already chosen, those predestined by God, who knew before the foundation of the world that they would be just."

St Cyprian of Carthage, *Letter to Florentius Pupianus* 66 (69), 8 (AD 254)
"There speaks Peter, upon whom the Church would be built, teaching in the name of the Church and showing that even if a stubborn and proud multitude withdraws because it does not wish to obey, yet the Church does not withdraw from Christ. The people joined to the priest and the flock clinging to their shepherd are the Church."

St Hilary of Poitiers, *The Trinity* 7, 4 (c. AD 357)
"The Church, instituted by the Lord and confirmed by the Apostles, is one for all men; but the frantic folly of the diverse impious sects has cut them off from her. It cannot be denied that this tearing asunder of the faith has arisen from the defect of poor intelligence, which twists what is read to conform to its opinion, instead of adjusting its opinion to the meaning of what is read. However, while individual parties fight among themselves, the Church stands revealed not only by her own doctrines, but by those also of her adversaries. And although they are all ranged against her, she confutes the most wicked error which they all share, by the very fact that she is alone and one."

St John Chrysostom, *On the Incomprehensible Nature of God* 3, 6 (c. AD 387)
"You cannot pray at home as at church, where there is a great multitude, where exclamations are cried out to God as from one great heart, and where there is something more: the union of minds, the accord of souls, the bond of charity, the prayers of the priests."

The Roman Catechism (1566)

Pt. I, Ch. X: The true Church is also to be recognized from her origin, which can be traced back under the law of grace to the Apostles; for her doctrine is the truth not recently given, nor now first heard of, but delivered of old by the Apostles, and disseminated throughout the entire world. Hence no one can doubt that the impious opinions which heresy invents, opposed as they are to the doctrines taught by the Church from the days of the Apostles to the present time, are very different from the faith of the true Church.

Catechism of the Catholic Church (1992)

No. 846: "Outside the Church there is no salvation."

> Basing itself on Scripture and Tradition, the Council teaches that the Church, a pilgrim now on earth, is necessary for salvation: the one Christ is the mediator and the way of salvation; he is present to us in his body which is the Church. He himself explicitly asserted the necessity of faith and Baptism, and thereby affirmed at the same time the necessity of the Church which men enter through Baptism as through a door. Hence they could not be saved who, knowing that the Catholic Church was founded as necessary by God through Christ, would refuse either to enter it or to remain in it.

No. 847: This affirmation is not aimed at those who, through no fault of their own, do not know Christ and his Church:

> Those who, through no fault of their own, do not know the Gospel of Christ or his Church, but who nevertheless seek God with a sincere heart, and, moved by grace, try in their actions to do his will as they know it through the dictates of their conscience — those too may achieve eternal salvation.

Infallibility of the Church

Objection: *"The Church is not infallible. It fell into error after Constantine when it began to teach pagan doctrines."*

The infallibility of the Church is a special supernatural prerogative given to her by God to preserve her from teaching error in her formal definitive dogmatic teaching in matters of faith and morals.

Infallibility involves not only the simple exemption from actual error but also exemption from the possibility of error. It is a divine assistance that is unrelated to the holiness, intelligence, wisdom, faults or failings of individual Church members or organs.

Infallibility must be distinguished from both 'inspiration' and 'revelation.' Inspiration involves more than simply preserving the author from the possibility of error, for God himself is the author of the utterance; revelation involves God making known supernatural truths otherwise entirely or morally beyond the scope of human observation.

In any discussion of infallibility, it must be first acknowledged that Jesus founded a Church as a visible and perfect society to govern, teach and sanctify his followers, and he obliged all that may come to know her to belong to and obey her: "And I tell you, you are Peter, and on this rock I will build my Church" (Mt 16:18); "if he refuses to listen even to the Church, let him be to you as a Gentile and a tax collector" (Mt 18:17). The only questions that need to be addressed then are whether, in what way, and to what extent Jesus' Church is infallible.

As the Church founded by Jesus is made up of teachers and believers, the gift of infallibility will protect her both in teaching and belief. Infallibility is thus found in the 'Church teaching' and in the 'Church believing.' The 'Church teaching' consists of the successors to the Apostles, namely, the Pope and all the bishops of the world united to him; the 'Church believing' is the entire body of all the faithful professing the Catholic Faith.

The Church may convey her infallible teaching either in 'solemn pronouncements' or through her 'ordinary teaching.' Her solemn pronouncements include all doctrines contained in the four great Creeds (*Apostles'*, *Nicene*, *Athanasian*, *Profession of Pius IV*), the definitions of the Popes, or General Councils deliberating under the Pope. The Church's ordinary teaching is that doctrine taught by the Pope and the bishops of the world in the everyday exercise of their pastoral office without interruption since Apostolic times.

Individual bishops of the Church are not infallible in themselves, but only when they teach definitively in union with the Pope. Furthermore, no individual member of the Church is infallible in belief, not even the Pope. The Pope's infallibility pertains only to his teaching office, not to his personal beliefs.

The object of the Church's infallibility is the 'Deposit of Faith.' This includes all doctrines delivered by Jesus and his Apostles and forming God's 'public' revelation to humanity. These doctrines are found in Sacred Scripture and Tradition. Scripture includes all the inspired books of the Old and New Testaments as contained in the Greek Septuagint version; Tradition embraces all those truths which have been passed on from age to age either orally, in the writings of the Church Fathers, in the Acts of the Martyrs, in early paintings and inscriptions, in the liturgy, in the practices and customs of the Universal Church, and in the definitions of Popes and Councils.

Before Jesus ascended into heaven from Mount Olivet, he commanded his disciples as follows: "Go therefore and make disciples of all nations, baptizing them in the name of the Father and of the Son and of the Holy Spirit, *teaching them to observe all that I have commanded you*" (Mt 28:19-20). These last words of Jesus contain the promise of doctrinal infallibility and were directed not only to St Peter and the other Twelve, but also to their lawful successors: "and behold, I am with you always, to the close of the age" (*ibid.*). If Jesus is with his Apostles and their successors to the end of time, it follows that their listeners are bound to receive their teaching as if it were Jesus' own. In other words, they are bound to accept it as infallible. It is idle to believe that Jesus' command to teach all nations could be effectively accomplished if the Church he established could at any time teach error on vital matters of faith and morals.

Also, in Matt. 16:18-20 we read the words, "and the gates of Hades shall not prevail against it." This is Jesus' promise that the Church will survive all infernal assaults from within and without to remain faithful to her divine commission until the end of the world. On this basis, it would again be a mockery to contend that the Church has erred in any of her dogmatic definitions, for if she has ever poisoned her children through the teaching of formal error then the gates of hell have prevailed against her and Jesus' promise has been rendered meaningless.

It is through the Holy Spirit that Jesus' perpetual assistance to the Church against hell and error is conveyed: "And I will pray the Father, and he will give you another Counselor, to be with you for ever ... the Spirit of truth ... he dwells with you, and will be in you ... the Counselor, the Holy Spirit, whom the Father will send in my name, he will teach you all things, and bring to your remembrance all that I have said to you" (Jn 14:16-17, 26). The Holy Spirit is responsible for the formal teaching of the Apostles and their successors in the realm of faith and morals. The consciousness of the Holy Spirit's corporate assistance to the Church is evident in the expression used by the Apostles during the Council of Jerusalem: "For it has seemed good to the Holy Spirit and to us to lay upon you no greater burden than these necessary things" (Acts 15:28). Consequently, as the Holy Spirit is responsible for Church teaching it is impossible for the Church which is the "Body of Christ" (Eph. 1:23) and the "pillar and bulwark of the truth" (1 Tim. 3:15) to apostatize into error or be destroyed.

Second objection: *"It was the Reformers of the sixteenth century who restored true doctrine."*

The following two quotes from Martin Luther and John Calvin respectively suffice as a response to such a claim:

> The tiresome devil begins to rage amongst the ungodly and to belch forth many wild and mazy beliefs and doctrines. This man will have nothing of baptism, that one denies the Sacrament, a third awaits another world between this and the Last Day; some teach that Christ is not God; some say this, some that, and there are as many sects and beliefs as there are heads; no peasant is so rude but that if he dreams or fancies

something, it must forsooth be the Holy Spirit which inspires him, and he himself must be a prophet.[1]

It is indeed important that posterity should not know of our differences; for it is indescribably ridiculous that we, who are in opposition to the whole world, should be, at the very beginning of the Reformation, at issue among ourselves.[2]

From these quotes, it is clearly evident that the Reformers restored no true doctrine but rather caused much of Christendom to be "tossed to and fro and carried about with every wind of doctrine" (Eph. 4:14).

Third objection: *"Infallibility is a failure. It has not prevented schisms and heresies among Christians."*

The Church was not endowed with infallibility to prevent schisms and heresies, but rather to ensure that she would always remain a fountain of truth and beacon of light among the tempests of error: "A city set on a hill cannot be hid" (Mt 5:14). The existence of a Church protected from error takes away all justification for schism and heresy. However, people remain free to disrupt the unity of faith in the same way they are free to reject any of the teachings or commandments of Jesus.

The Fathers

St Irenaeus of Lyons, *Against Heresies* **3, 4, 1 (c. AD 180)**
"When, therefore, we have such proofs, it is not necessary to seek among others the truth which is easily obtained from the Church. For the Apostles, like a rich man in a bank, deposited with her most copiously everything which pertains to the truth; and everyone whosoever wishes draws from her the drink of life. For she is the entrance to life, while all the rest are thieves and robbers. That is why it

---

[1] Antwerp Letter, April, 1525, Weim. ed., 18, p. 547.
[2] Letter to Philip Melanchthon, 28 November, 1552.

is surely necessary to avoid them, while cherishing with the utmost diligence the things pertaining to the Church, and to lay hold of the tradition of truth. What then? If there should be a dispute over some kind of question, ought we not have recourse to the most ancient Churches in which the Apostles were familiar, and draw from them what is clear and certain in regard to that question? What if the Apostles had not in fact left writings to us? Would it not be necessary to follow the order of tradition, which was handed down to those to whom they entrusted the Churches?"

Tertullian, *The Demurrer Against the Heretics* 28, 1 (c. AD 200)
"Grant, then, that all have erred; that the Apostle was mistaken in bearing witness; that the Holy Spirit had no such consideration for any one Church as to lead it into truth, although he was sent for that purpose by Christ, who had asked the Father to make him the Teacher of truth; that the Steward of God and Vicar of Christ neglected his office, and permitted the Churches for a time to understand otherwise and to believe otherwise than he himself had preached through the Apostles: now, is it likely that so many and such great Churches should have gone astray into a unity of faith?"

St Athanasius, *Letter on the Councils of Rimini and Seleucia* 5 (AD 361-362)
"Without prefixing Consulate, month, and day, (the Fathers) wrote concerning Easter, 'It seemed good as follows,' for it did then seem good that there should be a general compliance; but about the faith they wrote not, 'It seemed good,' but, 'thus believes the Catholic Church'; and thereupon they confessed how they believed, in order to show that their own sentiments were not novel, but Apostolic; and what they wrote down was no discovery of theirs, but is the same as was taught by the Apostles."

St Athanasius, *Synodal Letter to the Bishops of Africa* 2 (inter AD 368-372)
"But the word of the Lord which came through the Ecumenical Council at Nicaea remains forever."

St Ambrose of Milan, *Letter to the Emperor Valentinian II* **21, 14 (AD 386)**
"This (denial of the divinity of Christ) was written in the Council of Rimini, and I am right when I shiver at the thought of that Council. I follow the teaching of the Council of Nicaea, from which neither death nor the sword shall ever be able to separate me."

The Fathers of the Ecumenical Council of Chalcedon, *Letter to Pope St Leo I the Great* **98, 1 (AD 451)**
"For if where two or three are gathered together in his name, he says he is there in the midst of them, how much more will he not show his companionship with five hundred and twenty priests, who preferred the spread of knowledge concerning him to their own home and affairs, when you, as head to the members, showed your good will through those who represented you."

Pope St Gregory I the Great, *Letter to the Patriarchs of Constantinople, Alexandria, Antioch, Jerusalem* **1, 24 (AD 591)**
"But all persons that the aforesaid Councils (Nicaea, Constantinople I & II, Ephesus, Chalcedon) reject, I reject; those whom they venerate, I embrace; because, since those Councils were shaped by universal consent, anyone who presumes either to loose whom they bind or to bind whom they loose overthrows not them but himself. Whoever, therefore, deems otherwise, let him be anathema."

The Roman Catechism (1566)

Pt. II, Ch. VIII: For the Holy Ghost, who presides over the Church, governs her by no other ministers than those of Apostolic succession. This Spirit, first imparted to the Apostles, has by the infinite goodness of God always continued in the Church. And just as this one Church cannot err in faith or morals, since it is guided by the Holy Ghost; so, on the contrary, all other societies arrogating to themselves the name of *church*, must necessarily ... be sunk in the most pernicious errors, both doctrinal and moral.

Catechism of the Catholic Church (1992)

No. 890: The mission of the Magisterium is linked to the definitive nature of the covenant established by God with his people in Christ. It is this Magisterium's task to preserve God's people from deviations and defections and to guarantee them the objective possibility of professing the true faith without error. Thus, the pastoral duty of the Magisterium is aimed at seeing to it that the People of God abides in the truth that liberates. To fulfil this service, Christ endowed the Church's shepherds with the charism of infallibility in matters of faith and morals.

St Peter and Papal Primacy

Objection: *"St Peter was not the head of the other Apostles. All of them were equal in power and authority!"*

It has been said by many outside the Catholic Church that if you disprove the primacy of St Peter (i.e., show that he was not the leader of but only equal to the other Apostles), you undermine the Papacy and, therefore, the very foundations of Catholicism.

It is evident in numerous places in the Bible that St Peter was made by Jesus, and regarded by others, as the head of the Apostles:

(i) St Peter is the first of the disciples to confess the divinity of Jesus (Mt 16:16).

(ii) The keys of the kingdom of heaven to bind and loose on earth were given by Jesus to St Peter (Mt 16:19).

(iii) St Peter's name is listed first when he, St James and St John are mentioned as being with Jesus at the Transfiguration (Mt 17:1).

(iv) St Peter speaks on behalf of the other disciples when declaring that they had left everything to follow Jesus (Mt 19:21).

(v) Jesus made St Peter's home his headquarters while staying in Capernaum (Mk 1:29).

(vi) The resurrection of Jesus was first pronounced by the angel to St Peter (Mk 16:7).

(vii) Jesus twice instructs St Peter to let down his nets to catch the miraculous hauls of fish that follow (Lk 5:4-10; Jn 21:6).

(viii) Jesus prayed for St Peter alone and instructed him to "strengthen your brethren" (Lk 22:31-32).

(ix) After the resurrection, St Peter was the first of the Apostles to whom Jesus appeared (Lk 24).

(x) At his first meeting with St Peter, Jesus gave him the new name of "Cephas" (Rock) (Jn 1:42).

(xi) It was to St Peter that Jesus entrusted the care of his flock, lambs and sheep (Jn 21:15-17).

(xii) The election that chose St Matthias as the replacement for Judas was conducted by St Peter (Acts 1:25).

(xiii) The first miracle at the Temple was performed by St Peter (Acts 3).

(xiv) St Peter replied to the Sanhedrin on behalf of the Church (Acts 4).

(xv) The case of Ananias and Saphira was judged by St Peter (Acts 5).

(xvi) St Peter was the first to preach to the Jews (Acts 2:14) and to receive Gentiles into the Church (Acts 11).

(xvii) At the Council of Jerusalem, the multitudes "kept silence" after St Peter rose and spoke (Acts 15:12).

(xviii) After his conversion, St Paul first went to St Peter (Gal. 1:18).

(xix) The lists of Apostles in Matt. 10, Mark 3, Luke 6, and Acts 1 all place the name of St Peter first.

(xx) In the New Testament, St Peter is mentioned one hundred and ninety-five times. The other Apostles are together mentioned only one hundred and thirty times, with St John receiving twenty-nine mentions, St James the Greater twenty-four, Judas Iscariot twenty-three and Philip six.[1]

Second objection: *"Too much is made of Simon's name being changed to Peter. According to St Paul, Christ is the rock (1 Cor. 10:4)."*

In the Old Testament, we occasionally find God changing the names of certain men. This he does when he bestows a new mission on one of his close followers. So, with Abraham we read the following:

"Behold, my covenant is with you, and you shall be the father of a multitude of nations. No longer shall your name be Abram, but your name shall be Abraham; for I have made you the father of a multitude of nations" (Gen. 17:5).

---

[1] Fulton J. Sheen, *Life of Christ*, Doubleday Image, New York, 1958, p. 106.

Likewise, with Jacob:

"And he said to him, 'What is your name?' And he said, 'Jacob.' Then he said, 'Your name shall no more be called Jacob, but Israel, for you have striven with God and with men, and have prevailed'" (Gen. 32:27-28).

On first beholding Simon, Jesus changed his name to Cephas: "So you are Simon the son of John? You shall be called Cephas (Κεφᾶς)" (Jn 1:42). Cephas and Peter both mean rock. The significance of this name change cannot be ignored. It was to contrast what Simon Peter was before he met Jesus to what he would become afterwards, that is, the firm rock on which Jesus would build his Church (Mt 16:18ff.).

In six other verses of the New Testament, we find Simon being specifically called Cephas, or rock: 1 Cor. 1:12; 1 Cor. 3:22; 1 Cor. 9:12; 1 Cor. 15:5; Gal. 2:7, 11 & 14.

Third objection: *"But in Matthew 16:18 St Peter was called 'Petros,' meaning 'little stone' while Christ said he would build his Church on 'Petra,' or a 'massive rock.' Therefore, Christ did not intend to build his Church on Peter!"*

Undoubtedly, the different Greek words "Petros" (Πέτρος) and "Petra" (Πέτρα) appear in Matthew's Gospel. However, we must understand that when Jesus spoke to St Peter in 16:18 he spoke in Aramaic and not Greek. In Aramaic, Jesus would have said *"Anath-her kipha, v'all hode Kipha."* Numerous Protestant Biblical scholars today acknowledge this point, including the Baptist Professor D. A. Carson:

> ... the underlying Aramaic is in this case unquestionable; and most probably *Kepha* was used in both clauses ('you are *kepha*' and 'on this *kepha*'), since the word was used both for a name and for a 'rock' ... The Greek makes the distinction between *petros* and *petra* simply because it is trying to preserve the pun, and in Greek the feminine *petra* could not very well serve as a masculine name (*The Expositor's Bible Commentary: Vol. 8*, Grand Rapids, MI: Zondervan, 1984, p. 368).

If Jesus had intended to characterize St Peter as a 'little stone' — as distinct from a 'massive rock' — he could have chosen other more suitable words to signify such a contrast, such as *evna* in Aramaic, meaning "little stone." Likewise, had St Matthew really wanted to record in his Gospel that St Peter was only a "little stone" the more preferable and common word to use would have been *lithos*, which means "stone of virtually any size."

Fourth objection: *"Admittedly, St Peter is given the keys of the kingdom of heaven by Christ but didn't Christ also give the power to bind and loose to the other Apostles as well in Matthew 18?"*

Jesus gives to St Peter the keys of the kingdom of heaven in Matt. 16:19:

"I will give you the keys of the kingdom of heaven, and whatever you bind on earth shall be bound in heaven, and whatever you loose on earth shall be loosed in heaven."

This bestowal of the keys is made solely to St Peter as the word here for "you" in the Greek is the singular dative form soi (σοι), and the verbs "bind" and "loose" are the singular forms as well.

Jesus' bestowal of the keys on St Peter is reminiscent of the bestowal of authority upon the Chamberlain, or Vizier, in the Royal House of Israel in Isaiah 22:

"And I will place on his shoulder the key of the house of David; he shall open, and none shall shut; and he shall shut, and none shall open" (v. 22).

Undoubtedly, Is. 22 lies behind Matt. 16. The Chamberlain (Eliakim) in Is. 22 is given responsibility as a "father" (v. 21) over the "inhabitants of Jerusalem and to the house of Judah," while St Peter is given authority to govern the New Israel, or Jesus' Church. The symbol of the keys in both instances represents the authority of administrator and teacher, while the language of binding and loosing is a rabbinic expression for authoritative teaching and the declaring of what is permitted and what is not. The noted Lutheran Biblical scholar Oscar Cullman likewise sees the parallels:

In Matthew 16:19 it is presupposed that Christ is the master of the house, who has the keys to the Kingdom of Heaven, with which to open to those who come in. Just as in Isaiah 22:22 the Lord lays the keys of the house of David on the shoulders of his servant Eliakim, so Jesus commits to Peter the keys of his house, the Kingdom of Heaven, and thereby installs him as administrator of the house.[2]

The position of Chamberlain was established during the reign of King Solomon and continued under his successors throughout the history of Israel (in the case of Eliakim it had been received in succession from Shebna: see Is. 22:20). Likewise, St Peter too would have successors during the history of the new Israel, the difference being that his successors would always be under the one Davidic king, Jesus.

St Peter and his successors will hold the keys of the kingdom of heaven until Jesus visibly returns at the end of the world. But what of the other Apostles? What specific powers were they (and therefore their successors) given? Matthew 18:18 reads as follows:

"Truly, I say to you, whatever you bind on earth shall be bound in heaven, and whatever you loose on earth shall be loosed in heaven."

Matthew 18 is distinct from Matt. 16 in three important ways. First, Jesus in chapter 16 specifically promises to build his Church only on St Peter. Second, in 18:18 the first "you" that appears is the Greek plural *humin* (ὑμῖν), indicating that Jesus is talking to the Apostles as a whole. Third, chapter 18 makes no mention of keys together with the power to bind and loose.

Chapters 16 and 18 should be read together and are reconcilable in the following manner:

(i) The power of the keys is the wider power and authority that includes the power of binding and loosing. St Peter alone is

---

[2] *Peter: Disciple, Apostle, Martyr*, trans. Floyd V. Filson, Philadelphia: Westminster, 1953, p. 203.

Defend the Faith!

given the keys to exercise the power of binding and loosing in its fullness as Vicar of Christ.

(ii) St Peter holds individually and personally the power given to the Apostles in common. He can exercise this power and authority alone without reference to the other Apostles.

(iii) The Apostles share in the power of binding and loosing but can carry it out only in union with St Peter.

The pre-eminence of St Peter over the other Apostles is supported by Jesus' instruction to him to "Feed my lambs (ἀρνία)", "Tend my sheep (προβάτιά)", etc., in John 21:15-17. The word for "tend" in Greek is poimaine (ποίμαινε), which means to shepherd, rule or govern. The same may be said about Jesus' admonition to St Peter to "strengthen your brethren" (Lk 22:31-32). Commenting on Luke 22:31-32, Ethelbert Stauffer, a Lutheran scholar notes:

> What is the basis of Peter's unique position? Not upon any special qualification of the apostle, but upon the intercession of the Lord ... In praying specially for Peter, Jesus is protecting and delivering the young community as a whole. He prays for fallen Peter so that Peter uplifted might strengthen his brethren in the faith, and so all attain the goal reserved for them — the Kingdom. So in this one saying it is made clear that the only possible ground of the Church's existence and the very basis of its life is the mediatorial office of Christ, and also that Peter's own mediatorial function is to be co-ordinated with and subordinated to this Christological office of the mediator.[3]

It is unreasonable to assert that the unique power and authority held by St Peter was to die with him. To believe this would be to believe that Jesus would leave the Church on earth without central leadership for more than nineteen centuries. On the contrary, it has always been the universal view of Christendom that St Peter continues to govern the Church with the same power and authority given him by

---

[3] *New Testament Theology* (tr. John March), SCM Press, London, 1955, pp. 31-32.

Jesus in the person of his lawful successors, that is, those who occupy the See of Rome, the Popes.

Fifth objection: *"If St Peter was the head of the Church, then why was St James in charge of the Council of Jerusalem in Acts 15?"*

The Acts of the Apostles, more than any other book of the New Testament, supports the primacy of St Peter. In the first twelve chapters alone, St Peter is mentioned fifty-three times.

The Council of Jerusalem took place about AD 49 or 50. It displayed the same features of later ecumenical councils in the history of the Church: the rulers of the whole Church attend the Council; it promulgates decisions relating to faith and morals binding on all Christians; its decisions are recorded in written form and proclaimed universally.

In the first phase of the Council there was much discussion and debate over the entry of Gentiles into the Church: "But some believers who belonged to the party of the Pharisees rose up, and said, 'It is necessary to circumcise them, and to charge them to keep the law of Moses'" (v. 5). In the second phase St Peter got up and spoke authoritatively on the issue: "And God who knows the heart bore witness to them, giving them the Holy Spirit just as he did to us; and he made no distinction between us and them, but cleansed their hearts by faith" (vv. 8-9). Then there was silence as the multitude contemplated St Peter's words. In the third phase Sts Paul and Barnabas spoke, relating "what signs and wonders God had done through them among the Gentiles" (v. 12). Next, St James asked to be heard and echoed what St Peter had first said: "Therefore my judgment is that we should not trouble those of the Gentiles who turn to God, but should write to them to abstain from the pollutions of idols and from unchastity and from what is strangled and from blood" (vv. 19-20).

It is argued by Protestant apologists that St James' statement in v.13 ("Brethren, listen to me") is an ecclesiastical dictate denoting supreme authority over the Council, as he was bishop of Jerusalem. This is reinforced by his words in v. 19: "Therefore my judgment is that we should not trouble those of the Gentiles who turn to God." The consequence of such an argument is to show that St James was the final and undisputed decision-maker and St Peter had no absolute authority at all.

Such a conclusion, however, is totally unwarranted. The Greek for "listen to me" is *akousate* (ἀκούσατέ), which is not of itself an imperative connoting authority, but a word that can be used by any person seeking the attention of another. It is used hundreds of times in the New Testament in this sense. As for the words "my judgment," the original Greek words are *ego krino* (ἐγὼ κρίνω), which mean "I give my opinion, or voice." The fact that St James spoke in the first person singular ("My" or "I") suggests that he was only giving his opinion, conviction or recommendation, one that he urged be accepted by the rest of the Council.

Sixth objection: *"I don't see any significance in St Paul's visit to St Peter after spending three years in the desert."*

Some may see no significance, but St John Chrysostom certainly did:

> He says, "to visit Peter"; he does not say to see (heiden), but to visit and survey (historesai), a word which those who seek to become acquainted with great and splendid cities apply to themselves. Worthy of such trouble did he consider the very sight of Peter; and this appears from the Acts of the Apostles also (*Homily on Galatians* 1:18 [inter AD 393-397]).

Galatians 1:18-19 reads as follows:

"Then after three years I went up to Jerusalem to visit Cephas, and remained with him fifteen days. But I saw none of the other apostles except James the Lord's brother."

The words "visit" in relation to St Peter and "saw" for the other Apostles in Greek, are, respectively *historesai* (ἱστορῆσαι) and *eidon* (εἶδον). *Historesai* connotes more than just to visit; it also means "to question" or "to examine." Together, the words *"historesai Kephan"* (ἱστορῆσαι κηφᾶν) means "to get information from Cephas." St Paul spent more than two weeks with St Peter and in that time would have discussed a vast range of topics concerning the Christian faith with him. This he did not do with St James, the other Apostle he "saw" (*eidon*). Why? For St Peter alone was the Rock and head of the others.

Seventh objection: *"The primacy of the Roman popes based on St Peter began with Pope Gregory the Great. The early Church recognized no such primacy in the bishop of Rome!"*

There are numerous instances in early Church history when either individuals or groups, both orthodox and heretical, appealed to Rome for a decision or declaration in their favor, for example:

(i) The early Church historian Hegesippus travelled throughout the Empire to ascertain on behalf of Pope Anicetus (AD 155-166) whether the teachings of the various churches were in uniformity with Rome.
(ii) Tertullian states that the Montanist community dispatched letters to Rome seeking recognition (inter AD 173-180).
(iii) St Irenaeus of Lyons was delegated by the Church of Lyons to take to Pope St Eleutherius letters concerning the Montanist troubles (c. AD 178); and interceded with Pope St Victor I concerning the Paschal observance (c. AD 190-191).
(iv) Rome formally condemned Montanism in AD 212.
(v) The Priscillianists petitioned Pope Damasus for support (c. AD 381-382).
(vi) Faced with exile due to the machinations of Theophilus of Alexandria and the Empress Eudoxia, St John Chrysostom wrote an appeal to Pope Innocent I in AD 405.
(vii) St Prosper of Aquitaine travelled to Rome to obtain from Pope Celestine a condemnation of the semi-Pelagians (c. AD 430-431).
(viii) Pope St Leo I the Great condemned the Monophysite heresy in AD 451.

These examples are but a few. A more detailed study would reveal many more instances of Papal intervention. One thing is certain, both in the Empire and in the early Church all roads led to Rome.

The Fathers

Pope St Clement of Rome, *Letter to the Corinthians* Address (c. AD 98)
"The Church of God which sojourns in Rome to the Church of God which sojourns in Corinth ... Owing to the sudden and repeated calamities and misfortunes which have befallen us, we must acknowledge that we have been somewhat tardy in turning our attention to the matters in dispute among you."

St Irenaeus of Lyons, *Against Heresies* 3, 3, 2 (c. AD 180)
"... by pointing out here the successions of the bishops of the greatest and most ancient Church known to all, founded and organized at Rome by the two most glorious Apostles, Peter and Paul, that Church which has the tradition and the faith which comes down to us after having been announced to men by the Apostles. For with this Church, because of its superior origin, all Churches must agree, that is, all the faithful in the whole world; and it is in her that the faithful everywhere have maintained the Apostolic tradition."

Tertullian, *The Demurrer Against the Heretics* 22 (c. AD 200)
"Was anything hidden from Peter, who was called the Rock whereon the Church was to be built: who obtained the keys of the kingdom of heaven, and the power of loosing and binding in heaven and on earth?"

St Cyprian of Carthage, *Letter to all His People* 43 (40), 5 (AD 251)
"There is one God and one Christ, and one Church, and one Chair founded on Peter by the word of the Lord. It is not possible to set up another altar or for there to be another priesthood besides that one altar and that one priesthood. Whoever has gathered elsewhere is scattering."

Pope St Julius I, *Acknowledging Your Letter* [contained in St Athanasius' *Apology Against the Arians* 35] (AD 341)
"And above all, why was nothing written to us about the Church of the Alexandrians? Are you ignorant that the custom has been to write first to us, and then for a just decision to be passed from this place?"

St Jerome, *Letter to Pope Damasus* 15, 2 (inter AD 374-379)
"I speak with the successor of the fisherman and the disciple of the Cross. Though I acknowledge none as first except Christ, I am joined in communion with Your Holiness, that is to say, in communion with the Chair of Peter. I know that it is upon that rock that the Church has been built. Whoever eats the Lamb outside this house is profane."

St Augustine of Hippo, *Hymn Against the Donatists* 18 (AD 393)
"Run through the list of those priests who have occupied the See of Peter himself; and in that list of Fathers, see who succeeded to whom. This is the Rock which the proud Gates of Hell do not overcome."

The Roman Catechism (1566)

Pt. I, Ch. X: The Church has but one ruler and one governor, the invisible one, Christ, whom the eternal Father *hath made head over all the Church, which is his body*; the visible one, the Pope, who, as legitimate successor of Peter, the Prince of the Apostles, fills the Apostolic chair.

Catechism of the Catholic Church (1992)

No. 881: The Lord made Simon alone, whom he named Peter, the "rock" of his Church. He gave him the keys of his Church and instituted him shepherd of the whole flock. The office of binding and loosing which was given to Peter was also assigned to the college of apostles united to its head. This pastoral office of Peter and the other apostles belongs to the Church's very foundation and is continued by the bishops under the primacy of the Pope.

The Pope is Infallible

Objection: *"How can an ordinary man be infallible? This belongs to God alone. The Pope can commit sin like anyone else!"*

Jesus instructed the Apostles to "Go therefore and make disciples of all nations, baptizing them in the name of the Father and of the Son and of the Holy Spirit, teaching them to observe all that I have commanded you" (Mt 28:19-20). Together with this commission, Jesus promised the Apostles the protection of the Holy Spirit: "When the Spirit of truth comes, he will guide you into all the truth" (Jn 16:13).

For the Church of Jesus to fulfil its mission as teacher, she must never teach error with respect to faith or morals, otherwise she would be failing as a mother of souls and faithful spouse of Christ. Following from this, it is logical that the supreme head of the Church of Christ be also a perpetual source of truth. Jesus, foreseeing that false teachers would arise — "False Christs and false prophets will arise" (Mk 13:22) — endowed the supreme head of the Church with the power and authority to decide infallibly all controversies concerning written and unwritten doctrine (Mt 16:18-20). This supreme head of the Church on earth is the Pope.

Infallibility is a negative protection, the inability of the Church or Pope to teach error with respect to faith or morals when a formal teaching is proclaimed. It is distinct from *inspiration*, in that it does not help the Pope to know the truth or inspire him to teach it. The Pope must still work to know the truth and know it to an extraordinary level, considering his unique position. Infallible pronouncements are sparingly made, usually only when a key doctrine is doubted or denied.

Papal infallibility had its prefigurement in the Old Testament. In Exod. 28:30 the High Priest wore a special breastplate called the "Breastplate of Judgment" which carried two objects known as the *Urim and Thummim*. In Num. 27:21, 1 Sam. 14:41, Ezra 2:63 and Neh. 7:65 we see the High Priest use the Urim and Thummim to inquire of God, determine fault, obtain directions and settle disputes on behalf of the Jewish people. Whenever the High Priest used the Urim and Thummim his decisions were regarded as having come from God and therefore were unquestionable. Furthermore, this 'charism' operated irrespective of the High Priest's personal holiness.

In the New Testament, the texts of Scripture in support of the doctrine of Papal infallibility are as follows:

"And I tell you, you are Peter, and on this rock I will build my church, and the gates of Hades will not prevail against it" (Mt 16:18).

From these words, there is no doubt that St Peter (and logically his successors) was to be the rock-foundation of the Church and the source of its indefectibility against the forces of hell. This indefectibility must include, by implication, protection from doctrinal error, and this protection cannot be effectively secured without infallibility.

"Simon, Simon, behold, Satan demanded to have you, that he might sift you like wheat, but I have prayed for you that your faith may not fail; and when you have turned again, strengthen your brethren" (Lk 22:31-32).

This prayer of Jesus was for St Peter alone, conferring on him (and his successors) the office of authoritatively strengthening the brethren — that is, the other Apostles and the Church in general. As we cannot deny the efficacy of Jesus' prayer, the implication is that infallibility is also bestowed.

"When they had finished breakfast, Jesus said to Simon Peter, 'Simon, son of John, do you love me more than these?' He said to him, 'Yes, Lord; you know that I love you.' He said to him, 'Feed my lambs.' A second time he said to him, 'Simon, son of John, do you love me?' He said to him, 'Yes, Lord; you know that I love you.' He said to him, 'Tend my sheep.' He said to him the third time, 'Simon, son of John, do you love me?' Peter was grieved because he said to him the third time, 'Do you love me?' And he said to him, 'Lord, you know everything; you know that I love you.' Jesus said to him, 'Feed my sheep'" (Jn 21:15-17).

Jesus in these words bestows upon St Peter (and his successors) the supreme pastoral charge over all his flock, an authority that undoubtedly includes feeding the faithful with the true food of divine truth. However, this charge cannot effectively secure the unity of the Church in truth unless there is attached to it infallibility.

What has the Protestant denial of the Pope's infallibility produced except the creation of many thousands of Protestant 'popes' and an anarchy of private self-interpretation of the Bible?

Infallibility has nothing to do with the personal morality of the Pope. He is capable of committing sin like any other person. The history of the Church shows clearly that there were, sadly, several Popes who lived scandalous lives (though a distinct minority in contrast to the clear majority who led holy and even saintly lives). Nevertheless, no connection exists between the idea of *impeccability*, which means immunity from sin, and infallibility, which is freedom from error in teaching and defining the doctrines of Jesus.

Even so, Protestants should have no objection to the idea that sinners can be instruments of infallible teaching. The Bible itself provides the supreme example. All the writers, both Old and New Testaments, were sinners (and in the cases of David, Solomon and St Peter, even grievous sinners), but their writings are considered by Protestants of all types as not only infallible but also inspired. This shows that infallibility is a gift for the benefit of all the faithful in Christ, to ensure that believers receive the pure word of God irrespective of the defects existing in his chosen instruments.

Second objection: *"Catholics regard everything that the Pope says to be infallibly true!"*

The First Vatican Council (1870) defined Papal infallibility as follows:

> ... the Roman Pontiff, when he speaks *ex cathedra*, that is, when, in discharge of the office of pastor and teacher of all Christians, by virtue of his supreme Apostolic authority, he defines a doctrine regarding faith or morals to be held by the universal Church, is, by the divine assistance promised to him in Blessed Peter, possessed of that infallibility with which the divine Redeemer willed that his Church should be endowed in defining doctrine regarding faith or morals; and that, therefore, such definitions of the Roman pontiff are of

themselves, and not from the consent of the Church, irreformable.[1]

Consequently, the Pope is only infallible when:

(i) He speaks *ex Cathedra*, i.e., from the Chair of Peter as supreme teacher of the universal Church. He is not infallible in any other capacity.
(ii) When he *defines* a doctrine *absolutely* and *finally*.
(iii) When he treats of *faith* or *morals*.
(iv) When he clearly shows his intention of *binding the universal Church*.

Infallibility has nothing to do with the personal actions of Popes, their disciplinary decisions or even their unofficial comments or personal opinions, even on faith and morals. It should also be noted that Papal infallibility is a charism that is personal to the Pope and cannot be communicated, transferred or delegated to any other individual, tribunal or congregation. Even doctrinal decisions issued by Roman Congregations and approved by the Pope cannot be considered infallible. Only decisions issued by the Pope himself in his name and which satisfy all four of the above conditions are infallible.

Third objection: *"Was not the doctrine of Papal infallibility invented in 1870 by the First Vatican Council?"*

No. The First Vatican Council simply defined a doctrine that had always existed in the heart of the Church. This is proven by the fact that the Popes had made thirteen infallible pronouncements before 1870 — for example, that of the Immaculate Conception of the Blessed Virgin Mary by Pope Bl. Pius IX in 1854.

Furthermore, there exist numerous explicit and formal pronouncements by ancient ecumenical councils recognizing the finality, and therefore implicitly the infallibility, of Papal definitions:

---

[1] *Pastor Aeternus*, ch. 4, 1870.

(i) The Council of Ephesus (AD 431) declared that they "were compelled" to condemn Nestorius "by the letter of our holy father and co-minister, Celestine the Bishop of Rome."
(ii) The Council of Chalcedon (AD 451) – "Peter has spoken through Leo."
(iii) The Third Council of Constantinople (AD 680) – "Peter has spoken through Agatho."
(iv) The Fourth Council of Constantinople (AD 869-870) – "The Catholic Faith is preserved inviolable in the Apostolic See."
(v) The reunion Councils of Lyons (1274) and Florence (1438-1445) – "The Roman Pontiff ... to him in blessed Peter the full power of feeding, ruling and governing the universal Church was given by Our Lord Jesus Christ."

These are but a few of many statements from the early centuries that can be quoted in support of the supreme doctrinal authority and therefore the infallibility of the Pope. On the other hand, there existed no formal denial of papal authority until the first Eastern schism (that of Photius) in AD 862.

Fourth objection: *"How could St Peter as first Pope be infallible when it is clear from the Bible that on one occasion St Paul proved him wrong (Gal. 2:11-16)?"*

In this episode, which occurred in Antioch, St Paul withstood St Peter "to his face" because of his decision to withdraw from the table of the Gentiles for fear of offending the visiting Jews from Palestine who belonged to the "circumcision party." St Paul did accuse St Peter of error: "If you, though a Jew, live like a Gentile and not like a Jew, how can you compel the Gentiles to live like Jews?" (v.14). Nevertheless, infallibility was not involved as the issue concerned St Peter's personal actions, not the carrying out of his teaching office in matters relating to faith and morals. St Peter was not teaching others to do the same nor was he declaring his example to be binding upon the whole Church.

Fifth objection: *"There have been Popes who have taught heresy, Pope Liberius in the fourth century for example."*

No Pope has ever solemnly taught or endorsed heresy or any other kind of teaching contrary to Catholic faith and morals. Pope Liberius was imprisoned, threatened with death and treated with cruelty for two years by Arians who sought to extract a heretical statement in their favor. But none was forthcoming. The only evidence is that he may have signed a creed that did not include the full definition of Nicaea but contained no positive statement in favor of heresy. But, even then, he did not promulgate this creed to the whole Church. His alleged condemnation of St Athanasius as a heretic may also be discounted, for any Papal decision made in circumstances of coercion can never qualify as infallible.

Likewise, in the sixth century Pope Vigilius ascended to the Chair of St Peter with the help of the Empress Theodora because of his pro-Monophysite views. However, once Pope, Vigilius suddenly underwent a dramatic change and declared, "Formerly, I spoke wrongly and foolishly. Though unworthy, I am Vicar of Blessed Peter." In return for his fidelity to Catholic orthodoxy, Pope Vigilius was taken to Constantinople for eight years where he endured a 'white martyrdom' ending with death on his return journey to Rome.

Pope Honorius is often alleged to have taught Monothelitism, which held that in Jesus there was only one divine will and not two wills, human and divine. The reality is that he taught nothing at all on the issue, preferring (unwisely) to remain silent to maintain peace within the Church. However, infallibility is only involved when the Pope is defining a doctrine for the universal Church, not when he is not defining a doctrine. Honorius' condemnation by the Third Council of Constantinople (AD 680), which was approved by Pope Leo II, was based not on doctrinal grounds but on his moral failure to suppress a heresy early before it had the opportunity to spread.

Concerning the case of Galileo, since neither Popes Paul V nor Urban VIII promulgated the condemnation of the heliocentric system by the Holy Office as their own, Papal infallibility was not involved. As stated earlier, a Pope cannot delegate the exercise of infallible authority to any other Church congregation or organ.

The Fathers

Tertullian, *The Demurrer Against the Heretics* 23, 10 (c. AD 200)
"Moreover, if Peter was reproached [by Paul] because, after having lived with the gentiles, he later separated himself from their company out of respect for persons, the fault certainly was one of procedure and not of doctrine."

St Cyprian of Carthage, *Letter to Cornelius of Rome* 59 (55), 14 (AD 252)
"With a false bishop appointed for themselves by heretics, they dare even to set sail and carry letters from schismatics and blasphemers to the chair of Peter and to the principal Church, in which sacerdotal unity has its source; nor did they take thought that these are Romans, whose faith was praised by the preaching Apostle, and among whom it is not possible for perfidy to have entrance."

Pope St Zosimus, *Epistle to the Africans* 11 (AD 417)
"Although the tradition of the Fathers has assigned so great an authority to the Apostolic See, that no one should dare to dispute about a judgment given by it, and that See, by laws and regulations, has kept to this ... you know, dearest brethren, and as priests you are not ignorant, that we rule over his place, and are in possession also of the authority of his name, nevertheless, though so great be our authority that none may refuse our sentence, we have not done anything, which we have not, of our will referred by letter to your knowledge, conceding this to the Brotherhood."

St Augustine of Hippo, *Sermons* 131, 10 (inter AD 391-430)
"(On this matter of the Pelagians) two Councils have already been sent to the Apostolic See; and from there rescripts too have come. The matter is at an end; would that the error too might some time be at an end."

St Peter Chrysologus, *Letter to Eutyches* 25, 2 (AD 449)
"We exhort you in every respect, honorable brother, to heed obediently what has been written by the Most Blessed Pope of the City of Rome; for Blessed Peter, who lives and presides in his own see, provides the truth of faith to those who seek it. For we, by reason of our pursuit of peace and faith, cannot try cases on the faith without the consent of the Bishop of the City of Rome."

The Roman Catechism (1566)

Pt. I, Ch. X: So has (Christ) placed over his Church, *which he governs by his invisible Spirit*, a man to be his vicar and the minister of his power. A visible Church requires a visible head; therefore the Savior appointed Peter head and pastor of all the faithful, when he committed to his care the feeding of all his sheep, in such ample terms that he willed the very same power of ruling and governing the entire Church to descend to Peter's successors.

Catechism of the Catholic Church (1992)

No. 891: The Roman Pontiff, head of the college of bishops, enjoys this infallibility in virtue of his office, when, as supreme pastor and teacher of all the faithful — who confirms his brethren in the faith — he proclaims by a definitive act a doctrine pertaining to faith or morals ... The infallibility promised to the Church is also present in the body of bishops when, together with Peter's successor, they exercise the supreme Magisterium, above all in an Ecumenical Council. When the Church through its supreme Magisterium proposes a doctrine "for belief as being divinely revealed," and as the teaching of Christ, the definitions "must be adhered to with the obedience of faith." This infallibility extends as far as the deposit of divine Revelation itself.

Was St Peter Ever in Rome?

Objection: *"How can today's Pope, the Bishop of Rome, be the modern-day successor to St Peter when St Peter himself never visited Rome?"*

The Protestant case against St Peter ever being in Rome is stated bluntly by the Presbyterian minister Loraine Boettner in his book *Roman Catholicism*, the 'Bible' of anti-Catholic Fundamentalism:

> The remarkable thing, however, about Peter's alleged bishopric in Rome is that the New Testament has not one word to say about it. The word Rome occurs only nine times in the Bible, and never is Peter mentioned in connection with it. There is no allusion to Rome in either of his epistles. Paul's journey to the city is recorded in great detail (Acts 27 and 28). There is in fact no New Testament evidence, nor any historical proof of any kind, that Peter ever was in Rome. All rests on legend (p. 117).

Boettner's invective does not end there. He goes on to say:

> Not one of the early church fathers gives any support to the belief that Peter was a bishop in Rome until Jerome in the fifth century. Du Pin, a Roman Catholic historian, acknowledges that the primacy of Peter is not recorded by the early Christian writers, Justin Martyr (139), Irenaeus (178), Clement of Alexandria (190), or others of the most ancient fathers (p. 122).

On the other hand, at the end of his first epistle St Peter writes: "She who is at Babylon, who is likewise chosen, sends you greetings; and so does my son Mark" (1 Pet. 5:13). St Peter used Babylon here as an early Christian code word for Rome.

St John also uses the term Babylon in the Book of Revelation six times in the same way:

"Another angel, a second, followed, saying, 'Fallen, fallen is Babylon the great, she who made all nations drink the wine of her impure passion'" (14:8).

"The great city was split into three parts, and the cities of the nations fell, and God remembered great Babylon, to make her drain the cup of the fury of his wrath" (16:19).

"... and on her forehead was written a name of mystery: Babylon the great, mother of harlots and of earth's abominations" (17:5).

"... he called out with a mighty voice, 'Fallen, fallen is Babylon the great!'" (18:2).

"... they will stand far off, in fear of her torment, and say, 'Alas! Alas! you great city, you mighty city Babylon! In one hour has your judgment come'" (18:10).

"So shall Babylon the great city be thrown down with violence, and shall be found no more" (18:21).

Babylon in the book of Revelation can only refer to Rome as it was the only "great city" in the time of Jesus and the Apostles. Babylon proper in Mesopotamia had, by AD 100, been reduced to insignificance. Other extra-biblical works also refer to Rome as Babylon, such as the *Sibylline Oracles* (5:159ff.), the *Apocalypse of Baruch* (2:1) and 4 Esdras (3:1). Boettner, however, dismisses the argument that Babylon in 1 Peter is a code for Rome, preferring to believe that St Peter actually visited Babylon itself:

> While there is no Scriptural evidence at all that Peter went west to Rome, here is a plain statement of Scripture that he did go east to Babylon. Why cannot the Roman Church take Peter's word to that effect? ... there is no good reason for saying that Babylon means Rome (p. 120).

Boettner also asserts that St Peter wrote 1 Peter (and probably 2 Peter) while in Babylon. All credible Scripture scholars believe that St Peter wrote 1 Peter between AD 62 and 64. This is because St Peter seems to have known St Paul's letter to the Ephesians (written during St Paul's first Roman captivity which ended in AD 62) and because of the absence of any reference to an official Roman persecution of Christians, which began in August, AD 64. St Peter outlines the same duties for slaves, wives and husbands as in Eph. 5:22-33 and 6:5-8. To have such precise knowledge of this letter so soon after its composition, as well as being certain of its authenticity, St Peter must have been near St Paul — that is, in Rome with him, not in far-away Babylon.

Furthermore, in his final farewell in 1 Peter, St Peter mentions Silvanus and St Mark. Silvanus, the bearer of 1 Peter, was a constant companion of St Paul (Acts 15:22, 32-40; 2 Cor. 1:19; 1 Thess. 1:1; 2 Thess. 1:1) while St Mark was with St Paul in Rome during his first captivity (Col. 4:10). Why would Silvanus be in Babylon with St Peter if he normally travelled with St Paul and how could St Mark team up with St Peter and be in Babylon so soon after being mentioned in Col. 4:10 with St Paul in Rome? The more likely answer is that they were with St Paul and St Peter who were both in Rome at the same time.

So much is made also of the fact that St Paul never refers to St Peter being in Rome in Romans or in any of his Captivity Epistles. Boettner exclaims, "How strange for a missionary to write to a church and not mention the pastor! That would be an inexcusable affront" (p. 121). It is true that St Paul makes no direct reference to St Peter but it is strongly arguable that he makes an oblique one. St Paul refers to a "reason why I have so often been hindered from coming to you" (15:22). This reason is "lest I build on another man's foundation" (15:20). Who is this "another man" who has already laid the "foundation" in Rome? Tradition tells us that his name is Peter.

There is a prudential reason why St Paul does not directly mention St Peter in his Roman epistle. Christians were known and despised even before the first official persecution of Nero. The Emperor Claudius expelled all Christians and Jews from Rome in AD 50 because of their disputes over a man named "Chrestus," according to the ancient historian Suetonius.[1] St Peter was known as the leader of this seditious sect. Therefore, it was necessary to always conceal the identity and whereabouts of St Peter to protect both him and the Christians he visited. Roman officials routinely read mail for security reasons, hence the prudence on the part of early Christians, concealing the name of St Peter and even Rome in any important correspondence.

As for Boettner's claim that "Not one of the early church fathers gives any support to the belief that Peter was a bishop in Rome until Jerome in the fifth century," Herbert Cardinal Vaughan, Archbishop of Westminster back in 1895, set forth some of the early Patristic evidence in support of St Peter's presence in Rome[2]:

(i) Tertullian (AD 200) speaks of St Peter ordaining St Clement in Rome (*The Demurrer Against the Heretics* 32) and of St Peter baptizing in the Tiber River (*On Baptism* 4).

(ii) Clement of Alexandria (ante AD 217) speaks of St Peter proclaiming the word of God publicly in Rome (in Eusebius, *Ecclesiastical History* 6, 14).

(iii) Caius (AD 214) referred to Pope Victor as thirteenth bishop of Rome after St Peter (in Eusebius, *Ecclesiastical History* 5, 28).

(iv) St Hippolytus of Rome (AD 225) names St Peter as first bishop of Rome (fragment *On the Twelve Apostles* XLIX).

(v) St Cyprian of Carthage (AD 250) speaks of the "the place of Peter" (*Epistle to Antonianus*) and "the seat of Peter" (*Epistle to Cornelius*) when referring to Rome.

(vi) Firmilian of Caesaria (AD 257) speaks of the "succession of Peter" and "the chair of Peter" (*Epistle to Cyprian*) when referring to Rome.

(vii) The Council of Sardica (AD 342-343) "honors the memory of the Apostle Peter" by referring appeals to the See of Peter in Rome (*Can. IV* and *Epistle to Julius*).

---

[1] *Lives of the Caesars*, Claud. 25, 4. By "Chrestus" Suetonius clearly intended "Christus," which is Latin for Christ.

[2] Tenth Lecture at Free Trade Hall, Manchester, England, Autumn 1895.

(viii) Pope Julius I (AD 340), Bishop of Rome, referred to the doctrines received by him as coming from St Peter (*To the Eusebians at Antioch* 35).

(ix) St Athanasius (AD 358) called Rome "the Apostolic Throne" (*The Monk's History of Arian Impiety*, 35).

(x) St Optatus of Milevis says that the episcopal chair in Rome was first established by St Peter, in which chair sat St Peter himself (*On the Donatist Schism* II, 2).

(xi) Pope Damasus (AD 370) speaks of the "Apostolic Chair (in which the) holy Apostle sitting, taught his successors how to guide the helm of the Church" (*Epistle 9 to the Oriental Synod, in the presence of Theodoret*, V, 10).

(xii) St Ambrose (AD 387-390) refers to "Peter's chair" in Rome where "Peter, first of the apostles, first sat" (*On Penance*, I, 7-32).

The actual story of the discovery of St Peter's tomb and his skeletal remains spreads over centuries. On the site where St Peter's Basilica now stands stood originally a chariot racecourse track built by the Emperor Caligula. All that remains of that racetrack today is the tall Egyptian obelisk standing in the middle of the piazza. Nearby, at a short distance from the stone structure of the racetrack, along the Via Cornelia, was a pagan burial-ground lying in a knoll called Vaticanus. It was in this burial-ground that the bones of St Peter, wrapped in linen, were laid after his martyrdom.

St Anacletus, third Bishop of Rome, erected a shrine over St Peter's grave which was visible to all those who passed by Vatican Hill. This shrine, despite the persecutions, became a familiar meeting place for Christians from the beginning and was mentioned in the *Acts of St Sebastian*.

In the early fourth century, the Emperor Constantine allowed Pope St Sylvester I to construct a large new church over the burial place of St Peter and the remains of other early Popes now gathered there. The stones for this new church were quarried from the old racecourse and the structure of St Peter's shrine became the high altar. Begun in AD 326, this church was finally completed in AD 349. It contained five naves, fifty-two altars with seven hundred candles burning day and night, and golden mosaics decorating the walls and arches.

The actual bones of St Peter were ordered removed from their shrine by Constantine, covered in fine purple cloth interwoven with gold, put into a box and reposed in a niche of a nearby wall (Wall G) to protect them from humidity. This wall was later covered by red plaster. The original burial place of St Peter was also walled off to protect it from injury and the outside world, to become lost for the next one thousand six hundred years.

In 1506 it was decided, due to subsidence and decay, to replace the old church built by Constantine with a grand new basilica. In 1626, Bernini, testing the floor over St Peter's burial place for the erection of his weighty baldacchino, came across numerous skeletons. These skeletons were arranged like spokes of a wheel, pointing to a central spot under the high altar.

More than three hundred years later, Pope Pius XII, in March 1939, ordered an excavation under St Peter's to find "the foundations of our faith." In a radio broadcast on 23 December, 1950, the Pope announced to the world that the original tomb of St Peter had been discovered. It lay twenty-five feet beneath the high altar and was decorated with Christian mosaics, one of a fisherman with a rod, one of the Good Shepherd, and another of Jonah and the whale.

However, the bones of St Peter (as opposed to his tomb) remained missing. Dr Margherita Guarducci, a professor of Greek epigraphy, noticed that during the excavations for the tomb pieces of red plaster chipped off a nearby wall (Wall G) had Greek inscriptions carved on them. The Greek letters "pe" in the form of a monogram appeared on every line of the wall. By chance, on 2 August, 1951, a Jesuit excavator, Father Antonio Ferrua, noticed a piece one by three inches in size, with the words "*Petros eni*" (Peter is inside) on it and put it into his pocket and took it home. When Pius XII heard of this he ordered the Jesuit to return the fragment. Wall G also included many other references to St Peter, accompanied by the names of Jesus and Mary, the letters "pe" joined in the form of a key, and the name of Peter intersected by the names of Jesus and Mary. All this indicated that the bones of St Peter had to be nearby.

In fact, about ten years earlier, in 1942, an excavator named Giovanni Segoni had emptied the niche in Wall G. Included in the material collected were bones that were dusted and freed from the other rubble. Without informing the excavators, Monsignor Ludwig Kaas, the administrator of St Peter's Basilica, had the bones put into a wooden box and stored, first, in a damp area of the underground grotto and then in a cupboard of a basilica office. In 1962, these bones were analyzed by Venerando Correnti, one of Europe's most distinguished anthropologists. "The remains," he said, "are from a single male between sixty and seventy years, about five feet seven inches tall and of robust constitution. Judging from the soil, the body must have been buried in the earth. The bones — and not the body — were at some time wrapped in purple cloth." The fabric with the bones was interwoven with gold threads.

In February, 1964, Pope St Paul VI gave permission for further tests on the bones and the fabric. The analysis found, firstly, that the fabric was the same type used to wrap the bones of St Peter when they were transferred in the time of Constantine; secondly, the earth particles covering the bones were found to be identical in type to the soil in St Peter's original tomb. Other tests on the repository Wall G established that it was an ancient Roman work with absolutely no trace of later tampering or rebuilding. All the evidence pointed now to only one conclusion.

Pope St Paul VI announced to one of the excavators that "those bones are like gold to us." On 26 June, 1968, he surprised the world by announcing officially that the bones of St Peter had finally been rediscovered and identified: "The relics of St Peter have been identified in a manner which we believe convincing ... very patient and accurate investigations were made with the result which we believe positive." On the following day, the Pope, in a solemn ceremony, restored the sacred bones to their ancient resting-place.[3]

---

[3] Cf. J. E. Walsh, *The Bones of St Peter*, Doubleday, New York, 1982.

The Fathers

Dionysius of Corinth, *To Pope Soter* (c. AD 170) [Fragment in Eusebius, *Ecclesiastical History* 2, 25, 8 (c. AD 303)]
"You have also, by your very admonition, brought together the planting that was made by Peter and Paul at Rome and at Corinth; for both of them alike planted in our Corinth and taught us; and both alike, teaching similarly in Italy, suffered martyrdom at the same time."

St Irenaeus of Lyons, *Against Heresies* 3, 3, 2 (c. AD 180)
"... by pointing out here the successions of the bishops of the greatest and most ancient Church known to all, founded and organized at Rome by the two most glorious Apostles, Peter and Paul, that Church which has the tradition and the faith which comes down to us after having been announced to men by the Apostles. For with this Church, because of its superior origin, all Churches must agree, that is, all the faithful in the whole world; and it is in her that the faithful everywhere have maintained the Apostolic tradition."

Tertullian, *The Demurrer Against the Heretics* 36, 1 (c. AD 200)
"How happy is that Church ... where Peter endured a passion like that of the Lord, where Paul was crowned in a death like John's."

Clement of Alexandria (ante AD 217) [Fragment in Eusebius, *Ecclesiastical History* 6, 14 (c. AD 303)]
"When Peter preached the Word publicly at Rome, and declared the Gospel by the Spirit, many who were present requested that Mark, who had been for a long time his follower and who remembered his sayings, should write down what had been proclaimed."

Eusebius Pamphilus, *Ecclesiastical History* 2, 15, 4 (c. AD 303)
"It is said that Peter's first epistle, in which he makes mention of Mark, was composed at Rome itself; and that he himself indicates this, referring to the city figuratively as Babylon."

Eusebius Pamphilus, *The Chronicle* **Ad An. Dom. 42 (c. AD 303)**
"The second year of the two hundredth and fifth Olympiad (AD 42) the apostle Peter, after he has established the Church in Antioch, is sent to Rome, where he remains a bishop of that city, preaching the gospel for twenty-five years ..."

Eusebius Pamphilus, *The Chronicle* **Ad An. Dom. 68 (c. AD 303)**
"Nero is the first, in addition to all other crimes, to make a persecution against the Christians, in which Peter and Paul died gloriously in Rome."

St Peter of Alexandria, *Canonical Letter,* **Canon 9 (AD 311)**
"Peter, first chosen of the apostles, having been apprehended often and thrown into prison and treated with ignominy, at last was crucified in Rome."

The Roman Catechism (1566)

The Roman Catechism did not directly refer to the question of whether St Peter had ever been in Rome, but in Pt. I, Ch. X quotes the following from Optatus of Milevis (*De Schism. Donat.* ii. 2):

"You cannot be excused on the score of ignorance, knowing as you do that in the city of Rome the episcopal chair was first conferred on Peter, who occupied it as head of the Apostles ..."

Catechism of the Catholic Church (1992)

Likewise, the *Catechism of the Catholic Church* makes no direct statement on the question of whether St Peter ever visited Rome, but re-affirms that the Pope is "the Bishop of Rome and Peter's successor" (#882).

Apostolic Succession

Objection: *"No one is a successor to the Apostles and has their authority today. The possession of the Spirit is the factor that determined the Apostles' authority. How can anyone claim to have apostolic authority when not inspired by the Holy Spirit?"*

It is a central belief of Catholicism that there has been an unbroken line of bishops beginning immediately after the Apostles and continuing all the way to the present day. It follows that every current bishop in the Catholic Church can trace his ordination back in a continuous chain extending over twenty centuries to the Apostles themselves. This claim can be supported from Scripture, the Church Fathers and from historical investigation.

Jesus established his Church upon the foundation of the twelve Apostles, commissioning them to shepherd his people after his ascension back into heaven (Mt 10:1, 40; Mt 16:19; Mt 18:18). To receive and obey the Apostles was to receive and obey Jesus (Jn 13:20). To qualify as an Apostle, one had to be a witness to Jesus' public ministry, including his baptism, resurrection and ascension into heaven (Acts 1:21-26). The only exception was St Paul, who, though not a follower of Jesus during his years on earth (Acts 9) was made an Apostle by the risen Jesus approximately seven years after his ascension.

Even while still alive, the Apostles appointed others to different kinds of ministries to assist them. One of the first acts of St Peter was to appoint a successor to Judas, namely St Matthias. In the words of Scripture, "His office let another take" (Acts 1:20). Despite Judas' egregious sin, the remaining Apostles recognized the continuation of his office and the necessity that it be filled. St Matthias had been a witness to Jesus' ministry and resurrection (Acts 1:22). Elsewhere, we read of "elders" being appointed and having authority in the Church (Acts 11:30,14:23,15:2,15:22,16:4,20:17,21:18; 1 Tim. 4:14, 5:17; Tit. 1:5; Js 5:14; 1 Pet. 5:1). It was incumbent upon the "elders" ... "to feed the church of the Lord which he obtained with his own blood" (Acts 20:28). There was no pre-condition that an "elder" had to be a witness to Jesus' resurrection, only that they "be blameless ... a lover of goodness, master of himself, upright, holy, and self-controlled" (Tit. 1:7-8). There were also "deacons" ordained to assist in the daily distribution of food and drink among the brethren; the only prerequisite for their appointment was that they be "men of good repute, full of the Spirit and of wisdom" (Acts 6:3).

Soon enough, all the Apostles were to pass from the scene. Though Jesus could have appeared from time to time to appoint new Apostles, he chose not to do so. Government of the Church thereupon fell to the next highest-ranking officials appointed by the Apostles, namely the "elders." Over time, these "elders" were to be called bishops, from the Greek word *episcopos* (ἐπίσκοπος), or overseer (1 Tim. 3:1).

How did one formally acquire the office of elder/episcopos/bishop in the early Church? Essentially, after one was recognized as having the requisite moral and spiritual qualities, it was through the sacrament of ordination, today known as Holy Orders. This involved prayer, fasting and the laying on of hands, as evident in the Acts of the Apostles and several of St Paul's epistles:

"While they were worshiping the Lord and fasting, the Holy Spirit said, 'Set apart for me Barnabas and Saul for the work to which I have called them.' Then after fasting and praying they laid their hands on them and sent them off" (Acts 13:2-3).

"And when they had appointed elders for them in every church, with prayer and fasting, they committed them to the Lord in whom they believed" (Acts 14:23).

"Do not neglect the gift you have, which was given you by prophetic utterance when the council of elders laid their hands upon you" (1 Tim. 4:14).

"For this reason I remind you to rekindle the gift of God that is within you through the laying on of my hands" (2 Tim. 1:6).

As evident in the case of Sts Paul and Barnabas (Acts 13:2-3), the Apostles themselves ordained the first elders. Afterwards, the first elders would in turn ordain others to succeed them, and so on and so on. The fact that succession was intended in the office of elder from generation to generation is apparent in the following verses:

"*Do not be hasty in the laying on of hands, nor participate in another man's sins; keep yourself pure*" (1 Tim. 5:22).

"*You then, my son, be strong in the grace that is in Christ Jesus, and what you have heard from me before many witnesses entrust to faithful men who will be able to teach others also*" (2 Tim. 2:1-2).

"*This is why I left you in Crete, that you might amend what was defective, and appoint elders in every town as I directed you*" (Tit. 1:5).

It is also clear from Scripture that those ordained as elders possessed an authority that had to be respected and obeyed:

"*But we beg you, brethren, to respect those who labor among you and are over you in the Lord and admonish you, and to esteem them very highly in love because of their work*" (1 Thess. 5:12-13).

"*Let the elders who rule well be considered worthy of double honor, especially those who labor in preaching and teaching; for the Scripture says, 'You shall not muzzle an ox when it is treading out the grain,' and, 'The laborer deserves his wages'*" (1 Tim. 5:17-18).

"*Obey your leaders and submit to them; for they are keeping watch over your souls, as men who will have to give account*" (Heb. 13:17).

"*Likewise you that are younger be subject to the elders. Clothe yourselves, all of you, with humility toward one another, for 'God opposes the proud, but gives grace to the humble'*" (1 Pet. 5:5).

In conclusion, while it is a moral imperative that those claiming Apostolic authority live 'spirit-filled' lives, it is not "the possession of the Spirit" as such that determines whether one is a successor to the Apostles or not. Rather, as attested in Scripture, Apostolic authority is passed on through the laying on of hands, a process that began with the Apostles themselves and continues to our present day, and will so continue until the end of time. Unless persons claiming authority can show a link to this chain of Apostolic succession, they are not legitimate leaders in the Church Christ founded.

Second objection: *"The Apostles could speak with tongues, prophesy and work miracles. Catholic bishops today cannot do these things. How can they then be successors to the Apostles?"*

While all the Apostles spoke in tongues on Pentecost Day, there were over a hundred others also in the Upper Room who did likewise but were not Apostles. Similarly, there were others who could prophesy such as Agabus (Acts 11:28, 21:10) and perform miraculous wonders such as Stephen (Acts 6:8) who were not Apostles or even elders. At the same time, while all the Apostles possessed the power to perform miracles there is no conclusive evidence that all could also prophesy. The same goes for those ordained as elders by them. Hence, it cannot be said that speaking in tongues, prophesying and working miracles were or are indicative of, or essential prerequisites for, Apostolic authority or for being a legitimate successor to the Apostles.

Rather, speaking in tongues, prophesying and working miracles are charismatic gifts (*gratia gratis data*) given gratuitously by God to anyone he pleases for the spiritual benefit of others. As mentioned above, the Apostles were certainly given a share in these gifts, as were non-Apostles. We would normally expect such gifts to be given to people noted for their sanctity but they may even be granted to one who lacks God's favor (e.g., Balaam [Num. 22]). It is understandable why the Apostles would be so gifted, considering their pre-eminent calling as witnesses of the risen Jesus and their obligation to preach the Gospel to "all nations." The nascent early Church needed extraordinary assistance to establish and expand in the face of an incredulous and hostile world.

What qualified the Apostles to be Apostles was their witness of the risen Jesus and the power and authority specifically bestowed upon them by Jesus to continue his work of teaching, governing and sanctifying. The charismatic gifts were 'added extras' to enable them to better fulfil a mission already received from Jesus. What qualified the elders and those who came after them to be bishops was their calling by the Church and the power and authority to teach, govern and sanctify bestowed upon them through the laying of hands (the sacrament of Holy Orders). Again, charismatic gifts would be freely given by God to bishops to faithfully fulfil an office they already possessed through the laying of hands.

Even though bishops today do not usually "speak with tongues, prophesy and work miracles" it must be remembered that these are not the only kind of charismatic gifts, nor are they the most important or necessary for the discharge of their duties as is evident from the following:

"For as in one body we have many members, and all the members do not have the same function, so we, though many, are one body in Christ, and individually members one of another. Having gifts that differ according to the grace given to us, let us use them: if prophecy, in proportion to our faith; if service, in our serving; he who teaches, in his teaching; he who exhorts, in his exhortation; he who contributes, in liberality; he who gives aid, with zeal; he who does acts of mercy, with cheerfulness. Let love be genuine; hate what is evil, hold fast to what is good; love one another with brotherly affection; outdo one another in showing honor" (Rom. 12:4-10).

"Now you are the body of Christ and individually members of it. And God has appointed in the church first apostles, second prophets, third teachers, then workers of miracles, then healers, helpers, administrators, speakers in various kinds of tongues. Are all apostles? Are all prophets? Are all teachers? Do all work miracles? Do all possess gifts of healing? Do all speak with tongues? Do all interpret?" (1 Cor. 12:27-30).

From these quotes, it is clear that service, teaching, exhortation, liberality, zeal, mercy, cheerfulness and administration are also charismatic gifts and count just as much, if not more than 'miraculous' charismatic gifts. Teaching is certainly ranked by St Paul ahead of miracles, healing and tongues. These 'other gifts' should and can be had by any bishop today, as well as the most important gift of all, genuine charity.

Third objection: *"The Apostles witness to us today through their writings in the Bible and this is the only way their unerring guidance is transmitted to us."*

The above objection is typical of those who reject Apostolic succession, have no bishops, and subscribe to *Sola Scriptura* (the Bible alone). Certainly, the Scriptures are the inerrant word of God; nevertheless, no private individual can guarantee an inerrant interpretation of Scripture. What has *Sola Scriptura* and private interpretation of the Bible produced except a collection of over thirty-five thousand different denominations teaching a myriad of contradictory doctrines? Where is the original Apostolic witness to be found amid such chaos? Jesus left to his followers something better than private interpretation — a living teaching authority founded on St Peter and the Apostles that possesses his authority to teach, govern and sanctify, which continues to this day. It is this living teaching authority that throughout Christian history has guaranteed "one faith, one baptism" (Eph. 4:5) and continues today in the bishops of the world united to the Pope.

The importance of Apostolic succession in the preservation of authentic doctrine is illustrated in the following exhortation proffered by St Paul to St Timothy: "and what you have heard from me before many witnesses entrust to faithful men who will be able to teach others also" (2 Tim. 2:2). As an elder appointed by St Paul, St Timothy is exhorted to appoint succeeding elders who will preserve the original Apostolic faith. The preservation of the word of God was therefore to be intimately linked with the appointment of faithful and validly ordained elders, or bishops. However, was this model of passing on and preservation expected to endure for just three generations, being replaced by a Bible privately interpreted by each and every Christian? No, it was a model that was expected to endure until the end of the world.

We know that the latter was believed to be the case from the writings of the Church Fathers. Faced with a steady stream of heresies that regularly and skilfully appealed to the Scriptures for justification, the Fathers turned to Tradition to discover the authentic meaning of Scripture. But where was this Tradition to be found? In the succession of authentic Bishops stemming from the Apostles. St Irenaeus of Lyons and Origen are two examples of many Fathers exhibiting this belief:

> **St Irenaeus of Lyons,** *Against Heresies* **3, 4, 1 (c. AD 180)**
> If there should be a dispute over some kind of question, ought we not have recourse to the most ancient Churches in which the Apostles were familiar, and draw from them what is clear and certain in regard to that question? What if the Apostles had not in fact left writings to us? Would it not be necessary to follow the order of tradition, which was handed down to those to whom they entrusted the Churches?

> **Origen,** *Fundamental Doctrines* **1, Preface, 2 (c. AD 220)**
> Although there are many who believe that they themselves hold to the teachings of Christ, there are yet some among them who think differently from their predecessors. The teaching of the Church has indeed been handed down through an order of succession from the Apostles, and remains in the Churches even to the present time. That alone is to be believed as the truth which is in no way at variance with ecclesiastical and apostolic tradition.

At least one Anglican scholar, J.N.D Kelly, acknowledges the same:

> ... the original revelation is guaranteed by the unbroken succession of bishops in the great sees going back lineally to the apostles ... an additional safeguard is supplied by the Holy Spirit, for the message committed was to the Church, and the Church is the home of the Spirit (*Early Christian Doctrines*, p. 37).

Fourth objection: *"It seems very strange that the successor to a king is a king, the successor to a president is a president, and the successor to a governor is a governor, but the successor to an Apostle is a Catholic bishop or priest."*

As the saying goes, "a rose is still a rose by any other name." The word 'Apostle' means 'one who is sent,' an appropriate title to describe those sent by Jesus to convert the world; the word 'bishop' as stated earlier is derived from the Greek word for 'overseer' and appropriately describes the role of those inheriting the governance of the Church from the Twelve. Admittedly, there has been some confusion about the relationship between the Apostles and bishops, but there need not be.

Firstly, as already noted only the original Twelve plus St Paul were strictly Apostles for only they either witnessed the whole of Jesus' ministry on earth or were specifically commissioned and sent forth by the risen Lord. Coming afterwards, bishops serve not as Apostles but as their *successors*, receiving the governance of the Church immediately from the Twelve through the rite of ordination.

In addition to this point, the following are other differences that distinguish the offices of Apostle and bishop:

(i) Miraculous powers: each of the Apostles possessed the power to perform miracles to validate the credibility of their divine mission. Bishops ordinarily do not have the power to perform miracles.

(ii) Universal jurisdiction: Apostles possessed universal jurisdiction to serve Jesus and his faithful anywhere in the world. Bishops usually have territorial limitations on their authority to avoid overlap and confusion.

(iii) Infallibility: Each Apostle possessed personal teaching infallibility through the assistance of the Holy Spirit (Jn 14:26). Except for the Bishop of Rome under certain conditions, bishops today only possess infallibility when teaching as a body in union with the Pope.

Despite these differences, Catholic bishops are still legitimate successors to the Apostles as they and they alone can trace their ordinations along an unbroken chain back to the original Twelve and through them to Jesus himself.

Fifth objection: *"Catholic bishops are not the same as New Testament bishops, as the latter had to be married and oversaw only one local church. Catholic bishops are not married and oversee not just one church but a whole diocese of churches."*

One becomes a legitimate bishop through a valid ordination ceremony conducted by an authorized officiating bishop who:

(i) Lays hands on the baptized male candidate;
(ii) Pronounces the appropriate words;
(iii) Intends to do what the Church does.

These three requirements are essential to the validity of the rite of ordination and hence are 'not negotiable.' On the other hand, matters relating to the marital status of the candidate or territorial jurisdiction are 'accidental' matters that do not pertain to the validity of the rite of ordination. Being 'accidental,' they can be "bound" or "loosed" by the Church according to the perceived needs of the time. Regarding episcopal marriages, we find that in the early Church there were several married bishops but they separated from their wives upon their episcopal appointment (e.g., St Hilary of Poitiers, the father of Pope Damasus I, and Pope Hormisdas) and eventually Church legislation beginning with the councils of Elvira (AD 306) and Nicaea (AD 325) was enacted to forbid married bishops for pastoral or prudential reasons. Ultimately, in both the East and West clerical celibacy would be the norm for all bishops.

Those who claim that New Testament bishops "had to be married" usually cite St Paul's first letter to St Timothy, in which he insisted that a bishop should be "the husband of one wife ... (and) if a man does not know how to manage his own household, how can he care for God's church" (1 Tim. 3:2-5). The purpose of St Paul's words was to advise St Timothy on the qualities to look for when choosing candidates for ordination. If the candidate was already married, he had to have married only once. If the candidate was a widower, he was an eligible candidate for episcopal ordination so long as he did not intend to remarry, as a second wife would be regarded as a sign that the candidate did not have an episcopal calling. St Paul was certainly not insisting on marriage as a condition for ordination, for he himself never married (1 Cor. 7:8).

Territorial jurisdiction is likewise an accidental matter subject to the positive laws of the Church. It is neither here nor there for valid ordination whether a bishop has authority over one or more churches. In any case, it is mistaken to assert that all New Testament bishops oversaw only one local church. For example, St Paul left Titus in Crete to "amend what was defective, and appoint elders in every town" (Tit.

1:5). From this it is evident that Titus oversaw the whole church in Crete with responsibility to bring order and appoint leaders for all particular churches on that island. This model is no different to local bishops who today oversee a whole region "to amend what is defective and appoint priests in every town in their diocese." Through the power of the keys, the Church can arrange and change the territorial boundaries of all her dioceses and in the process determine how many particular parishes a bishop has jurisdiction over. She is also free to ordain any suitable man to the office of bishop without assigning to the same any territorial jurisdiction, as is the case with those many bishops working in church bureaucracies, particularly in the Vatican itself.

The Fathers

Pope St Clement of Rome, *Letter to the Corinthians* **42, 4-5; 44, 1-3 (c. AD 98)**
"Through countryside and city they preached; and they appointed their earliest converts, testing them by the spirit, to be the bishops and deacons of future believers. Nor was this a novelty: for bishops and deacons had been written about a long time earlier. Indeed, Scripture somewhere says: 'I will set up their bishops in righteousness and their deacons in faith' ... Our Apostles knew through our Lord Jesus Christ that there would be strife for the office of bishop. For this reason, therefore, having received perfect foreknowledge, they appointed those who have already been mentioned, and afterwards added the further provision that, if they should die, other approved men should succeed to their ministry."

Hegesippus, *Memoirs* **(AD 180), [Fragment in Eusebius,** *Ecclesiastical History* **4, 22 (c. AD 303)]**
"When I had come to Rome, I [visited] Anicetus, whose deacon was Eleutherus. And after Anicetus died], Soter succeeded, and after him Eleutherus. In each succession and in each city there is a continuance of that which is proclaimed by the law, the prophets, and the Lord."

Apostolic Succession

St Irenaeus of Lyons, *Against Heresies* **3, 3, 1 (c. AD 180)**
"It is possible, then, for everyone in every church, who may wish to know the truth, to contemplate the tradition of the apostles which has been made known to us throughout the whole world. And we are in a position to enumerate those who were instituted bishops by the apostles and their successors down to our own times, men who neither knew nor taught anything like what these heretics rave about."

Tertullian, *Demurrer Against the Heretics* **32 (AD 200)**
"But if there be any [heresies] which are bold enough to plant [their origin] in the midst of the apostolic age, that they may thereby seem to have been handed down by the apostles, because they existed in the time of the apostles, we can say: Let them produce the original records of their churches; let them unfold the roll of their bishops, running down in due succession from the beginning in such a manner that [their first] bishop shall be able to show for his ordainer and predecessor some one of the apostles or of apostolic men − a man, moreover, who continued steadfast with the apostles. For this is the manner in which the apostolic churches transmit their registers: as the church of Smyrna, which records that Polycarp was placed therein by John; as also the church of Rome, which makes Clement to have been ordained in like manner by Peter."

St Cyprian of Carthage, *Letters* **69 [75], 3 (AD 253)**
"[T]he Church is one, and as she is one, cannot be both within and without. For if she is with Novatian, she was not with [Pope] Cornelius. But if she was with Cornelius, who succeeded the bishop [of Rome], Fabian, by lawful ordination, and whom, beside the honor of the priesthood the Lord glorified also with martyrdom, Novatian is not in the Church; nor can he be reckoned as a bishop, who, succeeding to no one, and despising the evangelical and apostolic tradition, sprang from himself. For he who has not been ordained in the Church can neither have nor hold to the Church in any way."

St Augustine of Hippo, *Against the Letter of Mani* **4, 5 (AD 397)**
"[T]here are many other things which most properly can keep me in [the Catholic Church's] bosom. The unanimity of peoples and nations

keeps me here. Her authority, inaugurated in miracles, nourished by hope, augmented by love, and confirmed by her age, keeps me here. The succession of priests, from the very see of the apostle Peter, to whom the Lord, after his resurrection, gave the charge of feeding his sheep, up to the present episcopate, keeps me here."

The Roman Catechism (1566)

Pt. I, Ch. IX: That all, therefore, might know which was the Catholic Church, the Fathers, guided by the Spirit of God, added to the Creed the word *Apostolic*. For the Holy Ghost, who presides over the Church, governs her by no other ministers than those of Apostolic succession. This Spirit, first imparted to the Apostles, has by the infinite goodness of God always continued in the Church.

Catechism of the Catholic Church (1992)

No. 862: "Just as the office which the Lord confided to Peter alone, as first of the apostles, destined to be transmitted to his successors, is a permanent one, so also endures the office, which the apostles received, of shepherding the Church, a charge destined to be exercised without interruption by the sacred order of bishops." Hence the Church teaches that "the bishops have by divine institution taken the place of the apostles as pastors of the Church, in such wise that whoever listens to them is listening to Christ and whoever despises them despises Christ and him who sent Christ."

The Priesthood

Objection: *"We are all priests. There is no distinct ordained priesthood separate and apart from the laity."*

According to most Protestants, the early Church of the pre-Constantinian era was not characterized by any essential distinction between laity and clergy. There was no hierarchical structure of bishop, priest or deacon, let alone any 'pope' claiming universal jurisdiction over the whole Church. Rather, the Church was egalitarian and democratic with the members of local independent churches conferring their spiritual authority upon their own elected leaders.

Those who advocate such views normally rely on 1 Pet. 2:5-9, which reads as follows: "and like living stones be yourselves built into a spiritual house, to be a holy priesthood, to offer spiritual sacrifices acceptable to God through Jesus Christ ... But you are a chosen race, a royal priesthood, a holy nation, God's own people, that you may declare the wonderful deeds of him who called you out of darkness." It is contended that Jesus is not only the High Priest of the New Testament, but the *sole* priest as well. His passion and death on the Cross is the only sacrifice for Christians. Therefore, any other so-called priest offering material sacrifices such as the Eucharist is unnecessary. The only admissible sacrifices for Christians are the spiritual sacrifices of prayer and praise. All Christians without exception can offer these sacrifices, therefore all Christians are priests – the "universal priesthood of all believers."

The above objection is reminiscent of the story of Korah's rebellion: "... and they assembled themselves together against Moses and against Aaron, and said to them, 'You have gone too far! For all the congregation are holy, every one of them, and the Lord is among them; why then do you exalt yourselves above the assembly of the Lord?'" (Num. 16:3). Korah, Dathan and Abiram and two hundred and fifty followers then sought to offer incense before the Lord but the earth opened and fire came forth from the Tabernacle to swallow and consume them. God showed that these men were not to offer incense even though all the people of Israel according to Exod. 19:6 were priests. St Jude tells us that some Christians in his day (despite 1 Pet. 2:5-9) were guilty of the same sin when he states, "Woe to them! For they walk in the way of Cain, and abandon themselves for the sake of gain to Balaam's error, *and perish in Korah's rebellion*" (Jude 1:11).

In Old Testament Israel, there were three levels of priests: the people of Israel as a whole (Exod. 19:6), the ministerial priests chosen from the tribe of Levi (Num. 3:5), and the High Priest (Exod. 31:30). This three-tiered model of the priesthood was carried over and reflected in the people of God of the New Testament: the universal priests are now the entire body of the baptized (1 Pet. 2:5-9), the ministerial priests the ordained successors to the Apostles (Rom. 15:16), and the High Priest is Jesus Christ (Heb. 3:1). In both the Old and New Testaments, therefore, the fact that the entire body of believers were regarded as priests was no obstacle to the existence of a separate ministerial priesthood.

It is in the Catholic Church with her ordained hierarchical priesthood that the laity can be truly a "priesthood of all believers." It is the Catholic Church that encourages its membership to "take up their cross," to "drink his cup," to offer up their sufferings as a victim, to help orphans and widows, to abstain from the defilements of the world, and to give alms. These are regarded as acts of true worship and as sacrifices "acceptable and pleasing to God" (Phil. 4:18). A Christianity that does not demand moral change or good works to be justified, insisting simply on the sufficiency of fiducial faith, is more a denial of the common priesthood than the ministerial priesthood.

According to Catholic teaching, a man becomes a minister or priest through the imposition of hands made by a bishop who at the same time recites the solemn words of consecration as contained in the respective rites of ordination for deacon, priest and bishop. One ordained as a bishop receives the power to offer the Holy Sacrifice of the Mass, to forgive sins, to confirm and to ordain. The episcopate is not a sacrament distinct from the priesthood, but rather its full expression. A bishop also has authority to teach and guarantee the continuity of the Catholic Faith in his diocese and to decide on questions relating to faith and morals: "Take heed to yourselves and to all the flock, in which the Holy Spirit has made you guardians" (Acts 20:28). The bishops of the world together with the Pope form the

Hierarchy, with jurisdiction to teach and govern. The Pope is the successor to St Peter; the bishops, the other Apostles.

In spiritual power, the priesthood incorporates the diaconate; the episcopate incorporates the priesthood and diaconate. In fact, episcopal ordination is the norm of Orders as established by Jesus, while priesthood and diaconate are lesser degrees of the same sacrament of the Church. All three degrees were possessed by the Apostles and later, in conformity with the direction of Jesus, were passed on by them wholly or in part to others as the requirements of the growing Church demanded. Thus, we see in Scripture the Apostles, by a visible rite involving prayer and the laying of hands, ordaining assistants and successors separate and apart from the rest of the laity:

"'... pick out from among you seven men of good repute, full of the Spirit and of wisdom, whom we may appoint to this duty' ... These they set before the apostles, and they prayed and laid their hands upon them" (Acts 6:3-6).

"While they were worshiping the Lord and fasting, the Holy Spirit said, 'Set apart for me Barnabas and Saul for the work to which I have called them.' Then after fasting and praying they laid their hands on them and sent them off. So, being sent out by the Holy Spirit, they went down to Seleucia; and from there they sailed to Cyprus" (Acts 13:2-4).

"And after they had appointed elders for them in every church, with prayer and fasting, they committed them to the Lord in whom they believed" (Acts 14:23).

"I remind you to rekindle the gift of God that is within you through the laying on of my hands" (2 Tim. 1:6).

"This is why I left you in Crete, that you might amend what was defective, and appoint elders in every town as I directed you" (Tit. 1:5).[1]

---

[1] The Catholic priesthood is identical with this office of elder. In fact, the word "priest" is simply an abbreviated English rendering of the Latin transliteration (presbyter) of the Greek word for elder – *presbuteros*.

The above verses testify to the fulfilment of a prophecy uttered by Isaiah centuries earlier concerning the conversion of the Gentiles, when he said, *"And they shall bring all your brethren from all the nations as an offering to the Lord, upon horses, and in chariots, and in litters, and upon mules, and upon dromedaries, to my holy mountain Jerusalem, says the Lord, just as the Israelites bring their cereal offering in a clean vessel to the house of the Lord. And some of them also I will take for priests and for Levites, says the Lord"* (Is. 66:20-21).

Second objection: *"It appears that specific men were set apart and ordained to perform specialist functions but these functions were not of a sacrificial nature to qualify them as priests. They were simply ministers of the word of God and their sacrifices were prayer and praise."*

In all fairness, it must be recognized that the Greek word 'Hiereus,' used to describe the Jewish High Priest, is only used in the New Testament with respect to Jesus. It is for this reason that Protestants hold that Jesus is the only New Testament priest and that those who are elders or overseers hold no priestly office.

The question as to whether the ordained Christian clergy in the New Testament constituted a priesthood hinges on whether the Eucharistic Sacrifice of the Mass is a part of authentic Christian worship. This was recognized by the Council of Trent:

> Sacrifice and priesthood are, by the ordinance of God, so conjoined, that both have existed in every law. Therefore, whereas in the New Testament, the Catholic Church has received, from the institution of Christ, the holy visible sacrifice of the Eucharist, it must also be confessed that there is, in that Church, a new, visible and external priesthood into which the old has been translated.[2]

The Prophet Malachi in the Old Testament predicted that the Jewish priesthood and sacrifices would be replaced by Gentile ones:

---

[2] *Decree on the Sacrament of Order*, ch. I, 15 July 1563.

"I have no pleasure in you, says the Lord of hosts, and I will not accept an offering from your hand. For from the rising of the sun to its setting my name is great among the nations, and in every place incense is offered to my name, and a pure offering; for my name is great among the nations, says the Lord of hosts" (Mal. 1:10-11).

This Gentile sacrifice of a "pure offering" was inaugurated at the Last Supper when Jesus consecrated bread and wine into his Body and Blood and then told his Apostles to "Do this in remembrance of me" (Lk 22:19). The language of "body" and "blood" is the language of sacrifice and presupposes a slaying that has separated them. In other words, Jesus speaks of himself as a sacrifice. The separate displaying of the bread and wine reinforces this. The ex-Protestant convert James Akin makes this further point:

> This is true regardless of whether Christ is literally present in the sacrament or whether he is only symbolically present. Even if he is only symbolically present, then the Eucharist symbolizes a sacrifice. It is a symbolic sacrifice. Because elders have the duty of performing the sacraments, they have the duty of performing this sacrifice, again indicating the priestly character of their office.[3]

Furthermore, by the words "Do this in remembrance of me" Jesus commanded his Apostles to perform continually a liturgical action that would recall as a memorial before the Father the unique sacrifice of the Son, and make him present in this memorial. In this sense, they and their successors were to act as priestly "stewards of the mysteries of God" (1 Cor. 4:1) and did so as recorded as follows:

"And they held steadfastly to the apostles' teaching and fellowship, to the breaking of the bread and to the prayers" (Acts 2:42).

"And day by day, attending the temple together and breaking bread in their homes, they partook of food with glad and generous hearts" (Acts 2:46).

---

[3] http://www.catholicfidelity.com/apologetics-topics/priesthood-holy-orders/the-priesthood-debate-by-james-akin/

By being present at the Mass and partaking in the Body and Blood of Jesus, the common priesthood of all ages are enabled to offer the same sacrifice that Jesus as High Priest offered to God the Father. But this is only possible through the ministry of a separate and validly ordained Catholic priesthood.

The following verse of St Paul is also significant:

"But on some points I have written to you very boldly by way of reminder, because of the grace given me by God to be a minister (Leitourgon) of Christ Jesus to the Gentiles in the priestly service (hierorgounta) of the gospel of God, so that the offering of the Gentiles may be acceptable, sanctified by the Holy Spirit" (Rom. 15:16).

Leitourgos (λειτουργὸς) is the Greek parent from which is derived the modern word liturgy, understood as public religious worship or service. Protestants claim that *Leitourgos* here only refers to the public service of preaching the word of God. However, such an argument runs into difficulty in the light of Heb. 8:1-2 which uses the same word to describe the very priesthood of Jesus: "Now the point in what we are saying is this: we have such a high priest, one who is seated at the right hand of the throne of the Majesty in heaven, a minister *(Leitourgos)* in the sanctuary and the true tent which is set up not by man but by the Lord." Furthermore, the term *hierorgounta* (from *hiereus*, meaning priest) used to describe St Paul's Gospel work implies a work that is more than simple preaching, for the office of priest as understood by the Jews always involved the carrying out of material sacrifices.

However, the Sacrifice of the Mass shows only one side of the priesthood. The other side is the power of forgiving sins. That Jesus solemnly bestowed the power and authority on the Apostles to remit or retain sins is evident from John 20:21-23:

"As the Father has sent me, even so I send you ... Receive the Holy Spirit. If you forgive the sins of any, they are forgiven them; if you retain the sins of any, they are retained."

In this verse, we see that Jesus bestowed upon his Apostles the following: (i) mission (*"As the Father has sent me, so I send you ..."*); (ii) power (*"Receive the Holy Spirit"*) and (iii) discretion whether or not to exercise this power (*"If you forgive ...; if you retain"*). This verse cannot be explained away by claiming that the Apostles were simply authorized to go out and preach forgiveness according to the following injunction: "that repentance and forgiveness of sins should be preached in his name to all nations" (Lk 24:47). If such were the case, verse 23 would serve no purpose.

In claiming that her priests have the power to forgive sins, the Catholic Church is criticized and accused of carrying out a function that is proper to God alone. It is the same accusation Jesus the High Priest had to endure: "This man is blaspheming" (Mt 9:3). In forgiving sins, priests and bishops act as Jesus' ministers and instruments; the fact that they may be sinners themselves does not inhibit the exercise or effectiveness of this power.

Furthermore, we see a ministerial priesthood also operating in the administration of other sacraments. In Acts 8:17 we read that Sts Peter and John went to the Samaritans and "laid their hands on them and they received the Holy Spirit." Since time immemorial the ordinary minister of Confirmation has been only a Bishop (or at least one ordained to the priesthood as in the Eastern Rites), who places his hand on the candidate and anoints the forehead with Holy Oil mixed with balsam while saying the words, "Be sealed with the Gift of the Holy Spirit."

Finally, St James advises his readers to call upon the elders (presbyters) of the Church in times of life-threatening illness: "Is any among you sick? Let him call for the elders of the church, and let them pray over him, anointing him with oil in the name of the Lord; and the prayer of faith will save the sick man, and the Lord will raise him up; and if he has committed sins, he will be forgiven" (Js 5:14-15).

Far from being a usurpation of divine power and the role of the laity, the ministerial priesthood forms a foundational part of the whole structure of Christianity, the removal of which would result in the collapse of the whole edifice.

The Fathers

Pope St Clement of Rome, *Letter to the Corinthians* **40, 5 (c. AD 98)**
"To the high priest, indeed, proper ministrations are allotted, to the priests a proper place is appointed, and upon the levites their proper services are imposed. The layman is bound by the ordinances for the laity."

St Ignatius of Antioch, *Letter to the Trallians* **7, 2 (c. AD 110)**
"He that is within the sanctuary is pure; but he that is outside the sanctuary is not pure. In other words, anyone who acts without the bishop and the presbytery and the deacons does not have a clean conscience."

St Ignatius of Antioch, *Letter to the Smyrnaeans* **8, 1 (c. AD 110)**
"You must all follow the bishop as Jesus Christ follows the Father, and the presbytery as you would the Apostles. Reverence the deacons as you would the command of God. Let no one do anything of concern to the Church without the bishop. Let that be considered a valid Eucharist which is celebrated by the bishop, or by one whom he appoints. Wherever the bishop appears, let the people be there ... Nor is it permitted without the bishop either to baptize or to celebrate the agape; but whatever he approve, this too is pleasing to God, so that whatever is done will be secure and valid."

Tertullian, *An Exhortation to Chastity* **7, 3 & 5 (inter AD 208-212)**
"The authority of the Church and the dignity which pertains to those sanctified by God in the assembly of order has established a difference between those in orders and the laity ... So true is this, that unless the laity also observe the rules which pertain to those who are chosen as priests, how will there be any priests, since they are chosen from among laymen?"

St Gregory of Nyssa, *Sermon on the Baptism of Christ* **(c. AD 383)**
"This same power of the word also makes the priest venerable and honorable, separated from the generality of men by the new blessing bestowed upon him. Yesterday he was but one of the multitude, one of

the people; suddenly he is made a guide, a president, a teacher of piety, an instructor in hidden mysteries."

The Roman Catechism (1566)

Pt. II, Ch. VII: Regarding the internal priesthood, all the faithful are said to be priests, once they have been washed in the saving waters of Baptism. Especially is this name given to the just who have the spirit of God, and who, by the help of divine grace, have been made living members of the great High-priest, Jesus Christ; for, enlightened by faith which is inflamed by charity, they offer up spiritual sacrifices to God on the altar of their hearts. Among such sacrifices must be reckoned every good and virtuous action done for the glory of God ... The external priesthood, on the contrary, does not pertain to the faithful at large, but only to certain men who have been ordained and consecrated to God by the lawful imposition of hands and by the solemn ceremonies of holy Church, and who are thereby devoted to a particular sacred ministry.

Catechism of the Catholic Church (1992)

No. 1547: The ministerial or hierarchical priesthood of bishops and priests, and the common priesthood of all the faithful participate, "each in its own proper way, in the one priesthood of Christ." While being "ordered one to another," they differ essentially. In what sense? While the common priesthood of the faithful is exercised by the unfolding of baptismal grace — a life of faith, hope and charity, a life according to the Spirit —, the ministerial priesthood is at the service of the common priesthood. It is directed at the unfolding of the baptismal grace of all Christians. The ministerial priesthood is a means by which Christ unceasingly builds up and leads his Church. For this reason it is transmitted by its own sacrament, the sacrament of Holy Orders.

The Real Presence

Objection: *"The Catholic Church's belief in the Eucharist is confusing. Please explain what the Catholic Church teaches about the Eucharist."*

The sacrament of the Blessed Eucharist is the Body, Blood, Soul and Divinity of Jesus Christ under the appearances, or accidents, of bread and wine. Unlike the other sacraments, it not only bestows grace but also contains the Author of grace himself. So, by giving us his Body and Blood to drink, Jesus has left us the legacy of his very self: "He has caused his wonderful works to be remembered; the Lord is gracious and merciful. He provides food for those who fear him; he is ever mindful of his covenant" (Ps. 111:4-5).

Jesus first gave us his Body and Blood at the Last Supper:

"Now as they were eating, Jesus took bread, and blessed, and broke it, and gave it to the disciples and said, 'Take, eat; this is my body.' And he took a cup, and when he had given thanks he gave it to them, saying, 'Drink of it, all of you; for this is my blood of the covenant, which is poured out for many for the forgiveness of sins'" (Mt 26:26-28; cf. Mk 14:22; Lk 22:19; 1 Cor. 10:4-21).

The Church calls this mysterious change of the bread and wine into Jesus' Body and Blood *transubstantiation* (Lateran IV, 1215). The substances of the bread and the wine are changed respectively into the substances of Jesus' Body and Blood, while the accidents (i.e., color, shape, taste, etc.) of the bread and the wine remain unchanged.

In chapter 6 of John's Gospel, we find Jesus' great discourse concerning the future promise of the Eucharist. For our purposes, it is best to outline the principal verses in full:

"Jesus said to them, 'I am the bread of life; he who comes to me shall not hunger, and he who believes in me shall never thirst. But I said to you that you have seen me and yet do not believe. All that the Father gives me will come to me; and him who comes to me I will not cast out. For I have come down from

heaven, not to do my own will, but the will of him who sent me; and this is the will of him who sent me, that I should lose nothing of all that he has given me, but raise it up at the last day. For this is the will of my Father, that every one who sees the Son and believes in him should have eternal life; and I will raise him up at the last day.' The Jews then murmured at him, because he said, 'I am the bread which came down from heaven.' They said, 'Is not this Jesus, the son of Joseph, whose father and mother we know? How does he now say, 'I have come down from heaven'?' Jesus answered them, 'Do not murmur among yourselves. No one can come to me unless the Father who sent me draws him; and I will raise him up at the last day. It is written in the prophets, 'And they shall all be taught by God.' Every one who has heard and learned from the Father comes to me. Not that any one has seen the Father except him who is from God; he has seen the Father. Truly, truly, I say to you, he who believes has eternal life. I am the bread of life. Your fathers ate the manna in the wilderness, and they died. This is the bread which comes down from heaven, that a man may eat of it and not die. I am the living bread which came down from heaven; if any one eats of this bread, he will live for ever; and the bread which I shall give for the life of the world is my flesh.' The Jews then disputed among themselves, saying, 'How can this man give us his flesh to eat?' So Jesus said to them, 'Truly, truly, I say to you, unless you eat the flesh of the Son of man and drink his blood, you have no life in you; he who eats my flesh and drinks my blood has eternal life, and I will raise him up at the last day. For my flesh is food indeed, and my blood is drink indeed. He who eats my flesh and drinks my blood abides in me, and I in him. As the living Father sent me, and I live because of the Father, so he who eats me will live because of me. This is the bread which came down from heaven, not such as the fathers ate and died; he who eats this bread will live for ever.' This he said in the synagogue, as he taught at Capernaum. Many of his disciples, when they heard it, said, 'This is a hard saying; who can listen to it?' But Jesus, knowing in himself that his disciples murmured at it, said to them, 'Do you take offense at this? Then what if you were to see the Son of man ascending where he was before? It is the spirit that gives life, the flesh is of no avail; the words that I have spoken to you are Spirit and life. But there are some of you that do not believe.' For Jesus knew from the first who those were that did not believe, and who it was that would betray him. And he said, 'This is why I told you that no one can come to me unless it is granted him by the Father.' After this many of his disciples drew back and no longer went about with him. Jesus said to the twelve, 'Do you also wish to go away?' Simon Peter answered him, 'Lord, to whom shall we go? You have the words of eternal life; and we have believed, and have come to know, that you are the Holy One of God.' Jesus answered them, 'Did I not choose you, the twelve, and one of you is a devil?' He spoke of Judas the son of Simon Iscariot, for he, one of the twelve, was to betray him" (vv. 35-71).

Second objection: "When Jesus said 'This is my Body' he was meaning 'This is a symbol of my Body.' It still remained only bread."

The words "This is my body" in the Greek of Matthew's Gospel are *touto estin to soma* (τοῦτό ἐστιν τὸ σῶμά). The word "This" (*touto* – τοῦτο) is a neuter adjective. That being the case, it cannot be referring to bread (*arton* – ἄρτον) as arton in Greek is a masculine noun. The neuter "This" ought to refer to a neuter noun. That neuter noun is the Greek word for body (*soma* – σῶμά). In other words, the word "This" is not referring to bread but to the new substance it has become – Jesus' Body.

Third objection: "We are meant to understand Jesus' words in John 6 figuratively, not literally!"

The issue surrounding John 6:35-71 is how to determine whether Jesus was intending to speak literally or figuratively. Jesus himself gives us two basic rules to resolve this dilemma.

Rule number one: When Jesus spoke figuratively but was taken literally, he usually corrected the mistake of his listeners immediately.

Example (a): *"Take heed and beware of the leaven of the Pharisees and Sadducees"* (Mt 16:5).

The Apostles took these words literally and began to argue among themselves about the fact that they had no bread. Then Jesus said, "How is it that you fail to perceive that I did not speak about bread? ... Then they understood that he did not tell them to be aware of the leaven of bread, but of the teaching of the Pharisees and Sadducees" (vv.11-12).

Example (b): *"Our friend Lazarus has fallen asleep, but I go to awake him out of sleep"* (Jn 11:11).

The Apostles again took Jesus literally and said, "Lord, if he has fallen asleep, he will recover" (v.12). Immediately came the correction, "Lazarus is dead" (v.14).

Example (c): *"... unless one is born anew, he cannot see the kingdom of God"* (Jn 3:3).

Nicodemus automatically took these words literally and replied, "How can a man be born when he is old? Can he enter a second time into his mother's womb and be born?" (3:4). Jesus' answer immediately dispelled Nicodemus' error, showing that he meant a spiritual, not physical, rebirth: "Truly, truly, I say to you, unless one is born of water and the Spirit, he cannot enter the kingdom of God" (3:5).

Rule number two: When Jesus spoke literally, and those who heard him understood him correctly but refused to accept what he said, he reasserted the literal meaning again more forcibly.

Example (a): *"Take heart, my son; your sins are forgiven"* (Mt 9:2).

The Scribes at hearing these words were greatly disturbed and said among themselves, "This man is blaspheming" (9:3). However, Jesus did not try to water down or explain away his words but reasserted his claim to forgive sins by miraculously healing the paralytic before all.

Example (b): *"Your father Abraham rejoiced that he was to see my day"* (Jn 8:56).

The Jews correctly understood Jesus literally but rejected him asserting, "You are not yet fifty years old, and have you seen Abraham?" (8:57). Jesus' solemn reply, which brought forth the immediate wrath of the Jews and the risk of being stoned to death, was, "Truly, truly I say to you, before Abraham was, I am" (8:58-59).

The Real Presence

Keeping in mind these two rules, let us examine Jesus' discourse in John 6.

Jesus proclaims, "I am the bread of life. Your fathers ate the manna in the wilderness, and they died. This is the bread which comes down from heaven, that a man may eat of it and not die. I am the living bread which came down from heaven; if any one eats of this bread, he will live for ever; and the bread which I shall give for the life of the world is my flesh" (vv. 48-51). The Jews present understood Jesus literally but could not accept what he said: "The Jews then disputed among themselves, saying, 'How can this man give us his flesh to eat?'" (v. 52). But Jesus reinforced his literal meaning saying, "Truly, truly, I say to you, unless you eat the flesh of the Son of man and drink his blood, you have no life in you; he who eats my flesh and drinks my blood has eternal life, and I will raise him up at the last day. For my flesh is food indeed, and my blood is drink indeed. He who eats my flesh and drinks my blood abides in me, and I in him" (vv. 53-56).

Not satisfied with this, Jesus went further and solemnly invoked his Father's name to confirm his meaning: "As the living Father sent me, and I live because of the Father, so he who eats me will live because of me. This is the bread which came down from heaven, not such as the fathers ate and died; he who eats this bread will live for ever" (vv. 57-58). Nevertheless, the Jews continued in their disbelief, seeing in Jesus' words a literal meaning that contradicted the Mosaic prohibition against the consumption of blood (Lev. 17:14): "Many of his disciples, when they heard it, said, 'This is a hard saying; who can listen to it?'" (v. 60). But knowing their murmuring, Jesus again did not retreat or explain away his words, rather he implicitly asserted his own divine authority and future glorification: "Do you take offense at this? Then what if you were to see the Son of man ascending where he was before?" (v. 62).

By now this was too much for the Jews who "drew back and no longer walked with him" (v. 66). Jesus had now lost most of his longtime and closest followers but he allowed them to go even though he had earlier declared "that I should lose nothing of all that he has given me" (v. 39). Is it reasonable to believe that he would have allowed such a catastrophe over a simple misunderstanding, particularly considering his established habit of correcting past misunderstandings? He went further still and challenged the Apostles themselves, "Will you also go away?" (v. 67). Jesus was prepared to lose all human support rather than deny the literal truth of his words.

This was the first rupture from the Body of Christ recorded in history, a rupture which even claimed one of the Apostles: "For Jesus knew from the first who those were that did not believe, and who it was that would betray him" (v. 64). This rupture continues in the denials of Protestantism, which since the sixteenth century has repeatedly said of Catholic belief in the Real Presence, "This is a hard saying; who can listen to it?" Catholics, on the other hand, profess the faith of Simon Peter who, though not having full understanding himself, answered, "Lord, to whom can we go? You have the words of eternal life" (v. 68).

Fourth objection: *"Jesus' words in John 6 are simply a metaphor for having faith in him."*

Most Protestant authors claim that they can prove that Jesus was speaking only metaphorically by comparing his words in John 6:35 ("I am the bread of life") to verses such as John 10:9 ("I am the door") and John 15:1 ("I am the true vine"). The first problem with such an argument, however, is that there is no connection between John 6:35 and these latter verses. Furthermore, John 10:9 and 15:1 make sense as metaphors while, as we shall see, John 6:35 does not. In addition, Jesus himself takes John 6:35 beyond symbolism by repeating four times the injunction "to eat my flesh and drink my blood" and saying "For my flesh is food indeed, and my blood is drink indeed" (v. 55).

There is some truth in the assertion that such a phrase "to eat his flesh and drink his blood" had a metaphorical meaning in Jesus' day. However, in the cultures of the Middle East it meant to calumniate, revile, attack or insult someone unjustly. It is, therefore, nonsense to argue that Jesus would have used this phrase in such a sense, for that would have been tantamount to Jesus asking his followers to sin against him in order to inherit eternal life! It should also be noted that St John in chapter 6 uses words that are usually understood only literally. For example, he uses the word *phagete* (φάγητε) or it's like nine times to describe what we must do to Jesus' flesh. This word means to eat something and usually invites a literal rather than metaphorical interpretation. The same can be said for the verb *trogon* (τρώγων) (v. 58), which means to chew, crunch, nibble or gnaw. Furthermore, Jesus uses the word *sarx* (σάρξ) for his flesh, a word that Scripture invariably uses literally.

Fifth objection: *"Jesus' remark in John 6:63 that 'the words that I have spoken to you are spirit and life' prove that he was only speaking figuratively."*

John 6:63 reads in full as follows: "It is the spirit that gives life, the flesh is of no avail; the words that I have spoken to you are Spirit and life." This verse gives rise to two objections: (i) that the eating of flesh is of no spiritual value, and only faith can profit one unto eternal life; (ii) the word "spirit" in "spirit and life" indicates that Jesus was speaking only figuratively. The Catholic response is that Jesus was, firstly, making an appeal to his listeners to trust him on faith rather than try to rationalize his words to find their true meaning. In the previous verse (v. 62) Jesus infers that his listeners would have had no difficulty accepting his words if they had seen him in his original glory, that is, as the Son of God equal to the Father, for then his words would obviously be the words of God rather than the words of man. Secondly, the word "spirit" in "spirit and life" reinforce this latter point, namely, that Jesus' words are the words of God asking us to eat his flesh and drink his blood to have life in us.

Sixth objection: *"Besides John 6, there is no other evidence in the Bible that early Christians considered the Eucharist to be the literal body and blood of Christ."*

At this point it is timely to look at the words of St Paul in 1 Cor. 10 and 11. In these chapters he sternly chastises the Corinthians for their idolatry and their poor attitude towards reception of the Eucharist. His language is remarkably literal and blunt:

"I want you to know, brethren, that our fathers were all under the cloud, and all passed through the sea, and all were baptized into Moses in the cloud and in the sea, and all ate the same supernatural food and all drank the same

supernatural drink. For they drank from the supernatural Rock which followed them, and the Rock was Christ (10:1-4) ... Therefore, my beloved, shun the worship of idols ... The cup of blessing which we bless, is it not a participation in the blood of Christ? The bread which we break, is it not a participation in the body of Christ? Because there is one bread, we who are many are one body, for we all partake of the one bread (10:14-17) ... You cannot drink the cup of the Lord and the cup of demons. You cannot partake of the table of the Lord and the table of demons" (10:21-22).

In vv. 1-4, St Paul is regarding the manna, the water and the rock as types of things to come. This ties in with the words of Jesus in St John outlined earlier, "I am the bread of life. Your fathers ate the manna in the wilderness, and they died. This is the bread which comes down from heaven, that a man may eat of it and not die" (vv. 48-50). The early Christians saw the Eucharist as a fulfilment of the promised manna, but unlike those who ate the manna, he who eats the bread of the Eucharist will "live for ever" (v. 51).

The language of vv. 14-17 again is the type that excludes all sense of the figurative or symbolic. St Paul speaks directly of "participation in the blood and body of Christ." St Paul uses even more striking language in chapter 11:

"For I received from the Lord what I also delivered to you, that the Lord Jesus on the night when he was betrayed took bread, and when he had given thanks, he broke it, and said, 'This is my body which is for you. Do this in remembrance of me.' In the same way also the cup, after supper, saying, 'This cup is the new covenant in my blood. Do this, as often as you drink it, in remembrance of me.' For as often as you eat this bread and drink the cup, you proclaim the Lord's death until he comes. Whoever, therefore, eats the bread or drinks the cup of the Lord in an unworthy manner will be guilty of profaning the body and blood of the Lord. Let a man examine himself, and so eat of the bread and drink of the cup. For any one who eats and drinks without discerning the body eats and drinks judgment upon himself. That is why many of you are weak and ill, and some have died" (vv. 23-30).

Some scholars believe this written account of the institution of the Eucharist predates all the Gospel accounts. Stephen K. Ray, a convert to Catholicism from Evangelical Christianity, comments on vv. 23-31 as follows:

> Being guilty of someone's 'body and blood' was to be guilty of murder. How could one be guilty of murder if the body (bread) was only a symbol? The Real Presence of Christ's Body is necessary for an offense to be committed against it. How could one be guilty of the Body and Blood of Christ by simply eating a little bread and drinking a little wine? ... St Paul's words are meaningless without the dogma of the Real Presence.[1]

The Fathers

St Ignatius of Antioch, *Letter to the Smyrnaeans* 7, 1 (c. AD 110)

"They abstain from the Eucharist and from prayer, because they do not confess that the Eucharist is the Flesh of our Savior Jesus Christ, Flesh which suffered for our sins and which the Father, in his goodness, raised up again. They who deny the gift of God are perishing in their disputes."

St Justin Martyr, *First Apology* 66 (c. AD 155)

"For not as common bread nor common drink do we receive these; but since Jesus Christ our Savior was made incarnate by the word of God and had both flesh and blood for our salvation, so too, as we have been taught, the food which has been made into the Eucharist by the Eucharistic prayer set down by him, and by the change of which our blood and flesh is nourished is both the flesh and the blood of that incarnate Jesus ... The Apostles, in the Memoirs which they produced, which are called Gospels, have thus passed on that which was enjoined upon them: that Jesus took bread and, having given thanks, said, 'Do this in remembrance of Me; this is My Body.' And in like manner,

---

[1] Stephen K. Ray, *Crossing the Tiber – Evangelical Protestants Discover the Historic Church*, Ignatius Press, San Francisco, 1997, p. 211.

taking – the cup, and having given thanks, he said, 'This is My Blood.' And he imparted this to them only."

St Irenaeus of Lyons, *Against Heresies* 4, 33, 2 (c. AD 180)
"If the Lord were from other than the Father, how could he rightly take bread, which is of the same creation as our own, and confess it to be his Body, and affirm that the mixture in the cup is his Blood?"

Pectorius of Autun, *Funeral Inscription* (c. AD 200)
"Divine race of the heavenly fish preserve a pure heart having received among mortals the immortal source of Divine waters. Refresh, O friend, thy soul with the everflowing waters of treasure-bestowing wisdom. Receive the sweet food of the Saviour of the Saints, eat with delight holding the fish in thy hands. Nourish (thine) with the fish, I pray, Master and Saviour; Sweetly may mother slumber, I beseech thee, Light of the Dead. Ascandios father, beloved of my heart with sweet mother and my brothers in the peace of the fish remember Pectorius."

Origen, *Homilies on Exodus* 13, 3 (post AD 244)
"You who are wont to assist in the Divine Mysteries, know how, when you receive the body of the Lord you take reverent care, lest any particle of it should fall to the ground and a portion of the consecrated gift escape you. You consider it a crime – and rightly so – if any particle thereof fall down through negligence."

Origen, *Against Celsus* 8, 33 (c. AD 248)
"We give thanks to the Creator of all, and, along with thanksgiving and prayer for the blessings we have received, we also eat the bread presented to us; and this bread becomes by prayer a sacred body, which sanctifies those who sincerely partake of it."

St Cyril of Jerusalem, *Catechetical Lectures* 23, 15 (c. AD 350)
"Give us this day our supersubstantial bread. The bread which is of the common sort is not supersubstantial. But the Bread which is holy, that Bread is supersubstantial, as if to say, directed toward the substance of the soul. This Bread does not go into the belly, to be cast out into the

privy. Rather, it is distributed through your whole system, for the benefit of body and soul."

St Ephrem of Edessa, *Homilies* 4, 4 (ante AD 373)
"And extending his hand, he gave them the Bread which his right hand had made holy: 'Take all of you eat of this, which my word has made holy. Do not now regard as bread that which I have given you; but take, eat this Bread, and do not scatter the crumbs; for what I have called My Body, that it is indeed.' One particle from its crumbs is able to sanctify thousands and thousands, and is sufficient to afford life to those who eat of it. Take, eat, entertaining no doubt of faith, because this is My Body, and whoever eats it in belief eats in it Fire and Spirit."

St Augustine of Hippo, *Explanation of the Psalms* 33, 1 (c. AD 392-418)
"'And he was carried in his own hands.' But, brethren, how is it possible for a man to do this? Who can understand it? Who is it that is carried in his own hands? A man can be carried in the hands of another; but no one can be carried in his own hands. How this should be understood literally of David, we cannot discover; but we can discover how it is meant of Christ. For Christ was carried in his own hands, when, referring to his own Body, he said: 'This is My Body' for he carried that Body in his hands."

St Augustine of Hippo, *Explanation of the Psalms* 98, 9 (inter AD 392-418)
"He took flesh from the flesh of Mary. He walked here in the same flesh, and gave us the same flesh to be eaten unto salvation. But no one eats that flesh unless first he adores it ... and not only do we not sin by adoring, we do sin by not adoring."

The Roman Catechism (1566)

Pt. II, Ch. IV: When instituting this Sacrament, our Lord himself said: *This is my body*. The word *this* expresses the entire substance of the thing present; and therefore if the substance of the bread remained, our Lord could not have truly said: *This is my body* ... In St John, Christ the Lord also says: *The bread that I will give is my flesh, for the life of the world.* The bread which he promises to give, he here declares to be his flesh. A little after he adds: *Unless you eat the flesh of the Son of man, and drink his blood, you shall not have life in you.* And again: *My flesh is meat indeed, and my blood is drink indeed.* Since, therefore, in terms so clear and so explicit, he calls his flesh bread and *meat indeed,* he gives us sufficiently to understand that none of the substance of the bread and wine remains in the Sacrament.

Catechism of the Catholic Church (1992)

No. 1336: The first announcement of the Eucharist divided the disciples, just as the announcement of the Passion scandalized them: "This is a hard saying; who can listen to it?" The Eucharist and the Cross are stumbling blocks. It is the same mystery and it never ceases to be an occasion of division. "Will you also go away?": the Lord's question echoes through the ages, as a loving invitation to discover that only he has "the words of eternal life" and that to receive in faith the gift of his Eucharist is to receive the Lord himself.

The Holy Sacrifice of the Mass

Objection: *"The Mass is a blasphemous medieval superstition. There is no continual sacrifice for sin, Jesus having died 'once for all'!"*

What then is the Mass? Is it a holy sacrifice or is it meant to be just a simple memorial meal as claimed by Protestants?

The Catholic teaching on the Mass is often either grossly misunderstood or misrepresented by Protestants. It is necessary, therefore, to first outline exactly what the Catholic Church actually teaches on this subject. Vatican II succinctly outlined the Church's teaching on the Mass as follows:

> At the Last Supper, on the night he was betrayed, our Savior instituted the Eucharistic Sacrifice of his body and blood. He did this in order to perpetuate the sacrifice of the Cross throughout the centuries until he should come again, and so to entrust to his beloved spouse, the Church, a memorial of his death and resurrection: a sacrament of love, a sign of unity, a bond of charity, a paschal banquet in which Christ is consumed, the mind is filled with grace, and a pledge of future glory is given to us.[1]

In the on-going controversy between Catholics and Protestants over the Mass, debate initially centers around the meaning of Jesus' words *"This is my body"* used during the Last Supper:

"And he took bread, and when he had given thanks he broke it and gave it to them, saying, 'This is my body which is given for you. Do this in remembrance of me.' And likewise the cup after supper, saying, 'This cup which is poured out for you is the new covenant in my blood'" (Lk 22:19-20).

---

[1] *Sacrosanctum Concilium*, #47, 4 December, 1963.

The Greek words used in Luke 22:19-20 for "This is my body" are *Touto estin to soma mou* (τοῦτό ἐστιν τὸ σῶμά μου). The verb *estin* means "is." Depending on context, it can mean either "is really" or "is figuratively." The usual meaning is the former; Protestants, of course, insist on the latter meaning. However, to accept only a figurative meaning for *estin* would entail a rejection of the universal understanding held since Apostolic times and contradict directly the tenor of John chapter 6, where Jesus first promises the Eucharist:

"*'... the bread that I shall give for the life of the world is my flesh.' The Jews then disputed among themselves, saying, 'How can this man give us his flesh to eat?' So Jesus said to them, 'Truly truly, I say to you, unless you eat the flesh of the Son of man and drink his blood, you have no life in you ... For my flesh is food indeed, and my blood is drink in deed' ... Many of his disciples, when they heard it, said, 'This is a hard saying; who can listen to it?'*" (vv. 51-60).

In the above passage the Greek word used for flesh is *sarx* (σάρξ), which only means physical flesh, while the Greek word for 'eat' (*trogon* – τρώγων) literally means 'to gnaw.'

Another argument revolves around the claim that in Jesus' language, Aramaic, there was no separate word for 'represents,' and hence Jesus only used "is" because he was inhibited by a limited vocabulary. This argument, now outdated, was disposed of over a century ago by Cardinal Wiseman who showed that Aramaic possesses nearly forty different words for 'represents.' Therefore, there was no need for Jesus to use "is" if he intended only to speak figuratively.

Of critical importance also are the phrases "is given for you" and "is poured out" in Luke 22:19-20. In the original Greek, the phrase "is given for you" is *didomenon* (διδόμενον); the phrase "is poured out" is *ekchynnomenon* (ἐκχυννόμενον). Both Greek words are present participles, meaning that when Jesus spoke them he was literally giving his Body and Blood to the disciples in the present, not future, tense. If the Last Supper was not intended to be a sacrificial memorial, then St Luke would have used the word *mnemosynon* (μνημόσυνον) instead of *didomenon*, which is the word to describe non-sacrificial memorials (see Acts 10:4).

The Protestant rejection of the Mass as a sacrifice is based on various verses in Hebrews, chapters 7, 9 and 10:

"*He has no need, like those high priests, to offer sacrifices daily, first for his own sins and then for those of the people; he did this once for all when he offered up himself*" (7:27).

"*... he entered once for all into the Holy Place, taking not the blood of goats and calves but his own blood, thus securing an eternal redemption*" (9:12).

"*And by that will we have been sanctified through the offering of the body of Jesus Christ once for all. And every priest stands daily at his service, offering repeatedly the same sacrifices, which can never take away sins*" (10:10-11).

According to Protestants, by claiming that the Mass is a sacrifice, Catholics are adding another sacrifice to Jesus'. Therefore, Catholics hold that Jesus' sacrifice was not sufficient, perfect or complete enough to atone for all sin. Furthermore, by claiming that in the sacrifice of the Mass Jesus is being offered to the Father again and again, Catholics "crucify the Son of God on their own account and hold him up to contempt" (Heb. 6:6).

The Catholic Church, however, does not teach that the sacrifice of the Mass is another sacrifice in addition to Calvary or a re-crucifixion of Jesus. Rather, it is a *re-presenting of Jesus' original sacrifice*, making it present to all Christians in all places and at all times. The sacrifice of Calvary and the sacrifice of the Mass are one and the same sacrifice; only the manner in which they are offered is different. The Council of Trent expresses it thus:

> And inasmuch as, in this divine sacrifice which is celebrated in the Mass, that same Christ is contained and immolated in an unbloody manner, who once offered himself in a bloody manner on the altar of the cross: the holy synod teaches that this sacrifice is truly propitiatory, and that by means thereof this is effected that we obtain mercy, and find grace in seasonable aid ... For the victim is one and the same, the same now offering by the ministry of priests, who then offered

himself on the cross, only the manner of offering being different.[2]

The sacrifice of Jesus was accomplished once in time but to God it is an event eternally present before him. This we know from the following:

1. Heb. 6:20: Jesus is a "priest for ever according to the order of Melchizedeck."
2. Heb. 7:24: Jesus "holds his priesthood permanently, because he continues forever."
3. Heb. 8:2: Jesus is ministering in the "true tent."
4. Heb. 9:12: Jesus takes into the Holy Place "not the blood of goats and calves but his own blood."
5. Heb. 12:24: "Jesus, the mediator of a new covenant, and to the sprinkled blood that speaks more graciously than the blood of Abel."
6. Rev. 5:6: "And between the throne and the four living creatures and among the elders, I saw a Lamb standing, as though it had been slain."

Hebrews-Revelation combine to present a picture of Jesus as a living eternal priest appearing slain in sacrifice and yet ministering with his Blood before the Father. The words "priest," "ministering," "blood," "slain," "sacrifice" portray a Jesus currently offering a sacrifice to the Father. Jesus as priest can now be offering only one sacrifice to the Father and no other, namely his sacrifice on Mt Calvary. Mt Calvary thus transcends space and time — it has become a 'supra-temporal' reality. It is this reality that is made present before Christians in a sacramental and unbloody manner through the Mass. The Mass slices through time and re-presents this eternal sacrifice before us so all Christians may eat the flesh of the Eternal Lamb after it has been slain.

To the contrary, it is argued that the words in Luke 22:19-20, "*Do this in remembrance of me,*" testify that Jesus only intended to establish a memorial meal whereby Christians throughout all ages

---

[2] *Doctrine on the Sacrifice of the Mass*, Session XXII, 17 September, 1562.

would remember and give thanks for the 'once and for all' sacrifice of Calvary. However, the word for remembrance in Greek is *anamnesin* (ἀνάμνησιν), which means a remembering that makes something past become present. As ex-Protestant Max Thurian wrote before his conversion, "This memorial is not a simple objective act of recollection, it is a liturgical action ... which makes the Lord present ... which recalls as a memorial before the Father the unique sacrifice of the Son, and makes him present in his memorial."[3] The fact that the Mass is a sacrificial memorial is also given strength by Heb. 13:10, which says that Christians "have an *altar* (*thusiasterion* – θυσιαστήριον) from which those who serve the tent have no right to eat." The word "altar" is always associated with sacrifice.

The Old Testament predicted that the Messiah would offer a true sacrifice to God in the form of bread and wine, that Jewish sacrifices would one day be ended, and that in their stead the Gentiles would in every place offer a daily and pleasing sacrifice to God's name. In Gen. 14 we read that Melchizedek, the king of Salem and priest, offered sacrifice under the form of bread and wine:

"After his return from the defeat of Chedorlaomer and the kings who were with him, the king of Sodom went out to meet him at the Valley of Shaveh (that is, the King's Valley). And Melchizedek king of Salem brought out bread and wine; he was priest of God Most High. And he blessed him and said, 'Blessed be Abram by God Most High, maker of heaven and earth; and blessed be God Most High, who has delivered your enemies into your hand!'" (17-20).

Psalm 110 foretold that the Messiah would be a Priest "after the order of Melchizedek":

"The Lord says to my lord: 'Sit at my right hand, till I make your enemies your footstool ... The Lord has sworn and will not change his mind, You are a priest for ever after the order of Melchizedek'" (1:4).

---

[3] *The Eucharistic Memorial*, II, *The New Testament, Ecumenical Studies in Worship*: from Stephen K. Ray, *Crossing the Tiber – Evangelical Protestants Discover the Historic Church*, Ignatius Press, San Francisco, 1997, p. 210.

The author of the Letter to the Hebrews clearly identifies Jesus to be this priest:

"For it is evident that our Lord was descended from Judah, and in connection with that tribe Moses said nothing about priests. This becomes even more evident when another priest arises in the likeness of Melchizedek, who has become a priest, not according to a legal requirement concerning bodily descent but by the power of an indestructible life. For it is witnessed of him, 'Thou art a priest for ever, after the order of Melchizedek'" (7:14-17).

"After the order of Melchizedek" means 'in the manner of Melchizedek.' Melchizedek brought forth bread and wine and sacrificed them by offering them to Abraham to eat. Jesus is a priest after this manner by offering his Body and Blood under the veil of bread and wine for us to eat.

The Book of Daniel chapter 9 speaks of the end of the Jewish priesthood and its sacrifices:

"After the sixty-two weeks an anointed shall be cut down when he does not possess the city; And the people of a leader who will come shall destroy the sanctuary. Then the end shall come like a torrent; until the end there shall be war, the desolation that is decreed. For one week he shall make a firm compact with the many; Half the week he shall abolish sacrifice and oblation; On the temple wing shall be the horrible abomination until the ruin that is decreed is poured out upon the horror" (vv. 26-27).

The Jewish priesthood and sacrifices would be replaced by Gentile ones as predicted by the Prophet Malachi:

"'I have no pleasure in you, says the Lord of hosts, and I will not accept an offering from your hand. For from the rising of the sun to its setting my name is great among the nations, and in every place incense is offered to my name, and a pure offering; for my name is great among the nations, says the Lord of hosts" (Mal. 1:10-11).

Malachi's words found fulfillment in the worship of the early Christians:

"They held steadfastly to the apostles' teaching and fellowship, to the breaking of bread and to the prayers" (Acts 2:42).

"And day by day, attending the temple together and breaking bread in their homes, they partook of food with glad and generous hearts" (Acts 2:46).

"The cup of blessing that we bless, is it not a participation in the blood of Christ? The bread that we break, is it not a participation in the body of Christ?" (1 Cor. 10:16).

"For as often as you eat this bread and drink the chalice, you proclaim the Lord's death until he comes" (1 Cor. 11:26).

The early Christians were also warned that dire consequences await those who do not partake of this sacrificial bread and cup worthily:

"Whoever, therefore, eats the bread or drinks the cup of the Lord in an unworthy manner will be guilty of profaning the body and blood of the Lord. Let a man examine himself, and so eat of the bread and drink of the cup. For any one who eats and drinks without discerning the body eats and drinks judgment upon himself. That is why many of you are weak and ill, and some have died" (1 Cor. 11:27-30).

Where is the prophecy of Malachi fulfilled today? James Cardinal Gibbons answers as follows:

> We may divide the inhabitants of the world into five different classes of people, professing different forms of religion – Pagans, Jews, Mohammedans, Protestants and Catholics. Among which of these shall we find the clean oblation of which the prophet speaks? Not among the Pagan nations; for they worship false gods, and consequently cannot have any sacrifice pleasing to the Almighty. Not among the Jews; for they have ceased to sacrifice altogether, and the words of the prophet apply not to the Jews, but to the Gentiles. Not among the Mohammedans; for they also reject sacrifices. Not among any of the Protestants sects; for they all distinctly repudiate

sacrifices. Therefore, it is only in the Catholic Church that is fulfilled this glorious prophecy; for whithersoever you go, you will find the clean oblation offered on Catholic altars. If you travel from America to Europe, to Oceania, to Africa, or Asia, you will see our altars erected, and our Priests daily fulfilling the words of the prophets by offering the clean oblation of the body and blood of Christ.[4]

In October 1529 Luther and Zwingli met in Marburg, Germany, to resolve their differences concerning the Eucharist. The two leaders failed to reach an agreement. Ever since, Protestantism has been a house divided over the issue, with dozens of different interpretations of the words "This is my Body" appearing. How paradoxical that the very gift God gave to the world as a sign of the visible unity of Christians has become the source of so much dissension and division.

The Fathers

The Didache 14, 1 (inter AD 90-150)
"Assemble on the Lord's Day, and break bread and offer the Eucharist. But first make confession of your faults, so that your sacrifice may be a pure one ... For this is the offering of which the Lord has said, 'Everywhere and always bring me a sacrifice that is undefiled, for I am a great king, says the Lord and my name is the wonder of nations.'"

Pope St Clement of Rome, *Letter to the Corinthians* 44, 4 (c. AD 98)
"Our sin will not be small if we eject from the episcopate those who blamelessly and holily have offered its Sacrifices. Blessed are those presbyters who have already finished their course, and who have obtained a fruitful and perfect release."

---

[4] James Cardinal Gibbons, *The Faith of Our Fathers*, TAN Books and Publishers, Inc., Rockford, Illinois, 1980 Ed., p. 254.

St Ignatius of Antioch, *Letter to the Philadelphians* **4, 1 (c. AD 110)**
"Take care, then, to use one Eucharist, so that whatever you do, you do according to God: for there is one flesh of Our Lord Jesus Christ, and one cup in the union of his Blood; one altar, as there is one bishop with the presbytery and my fellow servants, the deacons."

St Irenaeus of Lyons, *Against Heresies* **4, 17, 5 (c. AD 180)**
"He took that created thing, bread, and gave thanks and said, 'This is My Body.' And the cup likewise, which is part of that creation to which we belong, he confessed to be his Blood, and taught the new oblation of the new covenant, which the Church, receiving from the Apostles, offers to God throughout the world ... concerning which Malachi, among the twelve prophets thus spoke beforehand: 'From the rising of the sun to the going down, my name is glorified among the gentiles, and in every place incense is offered to my name and a pure sacrifice' ... indicating in the plainest manner that in every place sacrifice shall be offered to him, and at that a pure one."

St Hippolytus of Rome, *Commentary on Daniel* **22 (AD 220)**
"For when the Gospel is preached in every place, the times being then accomplished ... the abomination of desolation will be manifested, and when he (the Antichrist) comes, the sacrifice and oblation will be removed, which are now offered up to God in every place by the Gentiles."

St Cyprian of Carthage, *Epistle to Caecilius on the Sacrament of the Cup of the Lord* **4 (AD 253)**
"In the priest Melchizedek we see prefigured the sacrament of the sacrifice of the Lord, according to what divine Scripture testifies, 'And Melchizedek, king of Salem, brought forth bread and wine' ... For who is more a priest of the most high God than Our Lord Jesus Christ, who offered a sacrifice to God the Father, and offered that very same thing which Melchizedek had offered, that is, bread and wine, to wit, his body and blood? ... In Genesis therefore, that the benediction ... might be duly celebrated, the figure of Christ's sacrifice precedes as ordained in bread and wine; which thing the Lord, completing and fulfilling,

offered bread and the cup mixed with wine, and so he who is the fullness of truth fulfilled the truth of the image prefigured."

St Ambrose of Milan, *Commentaries on Twelve of David's Psalms* 38, 25 (inter AD 381-397)
"We saw the Prince of Priests coming to us, we saw and heard him offering his blood for us. We follow, inasmuch as we are able, being priests; and we offer the sacrifice on behalf of the people. And even if we are of but little merit, still, in the sacrifice, we are honorable. For even if Christ is not now seen as the one who offers the sacrifice, nevertheless it is he himself that is offered in sacrifice here on earth when the Body of Christ is offered. Indeed, to offer himself he is made visible to us, he whose word makes holy the sacrifice that is offered."

St Augustine of Hippo, *Letter to Boniface, Bishop* 98, 9 (AD 408)
"Was not Christ immolated only once in his very Person? In the Sacrament, nevertheless, he is immolated for the people not only on every Easter Solemnity but on every day; and a man would not be lying if, when asked, he were to reply that Christ is being immolated. For if the Sacraments had not a likeness to those things of which they are Sacraments, they would not be Sacraments at all; and they generally take the names of those same things by reason of this likeness."

St Augustine of Hippo, *Sermon Against the Jews* 9, 13 (post AD 425)
"'From the rising of the sun even to its setting my name is great among the Gentiles, and in every place sacrifice is offered to my name, a clean oblation; for my name is great among the Gentiles, says the Lord Almighty.' What do you answer to that? Open your eyes at last, then, any time, and see, from the rising of the sun to its setting, the sacrifice of Christians is offered, not in one place only, as was established with you Jews, but everywhere; and not to just any god at all, but to him who foretold it, the God of Israel ... Not according to the order of Aaron, but according to the order of Melchizedek."

The Roman Catechism (1566)

Pt. II, Ch. IV: We therefore confess that the Sacrifice of the Mass is and ought to be considered one and the same Sacrifice as that of the cross, for the victim is one and the same, namely, Christ our Lord, who offered himself, once only, a bloody Sacrifice on the altar of the cross. The bloody and unbloody victim are not two, but one victim only, whose Sacrifice is daily renewed in the Eucharist, in obedience to the command of our Lord: *Do this for a commemoration of me.*

The priest is also one and the same, Christ the Lord; for the ministers who offer Sacrifice, consecrate the holy mysteries, not in their own person, but in that of Christ, as the words of consecration itself show, for the priest does not say: *This is the body of Christ,* but, *This is my body*; and thus, acting in the Person of Christ the Lord, he changes the substance of the bread and wine into the true substance of his body and blood.

Catechism of the Catholic Church (1992)

No. 1367: The sacrifice of Christ and the sacrifice of the Eucharist are one single sacrifice: "The victim is one and the same: the same now offers through the ministry of priests, who then offered himself on the cross; only the manner of offering is different." "And since in this divine sacrifice which is celebrated in the Mass, the same Christ who offered himself once in a bloody manner on the altar of the cross is contained and offered in an unbloody manner ... this sacrifice is truly propitiatory."

Your Sins are Forgiven

Objection: *"Why do Catholics go to a man to have their sins forgiven. Only God can forgive sins!"*

This is another common accusation directed against Catholics because of their well-known practice of confessing sins to priests. The insinuation is that Catholics are really practising a form of idolatry by ignoring God and preferring instead to go to a man for forgiveness. At the same time, the Catholic Church is accused of carrying out a function that is proper to God alone. It is a similar accusation to that which Jesus himself endured: "This man is blaspheming" (Mt 9:3).

No person claiming to be Christian doubts that Jesus had the power to forgive sins. The following incident in the Gospels testifies to this power:

"And behold, they brought to him a paralytic, lying on his bed; and when Jesus saw their faith he said to the paralytic, 'Take heart, my son; your sins are forgiven.' And behold, some of the scribes said to themselves, 'This man is blaspheming.' But Jesus, knowing their thoughts, said, 'Why do you think evil in your hearts? For which is easier, to say, 'Your sins are forgiven,' or to say, 'Rise and walk?' But that you may know that the Son of man has authority on earth to forgive sins' – he then said to the paralytic – 'Rise, take up your bed and go home.' And he rose and went home" (Mt 9:2-7).

For those who recognize that the Church is a divine institution founded by Jesus to continue his work of redemption in the world, there is no difficulty believing that she has the power to forgive sins. It follows that whatever Jesus the Head possesses, his Mystical Body, the Church, likewise possesses. We see recorded in the Acts of the Apostles the Church forgiving sins through the administration of Baptism to converts and Anointing to the sick:

"Peter said to them, 'Repent, and be baptized every one of you in the name of Jesus Christ so that your sins may be forgiven; and you shall receive the gift of the Holy Spirit'" (Acts 2:38).

"Rise and be baptized, and wash away your sins, calling on his name" (Acts 22:16).

"Is any among you sick? Let him call for the elders of the church, and let them pray over him, anointing him with oil in the name of the Lord; and the prayer of faith will save the sick man, and the Lord will raise him up; and if he has committed sins, he will be forgiven" (Js 5:14-15).

In addition, after his resurrection, Jesus appeared to the Apostles in the Upper Room and breathed on them saying:

"As the Father has sent me, even so I send you ... Receive the Holy Spirit. If you forgive the sins of any, they are forgiven; if you retain the sins of any, they are retained" (Jn 20:21-23).

Just as Jesus possesses the power to forgive sins as the Son of man, so he bestows the same power upon his Apostles and their successors. Like those who witnessed Jesus forgive sins in Matt. 9, we too should rejoice that God has "given such authority *to men*" (Mt 9:8). In describing this same gift, St Paul says that God "gave us the ministry of reconciliation" (2 Cor. 5:18).

Pope St John Paul II commented on John 20:21-23 as follows:

> Now this power to 'forgive sins' Jesus confers through the Holy Spirit upon ordinary men, themselves subject to the snare of sin, namely the Apostles ... This is one of the most awe-inspiring innovations of the Gospel! He confers this power on the Apostles also as something which they can transmit – as the Church has understood it from the beginning – to their successors, charged by the same Apostles with the mission and responsibility of continuing their work as proclaimers of the Gospel and ministers of Christ's redemptive work.[1]

---

[1] *Reconciliatio et Paenitentia*, #29, 2 December, 1984.

The power given to the Apostles in John 20:21-23 is reinforced by Jesus' following promise:

"Truly, I say to you, whatever you bind on earth shall be bound in heaven, and whatever you loose on earth shall be loosed in heaven" (Mt 18:18).

It is interesting to note that the only other time God breathed on man was when he first created Adam and "breathed into his nostrils the breath of life" (Gen. 2:7). The first breathing was to empower man with life; the second breathing was to empower man to restore life.

Second objection: *"But John 20:21-23 really means that the Apostles were simply authorized to go out and preach forgiveness according to the following injunction: 'that repentance and forgiveness of sins should be preached in his name to all nations' (Lk 24:47)."*

John 20:21-23 is an uncomfortable verse for most Protestants. Some try to explain it away as follows: "Jesus in John 20:21-23 was effectively commissioning the Apostles to go out and preach the Gospel to all creation. Those who believed in the Gospel would have their sins forgiven; those who did not would have their sins retained." Unfortunately, John 20:21-23 mentions nothing about preaching, nor of God forgiving sins directly himself. Rather, Jesus speaks of the Apostles forgiving or retaining sins and empowers them to do so.

Another tactic is to try and 'smother' John 20:21-23 by quoting numerous other verses that speak of God or Jesus forgiving sins directly without the intermediary of any Apostle or priest. Supposedly, the aim of this is to interpret John 20:21-23 in its proper context and conclude that God could not have appointed the Apostles as agents of forgiveness. However, none of these other verses relate directly to John 20:21-23, nor do they aim to interpret it or contradict it. To accept this approach would render John 20:21-23 utterly useless.

Third objection: *"What Jesus only did in John 20:21-23 was to give the Apostles the authority to declare that a person's sins have already been forgiven by God; he didn't actually give the Apostles the power to forgive sins themselves."*

People who use this line of argument tend to focus principally on the words *"they are forgiven them"* (*apheontai* – ἀφεώνται) ... *"they are retained"* (*kekratentai* – κεκράτηνται) arguing that because these are in the past tense the Apostles are dealing with sins that have already been forgiven by someone else, namely God; the only role left for them is to publicly declare that fact.

However, John 20:21-23 is clear that the actual forgiving is to be done *by the Apostles in the future*. The "you" in "you forgive" (*afete* – ἀφῆτε) and "you retain" (*kratete* – κρατῆτε) relates specifically and only to the Apostles and is in the future tense.

Fourth objection: *"Sure, the Apostles had the power and authority to forgive and retain sins but this authority ended with the death of the last Apostle. No-one possesses such an authority today."*

This argument might sound nice and neat but it is one that cannot be proved from Scripture nor from the historical data. On the contrary, a cursory glance at the writings of the Church Fathers would prove the contrary to be the case.

In any event, why would Jesus bestow such an outstanding gift upon the Apostolic Church only to allow it to disappear for future generations? The reality is that it did not disappear and continues to be available to all Christians today through the sacrament of Holy Orders.

Fifth objection: *"Catholics believe they can commit any sins and then simply go to confession whenever they like to have them forgiven. What an abuse!"*

Such would certainly be an abuse if it were true. However, in all cases we must make the clear distinction between use and abuse, remembering that abuse should never abolish use. If there have been or are Catholics who approach the sacrament of Penance with the above attitude, they can never have any of their sins forgiven. Only those who approach the sacrament with true sorrow for their sins and the intention never to commit them again are eligible for forgiveness.

For a valid reception of the sacrament, the penitent must perform three acts: *contrition, confession* and *satisfaction*.

Contrition is the most important condition for forgiveness. As stated, without true sorrow for sin there can be no possibility of pardon. Sorrow must be interior and genuine, not merely a hypocritical outward display. It must cover all mortal sins of which the penitent is aware. Sorrow for sin may be perfect, that is, out of charity, or love of God: "her sins, which are many, are forgiven, for she loved much" (Lk 7:47); or imperfect *attrition*, based on less perfect motives such as fear of hell, loss of heaven or the horror and ugliness of sin. Though imperfect, attrition is still regarded as true sorrow and pleasing to God.

With respect to confession, the penitent must declare to the Priest all mortal sins he or she can sincerely remember. The precise nature of the sin must be stated, not merely an evasive or generic reference. The exact number of times each sin has been committed must also be given (as far as memory serves). To the penitent who deliberately fails regarding any of these, the sacrament will be of no avail.

Satisfaction is the voluntary acceptance by the penitent of the penance imposed by the priest. Usually, the priest imposes prayers, acts of charity or other good works. The aim is to remit, in whole or in part, the debt of temporal punishment that often remains after the sin has been forgiven. Again, any person who has no intention during Confession to carry out the satisfaction imposed fails to receive the sacrament validly.

Sixth objection: *"According to the Presbyterian minister Loraine Boettner the practice of auricular confession was instituted only in 1215 by the Fourth Lateran Council."*

In his book *Roman Catholicism* Loraine Boettner claims many things, most of which are inaccurate, distorted or outrightly untrue. The Patristic evidence testifying to the practice of auricular confession in the early Church, even in the pre-Constantinian era, is indisputable. Origen, St Cyprian, Firmilian and Lactantius are but a few examples of this. These writers were not fringe figures in the early Church but – in the case of Origen and St Cyprian in particular – were outstanding leaders, apologists and martyrs. If the practice of auricular confession they had written about was merely an unbiblical invention imposed on faithful Christians against their will, then there should be records of protest and opposition dating from the same period. On the contrary, we find numerous other writers of even greater sanctity and intellect in the post-Nicene era writing about and promoting the same practice – for example, St Hilary, St Basil and St Jerome (see below).

Far from inventing the sacrament, what the Fourth Lateran Council in 1215 did was regulate the age-old practice of confession by requiring all Catholics to confess their sins *at least once a year* to an approved priest.

Seventh objection: *"Confession was invented by priests to have control of the people. And what about all the scandals associated with confession!"*

As shown above, the sacrament of Penance was 'invented' by no one except Jesus himself. Far from binding the people under a form of oppressive control, the sacrament of Penance has the real intention and effect of freeing them from the bonds of sin and the slavery of the devil. In addition to the wonderful spiritual benefits for the soul, frequent use of the sacrament of Penance can also give penitents genuine peace of mind by alleviating many of the mental difficulties arising from the subconscious fear of death and judgment. As multitudes discovered through St John Vianney in France in the nineteenth century, the sacrament of Penance is also an excellent means of obtaining sound spiritual advice from one experienced in the direction of souls.

In the history of the Church there have been cases when the seal of confession has been broken and information obtained from the penitent used for improper purposes – but this has occurred through eavesdropping by outsiders. St Joan of Arc was a victim of such an abuse. Nevertheless, even these cases are very rare. Attention should be given to examples such as St John Nepomucene (+1393), who preferred to die a horrible death rather than reveal what was said to him in confession. The Church's law, aimed at preserving the seal of confession, is perhaps one of its most rigorous: "A confessor who directly violates the sacramental seal incurs a *latae sententiae* [automatic] excommunication reserved to the Apostolic See."[2] This seal applies not only to the priest, but also to anyone who overhears or learns of confessional sins in any way.[3]

Concerning alleged scandals, again one must avoid the trap of abolishing use simply because of abuse. The theme of abuse and the sacrament of Penance seems to be an obsessive pre-occupation of those who produce tracts and pamphlets attacking this sacrament, perhaps in the hope of distracting the ignorant and gullible from realizing and appreciating its positive benefits. Loraine Boettner and other professional anti-Catholics of his kind seem to take delight in republishing the salacious charges of the nineteenth-century former Catholic priest, Father Charles Chiniquy.

Chiniquy called auricular confession "the modern Sodom," amid many other things. Any Catholic who has attended the sacrament of Penance faithfully for years would recognize his words as the sensationalist ravings of a revengeful man who had been disciplined by the Church for his own misdemeanors.

No reasonable person advocates the abolition of schools simply because there have been teachers who molest children, or of marriage because there are bad husbands who abuse their wives. Likewise, the legitimacy of the sacrament of Penance does not evaporate because some have used it for illicit purposes. Again, the Church's law here is severe: priests guilty of soliciting a penitent to commit a sin against the sixth commandment are liable to suspension, prohibitions and deprivations, and in more serious cases to dismissal from the clerical state.[4]

Finally, it should always be kept clearly in mind that as priests forgive sins "in the name of the Father and of the Son and of the Holy Spirit" it is really God himself who forgives the sins. The priest does not forgive sins in his own name or through his own power, but rather solely through the power of God. Hence, even if the priest himself is the most hideous sinner, this will not affect the validity of the sacrament and prevent the penitent's sins from being forgiven. This is a

---

[2] *Code of Canon Law* #1388; *Code of Canons of the Eastern Churches* #728.
[3] Canons #983; #984.
[4] Canons #1387; #728.

comforting thought for Catholics and gives them total confidence and certitude every time they approach the sacrament.

The Fathers

St Cyprian of Carthage, *The Lapsed* 29 (AD 251)
"I beseech you, brethren, let everyone who has sinned confess his sin while he is still in this world, while his confession is still admissible, while satisfaction and remission made through the priests are pleasing before the Lord."

Firmilian of Caesarea, *Letter to Cyprian* 75, 16 (c. AD 258)
"'Receive the Holy Spirit: if you forgive any man his sins, they shall be forgiven; and if you retain any man's sins, they shall be retained.' Therefore, the power of forgiving sins was given to the Apostles and to the Churches which these men, sent by Christ, established; and to the bishops who succeeded them by being ordained in their place."

Lactantius, *The Divine Institutions* 4, 30, 1 (inter AD 304-310)
"... let it be known: that is the true Church, in which there is confession and penance, and which takes a salubrious care of the sins and wounds to which the weak flesh is subject."

St Hilary of Poitiers, *Commentary on the Gospel of Matthew* 18, 8 (c. AD 354)
"In our present condition we are all subdued by the terror of that greatest dread. And now, out in front of that terror, he sets the irrevocable apostolic judgment, however severe, so that those whom they shall bind on earth, that is, whomsoever they leave bound in the knots of their sins; and those whom they loose, which is to say, those who by their confession receive grace unto salvation – these, in accord with the apostolic sentence, are bound or loosed also in heaven."

St Basil the Great, *Rules Briefly Treated* 229 & 288 (post AD 370)
"Just as the diseases of the body are not divulged to all, nor haphazardly, but to those who are skilled in curing them, so too our

declaration of our sins should be made to those empowered to cure them ... It is necessary to confess our sins to those to whom the dispensation of God's mysteries is entrusted. Those doing penance of old are found to have done it before the saints. It is written in the Gospel that they confessed their sins to John the Baptist; but in Acts they confessed to the Apostles, by whom also all were baptized."

St Pacian of Barcelona, *Letters to Sympronian* **1, 6 (inter AD 375-392)**
"God never threatens the repentant, rather he pardons the penitent. You will say that it is God alone who can do this. True enough, but it is likewise true that he does it through his priests, who exercise his power."

St Jerome, *Commentaries on Ecclesiastes* **4, 4 (c. AD 388-389)**
"If the serpent, the devil, bites someone secretly, he infects that person with the venom of sin. And if the one who has been bitten keeps silence and does not do penance, and does not want to confess his wound to his brother and to his master, who have the word that will cure him, they cannot very well assist him. For if the sick man is ashamed to confess his wound to the physician, medicine will not cure that to which it is not applied."

Pope St Leo I the Great, *Letter to the Bishops of Campania, Samnium and Picenum* **168, 2 (AD 459)**
"I decree also that the presumption contrary to the apostolic regulation, which I recently learned is being committed by some in an illegal usurpation, is by all means to cease. With regard to penance, certainly what is required of the faithful is not that the nature of individual sins be written in a document and recited in a public profession, since it is sufficient that the guilt of consciences be indicated to priests alone in a secret confession."

The Roman Catechism (1566)

Pt. II, Ch. V: After his Resurrection he breathed on the Apostles, assembled together, saying: *Receive ye the Holy Ghost, whose sins you shall forgive, they are forgiven; and whose sins you shall retain, they are retained.* Now in giving to priests the power to retain and forgive sins, it is evident that our Lord made them also judges in this matter ...

This doctrine the pastors should teach as defined by the holy Council of Trent, and handed down by the uniform doctrine of the Catholic Church. An attentive perusal of the Fathers will present passages throughout their works, proving in the clearest terms that this Sacrament was instituted by our Lord, and that the law of sacramental confession, which, from the Greek, they call *exomologesis*, and *exagoreusis*, is to be received as true Gospel teaching.

Catechism of the Catholic Church (1992)

No. 1441: Only God forgives sins. Since he is the Son of God, Jesus says of himself, "The Son of man has authority on earth to forgive sins" and exercises this divine power: "Your sins are forgiven." Further, by virtue of his divine authority he gives this power to men to exercise in his name.

No. 1444: In imparting to his apostles his own power to forgive sins the Lord also gives them the authority to reconcile sinners with the Church. This ecclesial dimension of their task is expressed most notably in Christ's solemn words to Simon Peter: "I will give you the keys of the kingdom of heaven, and whatever you bind on earth shall be bound in heaven, and whatever you loose on earth shall be loosed in heaven." The office of binding and loosing which was given to Peter was also assigned to the college of the apostles united to its head.

Veneration of the Blessed Virgin Mary as "Mother of God"

Objection: *"This so-called veneration of the Virgin Mary as 'Mother of God' is nothing but 'Mariolatry' and blasphemy!"*

"I will put enmity between you and the woman, and between your seed and her seed; he shall bruise your head, and you shall bruise his heel" (Gen. 3:15). This passage, called the *protoevangelion*, is the first promise of the Messiah, and the future defeat of the devil.

The woman in the above passage is the Blessed Virgin Mary, her offspring is Jesus Christ. There has been distinct controversy over the centuries between Biblical scholars as to whether the text should read *"she," "he"* or *"it shall bruise"* (or crush). St Jerome, who was fluent in the ancient Biblical languages of Hebrew and Greek, when translating the Bible into Latin rendered it as *Ipsa*, or "she shall crush," rather than *Ipse*, "he shall crush." So, likewise, did many other Fathers of the Church read this passage. In any case, the meaning is the same, as it is through her Son, Jesus, that the Virgin Mary crushes the devil.[1]

Genesis 3:15 together with the following passages form the basis for veneration of the Virgin Mary as Mother of God:

"Behold, a virgin shall conceive and bear a son, and his name shall be called Emmanuel (which means God with us)" (Mt 1:23; cf. Is. 7:14).

---

[1] It is also interesting to note that in two great Marian apparitions which have been officially approved by the Church, namely Guadalupe (1531) and Rue de Bac (1830), the Virgin Mary appeared standing triumphantly, crushing the head of a serpent. In fact, in the former of these apparitions the Virgin Mary actually announced herself to Juan Diego as "Our Lady of Tequatzacuepae," or "the Lady that crushes the Serpent."

"For to us a child is born, to us a son is given; and the government will be upon his shoulder, and his name will be called 'Wonderful Counselor, Mighty God, Everlasting Father, Prince of Peace'" (Is. 9:6).

"And he came to her and said, 'Hail, full of grace, the Lord is with you'" (Lk 1:28).

Luke 1:28 is also a source of much controversy. Most Protestants would prefer to render the original Greek *kecharitomene* (κεχαριτωμένε) as "highly favored" rather than "full of grace." *Kecharitomene* certainly relates to "grace" as its root word *charis* literally means "grace."[2] In fact, a strict translation of *kecharitomene* is "you who have been graced." Of the two options, "full of grace" is a more clear and definite rendering of the angel's words than is "favor." This conclusion is supported by the authority of the Latin Fathers; the Syriac and Arabic versions of the Bible; and even the writings of the heretics Wycliff, Coverdale and Tyndale.

"... and she exclaimed with a loud cry, 'Blessed are you among women, and blessed is the fruit of your womb! And why is this granted me, that the mother of my Lord should come to me?'" (Lk 1:42-43).

"... for he has regarded the low estate of his handmaiden. For behold, henceforth all generations will call me blessed" (Lk 1:48).

The Church distinguishes emphatically between *cultus duliae*, which translates as 'the homage of veneration,' and *cultus latriae*, which signifies 'the worship of adoration.' Veneration is paid to the Saints; a higher form of it, called *hyperdulia*, is given to the Mother of God; but adoration is given to God alone. Any attempt to give it to a creature would certainly be false worship – but the Catholic Church has never given it. She adores God and God only.

Most Protestants abhor the title "Mother of God" because for them it implies that Catholics believe the Virgin Mary existed before

---

[2] The King James Version of the Bible translates the word *charis* one hundred and twenty-nine times as "grace."

God, and that God only came into existence after being born from Mary. The term "Mother of God" is derived from the word *Theotokos* (God-beaer) and was approved by the Council of Ephesus (AD 431) in response to the Christological controversy ignited by Nestorius, then Patriarch of Constantinople. Nestorius held that in Jesus there existed not *one divine Person* with two natures, human and divine, but *two separate Persons, one human and one divine*, with two natures, human and divine. Consequently, the Virgin Mary, as she supplied only Jesus' human flesh and not his divinity, was only mother of Jesus' humanity and therefore in no sense could be called Mother of God. The Church, upholding that Jesus is one divine Person only, and noting that the Virgin Mary was the mother of this divine Person, defined dogmatically that she could properly be called *Theotokos*, or "Mother of God."

Surprisingly, John Calvin expressed precisely the same view when writing about Mary:

> It cannot be denied that God in choosing and destining Mary to be the Mother of his Son, granted her the highest honor ... Elizabeth calls Mary, Mother of the Lord, because the unity of the person in the two natures of Christ was such that she could have said that the mortal man engendered in the womb of Mary was at the same time the eternal God.[3]

Second objection: *"Mary is not so important; the Bible barely mentions her."*

Those who oppose or try to minimize the honor given to the Virgin Mary often raise this simple objection. Some even liken the role of the Virgin Mary to that of an eggshell. What is important is the content of the egg itself; the shell is disposable. The Virgin Mary was only important to bring Jesus into the world. Once Jesus had arrived his Mother was "no longer necessary." Such people even cite Matt. 12:46 ff. as evidence of Mary's alleged inconsequential role: "Who is my mother, and who are my brethren? ... For whoever does the will of my Father in heaven is my brother, and sister, and mother."

---

[3] *The Works of Calvin, Corpus Reformatorum*, Braunschweig-Berlin, 1863-1900, vol. 45, p. 348.

This passage, however, only reinforces the Virgin Mary's glory. Jesus was making the valid point that merit in the eyes of God the Father is based on obedience rather than blood ties. Not only was the Virgin Mary privileged for having been chosen to be the Mother of Jesus ("for he who is mighty has done great things for me": [Lk 1:49]) but she also perfectly fulfilled God's will throughout her entire life: "Behold, I am the handmaid of the Lord; let it be to me according to your word" (Lk 1:38).

Rather than being hardly mentioned in the Bible, the Virgin Mary is extensively mentioned in both the Old and New Testaments. In the Old Testament, besides Gen. 3:15 and Is. 7:14 mentioned above, Mary is mentioned under various 'types':

(i) *The Tree of Life*: planted by God in the middle of Paradise, this tree is a symbol of the Virgin Mary, who gave the world the holy fruit of life, namely, Jesus, to eat of and live forever (Gen. 3:22).

(ii) *The rainbow after Noah's flood*: this rainbow signified the covenant between God and Noah (Gen. 9:17). It symbolizes the Virgin Mary, the sign of the New Testament, from who came the one that would establish the "new and everlasting covenant."

(iii) *The burning bush*: God's word came forth from the burning bush unto Moses (Exod. 3:1-6). While burning, the bush was not consumed by the flames. Similarly, the Word of God came forth from the Virgin, and in the process, her virginity was not consumed.

(iv) *Elijah's little cloud*: this cloud watered Israel after years of drought (1 Kgs 18:41). It symbolizes the Virgin Mary who carried and brought the living water of Jesus to thirsty Israel.

(v) *The Holy of Holies*: contained the presence of God (the *Shekinah Kabod*), Who literally dwelt within it (1 Kgs 6:15-20). The Virgin Mary was the new Holy of Holies in whom dwelt the divine person of Jesus.

(vi) *Ezekiel's eastern gate*: Once the Lord God had entered in by this gate, it was shut; no man could afterwards pass through it (Ezek. 44:2). This represents how, after the Holy Spirit entered into Mary to impregnate her, no man would afterwards impugn her virginity.

In the New Testament, the Virgin Mary is the only person mentioned at every important point in the life of Jesus: at the annunciation (Lk 1:26); at the visitation to St Elizabeth (Lk 1:39); at Jesus' nativity (Lk 2:1); at his presentation in the Temple (Lk 2:22); during the flight to Egypt (Mt 2:13); during Jesus' childhood – the finding in the Temple (Lk 2:41); at the performance of his first miracle in Cana (Jn 2:1); following nearby during his public preaching (Mt 12:46); at the foot of the Cross (Jn 19:25); undoubtedly with him after his resurrection; and with the infant Church during the descent of the Holy Spirit at Pentecost (Acts 1:14).

Third objection: *"But isn't it a fact that Jesus called Mary 'woman' only because he was displeased with her interference at the wedding of Cana?"*

Contrary to what is believed and taught by some, the word "woman" used by Jesus towards his Mother in this context was not a disrespectful rebuke, but rather a term of respect, dignity and honor. An equivalent in modern-day English usage would be "Lady." Several Protestant Bible commentaries readily admit this fact, for example:

> Jesus' reply to Mary was not so abrupt as it seems. 'Woman' was a polite form of address. Jesus used it when he spoke to his Mother from the cross and also when he spoke to Mary Magdalene after the resurrection.[4]

> "In his reply, the use of 'woman' does not involve disrespect."[5]

In fact, Mary is called "woman" three times in the Bible:

---

[4] Frank E. Gaebelein, *Expositor's Bible Commentary*, Grand Rapids, MI: Zondervan, 1981, vol. 9, p. 42.
[5] C. F. Pfeiffer & E. F. Harrison, *Wycliffe Bible Commentary*, Chicago, Moody Press, 1979, p. 1076.

(i) "O woman, what have you to do with me? My hour has not yet come" (Jn 2:4).
(ii) "Woman, behold, your son!" (Jn 19:26).
(iii) "... a woman clothed with the sun" (Rev. 12:1).

By calling the Virgin Mary "woman" in the above verses, Jesus and St John identify her with the woman in Gen. 3:15 who would be at perpetual enmity with Satan: "I will put enmity between you and the woman." A closer examination of Gen. 3:15 and Rev. 12 reveals the striking similarities. There are three main characters in Gen. 3: the serpent, Adam and the woman; likewise, in Rev. 12 there is the dragon (the ancient serpent), the male child who is to rule the nations (the New Adam) and the woman (the Virgin Mary, or New Eve). The early Church Fathers themselves noticed this parallel between Eve and the Virgin Mary, especially those with a spiritual inheritance traceable to the Apostle John (e.g., St Irenaeus of Lyons).

Fourth objection: *"What about the following passage: 'As he said this, a woman in the crowd raised her voice and said to him, Blessed is the womb that bore you, and the breasts that you sucked! But he said, Blessed rather are those who hear the word of God and keep it!'"* (Lk 11:27-28).

The simple response one can give to this objection is that given by St Augustine of Hippo: The Virgin Mary was the only person who had both the privilege to bear and suckle the Christ-child and the distinction of hearing and keeping the word of God. Furthermore, if she had not persevered in keeping the word of God throughout her entire life she would not have been present at the foot of the Cross during the darkest hour or on Mt Olivet or in the Cenacle in the moments of final triumph and glory.

Regarding the quote itself, the ex-Protestant Catholic apologist James Akin makes the following valuable point:

> ... the Greek word here translated 'rather' (*menoun* – μενοῦν) does not have anything like the adversive force in Greek that 'rather' does in English. It is simply an emphatic particle normally rendered 'and.' Thus, if Bibles had italics for

emphasis, the passage would be better translated: 'He said, *And* blessed are those who hear the word of God and keep it!' He is not denying what she said, he is emphatically *adding* something to what she said. (*Internet Question Box*, 4/26/99).

In Phil. 3:7-8 the same word *menoun* (μενοῦν) again appears and is usually translated as "indeed," with the meaning of "yes, and in addition to."

Fifth objection: *"Isn't the belief that Mary is the 'Mother of the Church' a gross exaggeration?"*

St John would not agree. In his book of Revelation, he refers to those who obey God and believe in Jesus as children of "the woman": "the dragon was angry with *the woman*, and went off to make war on *the rest of her offspring, on those who keep the commandments of God and bear testimony to Jesus*" (Rev. 12:17). The woman St John saw is undoubtedly the Virgin Mary, for she is the mother of "a male child, one who is to rule all the nations" (12:5) — an obvious reference to Jesus.

Likewise, even the founder of Protestantism, Martin Luther, would not agree:

> Mary is the Mother of Jesus and the Mother of all of us ... If he is ours, we ought to be in his situation; there where he is, we ought also to be and all that he has ought to be ours, and his Mother is also our Mother.[6]

Eve is the natural and biological mother of humanity, but due to her disobedience and sin she contributed to the spiritual destruction of her children. The Virgin Mary, through her obedience opened the way for the coming of Jesus into the world and the subsequent spiritual restoration of humanity. How very true then is the ancient maxim, "Death through Eve, life through Mary."

When did "the woman" become the mother of Christians? When Jesus himself gave his Mother to be our Mother from the Cross itself. This we see in the verse cited earlier from John's Gospel:

---

[6] *Christmas Sermon*, 1529.

"Woman, behold your son! ... Behold your mother!" (Jn 19:26-27).

The first question that needs to be asked about this verse is why Jesus would instruct St John to call the Virgin Mary "mother" when St John's own biological mother (Salome) was still alive and standing nearby at the foot of the Cross (Mk 15:40). *Prima facie*, Jesus is entrusting his Mother into the care of St John, for St Joseph himself had long since passed away and the Virgin Mary had no other children to care for her. However, there has always existed the deeper understanding that St John was given to the Virgin Mary as a son, not in the capacity of a simple individual but as a disciple and Apostle representing the entire Church. If there is no symbolic significance in this passage, then why is the term "disciple" used instead of John's own name? Furthermore, why did Jesus use the term "woman" rather than "mother" when first addressing the Virgin Mary? As we have seen, the term "woman" has strong prophetic and symbolic connotations. The woman prophesied in Gen. 3:15 as the enemy of the serpent and who was present at the beginning of Jesus' public mission is now made Mother of the Church at the consummation of Jesus' mission. This certainly did not escape St John, which is why he would record that the "woman" he saw in Rev. 12 is the mother of *"those who keep the commandments of God and bear testimony to Jesus"* (v. 17).

To crown all the above, the Virgin Mary's motherhood is not only a spiritual motherhood of the Church but also a royal one. Jesus is King of heaven and earth and according to the Jewish Davidic tradition the King's mother occupied the role of *Giberah*, or "great lady." The "woman" in Rev. 12 is adorned with a "crown of twelve stars" (v. 1), which obviously conveys queenship. The twelve stars in Mary's crown means that she is queen of the people and kingdom of God, for the Old Testament people of God were founded upon the twelve tribes of Israel and the New Testament Church was founded upon the twelve Apostles.

Sixth objection: *"How can Catholics justify calling Mary 'mediatrix' and 'co-redemptrix' when 1 Tim. 2:5 says that there is only one mediator between God and man, the man Christ Jesus!"*

Understood properly, Jesus is the one *mediator of redemption*, for there is no other name under heaven by which any one can be saved. Only Jesus is true God and true man at the same time, therefore, only he could bridge the chasm between God and fallen humanity by offering a sacrifice of himself on behalf of the children of Adam that was infinitely pleasing to the Father. Nevertheless, Scripture itself attests that Jesus is not the sole *mediator of prayer*. For example, the Holy Spirit "intercedes for us with sighs too deep for words" (Rom. 8:26). Also, Scripture shows that God occasionally does not answer prayer without a mediator or intercessor. For instance, Abimelech and the friends of Job were only pardoned through the respective prayers of Abraham and Job (Gen. 20). St James makes the point that the "prayer of a righteous man has great power in its effects" (Js 5:16), and the Virgin Mary is certainly righteous. If having Jesus as our one mediator precludes the intercession of the Virgin Mary, then St Paul should never have recommended himself to the prayers of his brethren on earth, whose prayers would likewise lessen the importance of Jesus' mediatorship (Rom. 15:30; Heb. 13:18).

As for the term 'Co-Redemptrix,' this simply means "with the redeemer." By giving her free consent (*fiat*) to the Angel Gabriel, the Virgin Mary *co-operated with* God's plan of redemption. This consent was not only free but also absolutely essential to supply Jesus with the necessary humanity to be a son of Adam. Without this humanity, Jesus could not have died on the Cross for us; he would not have been eligible to be our redeemer.

Seventh objection: *"The Ark of the Covenant was lost during the time of Jeremiah. How is it that Catholics call the Virgin Mary 'Ark of the New Covenant'?"*

The original Ark of the Covenant was covered completely in gold and contained within itself a pot of manna, the priestly rod of Aaron, and the tablets of the Ten Commandments (Heb. 9:4). It was overshadowed (*episkiasai* – ἐπισκιάσαι) by a propitiatory – or mercy seat – upon which God himself dwelt (the *Shekinah Kabod*) between two statues of Cherubim (Exod. 25). The Ark accompanied the Jews into battle, being carried by four men handling two poles. It was forbidden for anyone without consecrated hands to touch the Ark (2 Sam. 6:7), or even to look inside it (1 Sam. 6:19), on pain of death.

The Ark of the Covenant was a symbolic type of the Virgin Mary. In fact, the Virgin Mary in comparison is a greater Ark, being a rational creature immaculately conceived who carried within her womb not simply the symbols of Jesus, but Jesus himself. Instead of being adorned in gold and gems she was adorned with grace and virtues. God, likewise, overshadowed (*episkiasai* – ἐπισκιάσαι) her when the Holy Spirit conceived Jesus within her after the Angel Gabriel had announced the glad tidings. Being a perpetual virgin, no one could, or did, touch her.

At the end of Rev. 11 we read the following verse:

"Then God's temple in heaven was opened, and the ark of his covenant was seen within his temple; and there were flashes of lightning, voices, peals of thunder, an earthquake, and heavy hail" (v. 19).

St John's Jewish audience would have been fascinated to hear about the Ark of the Covenant appearing in heaven and would have been eager for more information, but St John provides no further details, instead describing in the very next verse the "woman" crowned with twelve stars at the beginning of chapter 12. This juxtaposition of the "ark of his covenant" and the "woman" becomes more significant when we remember that St John did not record Revelation with chapter and verse divisions. Why Jesus revealed the two together is only understandable when we see the former as the shadow-type of the latter and greater reality. For Jesus, both the old and the new Arks are worthy of attention and veneration. Modern Catholic apologists also draw strong support for the Virgin Mary as the Ark of the New Covenant by comparing 2 Sam. 6 with Luke 1:

> In St Luke's account of the Visitation (Lk 1:39-56), it is clear that Mary is the new ark of the covenant. Mary, like David, heads to the hill country of Judah. As Mary, bearing Christ in her womb, approaches the home of Elizabeth, St John 'leaps' in Elizabeth's womb as she exclaims with a 'loud cry,' reminding us of David's leaping before the ark of the covenant and the shouts of the people of Israel. Elizabeth greets Mary

Veneration of the Blessed Virgin Mary as "Mother of God"

with words similar to those of David, '[W]hy is this granted me, that the Mother of my Lord [who is the new ark of the covenant] should come to me?' (v. 43).[7]

The following is an outline of 2 Sam. 6 and Luke 1, matching the corresponding verses:

2 Samuel 6	Luke 1
"David arose ... to bring up from there the ark of God" (v.2)	"Mary arose and went ... to a city of Judah" (v.39)
"How can the ark of the Lord come to me?" (v.9)	"And why is this granted me, that the mother of my Lord should come to me?" (v.43)
The house of Obededom the Gittite (v.10)	The house of Zechariah (v.40)
"The ark of the Lord remained in the house of Obededom the Gittite three months" (v.11)	"And Mary remained with her about three months" (v.56)
"David went and brought up the ark of God from the house of Obededom to the City of David with rejoicing" (v.12)	"Mary said, 'My soul magnifies the Lord, and my spirit rejoices in God my savior'" (vv.46-47)
"So David and all the house of Israel brought up the ark of the Lord with shouting, and with the sound of the horn" (v.15)	"Elizabeth was filled with the Holy Spirit and she exclaimed with a loud cry, 'Blessed are you among women, and blessed is the fruit of your womb'" (v.42).
King David leaping and dancing before the Lord (v.16)	"And when Elizabeth heard the greeting of Mary, the child leaped in her womb; and Elizabeth was filled with the Holy Spirit" (v.41)

---

[7] Timothy Gray, *Catholic for a Reason*, Ch. IX (Scripture's Revelation of Mary), Emmaus Road Publications, Steubenville, OH, 1997, p. 201.

Joshua prostrated himself and venerated the Ark for hours (Josh. 7:6). As "Joshua" means "Jesus" we have a type of Jesus venerating a type of Mary. Applying this to the New Testament figures themselves, it symbolizes the Son of God venerating his Mother.

The Fathers

St Justin Martyr, *Dialogue with Trypho the Jew* 100 (AD 155)
"For Eve, a Virgin and undefiled, conceived the word of the serpent, and bore disobedience and death. But the Virgin Mary received faith and joy when the angel Gabriel announced to her the glad tidings that the Spirit of the Lord would come upon her and the power of the Most High God. And she replied: 'Be it done unto me according to thy word.'"

St Irenaeus of Lyons, *Against Heresies* 3, 22, 4 (c. AD 180)
"Consequently, then, Mary the Virgin is found to be obedient, saying: 'Behold, O Lord, your handmaid; be it done to me according to your word.' Eve, however, was disobedient; and when yet a Virgin, she did not obey. So also Mary, betrothed to a man but nevertheless still a virgin, being obedient, was made the cause of salvation for herself and for the whole human race ... Thus, the knot of Eve's disobedience was loosed by the obedience of Mary. What the virgin had bound in unbelief, the Virgin Mary loosed through faith."

St Irenaeus of Lyons, *Against Heresies* 5, 19, 1 (c. AD 180)
"The Virgin Mary ... being obedient to his word, received from an angel the glad tidings that she would bear God."

Tertullian, *The Flesh of Christ* 17, 5 (c. AD 210)
"Likewise, through a Virgin, the Word of God was introduced to set up a structure of life. Thus, what had been laid waste in ruin by this sex, was by the same sex re-established in salvation. Eve had believed the serpent; Mary believed Gabriel. That which the one destroyed by believing, the other, by believing, set straight."

St Athanasius, *Apology Against the Arians* **3, 29 (c. AD 347)**
"It was for our sake that Christ became man, taking flesh from the Virgin Mary, Mother of God."

St Athanasius, *Homily of the Papyrus of Turin* **(ante AD 373)**
"O noble Virgin, truly you are greater than any other greatness. For who is your equal in greatness, O dwelling place of God the Word? To whom among all creatures shall I compare you, O Virgin? You are greater than them all, O Covenant, clothed with purity instead of gold! You are the Ark in which is found the golden vessel containing the true manna, that is, the flesh in which divinity resides."

St Epiphanius of Salamis, *The Well-Anchored Man* **30 (AD 374)**
"Without manly seed, he made himself of a holy body, taking it from the Theotokos Mary, 'born of a woman' according to the Scriptures, after he had taken our human nature. Then, as man, he could say: 'My God,' while, in his eternal nature as Son, he could say: 'My Father.'"

St Ambrose of Milan, *The Virgins* **2, 2, 6 (AD 377)**
"Mary's life should be for you a pictorial image of virginity. Her life is like a mirror reflecting the face of chastity and the form of virtue. Therein you may find a model for your own life ... showing what to improve, what to imitate, what to hold fast to."

St Cyril of Alexandria, *The Twelve Anathemas* **1 & 2 (AD 430)**
"If anyone does not confess that the Emmanuel is in truth God, and that the Holy Virgin is Mother of God, because she bore according to the flesh of the Word of God when he became flesh: let him be anathema."

"If anyone does not confess that the Word of God the Father is united hypostatically to the flesh, and that Christ with his own flesh is one, that is to say, the same one is God and man at the same time: let him be anathema."

St Cyril of Alexandria, *Scholia on the Incarnation of the Only-Begotten* 26 (post AD 431)
"The Word, then, was God, and he became also man; and since he was born according to the flesh for the sake of mankind, it is necessary that she who bore him is the Mother of God. For if she did not bear God, neither is he that was born of her to be called God. If the divinely inspired Scriptures name him God, as God having been made man and incarnate, he could not become man in any other way than through birth from a woman: how then should she who bore him not be the Mother of God?"

The Roman Catechism (1566)

Pt. I, Ch. IV: *Glory to God in the highest; and on earth peace to men of good will.* Then began the fulfilment of the splendid promise made by God to Abraham, that in his seed *all the nations of the earth should one day be blessed*; for Mary, whom we truly proclaim and venerate as Mother of God, because she brought forth him who is at once God and man, was descended from King David.

Catechism of the Catholic Church (1992)

No. 971: *"All generations will call me blessed"*: "The Church's devotion to the Blessed Virgin is intrinsic to Christian worship." The Church rightly honors "the Blessed Virgin with special devotion. From the most ancient times the Blessed Virgin has been honored with the title of 'Mother of God,' to whose protection the faithful fly in all their dangers and needs … This very special devotion … differs essentially from the adoration which is given to the incarnate Word and equally to the Father and the Holy Spirit, and greatly fosters this adoration." The liturgical feasts dedicated to the Mother of God and Marian prayer, such as the Rosary, an "epitome of the whole Gospel," express this devotion to the Virgin Mary.

Mary - the Immaculate Conception

Objection: *"St Paul clearly states that 'All have sinned and fall short of the glory of God' (Rom. 3:23). How can Catholics therefore claim that Mary was sinless?"*

The word 'immaculate' has its origins in the Latin word *macula*, meaning 'stain.' The Immaculate Conception is the Blessed Virgin Mary's glorious privilege of being preserved by a special grace of God from all stain of original sin through the future merits of Jesus Christ.

The Immaculate Conception of the Virgin Mary was solemnly defined and proclaimed by Pope Bl. Pius IX on 8 December 1854:

> The most Blessed Virgin Mary was, from the first moment of her conception, by a singular grace and privilege of almighty God and by virtue of the merits of Jesus Christ, Savior of the human race, preserved immune from all stain of original sin.[1]

Original sin itself is the deprivation of sanctifying grace – and the concomitant infused virtues and gifts – from our souls. It also involves the loss of the indwelling of the Blessed Trinity and thus spiritual death and separation from God. Furthermore, original sin 'wounded' our natural powers, leaving ignorance in the intellect, malice in the will, concupiscence in the concupiscible appetite, and debility in the irascible appetite. These wounds result in disordered desires and cravings that cause us to commit actual, personal sins.

Original sin is removed when we are "born anew" by baptism (Jn 3:5). The soul is re-generated through the infusion of sanctifying grace, which elevates it to the supernatural order so as to share in the divine life, or participation "in the divine nature" (2 Pet. 1:4-5). However, the disordered desires and cravings remain, only to be finally

---

[1] *Ineffabilis Deus*, #34, 1854.

vanquished by death and the glorious resurrection of the body. At the end of the world, therefore, all the Just will be rendered not only immaculate and free from original sin but also possessed of the gifts of the glorified body.

By being immaculately conceived, the Virgin Mary simply received in advance the full fruits of redemption and a participation in the wonderful gifts all the Just will enjoy one day. Why was such a grace bestowed upon the Virgin Mary in advance? It comes down to *appropriateness*. It was not fitting that she, who was to co-operate in the defeat of Satan, should ever be infected by his breath or be a slave to his kingdom of sin. St Bernardine of Siena (+1444) says, "we cannot think that the Son of God would have willed to be born of the Virgin Mary, or to have clothed himself with her flesh, if she had been stained with original sin."

That God should have created the Virgin Mary in a state of holiness as he had formed Eve and the angels is also befitting the honor of God: of the Father, whose daughter she is; of the Son, whose Mother she is; and of the Holy Spirit, who, in the incarnation, took Mary to be his spouse. Furthermore, as the 'new Eve' and Mother of the new Adam, the Virgin Mary cannot appropriately be anything less than the original Eve; on the contrary, as Jesus excelled Adam, so the Virgin Mary (though to a lesser degree) should excel Eve.

As for the quote from St Paul in Romans, the full text of it reads as follows:

"None is righteous, no, not one; no one understands, no one seeks for God. All have turned aside, together they have gone wrong; no one does good, not even one. Their throat is an open grave, they use their tongues to deceive. The venom of asps is under their lips. Their mouth is full of curses and bitterness. Their feet are swift to shed blood, in their paths are ruin and misery, and the way of peace they do not know. There is no fear of God before their eyes. Now we know that whatever the law says it speaks to those who are under the law, so that every mouth may be stopped, and the whole world may be held accountable to God. For no human being will be justified in his sight by works of the law, since through the law comes knowledge of sin. But now the righteousness of God has been manifested apart from law, although the law and the prophets bear witness to it, the righteousness of God through faith in Jesus Christ for all who believe.

For there is no distinction; since all (pantes – πάντες) have sinned and fall short of the glory of God, they are justified by his grace as a gift, through the redemption which is in Christ Jesus, whom God put forward as an expiation by his blood, to be received by faith" (Rom. 3:10-25).

To say that this passage is a proof-text for the universal sinfulness of humanity is a misuse of Scripture. St Paul is quoting from Ps. 14, which draws a distinction between the wicked, and the "generation of the righteous" (v. 5). The wicked are those who say in their hearts, "There is no God." They are the corrupt that do abominable deeds, which seek not after God and have gone astray. The words quoted by St Paul refer exclusively to them. On the other hand, God is with the righteous and is their refuge (v. 6). Similarly, the words "no one does good, not even one" come from Ps. 53 and refer exclusively to those who have fallen away from God. The faithful remnant on the other hand are those who do good.

In the context of his letter to the Romans, St Paul is quoting Ps. 14 to make the point that the Jews are no better off simply because they received the knowledge of the truth before the Gentiles. In saying that "all have sinned" St Paul is telling his readers that the Jews as well as the Gentiles labor under the power of sin (v. 9). He is not speaking of all *individuals* being in sin but of all *races* and gives the specific example of Greeks as well (*ibid.*). Though, collectively, races may be estranged from God that does not preclude the possibility of individuals within those races being exceptions.

In any case, even if St Paul's "all" (*pantes* – πάντες) refers to individuals it does not necessarily mean "every single person." Not every individual person is capable of sin; for example, infants who die soon after birth or those born mentally retarded. Also, we know from 1 Cor. 15:22 ("For as in Adam all [*pantes* – πάντες] die, so also in Christ shall all be made alive") and Rom. 5:12 ("so death spread to all [*pantas* – πάντας] men because all [*pantes* – πάντες] men sinned") that the word "all" can accommodate exceptions. Enoch and Elijah were translated from earth without death – God made them exceptions to the general law of death. It is God who makes the exceptions in lieu of the Cross of Jesus; and it is God who made the Virgin Mary exempt from the general law of sin in light of her vocation as Mother of God.

Second objection: *"There is nothing in the Bible about the Immaculate Conception, so why should I believe it?"*

The Church finds support for the doctrine of the Immaculate Conception in the words of the Angel Gabriel to the Virgin Mary: "Hail, *full of grace*, the Lord is with thee"; and of St Elizabeth: "Blessed are you among women" (Lk 1:28 & 42). Most Protestants would prefer to render the Greek *kecharitomene* (κεχαριτωμένε) as "highly favored" rather than "full of grace." *Kecharitomene* certainly relates to "grace" as its root word *charis* literally means "grace."[2] In fact, a strict translation of *kecharitomene* is "you who have been graced." Of the two options, "full of grace" is the more accurate rendering of the Angel's words and expressive of a characteristic quality. She, who was to conceive the Incarnate Word, the Holy of Holies, must herself be supremely holy and therefore be preserved not only from actual sin, but also from all stain of original sin. The Angel's words would not have been fully truthful had the Virgin Mary, for even one moment, been deprived of grace.

The Church, furthermore, asserts that God, immediately after Adam's sin, cursed Satan and said, "*I will put enmity between you and the woman, and between your seed and her seed; he shall bruise your head*" (Gen. 3:15). It was by the seed of the Virgin Mary, that is, Jesus, that the kingdom of Satan was demolished. The source of the *enmity* between the Virgin Mary and the serpent placed by God was her triumph over sin, her Immaculate Conception. Satan would for all time hate the one creature that would never be within his grasp. Conversely, the Virgin Mary's purity would have imbued her with the most intense hatred of sin and its author.

Third objection: *"Mary could not have been immaculately conceived for then she would not have needed redemption. Yet, she herself proclaims in the Magnificat that 'my spirit rejoices in God my Savior' (Lk 1:47)."*

---

[2] The King James Version of the Bible translates the word *charis* one hundred and twenty-nine times as "grace."

The Catholic Church does not deny that the Virgin Mary required salvation, for she was a child of Adam like the rest of humanity. However, her redemption was affected in another, more perfect manner, namely, *redemption by pre-emption*. One can be cured of a disease after having contracted it or one can be spared of that same disease by being inoculated against it in advance. The Virgin Mary's redemption was affected in this latter manner, sparing her from ever being under the dominion of Satan.

Fourth objection: *"But Mary herself admitted that she was a sinner when she presented herself in the Temple for purification in accordance with the Law of Moses: 'she shall take two turtledoves or two young pigeons, one for a burnt offering and the other for a sin offering; and the priest shall make atonement for her, and she shall be clean (Lev. 12:8)."*

The Virgin Mary observed this Law, not because she believed herself to be a sinner or defiled by giving birth to Jesus, but to give an example of humility and obedience in the fulfilment of all outward observances. Jesus himself was presented in the Temple to fulfil the Law of Moses as stated in Exod. 13:2: "Consecrate to me all the first-born; whatever is first to open the womb among the people of Israel" – although he, the divine Son of God, had no need to be consecrated. In any case, the Virgin Mary was strictly exempt from the rule of purification by virtue of what God himself had laid down in prefacing it: "If a woman having *received seed* shall bear a man child, she shall be unclean seven days" (Lev. 12:2). The conception and birth of Jesus was not due to the reception of male seed but rather to the power of the Holy Spirit. In no way can it be claimed that in conceiving, bearing and delivering Jesus, the Virgin Mary was made "unclean." In fact, the opposite would have occurred, that is, she would have received an augmentation of grace. Also, by presenting herself and her Son in the Temple, the Virgin Mary was avoiding any future opportunity for Jesus' enemies to calumniate him after the beginning of his public mission.

Fifth objection: *"If Mary was without sin then why did she suffer birth pangs while giving birth according to Rev. 12:2?"*

Pain in childbirth has traditionally been considered one of the specific punishments imposed upon womankind because of the sin of Eve (Gen. 3:16). Therefore, it follows that if the Virgin Mary endured birth pangs while giving birth to Jesus, she must have had original sin. However, in the language of apocalyptic literature we should not understand Rev. 12:2 as referring to the literal painful birth of Jesus but rather as symbolically depicting the birth of the Church and her members under the constant attacks of the devil.

In any case, the following prophecy from Isaiah indicates that the Virgin Mary gave birth to Jesus before (that is, without) experiencing any labor pains:

"Before she was in labor she gave birth; before her pain came upon her she was delivered of a son. Who has heard such a thing? Who has seen such things?" (Is. 66:7-8).

Sixth objection: *"Even St Thomas Aquinas, who Catholics claim as their greatest theologian, did not believe in the Immaculate Conception!"*

The opinion of St Thomas Aquinas against the Immaculate Conception is contained in his *Summa Theologica* (III, q. 27, a. 2, ad 3). There, he specifically says, "the time of her sanctification is unknown." No theologian, no matter how great, is the Church. If St Thomas was alive in 1854 he would have been the first to submit his views to the infallible definition of Pope Bl. Pius IX, so humble and faithful was he to the Church.

During the time of St Thomas it was not yet established exactly when the human soul was infused into the body. Different views abounded. One of the most common was that the soul was infused some weeks after conception. Holding this opinion, it followed for St Thomas that it was impossible for a person to be sanctified at conception when he had not yet received a rational soul. If a soul were to be sanctified it had to occur when or after it was infused, and therefore *after conception*.

Nevertheless, St Thomas in the same *Summa Theologica* certainly did express his belief in the personal sinlessness of the Virgin Mary based on her being sanctified *before her birth*:

> We must therefore confess simply that the Blessed Virgin committed no actual sin, neither mortal nor venial; so that what is written (Cant. 4:7) is fulfilled: "Thou art all fair, O my love, and there is not a spot in thee."[3]

Finally, writing near the end of his life, St Thomas expressed himself thus:

> For she was most pure in the matter of fault and incurred neither original nor mental nor venial sin.[4]

Interestingly, Martin Luther, who Protestants claim as their founder, certainly did believe in the Immaculate Conception:

> It is a sweet and pious belief that the infusion of Mary's soul was effected without Original Sin; so that in the very infusion of her soul she was also purified from Original Sin and adorned with God's gifts, receiving a pure soul infused by God; thus from the first moment she began to live, she was free from all sin.[5]

Seventh objection: *"The Immaculate Conception is another recent invention of Rome. It was not believed before 1854!"*

The Immaculate Conception has always been the belief of the Church, being *implicitly* contained in the Church's teaching on the Virgin Mary's absolute purity and sinlessness. Just as Jesus "grew in grace and wisdom," that is, manifested increasing signs of wisdom as he increased in years, so the Church, which possesses the wisdom of God from her origin, manifests it only according to the order of providence

---

[3] *Summa Theologica* III, q. 27, a. 4.
[4] *Expositio super Salutatione Angelica* (c. 1272-1273).
[5] Sermon, *On the Day of the Conception of Mary, the Mother of God* (8 December, 1527): quoted in Grisar, *Luther*, vol. 4, p. 238.

and her children's needs. If the Church did not believe in the Immaculate Conception before 1854, how was it that Popes and Councils over centuries made the following explicit references to the doctrine in their pronouncements:

(i) Pope Sixtus IV, Constitution *Cum Praeexcelsa* (1477); *Grave Nimis* (1483).
(ii) Council of Trent, *Decree on Original Sin* (1546).
(iii) Pope St Pius V, Bull *Ex Omnibus Afflictionibus* (1567).
(iv) Pope Alexander VII, Brief *Sollicitudo Omnium Ecclesiarum* (1661).

Finally, the Virgin Mary herself gave the infallible pronouncement of Pope Bl. Pius IX heavenly ratification when she appeared at Lourdes in France in 1858 and announced to St Bernadette Soubirous that she was *"the Immaculate Conception."* The subsequent flow of numerous miracles stemming from the waters of the Lourdes grotto attests to the authenticity of the Virgin Mary's apparitions and is a matter of public record for the entire world to examine.

The Fathers

Epitaph of Bishop Abercius (inter AD 180-216)
"I am a disciple of the chaste shepherd ... He taught me ... faithful writings. He sent me to Rome, to behold a kingdom and to see a queen with golden robe and golden shoes. There I saw a people bearing the splendid seal ... Having Paul as a companion, everywhere faith led the way and set before me for food the fish from the spring, mighty and pure, whom a spotless Virgin caught, and gave this to friends to eat, always having sweet wine and giving the mixed cup with bread."

St Ephrem of Edessa, *Prayers to the God-Bearer* (ante AD 373)[6]
"Most holy Lady, Mother of God, alone most pure in soul and body, alone exceeding all perfection of purity ... my Lady most holy, all-pure, all-immaculate, all-stainless, all-undefiled, all-incorrupt, all-inviolate."

St Gregory Nazianzus, *Sermons* 38, 13 (inter AD 379-381)
"He was conceived by the Virgin, who had first been purified by the Spirit in soul and body; for as it was fitting that childbearing should receive its share of honor, so it was necessary that virginity should receive even greater honor."

St Ambrose of Milan, *Commentary on the Gospel of Luke* 2, 7 (c. AD 389)
"Well: married but a virgin: because she is the type of the Church, which is also married but remains immaculate."

Liturgy of St James the Less (ante fifth century AD)
"Our most holy, immaculate, and most glorious Lady, Mother of God and ever Virgin Mary."

St Augustine of Hippo, *Nature and Grace* 36, 42 (AD 415)
"With the exception therefore of the Holy Virgin Mary, in whose case, out of respect for the Lord, I do not wish there to be any further question as far as sin is concerned, since how can we know what great abundance of grace was conferred on her to conquer sin in every way, seeing that she merited to conceive and bear him who certainly had no sin at all?"

St Epiphanius of Salamis, *Prayers in Praise of Mary* (ante AD 440)
"God alone excepted, she was superior to all ... to Cherubim and Seraphim, and the whole angelic host ... Hail full of grace, who satisfies the thirsty with the sweetness of the eternal fountain. Hail most holy Mother Immaculate, who brought forth Jesus."

---

[6] *Enchiridion Patristicum,* M. J. R. de Journel, SJ, no. 745.

Romanos the Melodist, *On the Birth of Mary* 1 (ante AD 560)
"Then the tribes of Israel heard that Anna had conceived the immaculate one. So everyone took part in the rejoicing. Joachim gave a banquet, and great was the merriment in the garden. He invited the priests and Levites to prayer: then he called Mary into the center of the crowd, that she might be magnified."

St Andrew of Crete, *Homilies on Mary's Nativity* 4 (ante AD 740)
"This is Mary the Theotokos, the common refuge of all Christians, the first to be liberated from the original fall of our first parents."

The Roman Catechism (1566)

Pt. I, Ch. IV: This immaculate and perpetual virginity forms, therefore, the just theme of our eulogy. Such was the work of the Holy Ghost, who at the Conception and birth of the Son so favored the Virgin Mother as to impart to her fecundity while preserving inviolate her perpetual virginity.

Catechism of the Catholic Church (1992)

No. 492: The "splendor of an entirely unique holiness" by which Mary is "enriched from the first instant of her conception" comes wholly from Christ: she is "redeemed, in a more exalted fashion, by reason of the merits of her Son." The Father blessed Mary more than any other created person "in Christ with every spiritual blessing in the heavenly places" and chose her "in Christ before the foundation of the world, to be holy and blameless before him in love."

Mary - Her Assumption and Coronation

Objection: *"The belief in the assumption of Mary is just another medieval Catholic invention. Mary died like everyone else. And in any case, there is no mention of it in the Bible!"*

Another aspect of the Virgin Mary's uniqueness and exceptional holiness is her assumption. The meaning of this doctrine is as follows: that by a special and singular privilege bestowed by God, the Virgin Mary was taken up *body and soul* into heavenly glory and re-united with Jesus Christ to henceforth live and reign with him in his kingdom forever.

Belief in the Virgin Mary's assumption can be traced back to the earliest days of the Church. In the ancient Church an account circulated that the Apostles had been divinely warned of the Virgin Mary's impending death. All, except St Thomas, managed to return in time for her death and funeral. For three days the Apostles and other faithful kept up a vigil outside her tomb, where they heard at times the distinct sound of heavenly music. When St Thomas finally arrived, he requested to see the Virgin Mary's body. To everyone's surprise, when the tomb was opened her body was not there, only flowers and her burial shroud being left in the sepulcher.

As early as the fifth century, Catholics were celebrating a 'memorial of Mary.' This primitive celebration eventually evolved into the Feast of the Dormition (falling asleep) of the Virgin, and during the sixth century, homilies on the Assumption appeared. In the sixth century also the following prayer was written for 15 August:

> May today's venerable festivity, O Lord, bring us salutary aid, whereon God's holy Mother underwent temporal death, yet, could not be held fast by the shackles of death, who gave birth to your Son made flesh of her (*The Gregorian Sacramentary*).

From the moment when the Virgin Mary's Immaculate Conception was defined as a dogma of the Faith, numerous petitions were sent to Rome asking for a definition of her assumption as the crowning glory of the privileges that stem from being Mother of God. After receiving over eighty-five thousand petitions from religious and clergy and over eight million from the lay faithful, Pope Pius XII infallibly proclaimed and defined the dogma of the Assumption on 1 November 1950:

> The Immaculate Mother of God, Mary Ever-Virgin, after her life on earth, was assumed, body and soul, into heavenly glory.[1]

This definition, though, left open the question as to whether the Virgin Mary died before being assumed into heaven. *Prima facie*, as the Virgin Mary was free from original sin due to being immaculately conceived, she would also have been free from all its consequences, including death. There are several great saints and theologians, however, such as St Louis de Montfort, who hold that the Virgin Mary did die before being assumed, due to her wish to be more conformed to her Son who died for all humanity. Yet this death, they say, was not accompanied by pain and suffering, but rather, according to St Francis de Sales, was a death of love, with her soul leaving her body out of her great desire to be re-united with Jesus.

The theological reasoning for belief in the assumption of Mary is as follows: The First Adam and the First Eve both shared the same fate due to their sin, namely death and decomposition into dust. It follows that the New Adam and the New Eve should also share the same reward for their fidelity. Jesus, by his glorious death, resurrection and ascension, gained a perfect victory over the devil, hell, sin and death. The Virgin Mary, as the immaculately conceived Mother of God, is most intimately associated with Jesus' perfect victory (Gen. 3:15). If there was no assumption of Mary, she would have been vanquished by death and that parallel to Jesus would, therefore, be destroyed.

No one can reasonably doubt that the Virgin Mary's soul is now in heaven; Jesus would not have it otherwise. She is pictured as

---

[1] *Munificentissimus Deus*, #44, 1950.

being in heaven by St John: "And a great sign appeared in heaven, a woman clothed with the sun, with the moon under her feet, and on her head a crown of twelve stars ... she brought forth a male child, who is to rule all the nations with a rod of iron" (Rev. 12:1 & 5). The doctrine of the Assumption is not contained explicitly in Scripture, but the fact that Scripture does not record an event is no absolute argument against it. The Bible does not record the death of St Joseph either, but all believe this did happen.

What Scripture does tell us, however, is that God has taken, in the past, other individuals both body and soul from the world and translated them into paradise. Such was the privilege granted to Enoch (Gen. 5:24; Heb. 11:5) and the Prophet Elijah (2 Kgs 2:1-13). St Jude may have believed that the same privilege was given to Moses by referring to the apocryphal work *Assumption of Moses* in his short epistle (v. 9). Considering such precedents, it is not unreasonable to believe that God would bestow upon the Virgin Mary an even more sublime privilege, namely a glorious assumption into heaven, in view of her fulfilment of her proportionately greater vocation as Mother of God. Such an opinion was certainly held by the sixteenth century Protestant Reformer, Heinrich Bullinger:

> Elijah was transported, body and soul, in a chariot of fire; he was not buried ... but mounted up to Heaven, so that ... we might know what immortality and recompense God prepares for his faithful prophets and for his most outstanding and incomparable creatures ... It is for this reason, we believe, that the pure and immaculate embodiment of the Mother of God, the Virgin Mary, the Temple of the Holy Spirit, that is to say, her saintly body, was carried up to heaven by the angels.[2]

The bodies of the glorious Apostles, the martyrs who shed their blood for Jesus, men and women noted for their holiness, have been carefully preserved and venerated in the Church from the beginning of Christianity. While the remains of Sts Peter and Paul are jealously possessed in Rome, no Christian city or center has ever claimed to possess the bodily remains of the Virgin Mary. No doubt her relics

---

[2] *On Original Sin*, 16, 1568.

would have been regarded of greater value than those of other Apostles or saints, so close was she to Jesus.

Of the Mother of God no relics were to remain. The Immaculate Conception, formed by the Holy Spirit, and which formed the body of Jesus, would not be allowed to see corruption. In her assumption, the Virgin Mary shows forth the fullness of redemption and is an example of what will happen to all one day. After all, as God took her glorified body into heaven, so will he take the glorified bodies of all the Just on the last day.

Second objection: *"The worship of Mary as Queen of Heaven is another form of Catholic idolatry similar to what the Prophet Jeremiah preached against before Jerusalem's destruction!"*

What the Prophet Jeremiah was preaching against was the rampant idolatry infecting Judah during the late seventh and early sixth centuries BC, involving Baal worship and human sacrifice: "The children gather wood, the fathers kindle fire, and the women knead dough, to make cakes for the queen of heaven; and they pour out drink offerings to other gods, to provoke me to anger" (Jer. 7:18). There can be no comparison between Catholic veneration given to the immaculate Mother of God and the hideous sacrificial worship of the Canaanites.

The recognition of the Virgin Mary as Queen of Heaven should not be surprising when we consider the great dignity accorded the Queen-mother in the Kingdom of Israel. Under the reign of the Davidic kings, the Queen-mother occupied the role of *Giberah*. In Hebrew, *Giberah* literally means "great lady." The Queen mother sat at the right hand of the king and intercession was a natural part of her office. Solomon showed great deference to his mother Bathsheba when she came to ask a favor of him (1 Kgs 2:19-20) and the ritual that surrounded her intercession suggests that it was a regular courtly event: "Then she said, 'I have one small request to make of you; do not refuse me.' And the king said to her, 'Make your request, my mother; for I will not refuse you'" (1 Kgs 2:20). In the later history of the Davidic dynasty the importance of the Queen-mother is testified by the careful recording of her name after the introduction of each new king (1 Kgs

14:21, 15:2, 22:42; 2 Kgs 8:26, 12:2, 14:1, 15:2, 18:2, 21:1, 22:1, 23:31) and by Jeremiah's remark, that the Queen-mother wears a diadem like the king (Jer. 13:18).

At the annunciation the Angel Gabriel told the Virgin Mary that the son to be born of her was of the royal line of David and would inherit his throne forever. We also acknowledge that Jesus is King of heaven: "King of kings and Lord of lords" (Rev. 19:16). It therefore follows that in the *Giberah* tradition Jesus' Mother should be Queen of Heaven. St Elizabeth acknowledged this queenship when greeting Mary not by her name but by saying, "And why is this granted me, that *the mother of my Lord* should come to me?" (Lk 1:43). St John saw the woman clothed with the sun wearing "on her head a crown of twelve stars" (Rev. 12:1). All the saved in heaven will wear crowns of glory, as is gathered from the words of St Paul: "From now on there is laid up for me the crown of righteousness, which the Lord, the righteous judge, will award to me on that Day" (2 Tim. 4:8). The Virgin Mary, having fulfilled the greatest of all vocations, namely, Mother of God, has been rewarded with the greatest crown; hence, her queenship over all other creatures in heaven.

Jesus himself crowned his Mother as Queen of heaven and earth after her assumption. Pope Pius XII officially proclaimed the universal queenship of Mary on 11 October 1954. He stated that the "maternity of Mary is without doubt the principal argument on which her royal dignity is based."[3] Thus was realized the dream of St Catherine Labouré: "Oh, how beautiful it will be to hear Mary is queen of the universe, especially of France, and each person in particular. She will be carried in procession and will go around the world."

The Queenship of Mary is not only a title and honorary distinction but also a "power of action and a principle of government." However, in the mind of God no one is ever raised to greatness for their own sake but only that they may serve others. The Queenship of Mary is not a sinecure but a noble bondage. In co-operation with the Most Holy Trinity, the Virgin Mary plays an invisible and wondrous role in the government of the universe. She has a word to say in the divine counsels and this word, without being a command, is a queenly

---

[3] *Ad Coeli Reginam* #34.

prayer capable of intimately moving the Most High. Cana is the first place where the Virgin Mary publicly performed her intercessory role (Jn 2:3). Such is the will of God who exalts the humble in reward for their fidelity. As Son and Mother were united in suffering on earth for the sake of our redemption, they are now united in heavenly splendor for the sake of our glorification.

The Fathers

St Epiphanius of Salamis, *Panacea Against all Heresies* 78, 23 (inter AD 374-377)

"If the holy Virgin is dead and has been buried, surely her dormition happened with great honor: her end was most pure and crowned by virginity. If she was slain, according to what is written: 'a sword shall pierce your soul,' then she obtained glory together with the martyrs, and her holy body, from which light shone forth for all the world, dwells among those who enjoy the repose of the blessed. Or she continued to live. For, to God, it is not impossible to do whatever he wills; on the other hand, no one knows exactly what her end was."

St Jerome, *Commentary on the Psalms* Ps. 44 (ante AD 420)

"('The Queen stood on the right hand in gilded clothing, surrounded with variety'). We read how the angels have come to the death and burial of some of the saints, and how they have accompanied the souls of the elect to heaven with hymns and praises. How much more should we believe that the heavenly army, with all its bands, came forth rejoicing in festal array, to meet the Mother of God, surrounded with her effulgent light, and led her with praises and canticles to the throne prepared for her from the beginning of the world."

St Gregory of Tours, *Eight Books of Miracles* 1, 4 (inter AD 575-593)

"And behold, the Lord Jesus came with his angels and, taking her soul, handed it over to the archangel Michael and withdrew. At dawn, the apostles lifted up her body on a pallet, laid it in a tomb, and kept watch over it, awaiting the coming of the Lord. And behold, again the Lord presented himself to them and ordered that her holy body be taken and carried up to heaven. There she is now, joined once more to her soul; she exults with the elect, rejoicing in the eternal blessings that will have no end."

St Germain I of Constantinople, *Sermon on the Dormition of the Blessed Virgin Mary* 2 **(ante AD 733)**
"Let death pass you by, O Mother of God, because you have brought life to men. Let the tomb pass you by, because you have been made the foundation stone of inexplicable sublimity. Let dust pass you by; for you are a new kind of formation, so that you may be mistress over those who have been corrupted in the very stuff of their potter's clay."

St Andrew of Crete, *Homilies on the Dormition* 2 **(ante AD 740)**
"Why is no body visible? And why are the burial wrappings missing from the tomb, if not because what had been entombed there escaped destruction, and because the treasure was transferred to another place?"

St John Damascene, *Second Homily on the Dormition of the Virgin* **10, 18 (inter AD 725-749)**
"From ancient tradition we have received that at the time of the glorious falling asleep of the Blessed Virgin, all the holy Apostles, traversing the whole earth for the salvation of all nations, were in one moment borne on high and carried to Jerusalem; and whilst they were there, they saw and heard angels; and thus amid divine glory, she yielded her soul into the hands of God. Her body, which God in some unutterable way has taken, was borne amid angelic and apostolic hymns, and was put in a tomb at Gethsemane, where angelic songs lasted for three consecutive days. The angelic singing ceasing after three days, the tomb was opened by the Apostles, who were then all together; for Thomas, the only one first absent, had come the third day, and desired to pay homage to the body which had received God. But nowhere could they find her body ... Astonished at this mysterious miracle, they could only conclude that he who was pleased from the Virgin Mary to take flesh and to become man ... the same was pleased, after her death, to preserve incorrupt her immaculate body, and to honor it, before the common and universal resurrection ..."

The Roman Catechism (1566)

The Roman Catechism made no reference to the Virgin Mary's assumption into heaven.

Catechism of the Catholic Church (1992)

No. 966: "Finally the Immaculate Virgin, preserved free from all stain of original sin, when the course of her earthly life was finished, was taken up body and soul into heavenly glory, and exalted by the Lord as Queen over all things, so that she might be the more fully conformed to her Son, the Lord of lords and conqueror of sin and death." The assumption of the Blessed Virgin is a singular participation in her Son's resurrection and an anticipation of the resurrection of other Christians:

> In giving birth you kept your virginity; in your Dormition you did not leave the world, O Mother of God, but were joined to the source of Life. You conceived the living God and, by your prayers, will deliver our soul from death (Byzantine Liturgy, Feast of the Dormition).

The Perpetual Virginity of Mary

Objection: *"Mary had other children besides Jesus. This is clear from the following passages of the Bible:*

"While he was still speaking to the people, behold, his mother and his brethren were stood outside, asking to speak to him" (Mt 12:46).

"Where did this man get this wisdom and these mighty works? Is not this the carpenter's son? Is not his mother called Mary? And are not his brethren James and Joseph and Simon and Judas? And are not all his sisters with us? Where then did this man get all this?" And they took offense at him" (Mt 13:54-57).

According to most Protestants, it appears clear from these passages that Jesus Christ had brothers and sisters, and that the Virgin Mary therefore did not remain a virgin all her life. Yet, it has been the belief of the Catholic Church since ancient times that the Virgin Mary was a virgin before, during, and perpetually after giving birth to Jesus (*ante partum, in partu, post partum*).

The so-called *Protoevangelium of St James* (written c. AD 170) says that the Virgin Mary was one of the women who, like the prophetess Anna, lived celibate lives in the Temple of Jerusalem, praying full-time: "(from the time she was three) Mary was in the temple of the Lord as if she were a dove that dwelt there" (4:7). A life of continual prayer and service to the Lord in the Temple meant that Mary could not live the ordinary life of a childbearing mother, and so she made a vow of perpetual virginity.

However, due to considerations of ceremonial cleanliness, it was eventually necessary for the Virgin Mary to have appointed a guardian who would respect her vow of virginity. Thus, St Joseph, an elderly widower who already had children, was chosen: "And Joseph [was chosen] ... And the priest said to Joseph, 'You have been chosen by lot to take into your keeping the Virgin of the Lord.' But Joseph refused, saying, 'I have children, and I am an old man, and she is a young girl'" (vv. 8-9). Nevertheless, St Joseph humbly resigned himself to the Lord's will.

The view of the *Protoevangelium* (whatever be its historical value) that the brethren of the Lord were Jesus' stepbrothers (children of St Joseph of another marriage) was the most popular one until the time of St Jerome, who argued that they were cousins instead. Whatever view one takes, any notion that the brethren of the Lord were other children of the Virgin Mary was certainly anathema to early orthodox Christianity, as can be gathered from the following statement of Pope St Siricius:

> Surely, we cannot deny that regarding the sons of Mary the statement is justly censured, and Your Grace has rightly abhorred it, that from the same virginal womb, from which according to the flesh Christ was born, another offspring was brought forth.[1]

The Lateran Council in AD 649 proclaimed emphatically the perpetual virginity of Mary:

> If anyone does not properly and truly confess according to the holy Fathers, that the holy Mother of God, the ever-Virgin and immaculate Mary, in these latter days, properly and truly conceived of the Holy Spirit without seed, namely, God the Word himself, who was born of God the Father before all ages, and that she bore him incorruptibly, her virginity remaining inviolable even after his birth, let him be condemned.[2]

Belief in the Virgin Mary's perpetual virginity was re-asserted during the first decades of the Protestant reformation:

> This immaculate and perpetual virginity forms, therefore, the just theme of our eulogy. Such was the work of the Holy

---

[1] *Accepi Litteras Vestras* (to Anysius, Bishop of Thessalonica) AD 392.
[2] Canon 3.

Ghost, who at the Conception and birth of the Son so favored the Virgin Mother as to impart to her fecundity while preserving inviolate her perpetual virginity.[3]

Ironically, the founders of Protestantism, unlike their modern-day disciples, strictly defended the same teaching. Martin Luther said:

> It is an article of faith that Mary is Mother of the Lord and still a virgin ... Christ, we believe, came forth from a womb left perfectly intact.[4]

> I am inclined to agree with those who declare that "brothers" really mean cousins here, for Holy Writ and the Jews always call cousins brothers.[5]

> She was, without doubt, a pure, chaste virgin before the birth, in birth, and after the birth, and she was neither sick nor weakened from the birth, and certainly could have gone out of the house after giving birth, not only because of her exemption under the Law, but also because of the uninterrupted soundness of her body. For her Son did not detract from her virginity but actually strengthened it; but, in spite of this, not only the Mother, but also the Son, both allowed themselves to be considered unclean according to the Law.[6]

Ulrich Zwingli, another major Protestant leader (1484-1531), even more adamantly stated:

> I firmly believe that Mary, according to the words of the gospel, as a pure Virgin brought forth for us the Son of God and in childbirth and after childbirth forever remained a pure, intact Virgin.[7]

---

[3] *The Roman Catechism*, 1566, Pt. I, Ch. IV.
[4] Weimer, *The Works of Luther*, Pelikan, Concordia, vol. 11, pp. 319-320.
[5] Ibid., vol. 22-23, pp. 214-215.
[6] Luther, *The Day of the Holy Innocents*, Sermon on Matthew, 2:13-23, 1541.
[7] *Zwingli Opera, Corpus Reformatorum*, Berlin, 1905, in Evang. Luc., vol. 1, p. 424.

According to Jewish custom at the time, there were two stages to marriage. The first stage, betrothal, was when the marriage was legally made (Exod. 21:9). The Virgin Mary and St Joseph had concluded this stage (Lk 1:27). The second stage of marriage was the social formality of the public celebration. A marriage would normally be consummated after the bringing of the bride to the husband's home. However, at the time of the annunciation it was obvious that the Virgin Mary and St Joseph had not consummated their marriage: "How can this be, since I have no husband?" (Lk 1:34). It may well be the case that the Virgin Mary and St Joseph also did not publicly celebrate their marriage in the usual manner due to their hastily arranged visit to St Elizabeth and Zachariah in Ein Karem (Luke 1:39ff.); nevertheless, this did not invalidate their marriage.

Like the *Protoevangelium of St James*, several distinguished Catholic commentators, including St Thomas Aquinas, also believed that the Virgin Mary had made a formal vow of perpetual virginity before being betrothed to St Joseph. The Jews, during the four centuries before Christ, had begun to develop a concept of consecrated virginity, particularly in the community of the Essenes. Having made a vow of virginity explains why Mary was so perplexed after the Angel Gabriel announced to her that she was about to bear a son.

The Catholic answer to Matt. 12:46 and 13:54 is detailed but decisive. There existed no special word in Hebrew or Aramaic for 'cousin.' The word 'brother' is used in these languages in a general sense, and does not necessarily imply that the children are from the same parent. There are many examples in the Old Testament when the word brother was applied to any sort of relations: nephew (Gen. 12:5, 13:8, 14:16); uncle (Gen. 29:15); husband (Sgs 4:9); a member of the same tribe (2 Kgs 9:13); of the same people (Exod. 2:21); an ally (Amos 1:9); a friend (2 Kgs 1:26); one of the same office (1 Sam. 9:13). In the New Testament, the other disciples are called St Peter's "brethren" (Lk 22:32), St Peter refers to the one hundred and twenty gathered in the Upper Room as "brethren" (Acts 1:15), and St Paul uses "brethren" and "kinsmen" interchangeably (Rom. 9:3).

The Perpetual Virginity of Mary

Second objection: *"This may well be the case but Matt. 1:25 says that Joseph 'knew her not until she had borne a son; and he called his name Jesus.' This implies that Mary, therefore, had sexual relations with Joseph after giving birth to Jesus."*

It would be well here to reproduce the footnote commentary on this verse from the Douai-Rheims version of the New Testament:

> St Jerome shows, by divers examples, that this expression of the Evangelist was a manner of speaking usual among the Hebrews, to denote by the word *until*, only what is done, without any regard to the future. Thus it is said, Genesis 8:6 and 7, that Noe sent forth a raven, which went forth, and did not return till the waters were dried up on the earth. That is, did not return anymore. Also Isaias 46:4, God says: I Am till you grow old. Who dare infer that God should then cease to be? ... God saith to his divine Son: Sit on my right till I make thy enemies thy footstool. Shall he sit no longer after his enemies are subdued?

Other examples from Scripture include:

"So they went up to Mount Zion with gladness and joy, and offered burnt offerings, because not one of them had fallen before they returned in safety" (1 Macc. 5:54).

Are we to read this verse to mean that the soldiers were killed after they returned from battle?

"And there was a prophetess, Anna, the daughter of Phanuel, of the tribe of Asher; she was of a great age, having lived with her husband seven years from her virginity, and as a widow till she was eighty-four" (Lk 2:36-37).

Does this mean that Anna was no longer a widow after the age of eighty-four?

Even John Calvin shared St Jerome's opinion:

There have been certain folk who have wished to suggest from this passage (Matthew 1:25) that the Virgin Mary had other children than the Son of God, and that Joseph then dwelt with her later; but what folly this is! For the gospel writer did not wish to record what happened afterwards; he simply wished to make clear Joseph's obedience and to show also that Joseph had been well and truly assured that it was God who had sent his angel to Mary. He had therefore never dwelt with her nor had he shared her company.[8]

Third objection: *"What about the fact that in some versions of Matt. 1:25 Jesus is called 'first-born.' Doesn't this imply that he was therefore the first-born of several?"*

According to the Jewish Law a child was called "first-born" irrespective of whether there were yet, or ever to be, other children born to the same mother. The law as stated in Exod. 13:2 required that "whatever is first to open the womb among the people of Israel" be consecrated to God thirty-one days after its birth. The child is designated "first-born" even though it is only thirty-one days old and hence impossible for it to have any brother or sister yet. John Calvin also conceded this fact:

> And besides this, Our Lord Jesus Christ is called the first-born. This is not because there was a second or a third, but because the gospel writer is paying regard to the precedence ... Scripture speaks thus of naming the first-born whether or not there was any question of the second.[9]

Another point of interest to note here is that the Gospels always refer to Jesus as "the" son of Mary, not "a" son of Mary (Mk 6:3).

Fourth objection: *"Psalm 69 is messianic and speaks of the Messiah as a stranger and an alien even unto his mother's children."*

---

[8] *Sermon on Matthew 1:22-25*, published 1562.
[9] *Ibid.*

The verse in question reads as follows: "I have become a stranger to my brethren, an alien to my mother's sons" (v. 8). There is no doubt that this psalm is messianic and in the New Testament it is referred to as a forecast of Jesus' experiences: Mt 27:34; Jn 15:25; Acts 1:20; and Rom. 15:3. The following verses specifically speak of Jesus:

"... *those who hate me without cause*" (v. 4).

"*For zeal for thy house has consumed me*" (v. 9).

"... *for my thirst they gave me vinegar to drink*" (v. 21).

However, the messianic interpretation of the psalm does not exclude the possibility that it also describes personal experiences of the psalmist. This must be the conclusion when considering the following other verses:

"*O God, thou knowest my folly; the wrongs I have done are not hidden from thee*" (v. 5).

"*Insults have broken my heart, so that I am in despair. I looked for pity, but there was none; and for comforters, but I found none*" (v. 20).

"*Add to them punishment upon punishment; may they have no acquittal from thee*" (v. 27).

The above words in v. 8 simply apply to David who considers the consequences of those sins he wails over in v. 5. It is in the other verses that he is carried on by the Holy Spirit to depict the ideal messianic sufferer.

Who, then, exactly were the brothers and sisters of Jesus? It is best to start by looking at Gal. 1:19. In Gal. 1 St Paul relates how, after spending three years in the wilderness of "Arabia," he returned to Jerusalem "to visit Cephas" (St Peter) (v.18). He goes on to mention that during his fifteen-day stay he "saw none of the other apostles except *James the Lord's brother*" (v.19). Note that St Paul describes *"James the Lord's brother"* as an "apostle." History tells us this is James the Less, the first bishop of Jerusalem. Of the twelve Apostles two were known by the name of James — James the Great, son of Zebedee and Salome and James the son of Alphaeus (Mt 10:2; Mk 3:16), the latter known also as James the Less. Neither of the two James were the son of St Joseph. Why then is James the Less, son of Alphaeus, called the Lord's brother?

The answer to this question begins with noting that the mother of James the Less, Mary, is described by St John as the "sister" of Mary the Mother of Jesus: "But standing by the cross of Jesus were his mother, *and his mother's sister, Mary the wife of Clopas*" (Jn 19:25). Clopas and Alphaeus are the same person as these different words are merely different transcriptions of the same Aramaic word "Halphai." This is confirmed when tying together Matt. 10:2, Mark 15:40 and John 19:25. James the Less is the son of Alphaeus in Matt. 10:2 and the son of Mary in Mark 15:40 ("*Mary the mother of James the younger ...*"). St John calls this same Mary the wife of Clopas in 19:25. The Mary described as the "mother of James" in Mark 15:40 is the same as Mary the wife of Clopas in John 19:25 and not Mary the "mother of Jesus" as the Virgin Mary is never mentioned by any other title in the Gospels except as "mother of Jesus."

Therefore, James the Less and Jesus were "brothers" because their respective mothers were "sisters" according to John 19:25. However, what was the nature of their sisterhood? The ancient second century Christian chronicler, Hegesippus, gives us a clue. He describes Clopas as "an uncle of the Lord," probably the brother of St Joseph. That makes the wives of St Joseph and Clopas sisters-in-law. Whichever way we look at it, James the Less and Jesus were no more than first cousins.

Scripture goes on to identify that two other "brothers" of Jesus, namely Joseph and Jude, were also his first cousins. St Mark tells us that in addition to James, Mary of Clopas was also the mother of a Joses (Joseph): "Mary the mother of James the younger and of Joses" (15:40). As for Jude, he describes himself at the beginning of his short epistle as "a servant of Jesus Christ and brother of James" (1:1). As for the fourth alleged brother of Jesus, Simon, Hegesippus describes him as "the son of Clopas, descended from the Lord's uncle, is made bishop, his election being promoted by all as being a kinsman of the Lord."

It is therefore conclusive from Scripture that there existed a family closely related to Jesus comprising of parents named Clopas (Alphaeus) and Mary, with sons named James, Joseph, Jude and Simon. Are we also to believe that Clopas had a brother named Joseph who also had a wife by the name of Mary and sons named James, Joseph, Jude and Simon? This would be greatly stretching credibility. One can safely state then that the "brothers" of Jesus – as mentioned in Matt. 13:54-57 being James, Joseph, Jude, Simon – are in fact the same James, Joseph, Jude and Simon who were his first cousins. One could expect, also, that after St Joseph died, the Virgin Mary would have gone with Jesus to live with or nearby her "sister," explaining why she was travelling with those mentioned in Matt. 12:46.

What about the "brethren" of the Lord who just six months before the crucifixion "did not believe in him" (Jn 7:5)? How could they be his disciples? Their unbelief was only relative. They believed Jesus to be the Messiah but had a faulty concept of messiahship, one that viewed the Messiah as a temporal ruler that should manifest his power to the world at large.

It is also important to examine closely three major events in Jesus' life mentioned in the Gospels: (i) the return of the Holy Family from Egypt to Nazareth after the death of Herod; (ii) the finding of the Child Jesus in the Temple after being lost for three days; and (iii) Jesus giving his Mother to the care of St John at his crucifixion. Jesus, according to the best of our knowledge, was about 2, 12 and 33 years of age respectively when each of these events occurred. Yet, never is there any mention of brothers or sisters of his being present, which one would naturally expect if they had actually existed.

The Fathers

Hegesippus, *Fragments from His Five Books of Commentaries on the Acts of the Church* Bk 5 (c. AD 170)

"James, the Lord's brother, succeeds to the government of the Church, in conjunction with the apostles. He has been universally called the Just, from the days of the Lord down to the present time ... The same historian mentions others also, of the family of one of the reputed brothers of the Savior, named Judas, as having survived until this same reign, after the testimony they bore for the faith of Christ in the time of Domitian, as already recorded ... And after James the Just had suffered martyrdom, as had the Lord also and on the same account, again Symeon the son of Clopas, descended from the Lord's uncle, is made bishop, his election being promoted by all as being a kinsman of the Lord."

St Athanasius, *On Virginity* (ante AD 373)
"But since she was a virgin, and was his Mother, he gave her as a Mother to his disciple, even though she was not really John's mother, because of his great purity of understanding and because of her untouched virginity."

St Ephrem of Edessa, *Prayers to the God-Bearer* (ante AD 373)
"... the rod of Aaron that budded, truly have you appeared as a stem those flower is your true Son, our Christ, my God and my Maker; you did bear according to the flesh God and the Word, did preserve your virginity before his birth, did remain a virgin after his birth, and we have been reconciled to God by Christ your Son."

St Basil the Great, *On the Holy Generation of Christ* 5 (ante AD 379)
"But since the lovers of Christ (the faithful) do not allow themselves to hear that the Mother of God ceased at a given moment to be a virgin, we consider their testimony to be sufficient."

Didymus the Blind, *The Trinity* 3, 4 (inter AD 381-392)
"It helps us to understand the terms first-born and only-begotten when the Evangelist tells that Mary remained a virgin 'until she brought forth her first-born son'; for neither did Mary, who is to be honored and praised above all others, marry anyone, nor did she ever become the Mother of anyone else, but even after childbirth she remained always and forever an immaculate virgin."

St Jerome, *Against Helvidius* 17 & 18 (c. AD 383)
"I now ask to which class you consider the Lord's brethren in the Gospel must be assigned. They are brethren by nature, you say. But

Scripture does not say so; it calls them neither sons of Mary, nor of Joseph. Shall we say they are brethren by race? ... The only alternative is to adopt the previous explanation and understand them to be called brethren in virtue of the bond of kindred, not of love and sympathy, nor by prerogative of race, nor yet by nature ... It is clear that our Lord's brethren bore the name in the same way that Joseph was called his father."

St John Chrysostom, *Homilies on the Gospel of St Matthew* **Hom. 1 (c. AD 390)**
"Joseph did not know her, until she gave birth, being unaware of her dignity: but after she had given birth, then did he know her (by way of acquaintance). Because by reason of her child she surpassed the whole world in beauty and dignity: since she alone in the narrow abode of her womb received him whom the world cannot contain."

St Augustine of Hippo, *Holy Virginity* **4, 4 (AD 401)**
"In being born of a Virgin who chose to remain a Virgin even before she knew who was to be born of her, Christ wanted to approve virginity rather than impose it. And he wanted virginity to be of free choice even in that woman in whom he took upon himself the form of a slave."

St Augustine of Hippo, *The Annunciation of the Lord* **3,** *Sermones Supp.* **195 (ante AD 430)**
"It is written (Ezek. 44:2): 'This gate shall be shut, it shall not be opened, and no man shall pass through it. Because the Lord the God of Israel has entered in by it.' What does this closed gate in the house of the Lord mean, except that Mary is to be ever inviolate? What does it mean that 'no man shall pass through it,' but that Joseph shall not know her? And what is this – 'The Lord alone enters in and goes out by it,' except that the Holy Spirit shall impregnate her, and that the Lord of Angels shall be born of her? And what means this – 'It shall be shut for evermore,' but that Mary is a Virgin before his birth, a Virgin in his birth, and a Virgin after his birth."

The Roman Catechism (1566)

Pt. I, Ch. IV: He is born of his Mother without any diminution of her maternal virginity, just as he afterwards went forth from the sepulcher while it was closed and sealed, and entered the room in which his disciples were assembled, the doors being shut; or, not to depart from every-day examples, just as the rays of the sun penetrate without breaking or injuring in the least the solid substance of glass, so after a like but more exalted manner did Jesus Christ come forth from his Mother's womb without injury to her maternal virginity. This immaculate and perpetual virginity forms, therefore, the just theme of our eulogy. Such was the work of the Holy Ghost, who at the conception and birth of the Son so favored the Virgin Mother as to impart to her fecundity while preserving inviolate her perpetual virginity.

Catechism of the Catholic Church (1992)

No. 500: Against this doctrine the objection is sometimes raised that the Bible mentions brothers and sisters of Jesus. The Church has always understood these passages as not referring to other children of the Virgin Mary. In fact James and Joseph, "brothers of Jesus," are the sons of another Mary, a disciple of Christ, whom St Matthew significantly calls "the other Mary." They are close relations of Jesus, according to an Old Testament expression.

The Holy Rosary of the Blessed Virgin Mary

Objection: *"Why pray the Rosary? It is not mentioned in the Bible."*

The Holy Rosary is a form of popular devotion that has its earliest origins in the Later Middle Ages. Since the time of the Church Fathers, it has been the common practice of laity to recite with clergy and religious the Liturgical Hours commonly known as the Divine Office. The most popular Hour is that of Vespers (6:00 p.m.). For the most dedicated laity, daily recitation of the Divine Office would involve praying all one hundred and fifty Psalms of David per week. According to Cassian and St Benedict of Nursia, certain religious even prayed all one hundred and fifty Psalms per day.

Throughout the Church's history, however, the Divine Office has been a prayer only for the literate or those who could memorize the Psalms. For the illiterate, the Holy Spirit would inspire a simpler but wonderful alternative. Thus, over time, another 'psalter' of one hundred and fifty prayers was developed and adopted by the learned and unlearned alike – the Psalter of Mary. Both the physical form of the Holy Rosary and the type and number of prayers have been changed over the centuries.[1]

Certainly, being a form of prayer first developed in the Middle Ages we do not find the Holy Rosary mentioned in the Bible. But of what ultimate consequence is this? There are hundreds, if not thousands, of excellent prayers used by both Catholics and Protestants that have been written only in recent centuries and not mentioned in the Bible either. Most of these are prayers to Jesus himself or the Holy Spirit, rather than to the Father. Should they, together with the Holy

---

[1] For example, the second half of the Hail Mary ("pray for us sinners, now and at the hour of our death. Amen.") only reached its final form in the Breviary promulgated by Pope St Pius V in 1568; the 'O my Jesus' prayer was added at the injunction of Our Lady at Fatima in 1917; Pope St John Paul II in October 2002 released *Rosarium Virginis Mariae*, adding the five 'Mysteries of Light.'

Rosary, be discarded simply because they are "not mentioned in the Bible"?

What is important is whether the doctrines underlying the prayers of the Holy Rosary are found in or are consistent with the Bible. In general, mainstream Protestants would have no objection to the contents of the Apostles' Creed, which is the first prayer of the Rosary. Nor would any reasonable Protestant object to the Lord's Prayer, the Trinitarian Doxology (the Glory Be)[2] or the contents of the 'O my Jesus' prayer.[3] The only real problems for Protestants are the prayers commonly known as the 'Hail Mary' and the 'Hail, Holy Queen.' Protestant objection to the Holy Rosary is essentially tied up with Protestant objection to Marian devotion in general. This is not the place to give a detailed defense of Marian devotion. All that needs to be said is that the Hail Mary and the Hail Holy Queen are simply intercessory prayers, having their foundation and legitimacy in the doctrine of the Communion of Saints (1 Cor. 12:26-27; Lk 15:10; Heb. 12:1).

Second objection: *"Catholics think that counting beads is going to get them to heaven!"*

Those who do not know what the Holy Rosary is often dismiss it as "counting beads." The Holy Rosary is a prayer that is both oral and mental. The Holy Rosary in its entirety recalls twenty events (otherwise known as 'mysteries' because of their sublimity) in the lives of Jesus and Mary that each teach a lesson in faith and virtue. These mysteries are divided into four groups of five. The first group is called the *Joyful Mysteries* (because of their joyous nature), the second the *Luminous Mysteries* (because they commemorate Jesus' revealing of himself and the announcement of his Kingdom), the third the *Sorrowful Mysteries* (because they commemorate Jesus in his passion and death) and the fourth the *Glorious Mysteries* (because they commemorate the triumph

---

[2] "Glory be to the Father, and to the Son, and to the Holy Spirit. As it was in the beginning, is now and ever shall be, world without end. Amen."

[3] "O my Jesus, forgive us our sins, save us from the fires of hell; lead all souls to heaven, especially those in most need of thy mercy."

of Jesus and Mary over the devil, sin and death). Each mystery consists of one 'Our Father,' ten 'Hail Marys,' one 'Glory be' and one 'O my Jesus' prayer. While these vocal prayers are recited, the person praying simultaneously meditates on the mystery at hand. Rosary beads are valued not only as a blessed sacramental, but also as an efficacious tool to help keep track of where one is up to in the recitation.

The *Joyful Mysteries* are:

(i) *The Annunciation*: This mystery calls to mind the visit of the Angel Gabriel to the Virgin Mary in Nazareth. Included among the virtues exemplified by this mystery are purity and obedience.

(ii) *The Visitation*: This mystery calls to mind the visit of the Virgin Mary to St Elizabeth in the hills of Judea. Included among the virtues exemplified by this mystery is the love of neighbor in service.

(iii) *The Nativity of Jesus*: This mystery calls to mind the birth of Jesus in Bethlehem. Included among the virtues exemplified by this mystery are love of God and poverty of spirit.

(iv) *The Presentation of the baby Jesus in the Temple*: This mystery calls to mind the purification of the Virgin Mary and the presentation of the baby Jesus in the Temple of Jerusalem. Included among the virtues exemplified by this mystery is obedience to God.

(v) *The Finding of the Child Jesus in the Temple*: This mystery calls to mind the finding of Jesus in the Temple of Jerusalem by the Virgin Mary and St Joseph. Included among the virtues exemplified by this mystery are the desire to always be in the presence of God and a love for Holy Wisdom.

The *Luminous Mysteries* are:

(i) *The Baptism of Jesus*: This mystery calls to mind the baptism of Jesus by John the Baptist in the River Jordan. Included among the virtues exemplified by this mystery is fidelity to our baptismal promises through the Holy Spirit.

(ii) *The Wedding at Cana*: This mystery calls to mind the first public miracle performed by Jesus through the intercession of his holy Mother. Included among the virtues exemplified by this mystery is trust in Jesus through Mary.

(iii) *The Proclamation of the Kingdom of God and the Call to Repentance*: This mystery calls to mind the proclamation by Jesus of his Father's Kingdom on earth. Included among the virtues exemplified by this mystery are repentance and trust in God.

(iv) *The Transfiguration*: This mystery calls to mind the manifestation of Jesus' divinity on Mount Tabor. Included among the virtues exemplified by this mystery are wonder and contempt of the world.

(v) *The Institution of the Eucharist*: This mystery calls to mind the institution of the Holy Eucharist by Jesus at the Last Supper. Included among the virtues exemplified by this mystery is adoration.

The *Sorrowful Mysteries* are:

(i) *The Agony in the Garden*: This mystery calls to mind the agony of Jesus in the Garden of Gethsemane. Included among the virtues exemplified by this mystery are obedience to God's will and sorrow for sin.

(ii) *The Scourging at the Pillar*: This mystery calls to mind the cruel scourging that Jesus received at the hands of the Romans. Included among the virtues exemplified by this mystery are the practise of penance and sorrow for sins of the flesh.

(iii) *The Crowning with Thorns*: This mystery calls to mind the crown of thorns that was placed on and pierced the sacred head of Jesus. Included among the virtues exemplified by this mystery is the practise of moral courage.

(iv) *The Carrying of the Cross*: This mystery calls to mind Jesus carrying his Cross to Mount Calvary. Included among the virtues exemplified by this mystery is perseverance in the love of God and in the spiritual life.

(v) *The Crucifixion on Mount Calvary*: This mystery calls to mind the crucifixion and death of Jesus on the Cross. Included among the virtues exemplified by this mystery are the love of God and the desire for a happy and holy death.

The *Glorious Mysteries* are:

(i) *The Resurrection*: This mystery calls to mind the resurrection on the third day of Jesus from the dead. Included among the virtues exemplified by this mystery are faith in God and hope of heaven.
(ii) *The Ascension*: This mystery calls to mind the ascension of Jesus by his own power into heaven. Included among the virtues exemplified by this mystery is a desire to be with Jesus.
(iii) *The Descent of the Holy Spirit*: This mystery calls to mind the descent of the Holy Spirit on the Virgin Mary and the Apostles on Pentecost Day. Included among the virtues exemplified by this mystery is a zeal for spreading the Faith.
(iv) *The Assumption of the Virgin Mary*: This mystery calls to mind the assumption of the Virgin Mary, body and soul, into heavenly glory by God. Included among the virtues exemplified by this mystery are a love of Mary and true devotion to her.
(v) *The Coronation of the Virgin Mary*: This mystery calls to mind the coronation of the Virgin Mary as Queen of heaven and earth. Included among the virtues exemplified by this mystery is a confident trust in the intercession of the Virgin Mary.

Simply counting beads certainly gets nobody into heaven, but the Holy Rosary is not about bead counting. It is about praying and meditating on the lives of the two greatest persons in history. Meditating on the deeds of the Lord is certainly an action praised by Scripture (Ps. 77:12; Lk 1:49). The sublimity of the first Joyful Mystery alone (the Incarnation) is a truth so awesome that it goes to the heart of God's own love for humanity. Catholics have, for over eight centuries, obtained many spiritual and temporal benefits from the faithful recitation of the Holy Rosary and know that, together with their baptism, faith in Jesus and obeying the Ten Commandments, it will help them get to heaven.

Third objection: *"The Bible condemns repetitious prayer, so how can repeating Hail Marys be right?"*

This objection is usually raised by those Protestants who use the *King James Version* of the Bible which incorrectly translates Matt. 6:7 as follows: "But when ye pray, use not vain repetitions, as the heathen do: for they think that they shall be heard for their much speaking."

The critical Greek word in Matt. 6:7 is *battalogesete* (βατταλογήσητε). It literally means to "babble." The *Revised Standard Version Second Catholic Edition* of the Bible more appropriately renders this verse in these words: "And in praying do not heap up *empty phrases* (babble) as the Gentiles do; for they think that they will be heard for their many words." Jesus was not intending to condemn repetitious prayers *per se* but rather the use of many *empty phrases*. We know this also from the fact that Jesus himself repeated the same prayer in the Garden of Gethsemane three times: "So, leaving them again, he went away and *prayed for the third time, saying the same words*" (Mt 26:44).

Furthermore, it was the custom of the Jews to praise God singing the Psalms in the Temple, in the synagogues and in Jewish homes. Jesus himself would have often sung the Psalms in public and in private. St Paul in Col. 3:16 exhorts Christians to continue in the singing of psalms. Jesus and the early Christians therefore would have often sung Ps. 136, a wonderful example of a prayer that praises God with the words "for his steadfast love endures for ever" repeated twenty-six times! Likewise, the heavenly court of angels continuously recite repetitious prayers before the throne of God: "and day and night they never cease to sing, Holy, holy, holy, is the Lord God Almighty, who was and is and is to come!" (Rev. 4:8).

Finally, Martin Luther had fond words for the *Hail Mary*, and certainly recommended his followers to recite it:

> We can use the Hail Mary as a meditation in which we recite what grace God has given her. Second, we should add a wish that everyone may know and respect her ... He who has no faith is advised to refrain from saying the Hail Mary.[4]

---

[4] Weimer, *The Works of Luther*, Pelikan, Concordia, vol. 43, pp. 39-41.

Fourth objection: *"Why ten Hail Marys and only one Our Father! Is Mary ten times more important for Catholics?"*

No, she is not. There is only one God for Catholics and he is infinitely "more important" than any creature, even one as great as the Virgin Mary. Listen to the words of St Louis Marie Grignon de Montfort (1673-1716), perhaps the greatest Marian devotee in the Church's history:

> I avow, with all the Church, that Mary, being a mere creature that has come from the hands of the Most High, is in comparison with his Infinite Majesty less than an atom; or rather, she is nothing at all, because only he is 'He who is.'[5]

It is erroneous to look at the Our Father and Hail Mary as if they were *ultimately* prayers to two different persons. The Our Father is a prayer *directly* to God the Father through Christ our Lord. The Hail Mary is a prayer *indirectly* to God the Father through the intercession of the Virgin Mary: *"pray for us* sinners, now and at the hour of our death. Amen." Who does the Virgin Mary pray to in heaven but God the Father; and through whom does she go to the Father but her son Jesus? If those in heaven are "a cloud of witnesses" (Heb. 12:1) then why is it wrong for Catholics to ask the Virgin Mary to pray for them, given that St Paul could ask for the prayers of his fellow earth-bound Christians who yet did not possess the vision of God (Rom. 15:30; Heb. 13:18)?

Lastly, as the Holy Rosary is a devotion honoring and invoking the Virgin Mary it should not be so surprising that it has such a pronounced Marian flavor to it. The fact that there are ten Hail Marys also gives ample time to the devotee to meditate on the mystery in question, mysteries which all relate to the lives of *Jesus and Mary*.

Fifth objection: *"The Rosary is a legacy of paganism; therefore the Catholic Church is pagan for promoting it!"*

---

[5] St Louis de Montfort, *True Devotion to Mary*, TAN Books and Publishers, Rockford, Illinois, 1985, ch. 1, #14.

This type of objection is often raised by those who habitually oppose Catholic practices not because there is anything intrinsically wrong with them, but simply because they are distinctly Catholic. Cardinal John Henry Newman (1801-1890) showed that many pagan practices have entered both Catholic and Protestant cultures – such as the use of wedding rings in marriage – without bringing with them elements of the pagan religion that begot them. The use of beads in prayer is also found in Islam and in Buddhism, for example, but there is no connection between such usage and the use of Rosary beads in Catholicism. Even if there were any connection, it could not be shown that any peculiar Islamic or Buddhist beliefs have thereby been incorporated into Catholicism. The claim that the Holy Rosary has pagan origins and is simply a mask to bring about the paganization of Christianity has no foundation whatsoever. In any case, the Holy Rosary is not based on the beads, but upon the prayers said and the mysteries meditated upon.

St Louis de Montfort relates the real origin of the Holy Rosary in his book *The Secret of the Rosary*:

> It was only in the year 1214, however, that the Church received the Rosary in its present form and according to the method we use today. It was given to the Church by St Dominic, who had received it from the Blessed Virgin as a means of converting the Albigensians and other sinners.[6]

The Albigensians were Gnostic heretics who believed in the existence of two Gods – one good God who created the spiritual world and one equally powerful evil god who created the physical world. The Albigensians were extremely violent and possessed a distinct hatred for Catholicism.

Saint Louis de Montfort continues:

> I will tell you the story of how he received it, which is found in the very well-known book *De Dignitate Psalterii*, by Blessed

---

[6] *The Secret of the Rosary*, TAN Books & Publishers Inc., Rockford, Illinois, 1987, Second Rose.

Alan de la Roche. Saint Dominic, seeing that the gravity of people's sins was hindering the conversion of the Albigensians, withdrew into a forest near Toulouse, where he prayed continuously for three days and three nights. During this time he did nothing but weep and do harsh penances in order to appease the anger of God. He used his discipline so much that his body was lacerated, and finally he fell into a coma ... At this point our Lady appeared to him, accompanied by three angels, and she said, 'Dear Dominic, do you know which weapon the Blessed Trinity wants to use to reform the world?' 'Oh, my Lady,' answered Saint Dominic, 'you know far better than I do, because next to your Son Jesus Christ you have always been the chief instrument of our salvation'... Then our Lady replied, 'I want you to know that, in this kind of warfare, the principal weapon has always been the Angelic Psalter, which is the foundation-stone of the New Testament. Therefore, if you want to reach these hardened souls and win them over to God, preach my Psalter (Rosary).'[7]

St Dominic then proceeded to preach the Holy Rosary and its popularity spread rapidly. However, due to the subsequent laxity of the people, it slowly fell out of popular use. It was not until the fifteenth century, after Blessed Alan de la Roche received a heavenly vision, that the use of the Holy Rosary was revived. In two separate revelations from Jesus and Mary, Blessed Alan was told of the great power that the Holy Rosary possessed to convert people and cultivate virtue. Jesus clearly teaches that a tree is known by its fruit (Lk 6:44). Nobody can deny that the greatest Catholic saints since the time of St Dominic were those who faithfully recited the Holy Rosary.

Sixth objection: *"The Catholic Church admits that the Rosary was invented by St Dominic in the thirteenth century. However, how is this consistent with the Church's teaching that there cannot be any new revelation after the death of the last Apostle?"*

In answering this objection one must first make clear the Church's distinction between *public* and *private* revelation. The

---

[7] *Ibid.*

Catholic Church certainly admits that public revelation ended with the death of the last Apostle, St John. Nothing can be added to the Deposit of Faith finally delivered once and for all by Jesus to the Apostles. All Christians without exception must accept and believe entirely what is contained in public revelation. What is allowed, however, is a legitimate 'development of doctrine,' that is, a deeper and greater understanding of truths already revealed and believed. One finds an example of this in the history of the doctrines of the Blessed Trinity and the divinity of Jesus. It was not until centuries after the Apostolic age that clear and unequivocal formal solemn definitions were made by the Church, delineating the precise parameters of these beliefs. None of these formal pronouncements, however, contradicted the explicit and implicit statements found in the Scriptures. The same is the case with regards the Marian dogmas.

Private revelation is another matter. Many apparitions of Jesus, Mary, and so on, are alleged to have occurred over the centuries. Often one or more individuals also claim to receive messages meant either for them or for the whole world. Such is the case with the apparitions of the Sacred Heart (1673-1689), Rue du Bac (1830), Lourdes (1858) and Fatima (1917), for example. Whether an apparition is from God or otherwise is a matter for the Church to determine. Even if the Church looks favorably upon an alleged apparition, it will simply declare that it is "worthy of belief." This does not constitute a formal positive declaration that the apparition did occur and that it is from God, but rather a negative declaration that the apparition and its purported messages contain nothing contrary to formal Church teachings and that the evidence for it has been carefully investigated. Consequently, there is no obligation on Catholics to believe in private apparitions even when approved.

Such is the case with the apparition of the Virgin Mary to St Dominic and the Rosary. The Catholic Church does not regard the Rosary and its recitation as being a part of or required by public revelation. The Church recommends the praying of it as worthy and beneficial for her children; she does not insist on its recitation as necessary for salvation. In any case, the Rosary is a pious devotion, not a doctrine.

The Fathers[8]

St Ephrem of Edessa, *Songs of Praise* **1, 1; 1, 2 (ante AD 373)**
"Awake, my harp, your songs
in praise of the Virgin Mary!
Lift up your voice and sing
the wonderful history
of the Virgin, the daughter of David,
who gave birth to the Life of the World.
Who loves you is amazed
and who would understand
is silent and confused,
because he cannot probe the Mother
who gave birth in her virginity.
If it is too great to be clarified
with words the disputants
ought not on that account
cross swords with your Son."

St Athanasius, *Homily of the Papyrus of Turin* **71:216 (ante AD 373)**
"O noble Virgin, truly you are greater than any other greatness. For who is your equal in greatness, O dwelling place of God the Word? To whom among all creatures shall I compare you, O Virgin? You are greater than them all, O Covenant, clothed with purity instead of gold! You are the Ark in which is found the golden vessel containing the true manna, that is, the flesh in which divinity resides."

Liturgy of St James the Less **(ante fifth century AD)**
"Our most holy, immaculate, and most glorious Lady, Mother of God and ever Virgin Mary."

---

[8] Being a development of medieval piety, the Holy Rosary was unknown to the Fathers. Nevertheless, the Fathers make countless references to the Blessed Virgin Mary and composed prayers praising her and invoking her intercession.

St Epiphanius of Salamis, *Prayers in Praise of Mary* **(ante AD 440)**
"God alone excepted, she was superior to all ... to Cherubim and Seraphim, and the whole angelic host ... Hail full of grace, who satisfies the thirsty with the sweetness of the eternal fountain. Hail most holy Mother Immaculate, who didst bring forth Jesus."

The *Akathist Hymn* **I, Oikos, Alpha (inter fifth-sixth century AD)**
Hail! by whom true hap had dawned.
Hail! by whom mishap has waned.
Hail! sinful Adam's recalling.
Hail! Eve's tears redeeming.
Hail! height untrodden by thought of men.
Hail! depth unscanned by angel's ken.
Hail! for the kingly throne thou art.
Hail! for who beareth all that thou bearest?
Hail! O star that bore the Sun.
Hail! the womb of God enfleshed.
Hail! through whom things made are all new made.
Hail! through whom becomes a Babe their Maker.
Hail! through whom the Maker is adorned.
HAIL! BRIDE UNBRIDED.

St Germain I of Constantinople, *Sermon on the Dormition of the Blessed Virgin Mary* **2 (ante AD 733)**
"Let death pass you by, O Mother of God, because you have brought life to men. Let the tomb pass you by, because you have been made the foundation stone of inexplicable sublimity. Let dust pass you by; for you are a new kind of formation, so that you may be mistress over those who have been corrupted in the very stuff of their potter's clay."

St John Damascene, *First Homily on the Dormition of the Virgin* **14 (inter AD 725-749)**
"We today also remain near you, O Lady. Yes, I repeat, O Lady, Mother of God and Virgin. We bind our souls to your hope, as to a most firm and totally unbreakable anchor, consecrating to you mind, soul, body, and all our being and honoring you, as much as we can, with psalms, hymns, and spiritual canticles."

The Roman Catechism (1566)[9]

Pt. IV, Ch. VI: To this sort of prayer belongs the first part of the Angelic Salutation, when used by us as a prayer: *Hail Mary, full of grace, the Lord is with thee, blessed art thou among women.* For in these words we render to God the highest praise and return him gracious thanks, because he has bestowed all his heavenly gifts on the most holy Virgin; and at the same time we congratulate the Virgin herself on her singular privileges.

To this form of thanksgiving the Church of God has wisely added prayers and an invocation addressed to the most holy Mother of God, by which we piously and humbly fly to her patronage, in order that, by her intercession, she may reconcile God to us sinners and may obtain for us those blessings which we stand in need of in this life and in the life to come. We, therefore, exiled children of Eve, who dwell in this vale of tears, should constantly beseech the Mother of mercy, the advocate of the faithful, to pray for us sinners. In this prayer we should earnestly implore her help and assistance; for that she is most desirous to assist us by her prayers, no one can doubt without impiety and wickedness.

Catechism of the Catholic Church (1992)

No. 2678: Medieval piety in the West developed the prayer of the rosary as a popular substitute for the Liturgy of the Hours. In the East, the litany called the *Akathistos* and the *Paraclesis* remained closer to the choral office in the Byzantine churches, while the Armenian, Coptic and Syriac traditions preferred popular hymns and songs to the Mother of God. But in the *Ave Maria*, the *theotokia*, the hymns of St Ephrem or St Gregory of Narek, the tradition of prayer is basically the same.

---

[9] The Roman Catechism made no reference to the Holy Rosary, but it did refer to the *Hail Mary* and highly extolled the value of Marian prayers.

Guardian Angels

Objection: *"As for guardian angels, they are a belief imported into Catholicism from the pagan Assyrians and Babylonians. God can help us without them!"*

God can certainly help us without the aid of any intermediary or creature. Nevertheless, that he wills to use intermediaries is evident in the Scriptures. It is Church teaching that every person has allotted to them a Guardian Angel by God. It is clear from both the Old and New Testaments that angels are God's ministers who carry out his will, and at appointed times are allotted special commissions to intervene in human affairs.

According to St Thomas Aquinas (S.T., I, q. 112, a. 4) only the lower five choirs of angels are sent to us as guardians. Guardian Angels can act upon our senses and our imaginations, and, through these faculties, upon our wills. Not only the baptized, but also every person, including children, receives a Guardian Angel, who remains with us even in heaven. In the opinion of many Church Fathers and other holy writers, every country, city, town and village also has a Guardian Angel. Altars, churches, parishes, dioceses and religious institutions do likewise. Even the Antichrist will have a Guardian Angel, who will restrain him from committing otherwise greater evils.

The good offices performed by the Guardian Angels on our behalf can be summarized as follows[1]:

(i) They preserve us from many unknown dangers to soul and body.
(ii) They defend us against the temptations of evil spirits.
(iii) They inspire in us holy thoughts and prompt us to deeds of virtue.
(iv) They warn us of upcoming spiritual dangers.

---

[1] See, The Benedictine Convent of Perpetual Adoration, *The Guardian Angels – Our Heavenly Companions*, TAN Books & Publishers Inc., Rockford, Illinois, 1996, pp. 8-10 & 16.

(v) They admonish us when we have sinned.
(vi) They unite their prayers with ours and offer them up to God.
(vii) They defend us at the hour of death against the last attacks of the demons.
(viii) They console the souls in Purgatory and conduct them to heaven after they have expiated their sins.

In Scripture, the doctrine of Guardian Angels is given no special consideration, but, is rather taken for granted:

"The two angels came to Sodom in the evening; and Lot was sitting in the gate of Sodom. When Lot saw them, he rose to meet them, and bowed himself with his face to the earth ... When morning dawned, the angels urged Lot, saying, 'Arise, take your wife and your two daughters who are here, lest you be consumed in the punishment of the city'" (Gen. 19:1 & 15).

"Behold, I send an angel before you, to guard you on the way and to bring you to the place which I have prepared. Give heed to him and hearken to his voice, do not rebel against him, for he will not pardon your transgression; for my name is in him" (Exod. 23:20-21).

"But now go, lead the people to the place of which I have spoken to you; behold, my angel shall go before you. Nevertheless, in the day when I visit, I will visit their sin upon them" (Exod. 32:34).

"The prayer of both was heard in the presence of the glory of the great God. And Raphael was sent to heal the two of them" (Tob. 3:16-17).

"The angel of the Lord encamps around those who fear him, and delivers them" (Ps. 34:7).

"For he will give his angels charge of you to guard you in all your ways" (Ps. 91:11).

"... but the prince (angel) of the kingdom of Persia stood in my way for twenty-one days, until finally Michael, one of the chief princes, came to help me. I left

him there with the prince of the kings of Persia, and came to make you understand what shall happen to your people in the days to come; for there is yet a vision concerning those days ... but I shall tell you what is written in the truthful book. No one supports me against all these except Michael, your prince" (Dan. 10:13-14, 21).

"At that time there shall arise Michael, the great prince, guardian of your people" (Dan. 12:1).

"When Maccabeus and his men got word that Lysias was besieging the strongholds, they and all the people, with lamentations and tears, besought the Lord to send a good angel to save Israel" (2 Macc. 11:6).

In the New Testament, the doctrine of Guardian Angels is stated more precisely:

"See that you do not despise one of these little ones; for I tell you that in heaven their angels always behold the face of my Father who is in heaven" (Mt 18:10).

"But the high priest rose up and all who were with him, that is, the party of the Sadducees, and filled with jealousy they arrested the apostles and put them in the common prison. But at night an angel of the Lord opened the prison doors and brought them out and said, 'Go and stand in the temple and speak to the people all the words of this Life'" (Acts 5:17-20).

"And Peter came to himself, and said, 'Now I am sure that the Lord has sent his angel and rescued me from the hand of Herod and from all that the Jewish people were expecting.' When he realized this, he went to the house of Mary, the mother of John whose other name was Mark, where many were gathered together and were praying. And when he knocked at the door of the gateway, a maid named Rhoda came to answer. Recognizing Peter's voice, in her joy she did not open the gate but ran in and told that Peter was standing at the gate. They said to her, 'You are mad.' But she insisted that it was so. They said, 'It is his angel!'" (Acts 12:11-15).

"Are they not all ministering spirits sent forth to serve, for the sake of those who are to obtain salvation?" (Heb. 1:14).

Nor does the ministry of the angels cease at death:

"The poor man died and was carried by the angels to Abraham's bosom" (Lk 16:22).

St Michael was the special protector of Israel and is now invoked as the guardian of the Christian faithful against the wickedness and snares of Satan. The Church sets aside 2 October to honor the Guardian Angels. How we should love our Guardian Angels and invoke their aid all the days of our lives!

> Angel of God, my guardian dear,
> to whom God's love commits me here,
> ever this day be at my side,
> to light and guard, to rule and guide.
> Amen.

The Fathers

The Shepherd of Hermas Parable 5, 6, 2 (inter AD 140-155)
"God planted the vineyard," (the shepherd) said: "that is, he created the people, and gave them over to his Son. And the Son appointed the angels to guard over them; and he himself cleansed them of their sins, laboring much and undergoing much toil."

Clement of Alexandria, *Miscellanies* 6, 17, 157, 4 (ante AD 217)
"The thoughts of virtuous men are produced by divine inspiration. The soul is disposed in the way it is, and the will of God is conveyed to human souls, by special divine ministers who assist in such service. For regiments of angels are distributed over nations and cities; and perhaps some even are assigned to particular individuals."

Origen, *Homilies on Luke* Hom. 12 (inter AD 233-254)
"To every man there are two attending angels, the one of justice and the other of wickedness. If there be good thoughts in our heart, and if righteousness be welling up in our soul, it can scarcely be doubted that

an angel of the Lord is speaking to us. If, however, the thoughts of our heart be turned to evil, an angel of the devil is speaking to us."

St Basil the Great, *Against Eunomius* **3, 1 (c. AD 364)**
"All the angels, having but one appellation, have likewise among themselves the same nature, even though some of them are set over nations, while others of them are guardians to each one of the faithful."

St Hilary of Poitiers, *Commentaries on the Psalms* **On Ps. 129:7 (c. AD 365)**
"We recall that there are many spiritual powers, to whom the name angels is given, or presidents of churches. There are, according to John, angels of the Churches in Asia. And there were, as Moses bears witness, when the sons of Adam were separated, bounds appointed for the peoples according to the number of the angels. And, as the Lord teaches, there are for little children, angels who see God daily. There are, as Raphael told Tobias, angels assisting before the majesty of God, carrying to God the prayers of suppliants. Mention is made of all this, because you might wish to understand these angels as the eyes, or the ears, or the hands, or the feet of God ... It is not the nature of God, but the weakness of men, which requires their service. For they are sent for the sake of those who will inherit salvation. God is not unaware of anything that we do; but in our weakness we are impoverished for a minister of spiritual intercession in the matter of beseeching and propitiating."

The Roman Catechism (1566)

Pt. IV, Ch. IX: By God's providence Angels have been entrusted with the office of guarding the human race and of accompanying every human being in order to preserve him from serious dangers ... our heavenly Father has placed over each of us an Angel under whose protection and vigilance we may be enabled to escape the snares secretly prepared by our enemy, repel the dreadful attacks he makes on us, and under his guiding hand keep to the right road, and thus be secure against false steps which the wiles of the evil one might cause us to make in order to draw us aside from the path that leads to heaven.

(Sacred Scripture shows) the benefits bestowed by God on man through the ministry and intervention of Angels, whom he deputes not only on particular and private occasions, but also appoints to take care of us from our very births. He furthermore appoints them to watch over the salvation of each one of the human race.

Catechism of the Catholic Church (1992)

No. 336: From infancy to death human life is surrounded by their watchful care and intercession. "Beside each believer stands an angel as protector and shepherd leading him to life." Already here on earth the Christian life shares by faith in the blessed company of angels and men united in God.

The Immortality of the Soul

Objection: *"Humans do not have souls; they are souls."*

The Catholic Church teaches that, as human beings, we have spiritual souls that make us in the image and likeness of God. This is inferred from the first chapter of Genesis, which says, "So God created man in his own image, in the image of God he created him; male and female he created them" (Gen. 1:27). Since God does not have a body by nature, we cannot be in his image and likeness in any physical sense; rather, given that God is pure spirit we must reflect him through having a spiritual element, or soul. The existence of the human soul is reinforced by the fact that the Old and New Testaments refer to it no less than two hundred and seventy-nine times.

However, there are some such as the Jehovah's Witnesses and Seventh-Day Adventists who deny that God created man with a living soul; rather, they believe God created man *as* a living soul. They base their arguments on Gen. 2:7, which says, "Then the Lord God formed man of dust from the ground, and breathed into his nostrils the breath of life; *and man became a living soul*." Therefore, there seems to be no distinction between man's body and soul — man with his living body *is* a soul. The same argue that the notion of the soul as a separate immaterial and immortal entity has its origins in the Egyptian and Babylonian belief in metempsychosis (transmigration of the soul) and was eventually imported into Christianity from Platonic and neo-Platonic writings by early Church Fathers such as Origen and St Augustine.

Nevertheless, despite such claims Scripture clearly speaks of the human soul or spirit in terms distinct from the body. For example:

"Watch and pray that you may not enter into temptation; the spirit indeed is willing, but the flesh is weak" (Mt 26:41).

"And I will say to my soul, 'Soul, you have ample goods laid up for many years; take your ease, eat, drink, be merry.' But God said to him, 'Fool! This night your soul is required of you; and the things you have prepared, whose will they be?' So is he who lays up treasure for himself, and is not rich toward God"* (Lk 12:19-21).

"So we do not lose heart. Though our outer man is wasting away, our inner nature is being renewed every day" (2 Cor. 4:16).

"Since we have these promises, beloved, let us cleanse ourselves from every defilement of body and spirit, and make holiness perfect in the fear of God" (2 Cor. 7:1).

"May the God of peace himself sanctify you wholly; and may your spirit and soul and body be kept sound and blameless at the coming of our Lord Jesus Christ" (1 Thess. 5:23).

Together, these verses speak of the spirit as something prone to conflict with the flesh, our outer (the body) and inner (the soul) natures as capable of moving in opposite directions of decay and renewal, and repeatedly call upon us to cleanse our bodies and spirit and keep them both blameless. How can such distinctions be made if the soul and the living body are one and the same thing?

Second objection: *"Scripture is clear that at death the soul is extinguished. It no longer knows anything for it no longer exists."*

There are two categories of persons who assert that the human soul does not consciously live on after death: (i) *hypnopsychites*, who believe that the departed soul passes into a state of unconsciousness at death; (ii) *thnetopsychites*, who believe that the departed soul is either permanently (in the case of the wicked) or temporarily (in the case of the Just) destroyed. The latter usually point to verses of Scripture such as Eccles. 9:5-6 in support, which says:

*"For the living know that they will die, but the dead know nothing, and they have no more reward; but the memory of them is lost. Their love and their hate

and their envy have already perished, and they have no more for ever any share in all that is done under the sun."

However, on closer inspection this verse does not actually assert that the souls of the dead are extinguished by death; rather, its purpose is to emphasize how the dead no longer have anything to do with the world or any part in the lives of those still living.

On the other hand, there are numerous verses of Scripture that clearly assert the opposite, that the soul after death still has existence, life and knowledge and will enjoy the vision of God and the companionship of Jesus:

"Precious in the sight of the Lord is the death of his saints" (Ps. 116:15).

How can the death of saints be "precious" in the sight of the Lord if the soul ceases to exist at death?

"The poor man died and was carried by the angels to Abraham's bosom. The rich man also died and was buried; and in Hades, being in torment, he lifted up his eyes, and saw Abraham far off and Lazarus in his bosom. And he called out, 'Father Abraham, have mercy upon me, and send Lazarus to dip the end of his finger in water and cool my tongue; for I am in anguish in this flame.' But Abraham said, 'Son, remember that you in your lifetime received your good things, and Lazarus in like manner evil things; but now he is comforted here, and you are in anguish'" (Lk 16:22-25).

How can Lazarus and the rich man be "carried," see "Father Abraham," "call out," be "comforted," and suffer in "anguish" if the soul ceases to exist at death?

"And as he was praying, the appearance of his countenance was altered, and his raiment became dazzling white. And behold, two men talked with him, Moses and Elijah, who appeared in glory and spoke of his departure, which he was to accomplish at Jerusalem" (Lk 9:29-31).

How could Moses, who died centuries before the coming of Jesus, appear "in glory" and speak to Jesus if the soul ceases to exist at death?

"Jesus said to her, 'I am the resurrection and the life; he who believes in me, though he die, yet shall he live, and whoever lives and believes in me shall never die. Do you believe this?'" (Jn 11:25-26).

How can those who die believing in Jesus "yet shall ... live" if the soul ceases to exist at death?

"For I am sure that neither death, nor life, nor angels, nor principalities, nor things present, nor things to come, nor powers, nor height, nor depth, nor anything else in all creation, will be able to separate us from the love of God in Christ Jesus our Lord" (Rom. 8:38-39).

How can "death" not separate the Christian from "the love of God" if the soul ceases to exist at death?

"And just as it is appointed for men to die once, and after that comes judgment" (Heb. 9:27).

How can men be judged after death if the soul ceases to exist at death?

"For Christ also died for sins once for all, the righteous for the unrighteous, that he might bring us to God, being put to death in the flesh but made alive in the spirit; in which he went and preached to the spirits in prison" (1 Pet. 3:18-19).

How could Jesus after his own death preach "to the spirits in prison" if the soul ceases to exist at death?

"For this is why the gospel was preached even to the dead, that though judged in the flesh like men, they might live in the spirit like God" (1 Pet. 4:6).

How could Jesus proclaim the gospel "even to the dead" if the soul ceases to exist at death?

"When he opened the fifth seal, I saw under the altar the souls of those who had been slain for the word of God and for the witness they had borne; they cried out with a loud voice, 'O Sovereign Lord, holy and true, how long before thou wilt judge and avenge our blood on those who dwell upon the earth?' Then they were each given a white robe and told to rest a little longer, until the number of their fellow servants and their brethren should be complete, who were to be killed as they themselves had been" (Rev. 6:9-11).

How could martyred Christians be "under the altar" and cry "out with a loud voice" to God for vengeance if the soul ceases to exist at death?

"And I heard a voice from heaven saying, 'Write this: Blessed are the dead who die in the Lord henceforth.' 'Blessed indeed.' says the Spirit, 'that they may rest from their labors, for their deeds follow!'" (Rev. 14:13).

How could the dead be "blessed" and have their "deeds follow them" if the soul ceases to exist at death?

Third objection: *"Since the soul is annihilated at death there is no eternal punishment for the wicked."*

Most who reject belief in eternal punishment for the wicked do so because they cannot reconcile such with belief in a loving and forgiving God. They either believe that hell is temporary, or everyone goes to heaven, or hell does not exist at all. The Jehovah's Witnesses go further, claiming that eternal punishment is a deceitful lie invented by the devil; rather, they believe hell is the grave, not fiery torment. Seventh-Day Adventists regard belief in eternal torment as a syncretic doctrine acquired from mythological and Gnostic writings. The reality is that Scripture has a host of passages that clearly teach that the wicked continue to exist after death and suffer eternal hell-fire. The following are just a few examples:

"I tell you, many will come from east and west and sit at table with Abraham, Isaac, and Jacob in the kingdom of heaven, while the sons of the kingdom will be thrown into the outer darkness; there men will weep and gnash their teeth" (Mt 8:11-12).

"And do not fear those who kill the body but cannot kill the soul; rather fear him who can destroy both soul and body in hell" (Mt 10:28).

"The Son of man will send his angels, and they will gather out of his kingdom all causes of sin and all evildoers, and throw them into the furnace of fire; there men will weep and gnash their teeth" (Mt 13:41-42).

"Woe to the world for temptations to sin! For it is necessary that temptations come, but woe to the man by whom the temptation comes! And if your hand or your foot causes you to sin, cut it off and throw it away; it is better for you to enter life maimed or lame than with two hands or two feet to be thrown into the eternal fire. And if your eye causes you to sin, pluck it out and throw it away; it is better for you to enter life with one eye than with two eyes to be thrown into the hell of fire" (Mt 18:7-9).

"Then he will say to those at his left hand, 'Depart from me, you cursed, into the eternal fire prepared for the devil and his angels' ... And they will go away into eternal punishment, but the righteous into eternal life" (Mt 25:41 & 46).

"The poor man died and was carried by the angels to Abraham's bosom. The rich man also died and was buried; and in Hades, being in torment, he lifted up his eyes, and saw Abraham far off and Lazarus in his bosom. And he called out, 'Father Abraham, have mercy upon me, and send Lazarus to dip the end of his finger in water and cool my tongue; for I am in anguish in this flame'" (Lk 16:22-24).

"And the beast was captured, and with it the false prophet who in its presence had worked the signs by which he deceived those who had received the mark of the beast and those who worshiped its image. These two were thrown alive into the lake of fire that burns with sulphur" (Rev. 19:20).

"Then I saw thrones, and seated on them were those to whom judgment was committed. Also I saw the souls of those who had been beheaded for their testimony to Jesus and for the word of God, and who had not worshiped the *beast or its image and had not received its mark on their foreheads or their hands. They came to life, and reigned with Christ a thousand years"* (Rev. 20:4).

"... and if any one's name was not found written in the book of life, he was thrown into the lake of fire" (Rev. 20:15).

Of all these verses, let us look briefly at how the Jehovah's Witnesses respond to just one, namely Matt. 25:46. In the Greek of this verse we find the word κόλασιν (kolasin), which is derived from κολάζω (kolazo), and means to prune, rest, or punish. The Jehovah's Witnesses' *New World Translation* translates κόλασιν in v. 46 as "everlasting cutting-off" rather than "eternal punishment." At first instance, such a translation is defensible as "cutting-off" is akin to "prune." However, the same *New World Translation* translates another derivative of κολάζω, namely κολάσωνται (kolasontai), in Acts 4:21 as "to punish." This is an obvious inconsistency in translation and brings into serious question both the sincerity of the Jehovah's Witnesses and the authenticity of their *New World Translation*.

Fourth objection: *"All souls are annihilated at death but the good are recreated at the end of the world for heaven or earthly paradise."*

This objection reflects the view of the *thnetopsychites* that the souls of the just are annihilated at death and will enjoy eternal life only after being resurrected at the end of the world. On the contrary, the following verses of Scripture prove that the souls of the Just continue to live on and receive their ultimate reward immediately after death:

"But the souls of the righteous are in the hand of God, and no torment will ever touch them. In the eyes of the foolish they seemed to have died, and their departure was thought to be an affliction, and their going from us to be their destruction; but they are at peace" (Wis. 3:1-3).

How can the "souls of the righteous" be "in the hand of God" and be "at peace" if they were annihilated at death?

"So we are always of good courage; we know that while we are at home in the body we are away from the Lord, for we walk by faith, not by sight. We are of good courage, and we would rather be away from the body and at home with the Lord. So whether we are at home or away, we make it our aim to please him. For we must all appear before the judgment seat of Christ, so that each one may receive good or evil, according to what he has done in the body" (2 Cor. 5:6-10).

How could St Paul desire to be "away from the body and at home with the Lord" if he believed that the soul is annihilated at death?

"For to me to live is Christ, and to die is gain. If it is to be life in the flesh, that means fruitful labor for me. Yet which I shall choose I cannot tell. I am hard pressed between the two. My desire is to depart and be with Christ, for that is far better" (Phil. 1:21-23).

How could St Paul desire to "depart and be with Christ" if he believed that the soul is annihilated at death?

"But you have come to Mount Zion and to the city of the living God, the heavenly Jerusalem, and to innumerable angels in festal gathering, and to the assembly of the first-born who are enrolled in heaven, and to a judge who is God of all, and to the spirits of just men made perfect" (Heb. 12:22-23).

How can there be an "assembly of the first-born" and "the spirits of just men made perfect" in "the heavenly Jerusalem" if the soul is annihilated at death?

Fifth objection: *"There is no such thing as a soul. Humans are only material beings."*

Atheism is steadily growing in the Western world and with it the denial of the spiritual, including the human soul. Those who deny the existence of the spiritual can be loosely termed 'materialists.' Materialists view the human person as simply an organized conglomeration of purely material elements, while thought, will and self-consciousness are nothing more than functions of organic matter.

On the other hand, the Catholic Church considers the human person to be a unity of body and soul and that the soul is spiritual in nature, meaning that it does not have component parts and does not occupy space (i.e., it is 'simple'). As souls do not have component parts they cannot be broken down like the body; hence, human souls by their very nature can live beyond the death of the body.

The Catholic Church also looks at the human activities of reasoning, reflecting and willing differently to materialists. How can a human have ideas and understand non-material spiritual concepts such as truth and justice if he/she is only a material being? A human can only have spiritual ideas and understandings if he/she has a non-material, spiritual side, or soul. The irony is that materialists reason and declare against the existence of the spiritual using spiritual powers – namely, the intellect and will.

Materialists are still struggling as to why there exists self-consciousness, thought, etc. For Christianity, it is clear – consciousness and personhood exist because God created humans in his image and likeness. Humans have a created ability to know, understand, judge and love that reflects the Creator who is Knowledge and Love.

The Fathers

St Irenaeus of Lyons, *Against Heresies* 5, 7, 1 (c. AD 180)
"For to die is to lose the vital ability and to become henceforth without breath and inanimate and incommunicative, and to melt away into those elements from which it had the beginning of substance. But this happens neither to the soul, for it is the breath of life, nor to the spirit, for it is simple spirit and not a composite, and cannot be decomposed, and is itself the life of those who receive it."

Tertullian, *The Soul* 58, 1 (inter AD 208-212)
"Therefore and on this account it is most fitting that the soul, without waiting for the flesh, be punished for what it did without the partnership of the flesh. And for pious and benevolent thoughts in

which it shared not with the flesh, without the flesh it shall be refreshed."

Origen, *Fundamental Doctrines* 1, Preface, 5 (ante AD 253-254)
"After these points, it is taught also that the soul, having a substance and life proper to itself, shall, after its departure from this world, be rewarded according to its merits. It is destined to obtain either an inheritance of eternal life and blessedness, if its deeds shall have procured this for it, or to be delivered up to eternal fires and punishments, if the guilt of its crimes shall have brought it down to this."

St Basil the Great, *Homilies on the Psalms* Ps. 7, no. 2 (ante AD 370)
"I think that the noble athletes of God, who have wrestled all their lives with the invisible enemies, after they have escaped all of their persecutions and have come to the end of life, are examined by the prince of this world; and if they are found to have any wounds from their wrestling, any stains or effects of sin, they are detained. If, however, they are found unwounded and without stain, they are, as unconquered, brought by Christ into their rest."

St Epiphanius of Salamis, *Against all Heresies* 75, 8 (inter AD 374-377)
"What is more timely or more excellent than that those who are still here should believe that the departed do live, and that they have not retreated into nothingness, but that they exist and are alive with the Master? And so that this most august proclamation might be told in full, how do they have hope, who are praying for the brethren as if they were but sojourning in a foreign land?"

St Augustine of Hippo, *The City of God* 21, 3, 1 (inter AD 413-426)
"Death will be eternal when the soul will not be able to possess God and live, nor to die and escape the pains of the body. The first death drives the soul from the body against her will; the second death holds the soul in the body against her will."

The Roman Catechism (1566)

Pt. I, Ch. XI: That in this Article the resurrection of mankind is called *the resurrection of the body*, is a circumstance which deserves special attention. It was not, indeed, so named without a reason; for the Apostles intended thus to convey a necessary truth, the immortality of the soul. Lest anyone, despite the fact that many passages of Scripture plainly teach that the soul is immortal, might imagine that it dies with the body, and that both are to be restored to life, the Creed speaks only of *the resurrection of the body*.

Catechism of the Catholic Church (1992)

No. 366: The Church teaches that every spiritual soul is created immediately by God – it is not "produced" by the parents – and also that it is immortal: it does not perish when it separates from the body at death, and it will be reunited with the body at the final Resurrection.

The Invocation of Saints

Objection: *"To worship saints, like Mary, is likewise idolatry!"*

No practice of the Catholic Church has received more attention and criticism from her opponents than the ancient custom of honoring the heroic servants of God. She is charged with idolatry and superstition.

The various Protestant denominations denounce the invocation of saints as follows:

> It cannot be proved from the Scriptures that we are to invoke the saints or seek help from them. "For there is one mediator between God and men, Christ Jesus" (1 Tim. 2:5) who is the only savior, the only high priest, advocate and intercessor before God.[1]

> (It is) the extreme of stupidity, not to say madness, to attempt to obtain access by means of others, so as to be drawn away from him without whom access cannot be obtained.[2]

> The Romish doctrine concerning ... (the) invocation of saints is a fond thing, vainly invented, and grounded upon no warranty of Scripture, but is rather, repugnant to the Word of God.[3]

The Church has been in existence nearly two thousand years. She has on her list of known saints many thousands of names of men and women to whom she pays real religious homage. However, never in her history has she given adoration to them. The Catholic Church makes a complete and clear distinction between the supreme worship that is given to God alone and the relative and inferior homage that is paid to the saints.

---

[1] *The Augsburg Confession*, Article 21 (Lutherans, 1530).
[2] John Calvin, *Institutes of the Christian Religion*, 28 (1559).
[3] *39 Articles of Religion*, Article 22 (Church of England, 1563).

Catholics have always distinguished emphatically between the *cultus duliae*, which translates as 'the homage of veneration,' and the *cultus latriae*, which signifies 'the worship of adoration.'

Veneration is paid to the saints. A higher form of it, called *hyperdulia*, is given to the Blessed Virgin Mary by virtue of her singular privilege as Mother of God; but adoration is given to God alone. Any attempt to give adoration to a creature would certainly be false worship – but the Catholic Church has never given it. She adores God and God alone.

It is noteworthy that while Jesus was dying on the Cross he cried out, *"Eli, Eli, lama sabachthani?"* (Mt 27:46). Due to the distance, the chief priests and scribes failed to discern that Jesus was in fact quoting the first verse of Ps. 21, thinking instead that he was calling upon the Prophet Elijah. Their response was not to condemn Jesus for idolatry, but rather to declare, "let us see whether Elijah will come to save him" (v. 49). The belief in the intercessory power of Elijah is still held by the Jews today, as Elijah is said to be invisibly present at all Brit Millah, or circumcision ceremonies.

Second objection: *"If the Catholic Church adores only God then why do Catholics speak of praying to the saints?"*

In traditional English usage, the word 'pray' simply meant to 'ask.' It was common for people to speak to each other in the following terms: "I pray thee, do tell;" or, "I pray thee, do grant me my request." In Shakespeare, the word "prithee" is often found – a contraction of "I pray thee." In the King James Version of the Bible, Bathsheba makes a request of King Solomon and says, "do not refuse me" (1 Kgs 2:20). We still find 'pray' being used in such a way in various courtrooms to this day. However, with the Protestantization of the English-speaking world, the word 'pray' lost its broader meaning and was restricted to God alone. This was in conformity with Protestant theology that refuses to make any distinction within the concept of worship between adoration and veneration.

Despite the persecution of Catholics in England, they never abandoned the older usage of the word 'pray.' When Catholics today speak of 'praying to the saints' they simply mean asking them to intercede on their behalf. There is no intention or desire to give them that worship which is due to God alone.

Third objection: *"Nevertheless, there is only one mediator between God and man, Jesus Christ!"*

The most common Protestant objection to the intercession of the saints is that it diminishes the intercessory role of Jesus who is the "one mediator between God and men" (1 Tim. 2:5). Understood properly, Jesus is the one *mediator of redemption*, for there is no other name under heaven by which humanity is saved. Nevertheless, this does not prevent others from acting as *intercessors of prayer*. For in the same verse to St Timothy, St Paul says, "First of all, then, I urge that supplications, prayers, intercessions, and thanksgivings be made for all men, for kings and all who are in high positions, that we may lead a quiet and peaceable life, godly and respectful in every way. *This is good, and it is acceptable in the sight of God our Savior"* (2:1-3). It is God, therefore, who invites Christians by virtue of their baptismal priesthood to be intercessors, or 'subordinate mediators' with Jesus. Christian intercessory prayer is only possible because Jesus is the one mediator who allows us to go boldly into the Father's presence through him.

Furthermore, Scripture itself attests that the Holy Spirit "intercedes for us with sighs too deep for words" (Rom. 8:26). The Virgin Mary interceded with Jesus at the wedding of Cana (Jn 2:1-10). Abraham interceded on behalf of Sodom and Gomorrah (Gen. 18:16-32). An angel interceded on behalf of Jerusalem (Zech. 1:12). The Lord accepted the intercession of Job after he had prayed for his friends (Job 42:8). Moses also interceded for the people of Israel, asking God's mercy and grace, for the sake of the dead Patriarchs who were righteous:

"But Moses besought the Lord his God, and said, 'O Lord, why does thy wrath burn hot against thy people, whom thou hast brought forth out of the land of Egypt with great power and with a mighty hand? Why should the Egyptians say, 'With evil intent did he bring them forth, to slay them in the mountains, and to consume them from the face of the earth?' Turn from thy fierce wrath, and repent of this evil against thy people. Remember Abraham, Isaac, and Israel, thy

servants, to whom thou didst swear by thine own self, and didst say to them, 'I will multiply your descendants as the stars of heaven, and all this land that I have promised I will give to your descendants, and they shall inherit it for ever.' And the Lord repented of the evil which he thought to do to his people" (Exod. 32:11-14).

Jesus himself recommended that Christians should pray and intercede for others: "But I say to you, love your enemies and pray for those who persecute you" (Mt 5:44). St Paul continually recommended himself to the prayers of his brethren (Rom. 15:30; Heb. 13:18). St James declared that the prayer of "the righteous man has great power" (Js 5:16), and Simon Magus sought the intercession of St Peter to save him from the wrath of God (Acts 8:24). Finally, angels likewise act as intercessors:

"I am Raphael, one of the seven holy angels who present the prayers of the saints and enter into the presence of the glory of the Holy One" (Tob. 12:15).

"And another angel came and stood at the altar with a golden censer; and he was given much incense to mingle with the prayers of all the saints upon the golden altar before the throne; and the smoke of the incense rose with the prayers of the saints from the hand of the angel before God" (Rev. 8:3-4).

Fourth objection: *"The dead are dead. They cannot hear our prayers."*

The assertion that dead saints cannot hear our invocations rests on Ps. 115:17: "The dead do not praise the Lord ..." It should be noted that this psalm was written at a time when Jewish understanding of the after-life was not yet fully developed. In later centuries, the Jews would have a better understanding of both the after-life and the intercessory role of the dead. Consequently, Baruch could utter the following prayer:

"O Lord Almighty, God of Israel, hear now the prayer of the dead of Israel and of the sons of those who sinned before thee, who did not heed the voice of the Lord their God, so that calamities have clung to us" (Bar. 3:4).

The Jews would also record how Onias saw the deceased Prophet Jeremiah praying for Israel:

"What he saw was this: Onias, who had been high priest, a noble and good man, of modest bearing and gentle manner, one who spoke fittingly and had been trained from childhood in all that belongs to excellence, was praying with outstretched hands for the whole body of the Jews. Then likewise a man appeared, distinguished by his gray hair and dignity, and of marvelous majesty and authority. And Onias spoke, saying, 'This is a man who loves the brethren and prays much for the people and the holy city, Jeremiah, the prophet of God.' Jeremiah stretched out his right hand and gave to Judas a golden sword, and as he gave it he addressed him thus: 'Take this holy sword, a gift from God, with which you will strike down your adversaries'" (2 Macc. 15:12-16).

At the Transfiguration on Mount Tabor, Moses and Elijah appeared talking with Jesus (Mt 17:3). This would have been impossible if they had been "dead" according to the Protestant understanding of Ps. 115. In relating to the Pharisees the parable of the Lost Sheep, Jesus stated, "there is joy before the angels of God over one sinner who repents" (Lk 15:10). St Paul also says, "we have become a spectacle to the world, to angels and to men" (1 Cor. 4:9). Furthermore, in his discourse to the Sadducees, Jesus declared that the Just dead are "equal to angels" (Lk 20:36) for God "is not God of the dead, but of the living; for all live in him" (Lk 20:38). In Heb. 12:1 the Old Testament saints are called "a cloud of witnesses" (nephos marturon – νέφος μαρτύρων) that surround the believers in Jesus. Hence, it follows that both angels and humans in heaven are aware of what is happening on earth. This is because they possess the Beatific Vision that enables them to see in God whatever knowledge is relevant to them. That is, they become 'multi-scient': "Now I know in part; then I shall understand fully" (1 Cor. 13:12). In their glorified state the saints are capable of unimaginable things, including hearing multiple prayers in various languages. The devil himself, though he is finite, is aware of many things and is engaged in multiple evil activities simultaneously.

Consider also the following passage:

"But you have come to Mount Zion and to the city of the living God, the heavenly Jerusalem, and to innumerable angels in festal gathering, and to the assembly of the first-born who are enrolled in heaven, and to a judge who is God of all, and to the spirits of just men made perfect" (Heb. 12:22-23).

In this text, St Paul explains to the faithful that although they are still on earth, they are in communion with the heavenly Jerusalem and with the dead saints, those *just men made perfect*. The faithful on earth are not in communion with the bodies of the saints buried in peace, but with their souls. Death does not inhibit this communion.

Fifth objection: *"The dead in heaven are totally focused on God. They are not concerned with our prayers or with what is happening on earth."*

The Book of Revelation indicates otherwise:

"... the twenty-four elders fell down before the Lamb, each holding a harp, and with golden bowls full of incense, which are the prayers of the saints" (5:8).

"I saw under the altar the souls of those who had been slain for the word of God and for the witness they had borne; they cried out with a loud voice, 'O Sovereign Lord, holy and true, how long before thou wilt judge and avenge our blood on those who dwell upon the earth?'" (6:9-10).

"And the twenty-four elders who sit on their thrones before God fell on their faces and worshiped God, saying, 'We give thanks to thee, Lord God Almighty, who art and who wast, that thou hast taken thy great power and begun to reign. The nations raged, but thy wrath came, and the time for the dead to be judged, for rewarding thy servants, the prophets and saints, and those who fear thy name, both small and great, and for destroying the destroyers of the earth'" (11:16-18).

Sixth objection: *"But isn't speaking to the dead forbidden in the Old Testament?"*

The relevant passage in the Old Testament is Deut. 18:10-12:

"There shall not be found among you any one who burns his son or his daughter as an offering, any one who practices divination, a soothsayer, or an augur, or a sorcerer, or a charmer, or a medium, or a wizard, or a necromancer. For whoever does these things is an abomination to the Lord; and because of these abominable practices the Lord your God is driving them out before you."

What is forbidden is the *conjuring* of the dead through trances, mediums or séances to obtain supernatural or prophetic information. Instead, the Jews were to rely on God who would send Prophets and later the Messiah: "The Lord your God will raise up for you a prophet like me from among you, from your brethren – him you shall heed" (Deut. 18:15).

Practises used to conjure up the dead are essentially diabolical. The power employed is that of the devil. The persons contacted are either demons impersonating dead people or the souls of the damned. The information obtained is mixed with lies and deceptions. This is why the Catholic Church from earliest times down to the present has condemned necromancy.[4] It has no resemblance to the pious practice of calling upon those in heaven to pray to God to obtain his spiritual favors and blessings. When praying to the saints Catholics know that it is God who allows the prayer to be heard and answered. In fact, talking to those in heaven (in this case the angels) is practised in the Psalms:

"Bless the Lord, O you his angels, you mighty ones who do his word, hearkening to the voice of his word! Bless the Lord, all his hosts, his ministers that do his will!" (Ps. 103:20-21).

Again, when Jesus talked about his death to Moses and Elijah on Mount Tabor was he guilty of necromancy? (Lk 9:30). Some may argue that Elijah was not one of the dead as he was taken from the world in a fiery chariot; however, Moses did die (Deut. 34:5).

---

[4] CCC ##1852, 2110-2117.

The Fathers

Inscriptions from the Catacombs
"O Atticus, sleep in peace and in the security of thy salvation and pray earnestly for our sins" (Capitol Museum, Rome).

"Gentianus, faithful, in peace who lived twelve years, eight months and sixteen days. You will intercede for us in your prayers because we know that you are in Christ" (Lateran Museum, Rome).

Pectorius of Autun, *Funeral Inscription* (c. AD 200)
"Divine race of the heavenly fish preserve a pure heart having received among mortals the immortal source of Divine waters. Refresh, O friend, thy soul with the everflowing waters of treasure-bestowing wisdom. Receive the sweet food of the Saviour of the Saints, eat with delight holding the fish in thy hands. Nourish (thine) with the fish, I pray, Master and Saviour; Sweetly may mother slumber, I beseech thee, Light of the Dead. Ascandios father, beloved of my heart with sweet mother and my brothers in the peace of the fish remember Pectorius."

St Cyril of Jerusalem, *Catechetical Lectures* 23 (Mystagogic 5), 10 (c. AD 350)
"Then we make mention also of those who have already fallen asleep: first, the patriarchs, prophets, apostles, and martyrs, that through their prayers and supplications God would receive our petition; next, we make mention also of the holy fathers and bishops who have already fallen asleep, and, to put it simply, of all among us who have already fallen asleep; for we believe that it will be of very great benefit to the souls of those for whom the petition is carried up, while this holy and most solemn Sacrifice is laid out."

St Epiphanius of Salamis, *Against All Heresies* 75, 8 (AD 377)
"Furthermore, as to mentioning the names of the dead, how is there anything very useful in that? What is more timely or more excellent than that those who are still here should believe that the departed do live, and that they have not retreated into nothingness, but that they exist and are alive with the Master? And so that this most august

proclamation might be told in full, how do they have hope, who are praying for the brethren as if they were but sojourning in a foreign land? Useful too is the prayer fashioned on their behalf, even if it does not force back the whole of guilty charges laid to them."

St Augustine of Hippo, *Against Faustus the Manichean* 20, 21 (c. AD 400)

"A Christian people celebrates together in religious solemnity the memorials of the martyrs, both to encourage their being imitated and so that it can share in their merits and be aided by their prayers. But it is done in such a way that our altars are not set up to any one of the martyrs – although in their memory – but to God himself, the God of those martyrs ... That worship, which the Greeks call latria and for which there is in Latin no single term, and which is expressive of the subjection owed to Divinity alone, we neither accord nor teach that it should be accorded to any save to the one God."

St Jerome, *Against Vigilantius* 6 (AD 406)

"You say in your book that while we live we are able to pray for each other, but afterwards when we have died, the prayer of no person for another can be heard; and this is especially clear since the martyrs, though they cry vengeance for their own blood, have never been able to obtain their request. But if the Apostles and martyrs while still in the body can pray for others, at a time when they ought still be solicitous about themselves, how much more will they do so after their crowns, victories, and triumphs?"

St John Damascene, *Apologetical Sermons Against those who Reject Sacred Images* 3, 41 (post AD 725)

"We worship and adore the Creator and Maker alone, as God who by his nature is to be worshiped. We worship also the holy Mother of God, not as God, but as God's Mother according to the flesh. Moreover, we worship also the saints, as elect friends of God, and as having gotten ready audience with him."

The Roman Catechism (1566)

Pt. III, Ch. II: True, there is but one Mediator, Christ the Lord, who alone has reconciled us to the heavenly Father through his blood, and who, *having obtained eternal redemption, and having entered once into the holies, ceases not to intercede for us.* But it by no means follows that it is therefore unlawful to have recourse to the intercession of the Saints. If, because we have one Mediator Jesus Christ it were unlawful to ask the intercession of the Saints, the Apostle would never have recommended himself with so much earnestness to the prayers of his brethren on earth. For the prayers of the living would lessen the glory and dignity of Christ's Mediatorship not less than the intercession of the Saints in heaven.

Catechism of the Catholic Church (1992)

No. 956: *The intercession of the saints* "being more closely united to Christ, those who dwell in heaven fix the whole Church more firmly in holiness ... [T]hey do not cease to intercede with the Father for us, as they proffer the merits which they acquired on earth through the one mediator between God and men, Christ Jesus ... So by their fraternal concern is our weakness greatly helped."

Purgatory and Praying for the Dead

Objection: *"I don't believe in Purgatory, because it is not mentioned in the Bible. There exists only heaven and hell!"*

For Catholics, the strongest arguments for the existence of Purgatory include the ancient liturgies of the East and West, the numerous inscriptions on the walls of the Catacombs, the constant and universal writings of the early Church Fathers, and the pronouncements of the Councils of Florence (1438-45) and Trent (1545-63).

The Catholic Church teaches that Purgatory is a temporary process of purification, whereby those who have died undergo expiation to remove all temporal punishment due to mortal sin duly forgiven, or all stain of unrepentant venial sin. It is not a 'second chance' opportunity or a place where souls that are not-good-enough-for-heaven-but-too-good-for-hell go. All the selfishness, inordinate attachment to creatures, dross and impurities in our souls are burned away by the fiery love and holiness of Jesus Christ. Souls undergo Purgatory, as "nothing unclean can enter heaven" (Rev. 21:27). The word "unclean" (*koinon* – κοινὸν) refers to something profane that needs to be cleansed before it can behold the glorious and overwhelming light of the Beatific Vision.

Purgatorial cleansing is a passive process. We do nothing ourselves to purify our souls. The purification is done solely by God. Following immediately after death, the soul appears before the judgment seat of Jesus: "It is appointed unto a man once to die, and then the judgment" (Heb. 9:27). This judgment involves the burning away of all "wood, hay, and straw" and the refining of all "gold, silver and precious stones" (1 Cor. 3:13ff.). All this takes place before the soul enters heaven. All souls that undergo Purgatory are destined ultimately for heaven.

The Church does not formally teach that Purgatory is a particular region in the afterlife. We are unsure as to how space operates in the next world, in particular for disembodied spirits. Likewise, with regards to time; a different temporal modality – called *aeviternity* – operates in the next life for humans that is distinct from the ordinary flow of events experienced on earth. After the General Resurrection and Final Judgment, Purgatory will no longer operate and all humanity will be either in heaven or hell.

Christians can pray for the souls in Purgatory and assist them through good works and penances, especially the Holy Sacrifice of the Mass: "But if he was looking to the splendid reward that is laid up for those who fall asleep in godliness, it was a holy and pious thought. Therefore, he made atonement for the dead, that they might be delivered from their sin" (2 Macc. 12:45). Each good action of a just man possesses a double value – that of merit, and that of satisfaction or expiation. Merit is personal and cannot be transferred to another, but satisfaction can be applied for the benefit of others. God accepts the charitable acts of others to abate the temporal punishment of the souls in Purgatory and these same souls will pray for us out of gratitude when they reach heaven.

It should also be noted that Purgatory is not all pain. Since the soul is closer to God than when it was on earth, it experiences correspondingly greater joys. St Catherine of Genoa (1447-1510) wrote in her *Treatise on Purgatory*:

> An incessant communication with God renders their happiness daily more intense, and this union with God grows more and more intimate, according as the impediments to that union, which exist in the soul, are consumed ... With regard to the will of these souls, they can never say that these pains are pains, so great is their contentment with the ordinance of God, with which their wills are united in perfect charity.

The ex-Protestant convert, James Akin, lists some of the other 'advantages' of Purgatory:

(a) Freedom from the committing of sin.
(b) Freedom from the desire to sin.
(c) Closer unity with God and Christ.
(d) Certainty of one's final salvation in a way not possible in this life.
(e) A final and full appreciation of just how gracious God has been to one.
(f) A final and full appreciation of just how much God loves one.
(g) The unencumbered and pure love we will feel for God and for others.
(h) Partial rewards which may be given in anticipation of one's entrance into the full glory of heaven at the end of Purgatory.[1]

Second objection: *"Sure, but all this means nothing, for the Bible still says nothing about Purgatory!"*

Protestants are always very quick to assert that the doctrine of Purgatory is unbiblical, insisting that there is only heaven and hell. However, as we have just seen, 2 Macc. 12:43-45 shows that the Jews in the Old Testament certainly believed in a state where the dead could profit from the sacrifices and prayers of the living. The full text of this passage reads as follows:

"He also took up a collection, man by man, to the amount of two thousand drachmas of silver, and sent it to Jerusalem to provide for a sin offering. In doing this he acted very well and honorably, taking account of the resurrection. For if he were not expecting that those who had fallen would rise again, it would have been superfluous and foolish to pray for the dead. But if he was looking to the splendid reward that is laid up for those who fall asleep in godliness, it was a holy and pious thought. Therefore he made atonement for the dead, that they might be delivered from their sin."

Protestants deny the canonicity of the Maccabean books, nevertheless, their historical value cannot be denied. Even Jewish prayer

---

[1] http://www.ewtn.com/library/answers/how2purg.htm

books today contain prayers for the dead (the *Mourner's Qaddish*). If the Jews had invented the doctrine of Purgatory or prayers for the dead, undoubtedly Jesus would have condemned such, as he condemned them for a long list of changes in doctrine and discipline in Matt. 23. Furthermore, the doctrine of Purgatory is implied in the Gospels:

"And whoever says a word against the Son of man will be forgiven; but whoever speaks against the Holy Spirit will not be forgiven, either in this age or in the age to come" (Mt 12:32).

According to Pope St Gregory I the Great, these words of Jesus infer that there are some sins that can be forgiven "in the age to come" (*en to mellonti* – ἐν τῷ μέλλοντι), or the next life. Now, as this cannot be done in heaven or hell, Jesus must have had in mind another state – that which the Church calls Purgatory.

"And that servant who knew his master's will, but did not make ready or act according to his will, shall receive a severe beating. But he who did not know, and did what deserved a beating, shall receive a light beating" (Lk 12:47-48).

The master in this passage is Jesus, who when judging us will dispense various punishments, either severe or light. In heaven there will be no beatings; in hell only severe beatings. The light beatings are for those who will be punished in Purgatory for their venial sins.

"As you go with your accuser before the magistrate, make an effort to settle with him on the way, lest he drag you to the judge, and the judge hand you over to the officer, and the officer put you in prison. I tell you, you will never get out till you have paid the very last copper" (Lk 12:58-59).

The judge in this parable represents God, the accuser our neighbor. If we have not reconciled with our neighbor before death, God will hold us accountable for the wrong inflicted on him/her. However, it will be a punishment that is only temporary, as implied by the words *"you will never get out till you have paid the very last copper."*

"... each man's work will become manifest; for the Day will disclose it, because it will be revealed with fire, and the fire will test what sort of work each one has done. If the work which any man has built on the foundation survives, he will receive a reward. If any man's work is burned up, he will suffer loss, though he himself will be saved, but only as through fire" (1 Cor. 3:13-15).

The words "he himself will be saved, but only as through fire" indicate a temporary process of purification that takes place before the soul enters heaven. Some Protestants argue that this verse does not refer to Purgatory, for it is our works and not our souls that will be tested by fire. This might appear to be the case on the surface, nevertheless, it is the soul that will feel the consequences of that testing. This is borne out by the Greek word for "he will suffer loss" which is *zemiothesetai* (ζημιωθήσεται) and which always refers to punishment. Works cannot be punished; only persons. This is why St Paul says "he will receive a reward" and "he will suffer loss."

"But you have come to Mount Zion and to the city of the living God, the heavenly Jerusalem, and to innumerable angels in festal gathering, and to the assembly of the first-born who are enrolled in heaven, and to a judge who is God of all, and to the spirits of just men made perfect" (Heb. 12:22-23).

The "heavenly Jerusalem" is inhabited by "innumerable angels" and "the spirits of just men made perfect." These spirits are the souls of the Just, made perfect by the merits of Jesus applied through the mysterious purifying process the Church calls Purgatory.

"Otherwise, what do people mean by being baptized on behalf of the dead? If the dead are not raised at all, why are people baptized on their behalf" (1 Cor. 15:29).

This passage is one of the most difficult in the Scriptures to understand. The most plausible interpretation is that "baptized" in this context means sufferings and afflictions undergone on behalf of others (Mk 10:38-39; Lk 12:50). What St Paul was alluding to was the practice of the Apostolic Church to sacrifice, pray and fast for the souls of departed Christians.

"May the Lord grant mercy to the household of Onesiphorus, for he often refreshed me; he was not ashamed of my chains, but when he arrived in Rome he searched for me eagerly and found me – may the Lord grant him to find mercy from the Lord on that Day – and you well know all the service he rendered at Ephesus" (2 Tim. 1:16-18).

The sense of this passage is that Onesiphorus is dead at the time of writing and that St Paul is praying for his soul. It is a simple prayer, akin to our present-day funeral utterances, such as "may he rest in peace."

Finally, the Scriptures give one clear example of another place besides heaven and hell in the next world. St Peter tells us (1 Pet. 3:19) that after his death Jesus preached his redemption "to the spirits in prison." Based on this, the concept of another temporary, intermediate place such as Purgatory is not totally out of the question.

Third objection: *"But St Paul says, 'To be absent from the body is to be present with Christ' (2 Cor. 5:6-10). Therefore, when a true Christian dies he immediately goes to Christ. There is no half-way house or waiting room in the middle."*

Does St Paul actually say the above words? In reality he says the following:

"So we are always of good courage; we know that while we are at home in the body we are away from the Lord, for we walk by faith, not by sight. We are of good courage, and we would rather be away from the body and at home with the Lord. So whether we are at home or away, we make it our aim to please him. For we must all appear before the judgment seat of Christ, so that each one may receive good or evil, according to what he has done in the body."

St Paul in verse 6 says, *"while we are at home in the body we are away from the Lord."* No one doubts that while we are still on earth we are not in the immediate presence of Jesus. In v. 8 St Paul states, *"we would rather be away from the body and at home with the Lord."* This is an expression of a pious desire by St Paul. All good Christians would rather be with Jesus than to continue on through this valley of tears.

Nevertheless, what follows after we leave this body and come before Jesus is the particular judgment, where we must give an account for all our words and deeds and have them tested by fire!

Fourth objection: *"But Purgatory is unnecessary, for Christ has paid all debt of punishment for sin by his death on the Cross."*

One important reason why Protestants think Purgatory is "unneccesary" is their belief in the unscriptural doctrines of total depravity and non-imputation of sin formulated by Martin Luther and John Calvin. They taught that the sin of Adam so damaged humanity that we are now nothing more than wild beasts who's every action, no matter how good, is sinful. Since we are incapable of good actions, there is nothing we can do to remit our temporal punishments, either for ourselves or for anyone else. Only Jesus, therefore, can achieve this and this he did on the Cross. Furthermore, as our souls are already totally depraved, any additional sin on our part cannot leave a 'stain of sin' that needs to be purified in Purgatory. When we accept Jesus as our "personal Lord and Savior" God simply 'covers up' our sinful natures, making us fit to enter the kingdom of heaven.

Jesus' death on the Cross more than certainly sufficed to redeem humanity and free us from both the eternal damnation of hell and any additional temporal punishments. That being the case, why is there any obligation on the part of Christians to do penance to remit temporal punishment for sin? One reason is that God may choose to leave a temporal debt outstanding even after the eternal penalty for a sin has been remitted. For example, humanity is still subject to the temporal punishments of labor, pain, sickness and death even though we have now been redeemed and baptized. Also, Mary, the sister of Moses, was forgiven by God for complaining against her brother. Nevertheless, God still imposed upon her the temporal punishment of leprosy and seven days exile from the Chosen People (Num. 12). Moses was forbidden to enter the Promised Land after being forgiven for striking the rock twice at the Waters of Contradiction (Num. 20:12). Similarly, King David was afflicted with the temporal punishment of his infant son's death even after being forgiven for the murder of Uriah (2 Sam. 12:13ff.).

However, it may be further asked why God leaves temporal penalties in place after forgiving eternal penalties for sins. It is a question, first, of discharging a debt of honor, making a gesture of reparation even after the real reparation has already been completed. Penance also has a rehabilitative effect. It helps us to learn from our sins and restore the loss or damage caused by them. Finally, penance satisfies our innate need to mourn for tragedies and sin, especially mortal sin, which is the greatest tragedy that can befall a person.

The reality is that the purgatorial cleansing we endure for sin is in a special way a consequence of Jesus' sacrifice for us. Jesus' sufferings paid the price for our sanctification from beginning to end. Purgatory is our final sanctification. If Jesus had not suffered there would be no Purgatory and therefore no final sanctification at all. Rather, there would be only a permanent exclusion from heaven!

The Fathers

Tertullian, *The Soul* 58, 8 (inter AD 208-212)
"In short, if we understand that prison of which the Gospel speaks to be Hades, and if we interpret the last farthing to be the light offense which is to be expiated there before the resurrection, no one will doubt that the soul undergoes some punishments in Hades, without prejudice to the fullness of the resurrection, after which recompense will be made through the flesh also."

Tertullian, *The Crown* 3, 3-5 (AD 211)
"The Sacrament of the Eucharist, which the Lord commanded to be taken at meal times and by all, we take even before daybreak in congregations, but from the hand of none others except the presidents ... We offer sacrifices for the dead on their birthday anniversaries ... We take anxious care lest something of our Cup or Bread should fall upon the ground."

Tertullian, *Monogamy* 10, 1 (post AD 213)
"A woman, after the death of her husband, is bound not less firmly but even more so, not to marry another husband ... Indeed, she prays for his soul and asks that he may, while waiting, find rest; and that he may

share in the first resurrection. And each year, on the anniversary of his death, she offers the Sacrifice."

St Cyril of Jerusalem, *Catechetical Lectures* 23 (Mystagogic 5), 10 (c. AD 350)
"Then we make mention also of those who have already fallen asleep: first, the patriarchs, prophets, Apostles, and martyrs, that through their prayers and supplications God would receive our petition; next, we make mention also of the holy fathers and bishops who have already fallen asleep, and, to put it simply, of all among us who have already fallen asleep; for we believe that it will be of very great benefit to the souls of those for whom the petition is carried up, while this holy and most solemn Sacrifice is laid out."

St Gregory of Nyssa, *Sermon on the Dead* (AD 383)
"After his departure out of the body, he gains knowledge of the difference between virtue and vice, and finds that he is not able to partake of divinity until he has been purged of the filthy contagion in his soul by the purifying fire."

St John Chrysostom, *Homilies on First Corinthians* 41, 5 (c. AD 392)
"Let us help and commemorate them. If Job's sons were purified by their father's sacrifice, why would we doubt that our offerings for the dead bring them some consolation? Let us not hesitate to help those who have died and to offer our prayers for them."

St Augustine of Hippo, *Confessions* Bk. 9, 2 (AD 400)
St Augustine's mother, St Monica, on her death-bed said to him: "This one request I make of you, that, wherever you be, you remember me at the Lord's altar."

St Augustine of Hippo, *The Care that Should be Taken for the Dead* 1, 3 (AD 421)
"We read in ... Maccabees that the sacrifice was offered for the dead. But even if it were found nowhere in the Old Testament writings, the authority of the universal Church which is clear on this point is of no small weight, where in the prayers of the priest poured forth to the Lord God at his altar the commendation of the dead has its place."

The Roman Catechism (1566)

Pt. IV, Ch. VI: Prayers for the dead, that they may be liberated from the fire of Purgatory, are derived from Apostolic teaching ... (The Eucharist) ... its benefits extend not only to the celebrant and communicant, but to all the faithful, whether living with us on earth, or already numbered with those who are dead in the Lord, but whose sins have not yet been fully expiated. For, according to the most authentic Apostolic tradition, it is not less available when offered for them, than when offered for the sins of the living, their punishments, satisfactions, calamities and difficulties of every sort.

Catechism of the Catholic Church (1992)

No. 1032: This teaching is also based on the practice of prayer for the dead, already mentioned in Sacred Scripture: "Therefore [Judas Maccabeus] made atonement for the dead, that they might be delivered from their sin" (2 Maccabees 12:46). From the beginning the Church has honored the memory of the dead and offered prayers in suffrage for them, above all the Eucharistic sacrifice, so that, thus purified, they may attain the beatific vision of God. The Church also commends almsgiving, indulgences, and works of penance undertaken on behalf of the dead:

> Let us help and commemorate them. If Job's sons were purified by their father's sacrifice, why should we doubt that our offerings for the dead bring them some consolation? Let us not hesitate to help those who have died and to offer our prayers for them (St John Chrysostom, *Hom. in 1 Cor.* 41:5).

Indulgences

Objection: *"Indulgences are nothing more than a permission to sin. It is a money-making exercise through which Catholics think they can buy their way into heaven!"*

The doctrine of indulgences was the very doctrine that triggered the Protestant revolt in 1517. It is probably the least understood teaching of the Catholic Church. Only the ignorant or prejudiced take it to mean that the Church grants a license or permission to sin. What then is an indulgence?

An indulgence is simply a remission of the temporal punishment due for sins committed after God has remitted guilt and eternal punishment through the infinite merits of Jesus Christ and his saints.

An indulgence may be *plenary* or *partial* according to whether it removes all or part of the temporal punishment due to sin. The requirements laid down by the Church for gaining a plenary indulgence are: (i) performance of the indulgenced work – for example, adoration of the Blessed Sacrament for at least half an hour, devout reading of the Scriptures for at least half an hour, or praying the Rosary in a church, public oratory or family group; (ii) sacramental confession; (iii) Eucharistic communion, and (iv) prayer for the Pope's intentions. The last three conditions may be fulfilled several days before or after the performance of the prescribed work. However, it is fitting that communion is received and the prayer for the Pope's intentions is said on the same day the work is performed. If any of these conditions is not fulfilled, the indulgence gained will only be partial.

A partial indulgence is gained by any of the faithful who:

(i) In the performance of their duties and bearing the trials of life, raise their mind with humble confidence to God, adding some pious invocation;

(ii) In a spirit of faith and mercy, give of themselves or of their goods to serve their brothers and sisters in need;

(iii) In a spirit of penance, voluntarily deprive themselves of what is licit and pleasing to them.[1]

Works which can be performed for partial indulgences include the recitation of any of the following prayers: Profession of Faith, *De Profundis, Magnificat, Sub Tuum Praesidium, Memorare, Salve Regina, Adoro Te Devote, Angelus, Anima Christi, Te Deum,* Grace before and after meals, the Litanies, the Sign of the Cross – or, indeed, any prayer.

Indulgences are, therefore, a great aid to true devotion, fostering a spirit of prayer and sacrifice in the name of Jesus, not just for one's own benefit, but also for the benefit of all the faithful.

The charge that Catholics see indulgences as a means of buying their way into heaven is entirely without foundation. Anti-Catholics exploiting the ignorance of both Catholics and non-Catholics normally make such a charge. First, as indulgences relate only to the remission of temporal punishment, they have nothing to do with remitting eternal punishment in hell. Only God's forgiveness following true sorrow for sin can achieve that. Neither are indulgences permissions to commit or pardons in advance for future sins for, again, they relate only to the remission of temporal punishment remaining after *past* sins have been forgiven.

The abuses relating to indulgences in the time of Martin Luther involved almsgiving for the construction of the new St Peter's Basilica. The giving of alms, especially for the service of God, is a meritorious work in itself and a worthy condition for the granting of an indulgence. There was no outright selling of indulgences, though one could gain that impression. For this reason, the Council of Trent radically reformed the practice of granting indulgences and in 1567 Pope St Pius V abolished all grants of indulgences in return for alms. This abolition was another genuine attempt to attack abuses that had previously been condemned by Ecumenical Councils in 1215, 1245, 1274 and 1312.

Second objection: *"What is the Scriptural basis for Indulgences? I can't seem to find one."*

---

[1]*Enchiridion of Indulgences: Norms and Grants*, Vatican City, 1968, 1999.

The main bases for the doctrine of indulgences are certainly found in the Scriptures: vicarious atonement among Church members, the power of the Church to bind and loose, and penance.

Looking firstly at the Old Testament, we see that God blesses one person or persons as a reward to someone else. For example, God promised Abraham that nations and kings would descend from him, that God would enter a covenant with these descendants, and that they would accede to the Promised Land (Gen. 17:6-8). All these blessings were granted to Abraham's descendants as God's reward to him.

On occasions the specific blessing God vicariously grants is a reduction of the temporal penalties the sinner deserves. For example, Solomon's heart drifted from the Lord in the last years of his life, and God vowed to tear the kingdom away from him as a consequence: "Therefore the Lord said to Solomon, 'Since this has been your mind and you have not kept my covenant and my statutes which I have commanded you, I will surely tear the kingdom from you and will give it to your servant. Yet *for the sake of David your father* I will not do it in your days, but I will tear it out of the hand of your son. However, I will not tear away all the kingdom; but I will give one tribe to your son, *for the sake of David my servant* and for the sake of Jerusalem which I have chosen'" (1 Kgs 11:11-13). We see here that God mitigated the temporal punishment in two ways: by delaying the removal of the kingdom until the time of Solomon's son and by leaving the one tribe of Benjamin under the rule Judah. Why did God do this? It is clear that God did not do this for the sake of Solomon but "for the sake of your father David" who had pleased God and was promised certain things regarding his kingdom. This is an instance of God reducing a chastisement for the sake of one of his holy ones.

This idea is also found in the New Testament. In Matt. 15:22-28 Jesus exorcises a demon from a Canaanite girl (deliverance from a temporal condition) in response to the pleading of her mother. Elsewhere, St Paul says "As regards the gospel they [the Jews] are enemies of God, for your sake; but as regards election *they are beloved for the sake of their forefathers*. For the gifts and the call of God are irrevocable" (Rom. 11:28-29). St Paul indicated that his Jewish contemporaries were treated more gently than they otherwise would have been treated (God's gift and call were not removed from them) because their forefathers were beloved by God, who gave them irrevocable gifts.

That Jesus has given the Church the power of granting indulgences is implied in Scripture: "I will give you the keys of the kingdom of heaven, and whatever you bind on earth shall be bound in heaven, and whatever you loose on earth shall be loosed in heaven" (Mt 16:19). If Jesus gave his ministers the power to forgive the eternal penalty of sin (Jn 20:21-23), how much more would they be capable to remit the temporal punishments due to sin? As the context makes clear, binding and loosing involves Church discipline, which includes the imposition and removal of temporal penalties (such as excluding and readmitting individuals to the sacraments).

St Paul provides a clear example of the Church using this power with respect to the incestuous Corinthian upon whom he had imposed a severe penance. After learning of the Corinthian's fervent sorrow, St Paul absolved him of the penance which he had imposed, saying: "What I have forgiven, if I have forgiven anything, has been for your sake in the presence of Christ" (*en prosopo christou* – ἐν προσώπῳ Χριστοῦ) (2 Cor. 2:10).

In this example we have the elements of a true indulgence: (i) a penance (temporal punishment) imposed on the Corinthian by St Paul; (ii) sorrow on the part of the sinner for his crime; (iii) the relaxation of the penance by St Paul (the indulgence); (iv) the relaxation done in the "presence of Christ."

Third objection: *"Indulgences are a waste of time for we do not have to do any penance as temporal punishment as Christ paid all debt for sin when he died on the cross!"*

Only since the advent of Protestantism has anyone thought the system of penance and indulgences to be a waste of time. As the ex-Protestant convert James Akin explains:

> The system of penance goes back beyond the middle ages, through the patristic age, through the New Testament, and into the Old Testament. It has been part of the religion of Yahweh since before the time of Christ, it was part of the religion of Christ and his first followers, and it has been part

of Christianity ever since. It was not until the rise of Protestantism that anyone in Christendom thought to deny it.[2]

To re-iterate what was said in the previous chapter on Purgatory, Catholics certainly believe that Jesus' death on the Cross was infinitely meritorious and therefore superabundantly sufficient to redeem and free humanity from both eternal punishment in hell and any additional temporal punishments. However, God still wills that humanity endure temporal punishments in this world for sins that have been forgiven. Why is this the case? It is, firstly, a question of discharging a debt of honor, making a reparatory gesture after the real reparation has been completed. Secondly, penance has rehabilitative benefits. It teaches us to learn from our sins: "For the Lord disciplines him whom he loves, and chastises every son whom he receives ... he disciplines us for our good, that we may share his holiness" (Heb. 12:6-10). Penance also restores the loss or damage caused by sin. For example, a thief may be sorry for stealing a large sum of money from someone else, but is still required to return the money taken and even do time in prison. Finally, penance satisfies the human need to mourn for tragedies and sin, particularly mortal sin, which is the greatest tragedy.

Fourth objection: *"The idea of a 'treasury of merits' in heaven that can be drawn upon by the Church to remit the temporal punishment of forgiven sinners is a fiction not mentioned in Scripture."*

Jesus certainly spoke of a 'treasury of merits' in heaven as recorded by Matthew in his Gospel:

"Do not lay up for yourselves treasures on earth, where moth and rust consume and where thieves break in and steal, but lay up for yourselves treasures in heaven, where neither moth nor rust consumes and where thieves do not break in and steal" (6:19-20).

---

[2] http://www.ewtn.com/library/answers/penance.htm

Catholics believe that many of the faithful throughout the centuries – virgins, martyrs, confessors, saints – have performed penances and good works far in excess of what was due as temporal punishment for their own sins. Their merits, in union with the infinite merits of Jesus, form a 'spiritual treasury' which the Church can draw upon to assist other members of the Church in general or, in particular, pay the debt of temporal punishment both for the living and the dead. This can be done, for every good action possesses a double value – that of merit and that of satisfaction. The meritorious value of an act is the reward given by God to the performer of the act and cannot be transferred, while the satisfactory value of an act is the intention sought after by the petitioner which can be directed to benefit others. We see an example of this in the following words of St Paul: "Now I rejoice in my sufferings for your sake, and in my flesh I complete what is lacking in Christ's afflictions for the sake of his body, that is, the Church" (Col. 1:24). St Paul knew perfectly well that with regard to the eternal salvation of humanity, Jesus' afflictions were not only not "lacking" but that they were superabundant (i.e., more than enough) in value to save the whole world. Therefore, St Paul and other Christians who, through the communion of saints, offer up prayers, Masses or alms as penance for the remission of others' temporal punishment act as temporal saviors only. They unite their praiseworthy actions to those of the one eternal savior, Jesus Christ.

The Fathers

St Ignatius of Antioch, *Letter to the Philadelphians* 3 (c. AD 110)
"For as many as are of God and of Jesus Christ are also with the bishop. And as many as shall, in the exercise of penance, return into the unity of the Church, these, too, shall belong to God, that they may live according to Jesus Christ."

St Cyprian of Carthage, *The Lapsed* 17 (AD 251)
"The Lord alone is able to have mercy. He alone, who bore our sins, who grieved for us, and whom God delivered up for our sins, is able to grant pardon for the sins which have been committed against him ...

Certainly we believe that the merits of the martyrs and the works of the just will be of great avail with the Judge – but that will be when the day of judgment comes, when, after the end of this age and of the world, his people shall stand before the tribunal of Christ."

St Cyprian of Carthage, *Letters* **9, 2 (c. AD 253)**
"... sinners may do penance for a set time, and according to the rules of discipline come to public confession, and by imposition of the hand of the bishop and clergy receive the right of communion."

St Ambrose of Milan, *Penance* **1, 15, 80 (inter AD 387-390)**
"For he is purged as if by certain works of the whole people, and is washed in the tears of the multitude; by the prayers and tears of the multitude he is redeemed from sin, and is cleansed in the inner man. For Christ granted to his Church that one should be redeemed through all, just as his Church was found worthy of the coming of the Lord Jesus so that all might be redeemed through one."

St Augustine of Hippo, *Sermon to Catechumens on the Creed* **8, 16 (c. AD 395)**
"For those whom you see doing penance have committed crimes, either adultery or some other enormities. That is why they are doing penance. If their sins were light, daily prayer would suffice to blot them out ... In the Church, therefore, there are three ways in which sins are forgiven: in baptisms, in prayer, and in the greater humility of penance."

St Augustine of Hippo, *Homilies on the Gospel of John* **124, 5 (AD 416-417)**
"... man is obliged to suffer, even when his sins are forgiven, ... for the penalty is of longer duration than the guilt, lest the guilt should be accounted small, were the penalty also to end with it. It is for this reason ... that man is held in this life to the penalty, even when he is no longer held to the guilt unto eternal damnation."

St Caesarius of Arles, *Sermon* **261, 1 (ante AD 542)**
"Considering the number of sins, he sees that he is incapable of himself alone to make satisfaction for such grave evils; and so he is anxious to seek out the assistance of the whole people."

The Roman Catechism (1566)

This Catechism referred to canonical penances and works of satisfaction, but made no specific reference to Indulgences. The question of Indulgences was dealt with by the Council itself in its *Decree Concerning Indulgences*, Session XXV, 4 December, 1563:

> Since the power of conferring indulgences was granted by Christ to the Church; and she has, even in the most ancient times, used the said power, delivered unto her by God: the holy synod teaches and enjoins that the use of indulgences – most salutary for the Christian people, and approved of by the authority of sacred councils – is to be retained in the Church; and it condemns with anathema those who either assert that they are useless, or who deny that there is in the Church the power of granting them.

Catechism of the Catholic Church (1992)

No. 1478: An indulgence is obtained through the Church who, by virtue of the power of binding and loosing granted her by Christ Jesus, intervenes in favor of individual Christians and opens for them the treasury of the merits of Christ and the saints to obtain from the Father of mercies the remission of the temporal punishments due for their sins. Thus the Church does not want simply to come to the aid of these Christians, but also to spur them to works of devotion, penance, and charity.

Hell is Eternal

Objection: *"The idea of hell is for those who have an Old Testament mentality. It is unimaginable how the loving Christian God could condemn any one to hell for all eternity."*

According to classical Catholic theology all who die at enmity with God – that is, in a state of unrepentant mortal sin – are condemned to the eternal punishment of hell where all therein will suffer the unimaginable pains of loss and of sense.

The doctrine of an eternal hell is today assailed from both within and without the Catholic Church. Within the Church there are Catholics teaching the modernist notion of 'universal salvation,' which asserts that ultimately all will be admitted into the kingdom of heaven because God's mercy is so great that he could not allow otherwise. These Catholics forget that God is also a God of justice. On the other hand, Jehovah's Witnesses, for example, assert that the wicked have no eternal destiny, either in heaven or hell, but instead they will be 'annihilated' upon death. In holding such a view they deny the immortality of the human soul, asserting that such a belief is derived from the pagan Babylonians and Greeks.

However, the Old Testament certainly does refer to hell:

"A land of gloom and chaos, where light is as darkness" (Job 10:22).

"And they shall go forth and look on the dead bodies of the men that have rebelled against me; for their worm shall not die, their fire shall not be quenched, and they shall be an abhorrence to all flesh" (Is. 66:24).

"Many of those who sleep in the dust of the earth shall awake; some shall live forever, others shall be an everlasting horror and disgrace" (Dan. 12:2).

Despite the protestations of many, hell is also clearly spoken of in the New Testament, both by John the Baptist and Jesus himself:

"'Even now the axe is laid to the root of the trees; every tree therefore that does not bear good fruit is cut down and thrown into the fire. 'I baptize you with water for repentance, but he who is coming after me is mightier than I, whose sandals I am not worthy to carry; he will baptize you with the Holy Spirit and with fire. His winnowing fork is in his hand, and he will clear his threshing floor and gather his wheat into the granary, but the chaff he will burn with unquenchable fire'" (Mt 3:10-12).

"But I say to you that every one who is angry with his brother shall be liable to judgment; whoever insults his brother shall be liable to the council, and whoever says, 'You fool!' shall be liable to the hell of fire" (Mt 5:22).

"Every tree that does not bear good fruit is cut down and thrown into the fire" (Mt 7:19).

"I tell you, many will come from east and west and sit at table with Abraham, Isaac, and Jacob in the kingdom of heaven, while the sons of the kingdom will be thrown into the outer darkness; there men will weep and gnash their teeth" (Mt 8:11-12).

"And do not fear those who kill the body but cannot kill the soul; rather fear him who can destroy both soul and body in hell" (Mt 10:28).

"The Son of man will send his angels, and they will gather out of his kingdom all causes of sin and all evildoers, and throw them into the furnace of fire; there men will weep and gnash their teeth" (Mt 13:41-42).

"Woe to the world for temptations to sin! For it is necessary that temptations come, but woe to the man by whom the temptation comes! And if your hand or your foot causes you to sin, cut it off and throw it away; it is better for you to enter life maimed or lame than with two hands or two feet to be thrown into the eternal fire. And if your eye causes you to sin, pluck it out and throw it away; it is better for you to enter life with one eye than with two eyes to be thrown into the hell of fire" (Mt 18:7-9).

"But when the king came in to look at the guests, he saw there a man who had no wedding garment; and he said to him, 'Friend, how did you get in here *without a wedding garment?' And he was speechless. Then the king said to the attendants, 'Bind him hand and foot, and cast him into the outer darkness; there men will weep and gnash their teeth'"* (Mt 22:11-13).

"And cast the worthless servant into the outer darkness; there men will weep and gnash their teeth" (Mt 25:30).

"Then he will say to those at his left hand, 'Depart from me, you cursed, into the eternal fire prepared for the devil and his angels'" (Mt 25:41).

"Whoever causes one of these little ones who believe in me to sin, it would be better for him if a great millstone were hung round his neck and he were thrown into the sea. And if your hand causes you to sin, cut it off; it is better for you to enter life maimed than with two hands to go to hell, to the unquenchable fire. And if your foot causes you to sin, cut it off; it is better for you to enter life lame than with two feet to be thrown into hell. And if your eye causes you to sin, pluck it out; it is better for you to enter the kingdom of God with one eye than with two eyes to be thrown into hell, where their worm does not die, and the fire is not quenched" (Mk 9:42-48).

"The poor man died and was carried by the angels to Abraham's bosom. The rich man also died and was buried; and in Hades, being in torment, he lifted up his eyes, and saw Abraham far off and Lazarus in his bosom. And he called out, 'Father Abraham, have mercy upon me, and send Lazarus to dip the end of his finger in water and cool my tongue; for I am in anguish in this flame'" (Lk 16:22-24).

"I am the vine, you are the branches. He who abides in me, and I in him, he it is that bears much fruit, for apart from me you can do nothing. If a man does not abide in me, he is cast forth as a branch and withers; and the branches are gathered, thrown into the fire and burned" (Jn 15:5-6).

"And the beast was captured, and with it the false prophet who in its presence had worked the signs by which he deceived those who had received the mark of the beast and those who worshiped its image. These two were thrown alive into the lake of fire that burns with sulphur" (Rev. 19:20).

"... and if any one's name was not found written in the book of life, he was thrown into the lake of fire" (Rev. 20:15).

Biographers of the founder of the Jehovah's Witnesses, Charles Taze Russell, all agree that his rejection of an eternal hell was based on his inability to reconcile the existence of such with the teaching that "God is love" (1 Jn 4:16). He preferred to believe that the souls of the wicked were simply annihilated at death. The following quote sums up the Witnesses' objection to the doctrine of hell:

> The doctrine of a burning hell where the wicked are tortured eternally after death cannot be true, mainly for four reasons: (i) It is wholly unscriptural; (ii) it is unreasonable; (iii) it is contrary to God's love; and (iv) it is repugnant to justice (*Let God be True*, p. 99).

The Jehovah's Witnesses claim that the Hebrew word *sheol* (and its Greek equivalent *hades*) actually refers not to hell but to "the grave." It is true that in certain contexts *sheol* does have that meaning (e.g., Gen. 37:35; 1 Kgs 2:6; Job 21:13) but to claim that this is its only meaning is inaccurate. *Sheol* has a wider range of meanings such as the "pit" of the nether world (Job 33:24-28; Ps. 88:4; Is. 38:18), "gates of death" (Job 38:17) or "chambers of death" (Prov. 7:27). In all these verses *sheol* is a place where the souls of the dead go. But in the parable of Lazarus and Dives (Lk 16:23) St Luke uses the word *hades* (ᾅδη) to describe specifically a place of punishment indistinguishable from hell, as it is traditionally understood.

The Hebrew *gehenna* is another word which means hell. It appears twelve times in the New Testament and is derived from *ge-hinnom*, the name for the valley southwest of Jerusalem where altars were erected for human sacrifices to Moloch (2 Kgs 23:10). This valley was also used by potters for their sulphur furnaces and in the time of Jesus it was employed as a dump for everything unclean. With its history of idolatry, uncleanness and sulphur fires, Gehenna provided the ideal symbol for the ultimate punishment that will befall the wicked, and it is used in this sense in the New Testament.

Hell is Eternal

However, in accordance with their denial of the soul's immortality, the Jehovah's Witnesses hold that *gehenna* with its fire and brimstone is instead a symbol of the wicked soul's total annihilation. They quote Matt. 10:28 for support: "rather fear him who can *destroy* both soul and body in hell (gehenna)." The Greek word in Matt. 10:28 for destroy is *apolesai* (ἀπολέσαι). The Witnesses translate each usage of *apolesai* in the New Testament as "destroy" but this can lead to absurd conclusions such as in Matt. 2:13 where St Joseph is warned of Herod's plan to "search for the young child to destroy (*apolesai*) him." There is no question of Herod here trying to annihilate Jesus, only to kill him. Likewise, in Matt. 10:28 *apolesai* does not mean annihilation, but the destruction of all hope due to exclusion from God's presence.

As for the eternity or otherwise of hell, a closer examination of Scripture assures us that it is eternal. The Book of Revelation, for example, uses the words *aionas aionon* (αἰῶνας αἰώνων) to describe the duration of hell "for ever and ever" (14:11). The Jehovah's Witnesses attempt to water down the force of these words by claiming that they simply refer to an indefinite period of time. However, such an argument crumbles in the light of Matt. 25:46 which uses virtually the same word *aionion* (αἰώνιων) to describe both the eternal duration of the reward for the good and the eternal duration of the punishment for the wicked respectively. Even the Witnesses' own version of the Bible, *The New World Translation*, contains passages that assert the eternity of hell:

"... *cannot be put out*" (Mt 3:12)

"... *everlasting cutting-off*" (Mt 18:8)

"... *cannot be put out*" (Mk 9:43)

"... *tormented day and night forever and ever*" (Rev. 20:10)

The Jehovah's Witnesses stand contradicted out of their own mouths.

The Fathers

St Ignatius of Antioch, *Letter to the Ephesians* 16, 1 (c. AD 110)
"My brethren: the corrupters of families will not inherit the kingdom of God. And if they who do these things according to the flesh suffer death, how much more if a man corrupt by evil teaching the faith of God, for the sake of which Jesus Christ was crucified? A man become so foul will depart into unquenchable fire; and so also will anyone who listens to him."

St Justin Martyr, *First Apology* 52 (c. AD 155)
"He shall come from the heavens in glory with his angelic host; when he shall raise the bodies of all the men who ever lived. Then he will clothe the worthy in immortality; but the wicked, clothed in eternal sensibility, he will commit to the eternal fire, along with the evil demons."

St Cyprian of Carthage, *Letter to the People of Thibar* 58 (56), 10 (AD 253)
"Oh, what a day that will be, and how great when it comes, dearest brethren! When the Lord begins to survey his people and to recognize by examining with divine knowledge the merits of each individual! To cast into hell evildoers, and to condemn our persecutors to the eternal fire and punishing flame! And indeed, to present to us the reward of faith and devotion."

Aphraates the Persian Sage, *Treatises* 22, 22 (inter AD 336-345)
"And again, in regard to punishment, I say that not all men are equal. He that sinned much is much tormented. He that offended not so much is less tormented. Some shall go into outer darkness, where there is weeping and gnashing of teeth. And others shall be cast into the fire, in accord with their deserts; for it is written that they shall gnash their teeth, nor is that place accounted as dark. And some shall be cast into another place, a place where the worm shall not die and their fire shall not be quenched; and they shall be a wonder to all flesh. Others shall have the door closed in their faces, and to them the judge will say, 'I do not know you.'"

St Augustine of Hippo, *Enchiridion of Faith, Hope and Love* **29, 112 (AD 421)**

"In vain, therefore, do some men, indeed, very many, because of human sentiment, bewail the eternal punishment, of the damned and their perpetual, unending torments, without really believing that it shall be so ... But let them suppose, if it pleases them, that the punishments of the damned are, at certain periods of time, somewhat mitigated. For even thus it can be understood that they remain in the wrath of God that is, in damnation itself, for it is this that is called the 'wrath of God,' not some disturbance in the divine mind: that in his wrath, that is, by their abiding in his wrath, he does not shut up his mercies; yet he does not put an end to their eternal punishment, but only applies or interposes some relief to their torments."

St John Damascene, *The Source of Knowledge* **3, 4, 27 (inter AD 743-749)**

"We shall rise again, therefore, our souls united again to our bodies, the latter now made incorruptible and having put corruption aside; and we shall stand before the awesome tribunal of Christ. And the devil and his demons, and the man that is his, the Antichrist, and the impious and the sinners shall be consigned to everlasting fire, not material fire such as we know, but such fire as God would know."

The Roman Catechism (1566)

Pt. I, Ch. VIII: The first words, *depart from me,* express the heaviest punishment with which the wicked shall be visited, their eternal banishment from the sight of God, unrelieved by one consolatory hope of ever recovering so great a good. This punishment is called by theologians the *pain of loss,* because in hell the wicked shall be deprived forever of the light of the vision of God ... The next words, *into everlasting fire,* express another sort of punishment, which is called by theologians the *pain of sense,* because, like lashes, stripes or other more severe chastisements, among which fire, no doubt, produces the most intense pain, it is felt through the organs of sense. When, moreover, we reflect that this torment is to be eternal, we can see at once that the punishment of the damned includes every kind of suffering.

Catechism of the Catholic Church (1992)

No. 1034: Jesus often speaks of "Gehenna," of "the unquenchable fire" reserved for those who to the end of their lives refuse to believe and be converted, where both soul and body can be lost. Jesus solemnly proclaims that he "will send his angels, and they will gather ... all evil doers, and throw them into the furnace of fire," and that he will pronounce the condemnation: "Depart from me, you cursed, into the eternal fire!"

Sunday Worship

Objection: *"The Commandments speak of remembering the Sabbath day, and keeping it holy (Gen. 2:3; Exod. 20:8). The Sabbath is Saturday, so why do Catholics worship publicly on the first day of the week, that is, Sunday?"*

This is a question normally posed by those – such as the Seventh-Day Adventists – who regard Sunday worship as a mark of the Apostate Church of the Beast. For such people, Sunday worship originated in paganism and is an abomination relating to sun worship. It is a commandment of men that contradicts the clear commandment of God.

The Seventh-Day Adventists were founded in 1831 under the original name of "The Adventists" by William Miller, an American farmer. He was obsessed with the second coming of Jesus and predicted its occurrence for October 1843 and then October 1844. When these dates failed, Miller abandoned his own movement. However, from among the Adventists arose a 'prophetess,' Mrs Ellen Gould Harmon White, who declared that she had been taken up to heaven and shown the truth of Sabbath observance. In reality, E. G. H. White had picked up the idea of reinstituting observance of the Jewish Sabbath from a Miss Preston, who was a member of the Seventh-Day Baptists diffusing her ideas throughout Washington in 1844. In 1845, E. G. H. White reorganized the Adventists and gave them the new name of "Seventh-Day Adventists."

Currently, the Seventh-Day Adventists are engaged in a public campaign alleging that the Catholic Church is involved in a worldwide conspiracy to introduce laws enforcing Sunday observance. As they state:

> Soon international law will require the observance of Sunday, the pagan day of sun worship, as a day of rest and worship for everybody. The United States of America will be the first to enact and later enforce a National Sunday Law in defiance of God's Commandments. National apostasy will be followed by national ruin (*Eternity Publications*, Grenfell, NSW, Australia).

Satan himself will appear as a majestic being of dazzling brightness, performing false miracles and commanding Sunday worship. The true Sabbath-keepers who resist will be put to death.

Jesus declared that he was Lord of the Sabbath and that it was made for humanity's benefit: Mt 12:1-8; Mk 2:24-26; Lk 6:5; Jn 5:10-11. Therefore, the early Church, in order to distinguish itself from the worship of the Synagogue, was free to depart from the Jewish Sabbath and worship God on another day of the week. This is evident from the words of St Paul to the Colossians: "Therefore let no one pass judgment on you in questions of food and drink or with regard to a festival, new moon, or a *sabbath*. These are only a shadow of what is to come, but the substance belongs to Christ" (2:16-17). There is no command or injunction in the New Testament that the followers of Jesus must continue to observe Saturday.

If Jesus himself had the power to "dispose" of the Sabbath, so too does his Church which is his Body. The power of the Church to make such a change is specifically found in Jesus' words to St Peter: "I will give you the keys of the kingdom of heaven, and whatever you bind on earth shall be bound in heaven, and whatever you loose on earth shall be loosed in heaven" (Mt 16:19).

From the outset of the Church's history Christians replaced the Sabbath day with a new day of public worship in commemoration of Jesus' resurrection from the dead. This occurred on a Sunday, the first day of the week:

"But on the first day of the week, at early dawn, they went to the tomb, taking the spices which they had prepared. And they found the stone rolled away from the tomb" (Lk 24:1-2).

"Early on the first day of the week ... Mary Magdalene came to the tomb and saw that the stone had been removed from the tomb" (Jn 20:1).

Early Christians such as St Ignatius of Antioch (*Letter to the Magnesians* 9, 1, AD 110) recognised Sunday as the *Lord's Day*: "Those who lived according to the old order of things have come to a new hope, no longer keeping the Sabbath, but the Lord's Day, in which our life is blessed by him and by his death."

The official 'birthday' of the Church, Pentecost Sunday, also fell on the first day of the week: Acts 2:1.

The apostolic Christians celebrated the Eucharist on Sunday:

"On the first day of the week, when we were gathered together to break bread ..." (Acts 20:7).

Collections supporting the Church were gathered on Sunday:

"On the first day of every week, each of you is to put something aside and store it up, as he may prosper, so that contributions need not be made when I come" (1 Cor. 16:2).

St John received his Revelation on a Sunday:

"I, John, your brother who share with you in Jesus the tribulation ... was on the island called Patmos ... I was in the Spirit on the Lord's ..." (Rev. 1:9-10).

In response, Seventh-Day Adventists cite the following passages as proof that the early Christians worshiped on the Sabbath:

"The women who had come with him ... saw the tomb, and how his body was laid; then they returned, and prepared spices and ointments. On the sabbath they rested according to the commandment" (Lk 23:55-56).

"As they went out, the people begged that these things might be told them the next sabbath. And when the meeting of the synagogue broke up, many Jews and devout converts to Judaism followed Paul and Barnabas, who spoke to them and urged them to continue in the grace of God. The next sabbath almost the whole city gathered together to hear the word of God" (Acts 13:42-44).

"And he argued in the synagogue every sabbath, and persuaded Jews and Greeks. When Silas and Timothy arrived from Macedonia, Paul was occupied with preaching, testifying to the Jews that the Christ was Jesus" (Acts 18:4-5).

However, in Luke 23 the resurrection of Christ had not yet occurred and therefore the significance of the Lord's Day was not yet a reality. In any case, the Jewish authorities would have prohibited work on Jesus' body even if the holy women had wanted to do some. Furthermore, from a closer reading of Acts it is obvious that St Paul went to the synagogues on the Sabbath not to actually worship but because the gatherings of Jews there provided an ideal forum in which to preach Jesus. These synagogue gatherings only occurred on the Sabbath and were solely for Jews who had not yet accepted Jesus.

Finally, it is important to note that, in changing the Sabbath law, the Church did not make a change in the divine law obliging men and women to worship God but merely a change in the day on which it was to be offered. That is, only a change in the positive ceremonial law. The law obliging men and women to worship God is a law based both on God's own nature and ours, as Creator and creature respectively. As natures cannot change, natural laws are irrevocable. On the other hand, all divine positive laws are based not on God's nature but on God's Will, and hence can be altered or revoked by God directly or through his Church according to changes in time, circumstance or place.

The Fathers

The Didache 14, 1 (inter AD 90-150)
"On the Lord's Day of the Lord gather together, break bread and give thanks, after confessing your transgressions so that your sacrifice may be pure ..."

St Ignatius of Antioch, *Letter to the Magnesians* 9, 1 (AD 110)
"Those who lived according to the old order of things have come to a new hope, no longer keeping the Sabbath, but the Lord's Day, in which our life is blessed by him and by his death."

Letter to Diognetus 4, 1 (inter AD 125-200)
"Furthermore, I do not suppose that you need to learn from me how ridiculous and unworthy of any argument are their scruples about food, their superstition about the Sabbath, their pride in circumcision, and their sham in fasting."

St Justin Martyr, *First Apology* **67 (c. AD 155)**
"We all gather on the day of the sun, for it is the first day (after the Jewish Sabbath, but also the first day) when God, separating matter from darkness, made the world; and on this same day Jesus Christ our Savior rose from the dead."

St Augustine of Hippo, *Against Faustus* **18, 4 (c. AD 400)**
"The things in the Law and in the Prophets which Christians do not observe are those which did but signify the things they do observe. They were but figures of things to come, which figures, now that the things themselves have been revealed and made present by Christ, must be removed, so that in the very fact of their removal the Law and the Prophets may be fulfilled."

The Roman Catechism (1566)

Pt. III, Ch. IV: But the Church of God has thought it well to transfer the celebration and observance of the Sabbath to Sunday. For, as on that day light first shone on the world, so by the Resurrection of our Redeemer on the same day, by whom was thrown open to us the gate to eternal life, we were called out of darkness into light; and hence the Apostles would have it called *the Lord's Day*.

We also learn from the Sacred Scriptures that the first day of the week was held sacred because on that day the work of creation commenced, and on that day the Holy Ghost was given to the Apostles.

Catechism of the Catholic Church (1992)

No. 2175: Sunday is expressly distinguished from the sabbath which it follows chronologically every week; for Christians its ceremonial observance replaces that of the sabbath. In Christ's Passover, Sunday fulfils the spiritual truth of the Jewish sabbath and announces man's eternal rest in God. For worship under the Law prepared for the mystery of Christ, and what was done there prefigured some aspects of Christ.

Statues and Images

Objection: *"Why are Catholic Churches and homes decorated with statues and images in clear breach of the Ten Commandments?!"*

God prohibits in the Ten Commandments the making of idols and the worshiping of them: "You shall not make for yourself a graven image, or any likeness of anything that is in heaven above, or that is in the earth beneath, or that is in the water under the earth; you shall not bow down to them or serve them ... for I the Lord your God am a jealous God" (Exod. 20:4-5). At first instance, it appears that this commandment imposes an absolute prohibition against the making and use of all images *per se*. However, a thorough examination of the Old Testament precludes such an interpretation, as this would necessitate God prohibiting what he allows and commands elsewhere, especially concerning the Temple of Jerusalem itself.

It follows that if the Commandments prohibited the making of all images whatsoever, Protestants ought to remove and destroy all their statues of political, military, artistic and sporting heroes, as well as all their pictures of relatives and friends. Common sense, though, tells us that such would be an absurd outcome.

The Catholic doctrine on the veneration of images was fully outlined by the Second Council of Nicaea in AD 787:

> Proceeding as it were on the royal road and following the divinely inspired teaching of our holy Fathers, and the tradition of the Catholic Church (for we know that this tradition is of the Holy Spirit which dwells in the Church), we define with all care and exactitude, that the venerable and holy images are set up in just the same way as the figure of the precious and life-giving cross; painted images, and those in mosaic and those of other suitable materials, in the holy churches of God, on holy vessels and vestments, on walls and in pictures, in houses and by the roadsides; images of our Lord God and Savior Jesus Christ and of our undefiled Lady, the holy God-bearer, and of the honorable angels, and of saintly and holy men. For the more frequently these are observed by

means of such representations, so much the more will the beholders be aroused to recollect the originals and to long after them, and to pay the images the tribute of an embrace and a reverence of honor, not to pay to them the actual worship which is according to our faith, and which is proper only to the divine nature: but as to the figure of the venerable and life-giving cross, and to the holy Gospels and the other sacred monuments, so to those images to accord the honor of incense and oblation of lights, as it has been the pious custom of antiquity. For the honor paid to the image passes to its original, and he that honors an image honors in it the person depicted thereby.

The real purpose of the commandment is to steer the people of God away from *idolatry*, that is, the worship of any false god. Consider the following passages:

"For they would turn away your sons from following me, to serve other gods; then the anger of the Lord would be kindled against you, and he would destroy you quickly. But thus shall you deal with them: you shall break down their altars, and dash in pieces their pillars, and hew down their Asherim, and burn their graven images with fire" (Deut. 7:4-5).

"And the people of Israel did secretly against the Lord their God things that were not right. They built for themselves high places at all their towns, from watchtower to fortified city; they set up for themselves pillars and Asherim on every high hill and under every green tree; and there they burned incense on all the high places, as the nations did whom the Lord carried away before them. And they did wicked things, provoking the Lord to anger, and they served idols, of which the Lord had said to them, 'You shall not do this'" (2 Kgs 17:9-12).

God obviously abhors idolatry; however, in the same Scriptures we see the Jews making statues for legitimate religious purposes, and under God's command:

"And the Lord said to Moses, 'Make a fiery serpent, and set it on a pole; and every one who is bitten, when he sees it, shall live.' So Moses made a bronze

serpent, and set it on a pole; and if a serpent bit any man, he would look at the bronze serpent and live" (Num. 21:8-9).

When the bronze serpent was later adored by some Jews, rather than simply venerated, it was destroyed:

"He [Hezekiah] removed the high places, and broke the pillars, and cut down the Asherah. And he broke in pieces the bronze serpent that Moses had made, for until those days the people of Israel had burned incense to it; it was called Nehushtan" (2 Kgs 18:4).

In the construction of the Ark of the Covenant God gave the following instructions:

"And you shall make two cherubim of gold; of hammered work shall you make them, on the two ends of the mercy seat. Make one cherub on the one end, and one cherub on the other end; of one piece with the mercy seat shall you make the cherubim on its two ends. The cherubim shall spread out their wings above, overshadowing the mercy seat with their wings, their faces one to another; toward the mercy seat shall the faces of the cherubim be turned toward the mercy seat" (Exod. 25:18-20).

The Temple of Jerusalem was thoroughly decorated with statues of all kinds:

"In the inner sanctuary he made two cherubim of olivewood, each ten cubits high" (1 Kgs 6:23).

"The height of one cherub was ten cubits, and so was that of the other cherub. He put the cherubim in the innermost part of the house; and the wings of the cherubim were spread out so that a wing of one touched the one wall, and a wing of the other cherub touched the other wall; their other wings touched each other in the middle of the house" (1 Kgs 6:26-27).

"... and on the panels that were set in the frames were lions, oxen, and cherubim. Upon the frames, both above and below the lions and oxen, there were wreaths of beveled work" (1 Kgs 7:29).

"... for the altar of incense made of refined gold, and its weight; also his plan for the golden chariot of the cherubim that spread their wings and covered the ark of the covenant of the Lord" (1 Chron. 28:18).

"In the most holy place he made two cherubim of wood and overlaid them with gold" (2 Chron. 3:10).

"Under it were figures of gourds, for thirty cubits, compassing the sea round about; the gourds were in two rows, cast with it when it was cast. It stood upon twelve oxen, three facing north, three facing west, three facing south, and three facing east; the sea was set upon them, and all their hinder parts were inward" (2 Chron. 4:3-4).

"It was formed of cherubim and palm trees, a palm tree between cherub and cherub. Every cherub had two faces" (Ezek. 41:17-18).

The Temple with all these statues was built by Solomon. What is remarkable is that just after construction was begun God spoke to Solomon as follows:

"Now the word of the Lord came to Solomon, 'Concerning this house which you are building, if you will walk in my statutes and obey my ordinances and keep all my commandments and walk in them, then I will establish my word with you, which I spoke to David your father. And I will dwell among the children of Israel, and will not forsake my people Israel.'" (1 Kgs 6:11-14).

What does Solomon do in the light of God's admonition to "walk in my statutes and obey my ordinances and keep all my commandments"? He carves statues for the house of the Lord, and to the Lord's delight:

"When Solomon had finished building the house of the Lord and the king's house and all that Solomon desired to build, the Lord appeared to Solomon a second time, as he had appeared to him at Gibeon. And the Lord said to him, 'I have heard your prayer and your supplication, which you have made before me; I have consecrated this house which you have built, and put my name there for ever; my eyes and my heart will be there for all time'" (1 Kgs 9:1-3).

The ancient Jewish objection to images, etc., was very strict, for they were prone to imitate the idolatry of the pagans around them. The early Christians, who lived in the age of the Incarnation, had no such difficulty. So, the Catacombs are a treasury of paintings, gilded glasses, depicting scenes from the lives of Jesus, his Mother, the Apostles and other persons of the Old and New Testaments. The mind of the early Christians was clearly a Catholic mind.

Objection two: *"But I have seen Catholics worshiping statues by kissing and bowing before them."*

The acts of kissing and bowing are not in themselves exclusively acts of adoration or idolatry. Scripture again gives examples of legitimate bowing done in honor and love of angels and human beings, even of the Temple itself:

"The two angels came to Sodom in the evening; and Lot was sitting in the gate of Sodom. When Lot saw them, he rose to meet them, and bowed himself with his face to the earth ..." (Gen. 19:1).

"Let peoples serve you, and nations bow down to you. Be lord over your brothers, and may your mother's sons bow down to you. Cursed be every one who curses you, and blessed be every one who blesses you!" (Gen. 27:29).

"He himself went on before them, bowing himself to the ground seven times, until he came near to his brother. But Esau ran to meet him, and embraced him, and fell on his neck and kissed him, and they wept" (Gen. 33:3-4).

"Now Joseph was governor over the land; he it was who sold to all the people of the land. And Joseph's brothers came, and bowed themselves before him with their faces to the ground" (Gen. 42:6).

"When Joshua was by Jericho, he lifted up his eyes and looked, and behold, a man stood before him with his drawn sword in his hand; and Joshua went to him and said to him, 'Are you for us, or for our adversaries?' And he said, 'No; but as commander of the army of the Lord I have now come.' And Joshua fell

on his face to the earth, and worshiped, and said to him, 'What does my lord bid his servant?'" (Josh. 5:13-14).

"Then Joshua ... fell to the ground upon his face before the ark of the Lord until the evening" (Josh. 7:6).

"And they told the king, 'Here is Nathan the prophet.' And when he came in before the king, he bowed before the king, with his face to the ground" (1 Kgs 1:23).

"Now when the sons of the prophets who were at Jericho saw him over against them, they said, 'The spirit of Elijah rests on Elisha.' And they came to meet him, and bowed to the ground before him" (2 Kgs 2:15).

"I bow down toward thy holy temple and give thanks to thy name for thy steadfast love and thy faithfulness; for thou hast exalted above everything thy name and thy word" (Ps. 138:2).

"Then King Nebuchadnezzar fell down and worshiped Daniel and ordered sacrifice and incense offered to him" (Dan. 2:46).

"Behold, I will make those of the synagogue of Satan who say that they are Jews and are not, but lie - behold, I will make them come and bow down before your feet, and learn that I have loved you" (Rev. 3:9).

If someone kisses the photograph of his mother is he paying respect to a piece of cardboard, or is he making an act of love offered to his mother? Catholics pay respect to images and statues only because they remind us of God, Jesus, Mary or the saints. The homage given to the image refers to the prototype it represents. Pagans either adore the statue/image itself or the statue/image represents a being that has no existence. A Catholic kisses a crucifix, not to worship the actual metal or wood, but because it represents Jesus and what he did for us. Christians see in the Cross of Jesus the great love he had for us and with St Paul would say, "But far be it from me to glory except in the cross of our Lord Jesus Christ, by which the world has been crucified to me, and I to the world" (Gal. 6:14). Thus, we see the value of the

Catholic practice of placing an image of Jesus upon crosses to form the image of the crucifix. It is a means by which we "preach Christ crucified" and show forth "the power of God and the wisdom of God" (1 Cor. 1:23-24).

The Fathers

St Basil the Great, *The Holy Spirit* 18, 45 (AD 375)

"It does not follow that there are two kings because we speak of a king and a king's image. The authority is not split nor is the glory divided. The sovereignty and power to the authority which we are subject is one, just as the glory we ascribe thereto is not plural but one; for the honor paid to the image passes to the prototype."

St Cyril of Alexandria, *Commentary on the Psalms* On Ps. 113B (115), 16 (ante AD 429)

"Even if we make images of pious men it is not so that we might adore them as gods but that when we see them we might be prompted to imitate them; and if we make images of Christ, it is so that our minds might wing aloft in yearning for him."

St John Damascene, *Apologetical Sermons Against Those Who Reject Sacred Images* 2, 5 (inter AD 725-749)

"We would certainly be in error if we were making an image of the invisible God; for what is incorporeal and invisible and uncircumscribable and without defined figure is not able to be depicted. And again, if we were making images of men and thought them gods, certainly we would be impious. But we do not do any of these things."

The Second Council of Nicaea, *Letter of the Synod to the Byzantine Emperor and Empress* (AD 787)

"The things which we have decreed, being thus well supported, it is confessedly and beyond all question acceptable and well-pleasing before God, that the images of our Lord Jesus Christ as man, and those of the undefiled Mother of God, the ever-virgin Mary, and of the honorable

Angels and of all Saints, should be venerated and saluted. And if anyone does not so believe, but undertakes to debate the matter further and is evil affected with regard to the veneration due the sacred images, such an one our holy ecumenical council (fortified by the inward working of the Spirit of God, and by the traditions of the Fathers and of the Church) anathematizes."

The Roman Catechism (1566)

Pt. III, Ch. II: Let no one think that this Commandment entirely forbids the arts of painting, engraving or sculpture. The Scriptures inform us that God himself commanded to be made images of Cherubim, and also the brazen serpent. The interpretation, therefore, at which we must arrive, is that images are prohibited only inasmuch as they are used as deities to receive adoration, and so to injure the true worship of God.

Catechism of the Catholic Church (1992)

No. 1161: All the signs in the liturgical celebrations are related to Christ: as are sacred images of the holy Mother of God and of the saints as well. They truly signify Christ, who is glorified in them. They make manifest the "cloud of witnesses" who continue to participate in the salvation of the world and to whom we are united, above all in sacramental celebrations. Through their icons, it is man "in the image of God," finally transfigured "into his likeness," who is revealed to our faith. So too are the angels, who also are recapitulated in Christ.

Relics

Objection: *"The veneration of relics is vain and superstitious. It amounts to nothing less than another form of Catholic idolatry!"*

The modern word 'relic' is derived from the Latin *reliquiae*, which means an extant part of a deceased person's body or clothing. In Catholic tradition, the word relic is normally used only in relation to a portion of body or clothing of a declared blessed or saint.

The veneration of relics of deceased saints has always been an approved practice of the Catholic faithful. For example, during the centuries of imperial Roman persecution the early Christians were meticulous in their collection and veneration of the remains of martyrs. As early as the mid-second century AD the Smyrnaeans "took up his (St Polycarp's) bones, more precious than costly gems and finer than gold, and put them in a suitable place" (*The Martyrdom of St Polycarp* 17, 3). In contrast to pagan Roman practice, dead Christian bodies were not cremated; rather, they were usually carefully buried in such places as the Catacombs. Eventually, the practice developed whereby relics were placed beneath the altars on which Mass was offered to honor the saints and martyrs seen by St John praying under the heavenly altar in Rev. 6:9.

The underlying reason for the veneration of relics lies in the Christian attitude towards the human body. Christians regard the body as something good in itself, an essential part of human nature created by God. More particularly, while alive on earth the Christian was a "temple of the Holy Spirit" (1 Cor. 6:19). Furthermore, as the body participated in the good or evil actions of the Christian, so after the general resurrection will it participate with the soul in either its eternal glory or condemnation.

Rather than being a superstitious practice, both Scripture and history testify to the marvellous prodigies God has rendered through the use and veneration of relics:

"... as soon as the man touched the bones of Elisha, he revived, and stood on his feet" (2 Kgs 13:21).

"... *so that they even carried out the sick into the streets, and laid them on beds and pallets, that as Peter came by at least his shadow might fall on some of them*" (Acts 5:15).

"... *so that handkerchiefs or aprons were carried away from his* (St Paul's) *body to the sick, and diseases left them and the evil spirits came out of them*" (Acts 19:12).

Miracles were also wrought through relics belonging to Old Testament saints while they were still alive: Elias' mantle parted the Jordan River (2 Kgs 2:8-14); and the rod of Moses performed prodigies in the presence of Pharaoh (Exod. 7:10).

We may add to these examples the veneration shown to the bones of Moses (Exod. 13:19; Josh. 24:32) in stark contrast to the Jewish ceremonial laws against contact with the dead (Num. 19:11ff.).

Faithful Jews also sought miracles through materials belonging to Jesus:

"*And behold, a woman who had suffered from a hemorrhage for twelve years came up behind him and touched the fringe of his garment; for she said to herself, 'If I only touch his garment, I shall be made well.' Jesus turned, and seeing her he said, 'Take heart, daughter; your faith has made you well.' And instantly the woman was made well*" (Mt 9:20-22).

"*And wherever he came, in villages, cities, or country, they laid the sick in the market places, and besought him that they might touch even the fringe of his garment; and as many as touched it were made well*" (Mk 6:56).

There exist, literally, thousands of cases of miracles worked through relics. In the writings of the Church Fathers, we find both St Ambrose and St Augustine relating miraculous stories, not only stories they heard and read, but also miracles they themselves had personally witnessed at the tombs of martyrs (St Ambrose: *Epist.* 22, 2 & 17; St Augustine: *Serm.* 284, 5; *City of God* 22, 8; *Confessions* 9, 7). The Protestant historian Harnack in his *History of Dogmas* is forced to admit, "no Church doctor of repute restricted it (veneration of relics). All of them, even the Cappadocians, countenanced it" (IV, 313).

Even in more modern times the Church still proclaims to the world in her beatification and canonization ceremonies accounts of unquestionable miracles that have occurred through the deceased's intercession. Often, the certified miracle is one that occurred when a relic of the deceased was physically applied to an afflicted part of the favored person's body. Such miracles are on the public record and all have been thoroughly investigated and analyzed by doctors and scientists of repute.

The Council of Trent articulated the official Catholic teaching on the veneration of relics in the sixteenth century:

> Also that the holy bodies of holy martyrs, and of others now living with Christ, which bodies were the living members of Christ and the temple of the Holy Spirit, and which are by him to be raised unto eternal life and to be glorified, are to be venerated by the faithful, through which (bodies) many benefits are bestowed by God on men; so that they who affirm that veneration and honor are not due to the relics of saints; or that these and other sacred monuments are uselessly honored by the faithful; and that the places dedicated to the memory of the saints are in vain visited with the view of obtaining their aid, are wholly to be condemned.[1]

There is nothing in the above paragraph that smacks of idolatry. The first commandment not only obliges us to honor and love God (*latria*), but also to honor and revere everything belonging to him (*dulia*). This is the reason why the Church venerates the bodies and relics of saints, for their bodies were the living members of Jesus and temples of the Holy Spirit. The Church has always approved the relatively inferior nature of the honor due to relics. As St Jerome says, "We do not worship, we do not adore, for fear that we should bow down to the creature rather than to the Creator, but we venerate the relics of the martyrs in order the better to adore him whose martyrs they are."[2] Neither does the Church promote the belief that there exists

---

[1] *On the Invocation, Veneration, and Relics of Saints, and on Sacred Images*, 4 December, 1563.
[2] Epistle 109, *To Riparius* 1 (AD 404).

any magical or curative power dwelling in the relic itself. Relics are merely instruments, as the Council of Trent says, "through which many benefits are bestowed by God on men."

Second objection: *"The Catholic practice of relic veneration is copied from ancient pagan usages."*

Undoubtedly, the veneration of relics can be found in many other religious traditions besides that of Christianity. We possess numerous records detailing how ancient pagan cultures practised it and how modern pagan cultures likewise do today. But of what consequence is this? Where is the proof of a deliberate adoption of relic veneration from paganism? There is none. Rather, relic veneration is an instinctive pious practice rooted in human nature. In any case, the veneration of relics of pagan personages cannot be legitimately compared with the veneration of the relics of those who followed Jesus.

Furthermore, how is the Catholic practice of relic veneration any different to the veneration given by all peoples, including Protestants, to the relics of famous figures of history, politics, war or sport? All nations and peoples have monuments and museums set up in honor of national heroes. Items belonging to them, such as clothing, diaries, documents, weapons, etc., are carefully displayed for public viewing and respect. Anyone attempting to steal or damage such items would certainly have to face the wrath of public opinion. A *fortiori*, the Catholic Church can certainly claim the same privilege to honor her heroes, especially as God can and often has granted special blessings and miracles through their instrumentality.

Third objection: *"There are numerous abuses associated with relic veneration. And what about all those frauds passed off as true relics such as the Shroud of Turin?"*

In the same pronouncement of the Council of Trent quoted above, the Council also urged all pastors to ensure that "in the invocation of saints the veneration of relics and the sacred use of images, every superstition shall be removed and all filthy lucre abolished." Throughout the long history of the Church there have, unfortunately, been numerous instances of error and fraud in relation to relics. As early as the late fourth century, St Augustine of Hippo decried against impostor monks who profiteered from the sale of fake relics. Even the Catholic Encyclopedia admits "that many of the more ancient relics duly exhibited for veneration in the great sanctuaries of Christendom or even at Rome itself must now be pronounced to be either certainly spurious or open to grave suspicion" (Vol. XII, p. 737, ed. 1911).

Professional anti-Catholics such as Loraine Boettner and Bart Brewer attempt to make great headway from the existence of fraudulent relics. In their writings we find ridicule and derision directed not only against proven frauds but also against the very doctrine of relic veneration itself. For example, Bart Brewer in his life-story, *Pilgrimage from Rome*, states:

> It is said that if all the pieces of the cross displayed in Catholic churches were assembled together, it would take a ten-ton truck to carry them. It is clear that most 'relics' are frauds. Furthermore, there is nothing in the Bible that supports the veneration of relics, even if they are genuine.[3]

Despite the existence of frauds, it must always be remembered that abuse does not abolish use. Even if fraudulent relics of the True Cross or the Apostles exist, there are also genuine relics in both cases deserving of veneration. In any case, no one is obliged to pay homage to dubious relics, and even when people do so, no dishonor is done to God if the error has been passed down in perfect good faith over centuries.

The claim that there are enough fraudulent pieces of the True Cross to fill a "ten-ton truck" was examined and refuted by Rohault de Fleury in the late nineteenth century. Despite long and arduous research, de Fleury could only discover enough relics to make up approximately one-third of a cross. This included three hundred and seventy cubic inches of relics that once allegedly existed but at the time no longer did.

---

[3] Bob Jones University Press, South Carolina, 1986, p. 132.

Critics of the Shroud of Turin say it is a medieval fraud, but their endeavors to produce conclusive proof have failed. This is partly due to the fact that the following questions have yet to be explained:

(i) Given the scientific certainty that the Shroud is not a painting, who using what methods in the Middle Ages could have produced a negative image when this technique only emerged in the mid nineteenth century?

(ii) If it was a forger who subjected his contemporary to the same sufferings as Jesus, how could he have obtained an image impressed on one side of the cloth only? And how, even at the beginning of the twenty-first century with all its scientific advances, does the method for producing this image remain unknown?

(iii) How could this forger implant into the cloth various microscopic grains of pollen coming from Palestine, Asia Minor, France and Italy?

(iv) How could the forger on the face on the Shroud produce details that only the modern invention of three-dimensional photography has been able to reveal, for instance, the imprint of two coins, one over the right eye and the other over the arch of the left eyebrow?

These and many other questions remain unanswered by the sceptic, but the faithful undoubtedly see the work and face of God before them.

Like all the wonderful relics of Christendom, this miraculous relic is in the possession of the Catholic Church and forms part of the treasures of history and an addendum to the treasure of the Deposit of Faith of which she is the custodian.

The Fathers

The Martyrdom of St Polycarp 17, 3 (c. AD 156)
"Christ we worship as the Son of God, but the martyrs we love as disciples and imitators of the Lord; and rightly so, because of their unsurpassable devotion to their own King and Teacher. With them

may we also become companions and fellow disciples. When the centurion saw the contentiousness caused by the Jews, he confiscated the body, and, according to their custom, burned it. Then, at least, we took up his bones, more precious than costly gems and finer than gold, and put them in a suitable place. The Lord will permit us, when we are able, to assemble there in joy and gladness, and to celebrate the birthday of his martyrdom, both in memory of those who have already engaged in the contest, and for the practice and training of those who have yet to fight."

St Jerome, *Letter to Riparius* 109, 1 (AD 404)
"... we honor the relics of the martyrs, that we may adore him whose martyrs they are. We honor the servants that their honor may be reflected upon their Lord who himself says: 'he that receives you receives me.' I ask Vigilantius, Are the relics of Peter and of Paul unclean? Was the body of Moses unclean, of which we are told (according to the correct Hebrew text) that it was buried by the Lord himself? And do we, every time that we enter the basilicas of apostles and prophets and martyrs, pay homage to the shrines of idols? Are the tapers which burn before their tombs only the tokens of idolatry?"

St Augustine of Hippo, *The City of God* Bk 1, Ch. 13 (ante AD 413)
"The bodies of the dead, nevertheless, are not to be despised and thrown aside, and least of all, those of the righteous and faithful, which were used in a chaste manner by the Spirit as the organs and vessels for all good works."

Theodoret of Cyr, *The Cure of Pagan Maladies* 8 (ante AD 449)
"The noble souls of the triumphant are sauntering around heaven, dancing in the choruses of the bodiless; and not one tomb for each conceals their bodies, but cities and villages divide them up and call them healers and preservers of souls and bodies, and venerate them as guardians and protectors of cities; and when they intervene as ambassadors before the Master of the universe the divine gifts are obtained through them; and though the body has been divided, its grace has continued undivided. And that little particle and smallest relic has the same power as the absolutely and utterly undivided martyr."

Pope St Gregory I the Great, *Letter to the Empress Constantia Augusta* 4, 30 (AD 594)
"Let my Most Tranquil Lady know that it is not the custom of the Romans, when they give relics of the saints, to presume to touch any part of the body. But only a cloth is put into a box and placed near the most sacred bodies of the saints. When it is taken up again it is deposited with due reverence in the Church that is to be dedicated, and effects so powerful are thereby produced, that it is as if their bodies had actually been taken there."

The Roman Catechism (1566)

Pt. III, Ch. II: If the clothes, the handkerchiefs, and even the very shadows of the Saints, while yet on earth, banished disease and restored health, who will have the hardihood to deny that God can still work the same wonders by the holy ashes, the bones and other relics of the Saints? Of this we have proof in the restoration to life of the dead body which was accidentally let down into the grave of Eliseus, and which, on touching the body (of the Prophet), was instantly restored to life.

Catechism of the Catholic Church (1992)

No. 1674: Besides sacramental liturgy and sacramentals, catechesis must take into account the forms of piety and popular devotions among the faithful. The religious sense of the Christian people has always found expression in various forms of piety surrounding the Church's sacramental life, such as the veneration of relics, visits to sanctuaries, pilgrimages, processions, the stations of the cross, religious dances, the rosary, medals, etc.

Celibacy of the Clergy

Objection: *"Where does it say in the Bible that priests cannot marry? In any case, the Bible states that, 'Therefore a man leaves his father and his mother and clings to his wife, and they become one flesh' (Gen. 2:24)."*

God created our original parents, Adam and Eve, in marital joy and placed them in the paradise of Eden: "and the rib which the Lord God had taken from the man he made into a woman and brought her to the man. Then the man said, 'This at last is bone of my bones and flesh of my flesh; she shall be called Woman, because she was taken out of Man'" (Gen. 2:22-23). The Fall, however, disrupted not only Adam's relationship with God but also introduced tension and disharmony into his relationship with Eve: "yet your desire shall be for your husband, and he shall rule over you" (Gen. 3:16).

Jesus Christ as Redeemer came to restore all things, including marriage. However, in the process of doing so, he introduced a new depth into the relationship between man and God – celibacy. It should be understood that, as true man, Jesus was certainly physically capable of marrying. However, the marriage he entered was not a marriage with one particular woman only. Through the love of a Bridegroom who was not only human but also divine, Jesus came to marry spiritually all he redeemed on the Cross.

This new spiritual and celibate love highlighted for the first time that there is another state of existence awaiting humanity after our earthly pilgrimage – the state of resurrection. The love of Jesus was of the kind the Just will finally and perfectly possess when they are united with God in the Beatific Vision. In heaven, there will be no bodily marriage, for our bodies will be completely absorbed in the spiritual marriage with the three Persons of the Blessed Trinity and a union of joy with the saints.

Celibacy is not a dogma of faith but a disciplinary law designed to increase the dignity of the priesthood. In the early Church there were many married men chosen for the offices of deacon, priest and bishop, but as the numbers of single, eligible men increased, more of them were ordained. Though widely practised since the beginning of the Church, celibacy was introduced as a mandatory rule in the Western Church only during the eleventh century, as part of the reforms of Pope St Gregory VII. The Church has the right to make (or unmake) such positive ecclesiastical laws on the basis of the power of the keys given to St Peter: "I will give you the keys of the kingdom of heaven, and whatever you bind on earth shall be bound in heaven, and whatever you loose on earth shall be loosed in heaven" (Mt 16:19). Unknown to many, the Eastern Rites of the Catholic Church have never changed their discipline and even to this day allow married men to become priests. However, once ordained, an Eastern Rite priest cannot marry, and only celibates can be chosen as bishops.

It was Jesus himself who first called some of his followers to celibacy:

"But he said to them, 'Not all men can receive this saying, but only those to whom it is given. For there are eunuchs who have been so from birth, and there are eunuchs who have been made eunuchs by men, and there are eunuchs who have made themselves eunuchs for the sake of the kingdom of heaven. He who is able to receive this, let him receive it'" (Mt 19:11-12).

Those who faithfully answer the call to practise celibacy for the sake of the Kingdom will receive a great reward:

"... let not the eunuch say, 'Behold, I am a dry tree.' For thus says the Lord: 'To the eunuchs who keep my sabbaths, who choose the things that please me and hold fast my covenant, I will give in my house and within my walls a monument and a name better than sons and daughters; I will give them an everlasting name which shall not be cut off'" (Is. 56:3-5).

"And he said to them, 'Truly, I say to you, there is no man who has left house or wife or brothers or parents or children, for the sake of the kingdom of God who will not receive manifold more in this time, and in the age to come eternal life'" (Lk 18:29-30).

Jesus clearly praises celibacy and promises to reward it abundantly when undertaken for his service and glory. The injunction to "be fruitful and multiply" in Gen. 1:28 is a general counsel for humanity; it is not obligatory for each individual, or Jesus would have been counselling and allowing people to live in a state of disobedience, including John the Baptist and most of the Apostles.

The teaching of the Apostle of the Gentiles, St Paul, is the same as Jesus'. He, like Jesus, led a life of celibacy and recommended it to others:

"I wish that all were as I myself am. But each has his own special gift from God, one of one kind and one of another. To the unmarried and the widows I say that it is well for them to remain single as I do. But if they cannot exercise self-control, they should marry. For it is better to marry than to be aflame with passion ... Now concerning the unmarried, I have no command of the Lord ... Are you bound to a wife? Do not seek to be free. Are you free from a wife? Do not seek marriage. But if you marry, you do not sin, and if a girl marries she does not sin" (1 Cor. 7:7-9, 25, 27-28).

Furthermore, he expressly states that celibacy is a higher state than the state of marriage:

"So that he who marries his betrothed does well; and he who refrains from marriage will do better" (v. 38).

In the light of the words and examples of Jesus and St Paul, how can anyone say that the celibate life is not an excellent one and therefore deny souls the opportunity of following more closely the footsteps of their Master?

St Paul in vv. 32-34 also gives a practical reason why the priests of Jesus should practise celibacy:

"The unmarried man is anxious about the affairs of the Lord, how to please the Lord; but the married man is anxious about worldly affairs, how to please his wife, and his interests are divided."

As a final point, the one hundred and forty-four thousand who sing the new canticle and follow the Lamb wherever he goes in the Book of Revelation are all virgins, as St John relates in chapter 14.

Second objection: *"But still, isn't celibacy against nature?"*

With God all things are possible. The true celibate is filled with joy and radiates his light and warmth to all others. Celibacy is not impossible, for its inspirer and guardian is the Holy Spirit: "Not all men can receive this saying, but only those to whom it is given" (Mt 19:11). It is the grace of God, not purely human effort, which keeps a celibate person pure. The abuses that occur are not due to celibacy itself, but to the lack of correspondence and fidelity to God's grace. God's gifts are never the cause of scandal when embraced and lived faithfully. In any case, abuse should never abolish use. Should marriage be discouraged because of the widespread prevalence of adultery and divorce? The Church is called to uphold the ideal, no matter how many may fail to live up to it.

Third objection: *"Did not St Paul insist that a Bishop should be 'a husband of one wife ... (and) if a man does not know how to manage his own household, how can he care for God's church' (1 Tim. 3:2-5)?"*

This is a favorite accusation raised by the most heated anti-Catholics, including Loraine Boettner in his work *Roman Catholicism* (p. 310). Boettner launches a series of attacks against so-called enforced celibacy, religious orders and the monastic system in general, together with his misinterpretation of St Paul's words to St Timothy. St Paul's obvious intent was to advise the younger St Timothy on the qualities to look for when choosing candidates for ordination. St Paul could not have been insisting on marriage as a necessary condition for ordination, for he himself – as mentioned earlier (1 Cor. 7:8) – never married.

One interpretation of St Paul's words is the following: If the candidate was a married man, he must not be in a second marriage that is adulterous. But if the candidate had been married and was now a widower, he was eligible, whereas a remarried man was not, since celibacy after widowhood was more highly regarded: "since he who refrains from marriage will do better" (1 Cor. 7:38); and "The unmarried man is anxious about the affairs of the Lord" (1 Cor. 7:32). An alternative interpretation is that continence, or abstinence, was demanded of clerics after ordination, and therefore a second marriage was a sign that a man could not live by such a discipline.

Fourth objection: *"But St Paul was married as well as the other Apostles according to 1 Cor. 9:5."*

The Revised Standard Version (Second Catholic Edition) of 1 Cor. 9:5 reads as follows: "Do we not have the right to be accompanied by a wife, as the other apostles and the brothers of the Lord and Cephas?" However, the Greek word translated as wife here is actually *gunaika* (γυναῖκα) that according to the Nestle-Aland Greek New Testament, 27th Ed., means a "woman," either betrothed, married or single. The root word for *gunaika* is *gune* (γυνη), which means a woman, wife or spouse. In either case the most common meaning of these two words is simply woman, and this is the sense in which it is used in John 2:4 when Jesus refers to his Mother as "woman" – the Greek word used here is *gune*. Also, the RSV for 1 Cor. 9:5 does not give a translation for the word *adelphen* (ἀδελφὴν) which is found in the original Greek of this verse and means sister. The Douai-Rheims gives a better translation of 1 Cor. 9:5 being, "Have we not power to bring about a woman, a sister, as well as the rest of the apostles, and the brethren of the Lord, and Cephas?"

Several the Fathers expressly denied that 1 Cor. 9:5 inferred St Paul had a wife (Tertullian, St Jerome and St Augustine). Rather, St Paul was asserting his claim to apostleship and the privileges that attached to it. The privileges given to those who gave their all for Jesus centered around being supported in their temporal needs, including food and drink (v. 4). To be accompanied by a wife could not be a privilege of apostleship for that is a right for all men in general. The privileges of apostleship were exclusive and included having the attendance of holy women as Jesus himself had. Such was the custom in Judea at the time and was no cause for scandal. These women were generally single, widows or elderly. If they were married to a Prophet or Apostle they did not live normal marital lives but sacrificed such for the sake of their husband's mission. To return to St Paul himself, "To the unmarried and the widows I say that it is well for them to remain single as I do" (1 Cor. 7:8).

Fifth objection: *"Did not St Paul also say that to 'forbid marriage' was one of the 'doctrines of demons' (1 Tim. 4:1-3)?"*

St Paul did make such a statement; however, he was not condemning the Catholic Church, but Gnostic heretics of his time and in the future who believed and taught that marriage was evil in itself. These Gnostics believed matter to be the creation of the Evil Principle and so also evil. As marriage led to the bringing into the world of human souls trapped in material bodies, it had to be condemned. On the other hand, in addition to extolling the superiority of consecrated celibacy the Catholic Church has always regarded marriage as a sacrament of Jesus and indissoluble (Mt 19:6). Protestantism, as much as it extols the virtues of marriage in contrast to celibacy, preaches a form of marriage that does not strictly meet the Christian ideal. Together with eliminating consecrated celibacy, the so-called Reformers of the sixteenth century introduced divorce (Henry VIII) and even sanctioned polygamy (Luther and the Landgrave of Hesse). Going further, since the Lambeth Conference of 1930 Protestantism has allowed contraception to artificially limit procreation, one of the essential purposes of marriage as ordained by God.

The Church forces no one into celibacy for it is a state of life that must be freely chosen by the individual in response to the inspirations of the Holy Spirit. Neither has anyone a right to ordination to the priesthood. However, the Church by virtue of the power of the keys has the right and the power to determine which persons may be ordained to the priesthood and under what conditions. The Catholic Church over the centuries has come to realize that generally a celibate rather than married clergy does better work for God's people. Candidates seeking ordination know the conditions well in advance and are given on average seven years to discern God's will for them and make their final decision. Only those who know that they have been given the gift of celibacy and embrace it wholeheartedly are welcomed and ordained into the ministerial priesthood. Those who do not have the calling to celibacy are free to serve God in the other ministries available to lay people in the Church.

The Fathers

St Ignatius of Antioch, *Letter to Polycarp* 5, 2 (c. AD 110)
"If anyone is able to remain continent, to the honor of the flesh of the Lord, let him so remain without boasting."

Origen, *Against Celsus* 1, 26 (c. AD 248)
"Certain ones among the Christians, from a desire of excelling in chastity, and in order to worship God in greater purity, refrain even from physical pleasures as are in accord with the law."

St Ambrose of Milan, *Synodal Letter to Pope Siricius* 42, 3 (AD 389)
"They pretend to honor marriage; but what praise can be given marriage if there is no glory in virginity? Neither do we deny that marriage has been sanctified by Christ, since the divine word says: 'The two shall become one flesh' and one spirit. But we are born before we are brought to our goal, and the mystery of the divine operation is much more excellent than the remedy for human weakness. It is quite right that a good wife be praised, but even better that a pious virgin be preferred."

St John Chrysostom, *Virginity* 10 (c. AD 392)
"That virginity is good I do agree. But that it is even better than marriage, this I do confess and if you wish, I will add that it is as much better than marriage as heaven is better than earth, as much better as the angels are better than men. And if there were any other way in which I could say it even more emphatically, I would do so."

St Augustine of Hippo, *Heresies* 82 (AD 428)
"He (Jovinian) destroyed the virginity of Mary, saying that it was lost by her parturition. He equated the merits of chaste spouses and of the faithful with the virginity of consecrated women and the continence of the male sex in holy persons choosing a celibate life."

The Roman Catechism (1566)

Pt. II, Ch. VIII: The words *increase and multiply*, which were uttered by the Lord, do not impose on every individual an obligation to marry, but only declare the purpose of the institution of marriage. Now that the human race is widely diffused, not only is there no law rendering marriage obligatory, but, on the contrary, virginity is highly exalted and strongly recommended in Scripture as superior to marriage, and as a state of greater perfection and holiness.

Catechism of the Catholic Church (1992)

No. 1618: Christ is the center of all Christian life. The bond with him takes precedence over all other bonds, familial or social. From the very beginning of the Church there have been men and women who have renounced the great good of marriage to follow the Lamb wherever he goes, to be intent on the things of the Lord, to seek to please him, and to go out to meet the Bridegroom who is coming. Christ himself has invited certain persons to follow him in this way of life, of which he remains the model.

Call No Man Your Father

Objection: *"Why do Catholics call their priests 'Father' when the Bible clearly states 'call no man your father on earth, for you have one father, who is in heaven' (Mt 23:9)?"*

The above quote from Matthew's Gospel must be read in the context of the whole of chapter 23, in which Jesus denounces the pride and hypocrisy of the Scribes and Pharisees, the contrast between their words and their actions (v. 3), the heavy burdens they placed on the shoulders of the people without giving any assistance (v. 4) and their love to be seen and praised: "They do all their deeds to be seen by men; for they make their phylacteries broad and their fringes long, and they love the place of honor at feasts and the best seats in the synagogues, and salutations in the market places, and being called rabbi by men" (vv. 5-7).

Jesus used this hyperbole to provide a lesson in humility, exhorting his followers to realize that only the Heavenly Father is the principal Father, while all others simply partake, or reveal a part, of his Fatherhood. Those in positions of power or authority are not to lord it over others, imposing impossible burdens while seeking public recognition and praise. Jesus concluded his admonitions, saying, "whoever exalts himself will be humbled, and whoever humbles himself will be exalted" (v.12).

A literal understanding of Jesus' words would lead to an absurd conclusion, prohibiting us from calling our natural fathers "father," while allowing us to call our mothers "mother." Yet, such an interpretation would go against Scripture itself, where the Virgin Mary says to the Child Jesus, "And when they saw him they were astonished; and his mother said to him, 'Son, why have you treated us so? Behold, *your father* and I have been looking for you anxiously'" (Lk 2:48). It would also prevent us from calling anyone "teacher" for Jesus warned equally against the use of this title as well: "But you are not to be called rabbi, for you have one teacher, and you are all brethren" (Mt 23:8).

St Paul confirms that there are various types of fatherhood, all of which are based on the Fatherhood of God: "For this reason I bow my knees before the Father, from whom every *paternity* in heaven and on earth is named" (Eph. 3:15). Abraham is acknowledged as the father of all who have faith in numerous passages, even in the New Law:

"And he said, 'No, father Abraham; but if some one goes to them from the dead, they will repent'" (Lk 16:30).

"Your father Abraham rejoiced that he was to see my day; he saw it and was glad" (Jn 8:56).

"And Stephen said: 'Brethren and fathers, hear me. The God of glory appeared to our father Abraham, when he was in Mesopotamia, before he lived in Haran'" (Acts 7:2).

"He received circumcision as a sign or seal of the righteousness which he had by faith while he was still uncircumcised. The purpose was to make him the father of all who believe without being circumcised and who thus have righteousness reckoned to them" (Rom. 4:11).

"Was not Abraham our father justified by works, when he offered his son Isaac upon the altar?" (Js 2:21).

Jesus calls those who gave the Jews the practice of circumcision "the fathers":

"Moses gave you circumcision (not that it is from Moses, but from the fathers), and you circumcise a man upon the Sabbath" (Jn 7:22).

The angel Gabriel calls King David "father":

"He will be great, and will be called the Son of the Most High; and the Lord God will give to him the throne of his father David" (Lk 1:32).

The Virgin Mary says that God spoke to "our fathers":

"He has helped his servant Israel, in remembrance of his mercy, as he spoke to our fathers, to Abraham and to his posterity for ever" (Lk 1:54-55).

The Samaritan woman questions whether Jesus is greater than "our father" Jacob:

"Are you greater than our father Jacob, who gave us the well, and drank from it himself, and his sons, and his cattle?" (Jn 4:12).

The Acts of the Apostles records that the early Christians in their prayers likewise referred to King David as "our father":

"... who by the mouth of our father David, your servant, said by the Holy Spirit, 'Why did the Gentiles rage, and the peoples imagine vain things?'" (Acts 4:25).

St Paul addressed a crowd in Jerusalem as follows:

"Brethren and fathers, hear the defense which I now make before you" (Acts 22:1).

St Paul also applies the term "father" to himself, while on more than one occasion he writes to his own as his children:

"I do not write this to make you ashamed, but to admonish you as my beloved children. For though you have countless guides in Christ, you do not have many fathers. For I became your father in Christ Jesus through the gospel" (1 Cor. 4:14-15).

"Here for the third time I am ready to come to you. And I will not be a burden, for I seek not what is yours but you; for children ought not to lay up for their parents, but parents for their children" (2 Cor. 12:14).

"But Timothy's worth you know, how as a son with a father he has served with me in the gospel" (Phil. 2:22).

"... or you know how, like a father with his children, we exhorted each one of you and encouraged you and charged you" (1 Thess. 2:11).

"To Timothy, my true child in the faith. Grace, mercy, and peace from God the Father, and from Christ Jesus our Lord" (1 Tim. 1:2).

"To Titus my true child in a common faith: Grace and peace from God the Father and Christ Jesus our Savior" (Tit. 1:4).

"I appeal to you for my child, Onesimus, whose father I have become in my imprisonment" (Phile. 1:10).

In similar vein do the other Apostles themselves write:

"She who is at Babylon, who is likewise chosen, sends you greetings; and so does my son Mark" (1 Pet. 5:13).

"I am writing to you, little children, because your sins are forgiven for his sake. I am writing to you, fathers, because you know him who is from the beginning. I am writing to you, young men, because you have overcome the evil one. I write to you, children, because you know the Father" (1 Jn 2:12-13).

From these verses, it is evident that the title "father" was used not with any sense of pride, but rather to engender tenderness and affection within spiritual relationships. The Catholic Church wishes her children to act in the same way when addressing those who partake in God's Fatherhood through preaching the Gospel and sanctifying the faithful as "other Christs."

The Fathers

St Ignatius of Antioch, *Letter to the Trallians* 3, 1 (c. AD 110)
"Reverence them [the deacons] as Christ Jesus, of whose place they are the keepers, even as the bishop is the representative of the Father of all things, and the presbyters are the council of God, and assembly of the apostles of Christ."

St Irenaeus of Lyons, *Against Heresies* 4, 41, 2 (c. AD 180)
"He who has received the teaching from another's mouth is called the son of his instructor, and he is called his father."

St John Chrysostom, *Homilies on the First Epistle to Timothy* 6 (inter AD 392-397)
"... priests are the Fathers of all, it is their duty to attend to all their spiritual children, edifying them first by a holy life, and afterwards by salutary instructions."

Pope St Gregory I the Great, *Homilies on the Gospels* 17 (c. AD 592)
"Priests are Patres Christianorum (the Fathers of Christians)."

The Roman Catechism (1566)

Pt. III, Ch. V: In the first place, the prelates of the Church, her pastors and priests are called fathers, as is evident from the Apostle, who, writing to the Corinthians, says: *I write not these things to confound you; but I admonish you as my dearest children. For if you have ten thousand instructors in Christ, yet not many fathers* ... It is written in Ecclesiasticus: *Let us praise men of renown, and our fathers in their generation* ... Those who govern the State, to whom are entrusted power, magistracy, or command, are also called fathers; thus Naaman was called father by his servants ... The name father is also applied to those to whose care, fidelity, probity and wisdom others are committed, such as teachers, instructors, masters and guardians; and hence the sons of the Prophets called Elijah and Eliseus their father. Finally, aged men, advanced in years, we also call fathers.

Catechism of the Catholic Church (1992)

No. 1549: Through the ordained ministry, especially that of bishops and priests, the presence of Christ as head of the Church is made visible in the midst of the community of believers. In the beautiful expression of St Ignatius of Antioch, the bishop is *typos tou Patros*: he is like the living image of God the Father.

Fasting

Objection: *"Fasting is pointless. When one has faith it is useless for salvation! And doesn't St Paul say, 'For the kingdom of God does not mean food and drink but righteousness and peace and joy in the Holy Spirit' (Rom. 14:17)?"*

Most Evangelical and Fundamentalist Protestants generally see no value in fasting, due to their doctrine of justification by faith alone. It is sufficient simply to accept Jesus as one's "personal Lord and Savior" to be "saved" and have one's sinful nature "covered up" by the merits of Jesus. In addition, in accord with the doctrine of "total depravity," every action of man is considered sinful, including fasting. For other Protestants, though, fasting does have value, not towards justification but by way of appeasing God's wrath and deterring his just chastisements.

In contrast, the Catholic Church teaches that fasting is a meritorious action which not only deters God's wrath but goes to sanctify the Christian and assist him/her to achieve the ascendancy of the spirit over the flesh. As with all meritorious actions, fasting increases the life of sanctifying grace in the soul ("partakers of the divine nature": 2 Pet. 1:4) and remits temporal punishment due to sin.

Numerous passages both in the Old and New Testaments speak of fasting and its value for the People of God:

"'Yet even now', says the Lord, 'return to me with all your heart, with fasting, with weeping, and with mourning'" (Joel 2:12).

"Prayer is good when accompanied by fasting, almsgiving, and righteousness" (Tob. 12:8).

"And the people of Nineveh believed God; they proclaimed a fast, and put on sackcloth, from the greatest of them to the least of them" (Jon. 3:5).

"But I, when they were sick – I wore sackcloth, I afflicted myself with fasting. I prayed with head bowed on my bosom" (Ps. 35:13).

"I turned to the Lord God, pleading in earnest prayer, with fasting, sackcloth, and ashes" (Dan. 9:3).

Jesus himself spoke about fasting, giving us a more perfect understanding of how it should be practised:

"But when you fast, anoint your head and wash your face, that your fasting may not be seen by men but by your Father who is in secret; and your Father who sees in secret will reward you" (Mt 6:17-18).

"Jesus said to them, 'Can the wedding guests fast while the bridegroom is with them? As long as they have the bridegroom with them, they cannot fast. The days will come, when the bridegroom is taken away from them, and then they will fast in that day'" (Mk 2:19-20).

Jesus himself fasted forty days and forty nights in preparation before beginning his public mission:

"Then Jesus was led up by the Spirit into the wilderness to be tempted by the devil. And he fasted forty days and forty nights, and afterward he was hungry" (Mt 4:1-2).

Fasting, together with prayer, has from the beginning of the Church's history been part of her ceremonial worship:

"While they were worshiping the Lord and fasting, the Holy Spirit said, 'Set apart for me Barnabas and Saul for the work to which I have called them.' Then after fasting and praying they laid their hands on them and sent them off" (Acts 13:2-3).

"And when they had appointed elders for them in every church, with prayer and fasting they committed them to the Lord in whom they believed" (Acts 14:23).

Fasting gives added strength to the apostle and the servant of Jesus against the powers of the Evil One:

"Then came the disciples to Jesus secretly, and said: 'Why could not we cast it out?' He said to them: 'Because of your little faith ... But this kind is not cast out but by prayer and fasting'" (Mt 17:19-20).

Fasting is a sign of the suffering and penitential Christian:

"... but as servants of God we commend ourselves in every way: through great endurance, in afflictions, hardships, calamities beatings, imprisonments, tumults, labors, watching, hunger" (2 Cor. 6:4-5).

Second objection: *"Isn't the Catholic practice of abstaining from meat on Fridays one of the 'doctrine of demons' Paul spoke about to Timothy (1 Tim. 4:1-5)?"*

The full text of St Paul's words of warning reads as follows: "Now the Spirit expressly says that in later times some will depart from the faith by giving heed to deceitful spirits and doctrines of demons, through the pretensions of liars whose consciences are seared, who forbid marriage and *enjoin abstinence from foods* which God created to be received with thanksgiving by those who believe and know the truth" (1 Tim. 4:1-3).

The Catholic Church for several centuries enjoined abstinence from meat on Fridays. Since 1966, Friday is rather designated as a "day of penance"; abstinence from meat is now only compulsory on Ash Wednesday, Good Friday and Fridays during Lent. Nevertheless, it is still the common practice of many faithful Catholics to abstain from meat on Fridays. On other days, they eat meat as other people do.

That St Paul had in mind the Catholic practice of abstaining from meat on Fridays when he pronounced the above prophecy is out of the question, particularly in view of the well-known practice of the Prophet Daniel: "In those days, I, Daniel, mourned three full weeks. I ate no savory food, I took *no meat* or wine, and I did not anoint myself at all until the end of the three weeks" (Dan. 10:2-3). The Catholic practice is similar in essence to Daniel's, who undertook a temporary abstinence of meat for penitential reasons. Daniel was hardly one to practise a "doctrine of demons."

Rather, St Paul was speaking of future Gnostic heretics, such as the Manicheans and Albigensians, who would teach that matter was the creation of the Evil Principle and hence intrinsically evil. Consequently, they believed that the eating of meat was also evil and abstained from it perpetually. Many vegetarian 'New Agers' share a similar opinion, while Seventh-Day Adventists insist that pork, oysters, prawns, rabbits are forbidden meats. St Paul saw no difficulty with the idea of giving up meat, even permanently, so long as one did not regard the eating of it as intrinsically evil. He even advised giving meat up permanently if such would prevent the sin of scandal (1 Cor. 8:13) and praised the man who abstains in the Lord's honor: "He who observes the day, observes it in honor of the Lord. He also who eats, eats in honor of the Lord, since he gives thanks to God; while he who abstains, abstains in honor of the Lord and gives thanks to God" (Rom. 14:6).

Contrary to Gnosticism, the Catholic Church regards the eating of meat to be good and healthy, even a delicacy, which is why she recommends that it be given up, but only temporarily. By abstaining from something good the Christian learns to cultivate a spirit of humility and sacrifice, as well as exercising the spiritual discipline of subduing the wayward desires of the flesh, that is, the unruly inclinations of our lower nature. Fasting helps raise our hearts and minds to the contemplation of heavenly things, aiding us to fulfil the universal call to holiness. Conversely, the glutton is equated with being an enemy of Christ's Cross (Phil. 3:18).

Third objection: *"Catholic fasts are a farce. As the Presbyterian minister Loraine Boettner says, 'Rome's fasts are purely arbitrary and mechanical, not spiritual ... True fasting is a spiritual exercise usually connected with prayer, repentance and meditation' (Roman Catholicism, p. 276)."*

To outsiders, the days of fasting and abstinence appointed by the Church and their accompanying rules may seem arbitrary and without Biblical foundation. Nevertheless, Jesus bestowed upon the Church power to legislate, binding and loosing laws for the spiritual benefit of her children (Mt 16:18, 18:18). These are not simply 'man-made commandments' as some claim, but the obligatory commands of the Church of Christ: "He who hears you hears me, and he who rejects you rejects me, and he who rejects me rejects him who sent me" (Lk 10:16). Not only has the Church the power to make laws regulating fasting, she also has the moral responsibility to do so, setting down balanced standards in order to avoid extremes of laxity or excess. The Church in this regard acts purely as a mother, guiding her children and ensuring that all within her fold can undertake appropriate levels of fasting, taking into account factors such as the health and age of her children as well as the environment in which they live.

No one doubts that true fasting must be spiritual and connected with prayer, repentance and meditation. In this regard Boettner unwittingly echoes the Catholic Church's own teaching and the practice of her saints and numerous millions of other faithful throughout the centuries. However, he falls into the common error of attacking abuse while claiming to be attacking actual Catholic teaching. Let us abolish abuse, while remembering at the same time that abuse does not abolish use.

The Fathers

The Didache 7, 1; 8, 1 (inter AD 90-150)
"Before the Baptism, let the one baptizing and the one to be baptized fast, as also any others who are able. Command the one to be baptized to fast beforehand for one or two days ... Bless those who curse you, and pray for your enemies: fast for those who persecute you ... Do not let your fasts be with the hypocrites. They fast on Monday and Thursday; but you will fast on Wednesday and Friday."

Tertullian, *The Demurrer Against the Heretics* 19, 1 (c. AD 206)
"Likewise, in regard to days of fast, many do not think they should be present at the sacrificial prayers, because their fast would be broken if they were to receive the Body of the Lord ... Will not your fast be more solemn if, in addition, you have stood at God's altar?"

St Ambrose of Milan, *Epistle to the Church of Vercellae* **63, 17 (AD 396)**
"Who then are these new teachers who reject the merit of fasting? Is it not the voice of heathen who say, 'Let us eat and drink?' whom the Apostle well ridicules, when he says: 'If after the manner of men I have fought with beasts at Ephesus, what advantage is it to me if the dead rise not?'... And, consequently, if all hope of the resurrection is lost, let us eat and drink, let us not lose the enjoyment of things present, who have none of things to come."

Pope St Leo I the Great, *Sermon* **12, 4 (inter AD 440-461)**
"... in prayer faith remains steadfast, in fastings life remains innocent, in almsgiving the mind remains kind. On Wednesday and Friday therefore let us fast: and on Saturday let us keep vigil with the most blessed Apostle Peter, who will deign to aid our supplications and fast and alms with his own prayers through our Lord Jesus Christ, who with the Father and the Holy Ghost lives and reigns for ever and ever."

The Roman Catechism (1566)

Pt. IV, Ch. VI: To prayer let us unite fasting and almsdeeds. Fasting is most intimately connected with prayer. For the mind of one who is filled with food and drink is so borne down as not to be able to raise itself to the contemplation of God ...

Catechism of the Catholic Church (1992)

No. 1434: The interior penance of the Christian can be expressed in many and various ways. Scripture and the Fathers insist above all on three forms, *fasting, prayer, and almsgiving,* which express conversion in relation to oneself, to God, and to others. Alongside the radical purification brought about by Baptism or martyrdom they cite as means of obtaining forgiveness of sins: efforts at reconciliation with one's neighbor, the intercession of the Saints, and the practice of charity "which covers a multitude of sins."

The Sign of the Cross

Objection: *"According to the Presbyterian minister, Loraine Boettner, the 'sign of the cross' was introduced into Catholic worship from paganism in the late third century. Indeed, the cross is a detestable thing, a pagan symbol of sin and shame!"*

Anyone of objective mind and fairness cannot take such claims seriously. There is no doubt that the cross as an instrument of execution was considered hideous and fearful in its day. It was the most painful and degrading punishment inflicted by the ancient Romans on criminals and prisoners. After the Christianization of the Empire, crucifixion was abolished.

However, "The earth is the Lord's and the fulness thereof" (Ps. 24:1; 1 Cor. 10:26). Therefore, the Church of Christ has the power and authority to take any appropriate object created by God and attribute to it a Christian meaning, that is 'baptize it,' and employ it in her official worship. Simply because ancient pagan cultures engaged in certain practices or used certain objects in their worship does not of itself render those same practices or objects illicit for all time. Certain pagans would have prayed with the hands outstretched or used incense in their worship. Should Christians refrain from doing likewise simply because of that fact? Obviously not.

What was sinful was that such practices and objects were employed in idolatrous worship. This was the case when incense was offered to worship Baal, Astarte or Caesar. Nevertheless, Scripture testifies to the use of incense in the worship of the true God by the heavenly court: "And another angel came and stood at the altar with a golden censer; and he was given much incense to mingle with the prayers of all the saints upon the golden altar before the throne" (Rev. 8:3). Therefore, what meaning an object or practice had for pagans is of no relevance for Christians in their worship.

It testifies to the glory and power of Jesus that he could take the most abject of objects and cause it to become the most glorious of all symbols. For early non-Christians, the Cross was a "stumbling block" (Gal. 5:11) and a "shame" (Heb. 12:2). However, as Christians saw in the Cross of Jesus the great love he had for us, the symbol of the Cross began to take on a deep spiritual meaning. As St Paul would say, "But far be it from me to glory except in the cross of our Lord Jesus Christ, by which the world has been crucified to me, and I to the world" (Gal. 6:14). For Christians, the Cross only has significance because Jesus died upon it. Apart from this fact, the Cross has only a pagan or historical significance. Thus, we see the value of the Catholic practice of placing an image of Jesus upon crosses to form the image of the crucifix. It is a means to "preach Christ crucified" and to show forth "the power of God and the wisdom of God" (1 Cor. 1:23).

Many Protestants use crosses in their churches and homes but object to having crucifixes because they regard three-dimensional images to be idols in breach of their second commandment. However, there exists a strange inconsistency in all this, for if one peruses their children's Bible-story books one would discover many two-dimensional pictures of the crucifixion!

Second objection: *"Crucifixes should not be used because we worship Christ risen, not crucified."*

Jesus ought to be worshiped both as crucified and as risen. This is the spirit shown by St Paul in Gal. 6:14 and 1 Cor. 1:23 quoted above. Indeed, Christians should worship him in all the stages of his incarnation, as he is the divine Son of God at all times. The above objection fails to give full significance to the crucifixion as the event (rather than the resurrection) that paid the price for our sins. St Paul himself said, "For I decided to know nothing among you except Jesus Christ and him crucified" (1 Cor. 2:2).

There are some who claim that Jesus was in fact not crucified on a cross at all, but instead was impaled to a punishment stake with his two hands nailed together above his head rather than stretched outwards to his right and left. The Jehovah's Witnesses have been propagating this opinion since 1930 (previously, from their foundation in 1879 they had held the Catholic position). Needless to say, there is nothing in Scripture to support such a novel view. Rather, there are numerous quotes that can be cited to the contrary, for example:

"... he who does not take his cross and follow me is not worthy of me" (Mt 10:38).

"And they compelled a passer-by, Simon of Cyrene, who was coming in from the country, the father of Alexander and Rufus, to carry his cross" (Mk 15:21).

"And he said to all, 'If any man would come after me, let him deny himself and take up his cross daily and follow me'" (Lk 9:23).

"So they took Jesus, and he went out, bearing his own cross, to the place called the place of a skull, which is called in Hebrew Golgotha" (Jn 19:17).

"And being found in human form he humbled himself and became obedient unto death, even death on a cross" (Phil. 2:8).

There is no direct reference to the use of the Sign of the Cross in worship in Scripture. Nevertheless, it would be highly presumptuous to denigrate this holy practice simply because of this fact, particularly given that Scripture speaks so highly of the Cross as the instrument of our salvation. The Church employs the Sign of the Cross when she wishes to bestow the blessings of God on animate and inanimate creatures. It has also always been used to mark out Jesus' faithful. In this it has its prefigurement in the Old Testament: "And the Lord said to him: 'Go through the city, through Jerusalem, and put a mark upon the foreheads of the men who sigh and groan over all the abominations that are committed in it ... slay old men outright, young men and maidens, little children and women, but touch no one upon whom is the mark. And begin at my sanctuary" (Ezek. 9:4 & 6). The "mark" Ezekiel refers to was T-shaped. From the very beginning, Christians have seen in the Ezekiel's "mark" a prefigurement of Jesus' own Cross, and its application on people's foreheads, the Sign of the Cross.

Ezekiel 9:4 has its echo in Rev. 7:3: "Do not harm the earth or the sea or the trees, till we have sealed the servants of our God upon their foreheads." Can this *seal* be possibly any different from the "sign of the Son of man" (Mt 24:30), which is the Cross?

The early Christians were always eager to develop signs and symbols that summarized the great mysteries of the Faith. In the Sign of the Cross, two immense truths are signified together, namely the mystery of the Blessed Trinity, Father, Son and Holy Spirit, and the misery and humiliation of the crucifixion. Spontaneously they drew this holy sign everywhere, accompanied by any one of the following words: "Sign of Christ"; "In the Name of Jesus"; or "In the Name of the Father and of the Son and of the Holy Spirit."

Constantine, before his great victory in the battle of Milvian Bridge (28 October, AD 312), which brought him to power as the first Christian Roman Emperor, saw in the sky a cross with the words *"In Hoc Signo Vinces"* – "In this sign you shall conquer." The victory of every Christian is achieved always through the power of the Cross.

The Fathers

Tertullian, *The Crown* 3, 2 (AD 211)
"At every forward step and movement, when coming in and going out, when putting on our clothes, when putting on our shoes, when bathing, when at table, when lighting the lamps, when reclining, when sitting, in all the ordinary occupations of our daily lives, we furrow our forehead with the sign."

St Athanasius, *Treatise on the Incarnation of the Word* 47, 2 (c. AD 318)
"And while in times past demons, occupying springs or rivers or trees or stones, cheated men by deceptive appearances and imposed upon the credulous by their juggleries, now, after the divine coming of the Word, an end is put to their deceptions. For by the sign of the cross, a man but using it, their wiles are put to flight."

St Cyril of Jerusalem, *Catechetical Lectures* 15, 22 (c. AD 350)
"But what – lest a hostile power dare to counterfeit it – is the sign of his coming? 'And then shall appear,' he says, 'the sign of the Son of Man in the heavens.' Christ's own true sign is the cross. The sign of a luminous cross shall go before the King, pointing out him that was formally crucified."

St Basil the Great, *The Holy Spirit* 27, 66 (AD 375)
"Indeed, were we to try to reject unwritten customs as having no great authority, we would unwittingly injure the Gospel in its vitals; or rather, we would reduce Kerygma to a mere term. For instance, to take the first and most general example, who taught us in writing to sign with the sign of the cross those who have trusted in the name of our Lord Jesus Christ?"

St Augustine of Hippo, *Homilies on John* 11, 3 (AD 416-417)
"If we should say to a catechumen: 'Do you believe in Christ,' he will answer, 'I do believe,' and he will sign himself. He already carries the cross of Christ on his forehead, and he is not ashamed of the cross of the Lord."

The Roman Catechism (1566)

Pt. II, Ch. III: Besides, that mark by which the Christian is distinguished from all others, as the soldier is by certain badges, should be impressed on the more conspicuous part of the body.

Catechism of the Catholic Church (1992)

No. 617: The Council of Trent emphasizes the unique character of Christ's sacrifice as "the source of eternal salvation" and teaches that "his most holy Passion on the wood of the cross merited justification for us." And the Church venerates his cross as it sings: "Hail, O Cross, our only hope."

The Rapture

Objection: *"The Rapture is an authentic Christian belief with solid support in the Bible. Why don't Catholics believe in it?"*

For most people who believe in the Rapture it is the idea that Jesus Christ will soon secretly return to invisibly snatch away true Christians and innocent children, whether living or dead, and take them to heaven before the appearance of the Antichrist and the period of the 'Great Tribulation.' The sudden disappearance of all true Christians will cause worldwide confusion and turmoil. Once all true Christians have disappeared, the Antichrist will be free to take control of the world and impose his reign of terror. Of the people remaining on earth during this terrible time only those who resist the Antichrist and die as martyrs for Jesus will be saved. After seven years of tribulation, Jesus will return yet again, this time visibly and in glory to destroy the Antichrist and his followers and institute his thousand-year public reign, known as 'the Millennium.' Belief in a secret Rapture has become increasingly popular in recent decades through the publications of works such as *The Late Great Planet Earth* by Hal Lindsey (1969) and the *Left Behind* series by Tim LaHaye and Jerry B. Jenkins (1995-2001).

However, does this view of the 'end-times' accurately reflect the Biblical data, or is it an interpretation tainted by peculiar theological beliefs? The advocates of 'secret Rapture doctrine' insist that their beliefs are simply the plain understanding of Scripture and point to passages such as 1 Thess. 4:15-17 for support:

"For this we declare to you by the word of the Lord, that we who are alive, who are left until the coming of the Lord, shall not precede those who have fallen asleep. For the Lord himself will descend from heaven with a cry of command, with the archangel's call, and with the sound of the trumpet of God. And the dead in Christ will rise first; then we who are alive, who are left, shall be caught up together with them in the clouds to meet the Lord in the air; and so we shall always be with the Lord."

The words "caught up" in the above verse originally read *rapiemur* in the Latin Vulgate, from which "rapture" is derived. In the original Greek, the relevant word is ἁρπαγησόμεθα (harpagesometha), meaning, "shall be seized." The meaning is nevertheless the same; Jesus will one day return and his followers, living and dead, will be lifted up to meet him in the air.

Nevertheless, does 1 Thess. 4:15-17 really describe a secret event? Not at all. Rather, it describes an awesome public event, one involving the descent of Jesus amidst *"a cry of command, with the archangel's call, and with the sound of the trumpet of God."* There is nothing secret about cries, calls and trumpets! The public nature of Jesus' second coming is reinforced by other verses of Scripture, including Matt. 24:30 and Rev. 1:7:

"... then will appear the sign of the Son of man in heaven, and then all the tribes of the earth will mourn, and they will see the Son of man coming on the clouds of heaven with power and great glory ..."

"Behold, he is coming with the clouds, and every eye will see him, every one who pierced him; and all tribes of the earth will wail on account of him. Even so. Amen."

The second problem with secret Rapture doctrine is its belief in two 'second comings' of Jesus – the first to secretly snatch away the true Christians; the second in glory to defeat the Antichrist. Yet, the Bible consistently speaks of one and only one second coming of Jesus. For example, 1 Thess. 4:15 cited above says *"the* coming," not *"a* coming."

The third problem with secret Rapture doctrine is that nowhere in 1 Thess. 4:15-17 does it say that Jesus will descend and then do a 'u-turn' back into heaven. Rather, Jesus will return and establish his Kingdom, which will descend like a bride adorned for her wedding:

"And I saw the holy city, new Jerusalem, coming down out of heaven from God, prepared as a bride adorned for her husband" (Rev. 21:2).

The fourth problem with secret Rapture doctrine is the assertion that true Christians will be spared the Great Tribulation and all its attendant sufferings. Yet, Matt. 24:21-22 indicates otherwise:

"For then there will be great tribulation, such as has not been from the beginning of the world until now, no, and never will be. And if those days had not been shortened, no human being would be saved; but for the sake of the elect those days will be shortened."

Why would the days of misery be shortened for the sake of the elect unless the elect were still on earth during the Great Tribulation?

The fifth problem with secret Rapture doctrine is its assertion that Jesus will secretly come *before* the appearance of the Antichrist, while 2 Thess. 2:3-4 & 8 is clear that Jesus' one and only return will occur *after* the Antichrist's appearance and reign:

"Let no one deceive you in any way; for that day will not come, unless the rebellion comes first, and the man of lawlessness is revealed, the son of perdition, who opposes and exalts himself against every so-called god or object of worship, so that he takes his seat in the temple of God, proclaiming himself to be God ... And then the lawless one will be revealed, and the Lord Jesus will slay him with the breath of his mouth and destroy him by his appearing and his coming."

The sixth problem with secret Rapture doctrine is the belief that the righteous dead are raised to meet Jesus at the time of his secret second coming. Afterwards, there will be seven years of the Antichrist's reign before Jesus' final coming in glory. Yet, we know from John 6:54 that the dead will only be raised on the "last day":

"He who eats my flesh and drinks my blood has eternal life, and I will raise him up at the last day."

The seventh problem with secret Rapture doctrine lies in the verse of Scripture used as the basis for unbelievers being 'left-behind,' namely Matt. 24:37-41:

"As were the days of Noah, so will be the coming of the Son of man. For as in those days before the flood they were eating and drinking, marrying and giving in marriage, until the day when Noah entered the ark, and they did not know until the flood came and swept them all away, so will be the coming of the Son of man. Then two men will be in the field; one is taken and one is left. Two women will be grinding at the mill; one is taken and one is left."

The above verse tells us that in the days of Noah the unrighteous were swept away, while the righteous were left behind. This is the opposite of what Rapture doctrine says will happen when Jesus returns secretly. If the 'end-times' are meant to be like the days of Noah, then what Matt. 24:37-41 means is that the unrighteous will be "taken" by death (presumably to damnation) and that the righteous will be left behind to be raptured when Jesus returns in public glory.

The eighth problem with secret Rapture doctrine is its reliance on the words "twinkling of an eye" in 1 Cor. 15:52 in support of a secret rapture. The full text of 1 Cor. 15:50-52 reads as follows:

"Behold! I tell you a mystery. We shall not all sleep, but we shall all be changed, in a moment, in the twinkling of an eye, at the last trumpet. For the trumpet will sound, and the dead will be raised imperishable, and we shall be changed."

St Paul's purpose in the above passage was to teach the Corinthians how Christians will be mysteriously and instantly glorified in their bodies at the return of Jesus, not that they will be secretly snatched off the earth prior to the Tribulation. At the sound of "the last trumpet" both the living and the dead faithful in Jesus will be transformed. The sounding of this "trumpet" is evidence enough that St Paul is speaking of a public event. This is the same "last trumpet" heralding the public second coming of Jesus in Matt. 24:31.

The final problem with secret Rapture doctrine is the fact that none of the leaders of the Protestant Reformation – Luther, Calvin, Zwingli, Knox, etc. – showed any evidence of belief in a secret second coming to steal away the elect. Rather, with the Catholic Church, they viewed 1 Thess. 4:15-17, etc., as referring to the *Parousia*, or Jesus' public second coming at the end of the world to judge the living and the dead.

The last word regarding secret Rapture doctrine should go to the pre-millennial Baptist theologian Dale Moody, who in his work *The Word of Truth* said the following[1]:

> Belief in a pre-tribulational rapture ... contradicts all three chapters in the New Testament that mention the tribulation and the rapture together (Mk 13:24-27; Mt 24:26-31; 2 Thess. 2:1-12) ... The theory is so biblically bankrupt that the usual defense is made using three passages that do not even mention a tribulation (Jn 14:3; 1 Thess. 4:17; 1 Cor. 15:52). These are important passages, but they have not had one word to say about a pre-tribulation rapture. The score is 3 to 0, three passages for a post-tribulational rapture and three that say nothing on the subject.

There will be a Rapture, however it will occur when Jesus makes his one and only second coming in power and glory at the end of the world to judge the living and the dead. The righteous will be caught up together to meet Jesus as he approaches the world in triumph. They will be joined by the angels and the saints who have been reigning with Jesus in heaven (Rev. 6:9-11). Together, all the righteous will welcome the King of Glory as he approaches to consummate all things.

Second objection: *"The Rapture was believed by the early Christians and the Fathers of the Church."*

Proponents of a secret Rapture such as LaHaye insist that all Christians who take the Bible literally believe in a pre-Tribulation Rapture. It is these same modern Christians who have allegedly restored belief in the Biblical doctrine of the 'pre-Trib' Rapture lost during the era of 'Romanism.' As evidence that early Christians believed in a 'pre-Trib' Rapture the writings of one Father known as Pseudo-Ephraem are cited. Anti-Rapture Christians, however, insist that there exists no evidence of belief in a secret Rapture by any

---

[1] Dale Moody, *The Word of Truth*, Grand Rapids: Eerdmans, 1981, pp. 556-557.

reputable Christian before the eighteenth century. Where, then, does such a belief spring?

Looking firstly at the early Church Fathers, we find that a significant number of them – including Papias, Justin Martyr, Irenaeus, Tertullian, Hippolytus, Methodius, Commodianus and Lactantius – were pre-millennialists who believed that Jesus would return to establish a visible, earthly reign of a thousand years. Belief in such a literal millennium is a necessary part of the secret Rapture end-times picture. However, as esteemed as most of these Fathers are, no one Church Father or group of Fathers is infallible in their teachings. The Church interprets the Millennium as the reign of Jesus through his Church beginning at Pentecost and ending with the Second Coming. In any case, none of these same Fathers displayed any sign of belief in a secret Rapture (even though they all lived through the persecutions of the Roman Empire!), whether before or during the seven-year period of Tribulation prior to the Second Coming. The same Justin Martyr, Irenaeus and also Augustine of Hippo are just a few of the many Fathers who wrote about the suffering of Christians during the Tribulation. It is little wonder then that when the Nicene Creed was composed in the first half of the fourth century AD there was no mention of a secret Rapture of Christians before the coming of Jesus.

What about the writings of Pseudo-Ephraem? The relevant quote comes from a work entitled *Sermon on the Last Times, the Antichrist and the End of the World* and reads:

> All the saints and the elect of God are gathered together before the tribulation which is to come, and are taken to the Lord, in order that they may not see at any time the confusion which overwhelms the world because of our sins.

Pseudo-Ephraem wrote sometime between AD 565 and 627 and claimed that the above quote belonged to a sermon written by St Ephraem himself (AD 306-373), the greatest figure of the ancient Syrian church. Patristic scholars such as C.P. Caspari and P.J. Alexander admit that such a claim has some plausibility as Pseudo-Ephraem was heavily influenced by Ephraem's genuine works.

What significance should be attached to Pseudo-Ephraem? Not much. Undoubtedly, the quote is 'pre-trib' in nature but goes against all other ancient Byzantine and Latin apocalyptic texts that advocated a shortening of the time of Tribulation to three and a half years as the ultimate reason why Christians will survive. Furthermore, scholars still debate whether St Ephraem originally authored the quote for two reasons: (i) the notion of a 'pre-trib' rapture does not appear in any of his genuine works; (ii) the quote is taken from a Latin translation that is later than the eighth century, is conflated as compared to the Syriac version, and borrows from Pseudo-Methodius.

It does not get any better for secret Rapture supporters in the thousand years plus between the fall of the Roman Empire and the Protestant Reformation. No theologian or Scripture commentator of note makes mention of it. Both Martin Luther (*Preface to the Revelation of St John*) and John Calvin (*Institutes of the Christian Religion*, IV, vii, 25: III, xx) wrote that Christians would endure the end-times on earth. They can hardly be accused of not reading or ignoring Scripture for their failure to acknowledge the so-called truth of the secret Rapture.

The first vague notions of a secret Rapture were espoused by Puritan preachers Increase (1639-1723) and Cotton Mather (1663-1728) who taught that Christians would be "caught up in the air" before the final fiery judgment. They were followed by the Baptist pastor Morgan Edwards who in 1788 published an essay promoting the idea that Christians would be snatched up into heaven three and a half years before Jesus' final return.

Surprisingly enough, the next to write about the snatching up of Christians from the earth before the end of the world was a Chilean Jesuit by the name of Manuel Lacunza. His 1812 book, *The Coming of the Messiah in Glory and Majesty*, concluded that Jesus would snatch up Christians who regularly received the Eucharist and keep them safe for forty-five days while the world was punished with terrible chastisements. Lacunza's book was eventually condemned by Rome and placed on the Index of Forbidden Books. Nevertheless, Edward Irving, the founder of the "Catholic Apostolic Church," a forerunner of modern Pentecostalism, translated it into English in 1827. Under the influence of Lacunza's book, Irving began to preach that a secret Rapture would occur three and a half years before Jesus' final return.

Around 1830, a member of the British Plymouth Brethren sect by the name of John Nelson Darby began similarly to preach a secret

Rapture within a novel belief system called *Dispensationalism*. Dispensationalism is the belief that God plans to unravel revelation to humanity in seven progressive 'dispensations' over seven thousand years. It is said that we are currently living near the end of the sixth dispensation with the secret Rapture, the seven-year Tribulation and Jesus' public return imminent. The seventh dispensation will be the one-thousand-year public reign of Jesus, or 'Millennium.'

Darby popularized his Dispensationalism-Rapture beliefs during seven trips to Canada and the United States between 1859 and 1874, speaking at influential 'Bible Prophecy' conferences attended by tens of thousands of American Protestants. Eventually, several popular Evangelical Protestant leaders came under Darby's influence, including the famous revivalist Dwight L. Moody.

One of Moody's friends was Cyrus I. Schofield. Originally a hard-drinking lawyer, Schofield became an enthusiastic convert to Darby's beliefs and later in 1909 published his own commentary on the King James Version of the Bible known popularly as *The Schofield Reference Bible*. Schofield's copious marginal notes and commentaries advocating a secret Rapture were soon being read and believed by millions of ordinary Americans.

In the years that followed, Schofield's Bible and emotional revival meetings would spread secret Rapture belief into isolated, independent, Methodist, Baptist and Pentecostal churches across America. Respected centres of education such as the Dallas Theological Seminary and Moody Bible Institute would also embrace secret Rapture belief and send forth thousands of newly trained ministers to preach the same to countless people weary of economic depression and two world wars.

The re-establishment of Israel in 1948, the Cold War, the nuclear arms race, the Vietnam War, the 1960's student revolts, the Watergate scandal, etc., together all heightened interest in the end-times and Biblical prophecy. Concerned Christians became more than ever focussed on the 'promise' of an escape from a hell-bent world. In this context appeared *The Late Great Planet Earth* by Hal Lindsey in 1969. A former student at Dallas Theological Seminary, Lindsey presented his secret rapture beliefs in a book full of selected Bible quotes, news clippings, tantalizing chapter titles and sensationalist dire predictions. All up, Lindsey would eventually sell over forty million copies and become one of the best-selling American authors of the 1970s.

Countless imitators have since followed Lindsey, trying both to forewarn the world of the imminent secret Rapture and cash in where possible. The most successful of these imitators have been Tim LaHaye and Jerry B. Jenkins, whose twelve-volume *Left Behind* series published between 1995-2001 has since sold over fifty-five million copies. Undoubtedly, events surrounding the World Trade Center terrorist attack in 2001 re-energized end-times fears and belief in a secret Rapture. With continual wars and upheavals across the Middle East, the Global Financial Crisis, changing weather patterns, the COVID-19 pandemic, etc., these fears continue unabated to this day.

More than ever the world needs an authentic end-times catechesis that is truly Apostolic and Scriptural.

Third objection: *"The Church is God's 'Plan B' for Christians; 'Plan A' is still to be fulfilled for the Jews."*

The above comment reflects the standard conviction of all Dispensationalists who subscribe to belief in a secret Rapture. Dispensationalists believe that Jesus initially came to offer the Jews a material and worldly Kingdom, but the Jews rejected him. Consequently, Jesus set up the Church and returned to heaven to become "wholly a heavenly person." In the words of one popular Dispensationalist, Lewis S. Chafer (1871-1952), "The present age of the Church is an intercalation into the revealed calendar or program of God as that program was foreseen by the prophets of old. Such, indeed, is the precise nature of the present age." As long as the present "Church age" continues, the Old Testament promises made to Israel are suspended, waiting to be fulfilled.

The Church for Dispensationalists, therefore, is not the "New Israel" spoken of by St Paul (Gal. 6:16). It is only one of two separate peoples of God: the Jews (the "earthly people") and the Christians (the "heavenly people"). The secret Rapture is necessary to remove the Christians from earth so that God's plan for the Jews can be resumed. That plan will see the Jews being chastised during the Tribulation, resulting in most being killed and the remaining converting to Christianity. Once the Millennium arrives, Jesus will rule an earthly kingdom of Israel, with Jerusalem as its capital. The Temple of Jerusalem will be rebuilt and the ancient animal sacrifices will be resumed. These sacrifices will have salvific value, befitting the theocratic nature of the kingdom and society.

None of the above is compatible with Scripture and Catholic doctrine. Jesus did not 'fail' nor did all the Jews reject him; many accepted him as the Messiah. Nor did Jesus ever offer a worldly kingdom; rather, his kingdom was "not of this world" (Jn 18:36). Rather than being a "Plan B," the Church is Jesus' Body (Eph. 5:23) and the Bride of Christ (Rev. 19:7). Rather than two separate peoples of God, Jesus prayed that "they may be one" (Jn 17:11) and gave us baptism so that all may be "baptized into one body" (1 Cor. 12:13). In the words of St Paul, "There is one body and one Spirit, just as you were called to the one hope that belongs to your call, one Lord, one faith, one baptism, one God and Father of us all, who is above all and through all and in all" (Eph. 4:4).

Fourth objection: *"The Rapture doctrine helps me to focus on what is important – my salvation!"*

Secret Rapture doctrine might help certain individuals to focus on their salvation, but for many that focus often fails to understand the deeper meaning of suffering and deteriorates to a selfish disregard of the here and now and the immediate needs of others.

Undoubtedly, the thought of Jesus' imminent return is attractive and intoxicating; so too the prospect of escaping suffering, torture and martyrdom during the reign of the Antichrist. While one is free to believe in the imminent return of Jesus, escape from all forms of suffering is not a legitimate option for Christians. Rather, the Apostles viewed suffering and death for the "name of Jesus" as a great honor (Acts 5:40). Suffering is both a good and necessary thing because it draws the believer closer to God (Mt 10:22-23; Jn 16:33) and enables Christians to imitate their Lord more closely through the taking up of their own crosses (Mt 16:24). In any case, why should latter-day

Christians be exempt from torture and death when millions of other Christians over the past twenty centuries were afforded no such luxury?

Selfishness is the other offspring of secret Rapture escapism. Regular Rapture preaching usually does not result in vast numbers of Christians volunteering for soup kitchens or enlisting in social and political activism. Why bother struggling against poverty, hunger, immorality, the culture of death, etc., if the secret Rapture is imminent? Worse still, events such as droughts, floods, famine, earthquakes and wars are not only welcomed by millions but even encouraged to hasten the predicted apocalypse.

Any person who is worried about their salvation would do better to read the Last Judgment scene in Matt. 25 than listen to sermons on the secret Rapture.

Fifth objection: *"The Catholic Church neither believes in the Rapture nor in Jesus' imminent return."*

It might come as a surprise to many non-Catholic Christians, but the Catholic Church certainly does believe in a Rapture, "a final trial", a "supreme religious deception ... of the Antichrist" (*Catechism of the Catholic Church* #675), and Jesus' return.

The Catholic Church's official teachings on the end-times are contained in the Nicene Creed and the *Catechism of the Catholic Church* paras 668-682. In short, the second coming of Jesus is associated with the end of the world and the Last Judgment, not with a secret Rapture or the establishment of a temporary 'Millennium.' Jesus' Second Coming will be triumphant and ever-lasting, not temporal and limited.

From the *Catechism* (CCC 673-677), the order of events we can expect for the end-times are:
- The full number of Gentiles to enter the Church.
- The "full inclusion of the Jews in the Messiah's salvation, in the wake of the full number of the Gentiles."
- A final trial conducted by the Antichrist against the Church "in the form of a religious deception offering men an apparent solution to their problems at the price of apostasy from the truth."

- Jesus' victory over this final trial through his glorious return and the Last Judgment.

Amid all this, the Catholic Church believes that the Rapture will occur on the Last Day, when Jesus returns to judge the living and the dead, after the dead have been raised. On that day, all the faithful will go to meet Jesus and be with him forever (1 Thess. 4:17).

The Fathers

St Irenaeus of Lyons, *Against Heresies* **5, 28, 4 (c. AD 180)**
"And for this cause tribulation is necessary for those who are saved, that having been after a manner broken up, and rendered fine, and sprinkled over by the patience of the word of God, and set on fire [for purification] they may be fitted for the royal banquet."

St Irenaeus of Lyons, *Against Heresies* **5, 29, 1 (c. AD 180)**
[Speaking on Matt. 24:21] "For this is the last contest of the Righteous, in which, when they overcome, they are crowned with incorruption."

St Hippolytus of Rome, *Commentary on the Book of Daniel,* **60 (c. AD 204)**
"Now concerning the tribulation of the persecution which is to fall upon the Church from the adversary, John also speaks thus, [then he writes out Rev. chapter 12]. After this, he writes about the time, times, and half a time the woman is hid, and says, 'That refers to the one thousand two hundred and threescore days [the half of the week] during which the tyrant is to reign and persecute the Church, which flees from city to city to seek concealment in the wilderness."

St Cyril of Alexandria, *Against the Anthropomorphites* **16 (post AD 441)**
"The Divine Scripture says that the judgment is to take place after the resurrection of the dead. But the resurrection is not to take place until Christ returns to us from heaven in the glory of the Father with the holy angels."

The Roman Catechism (1566)

Pt. I, Ch. VIII: Hence, speaking of the last day, our Lord and Savior declares that a general judgment will one day take place, and he describes the signs of its approach, that seeing them, we may know that the end of the world is at hand. At his Ascension also, to console his Apostles, overwhelmed with grief at his departure, he sent angels, who said to them: *This Jesus who is taken up from you into heaven, shall so come, as you have seen him going into heaven.*

Catechism of the Catholic Church (1992)

No. 673: Since the Ascension Christ's coming in glory has been imminent ... This eschatological coming could be accomplished at any moment, even if both it and the final trial that will precede it are "delayed."

No. 677: The Church will enter the glory of the kingdom only through this final Passover, when she will follow her Lord in his death and Resurrection. The kingdom will be fulfilled ... by God's victory over the final unleashing of evil, which will cause his Bride to come down from heaven. God's triumph over the revolt of evil will take the form of the Last Judgement after the final cosmic upheaval of this passing world.

The Antichrist

Introduction

The word 'Antichrist' appears only four times in the Bible (1 Jn 2:18, 2:22, 4:3 & 2 Jn 1:7), yet he is a person and theme that has intrigued the minds of Christians for most of the past two thousand years. Nearly all Scripture commentators of repute, or otherwise, have attempted to identify this figure of dread, though there is precious little agreement as to who (or what) he is or when he will make his appearance.

Despite receiving only limited mention in the Johannine epistles, commentators generally agree that the Antichrist appears under other names elsewhere in the Bible. These include the "little horn" (Dan. 8:9), the "desolating sacrilege" (Mt 24:15), the one who "comes in his own name" (Jn 5:43), and the "lawless one" (2 Thess. 2:8). Confusion has arisen, however, as to the Antichrist's identity in the Apocalypse. Some see him as the "beast" of 11:7, others as the "beast" of 13:11, others still as the "red dragon" of 12:3. Other speculators have believed that the Antichrist is a demon or the devil himself in human form that will be "released from his prison" (Apoc. 20:7) during the end times to seduce the nations.

The contention that the Pope or Papacy is the Antichrist was first espoused in the Middle Ages by such groups as the Albigensians, Waldensians and the Fraticelli. Wycliffe and Huss followed them in the fourteenth and fifteenth centuries. In the sixteenth century, the Protestant reformers, needing to disparage the large, international system of religion they had rejected, soon came to portray the Pope as the Antichrist and the Catholic Church as the Whore of Babylon:

Thomas Cranmer (Anglican):

> Whereof it followeth Rome to be the seat of antichrist, and the pope to be very antichrist himself. I could prove the same by many other scriptures, old writers, and strong reasons (*Works by Cranmer*, vol. 1, pp. 6-7).

The Lutheran *Book of Concord*:

> The Pope is the real Antichrist who has raised himself over and set himself against Christ ... Accordingly, just as we cannot adore the devil himself as our lord or God, so we cannot suffer his apostle, the Pope or Antichrist, to govern us as our head or lord (2:4:10, 14).

The Presbyterian *Westminster Confession*:

> There is no other head of the church but the Lord Jesus Christ; nor can the Pope of Rome in any sense be the head thereof; but is that Antichrist, that man of sin, and that son of perdition, that exalteth himself in the church against Christ, and all that is called God (25:6).

John Wesley (founder of Methodism):

> He is in an emphatical sense, the Man of Sin, as he increases all manner of sin above measure. And he is, too, properly styled the Son of Perdition, as he has caused the death of numberless multitudes, both of his opposers and followers ... He it is ... that exalteth himself above all that is called God, or that is worshiped ... claiming the highest power, and highest honor ... claiming the prerogatives which belong to God alone (*Antichrist and His Ten Kingdoms*, p. 110).

It is intended in this chapter to:

(i) Refute three popular modern-day theories that allege that the Pope is the Antichrist;
(ii) Establish that the Whore, the Beast and the Antichrist are three separate organizations/persons belonging to different ages; and,
(iii) Provide a credible theory for who the Whore, Beast and the Antichrist really are.

Papal Antichrist theories

While many Protestants hold that the Pope is the Antichrist, there is a variety of so-called 'Papal Antichrist theories' circulating the rounds. The following three are some of the most popular:

'Seventh-Day Adventist theory':

The Seventh-Day Adventists advance their Papal Antichrist theory heavily on the books of Daniel and Revelation. Daniel 2 provides a prophetic blueprint of history outlining the succession of great world powers in the following order: Babylon, Medo-Persia, Greece, Rome, the ten divisions of Rome, and the Kingdom of the Stone. The Adventists claim that the ten divisions of the Roman Empire after it fell were: (1) the Anglo-Saxons (England); (2) the Alemanni (Germany); (3) the Visigoths (Spain); (4) the Suevi (Portugal); (5) the Lombards (Italy); (6) the Burgundians (Swiss); (7) the Franks (France); (8) the Vandals; (9) the Ostrogoths; and (10) the Heruli. These ten divisions are symbolized by the "ten horns" in Dan. 7:7.

Amid these ten horns emerges another "little horn" (Dan. 7:8). The Adventists claim this "little horn" symbolizes the emergence of the Papacy amidst the ten tribal divisions of Rome. The Papacy then becomes a political power in AD 538 thanks to a decree of the Emperor Justinian. The Adventists see the Papacy in the remainder of Dan. 7 as follows:

(i) The "three of the previous horns were torn away" (Dan. 7:8). These are said to be the Vandals, Ostrogoths and Heruli who were allegedly destroyed by pagan Roman armies at the instigation of the Papacy.

(ii) "... had eyes like a man, and a mouth that spoke arrogantly" (Dan. 7:8). This is said to be the Pope purporting to teach the entire world.

(iii) "... made war with the holy ones" (Dan. 7:21). This is said to be the Papacy's persecution of true Christians from the Dark Ages onwards through inquisitions, etc., resulting in the death of fifty to ninety-five million innocent victims.

(iv) "... he shall be "Different from those before him" (Dan. 7:24). This is the Papal "little horn" who is different from the other ten horns for it alone is a religious-political power.

(v) "He shall speak against the Most High" (Dan. 7:25). These are the alleged boastful and blasphemous claims of the Papacy to be the Vicar of Christ having total power.

(vi) "... thinking to change the feast days and the law" (Dan. 7:25). This is the Papacy's changing of the Sabbath from Saturday to Sunday and the deletion of the Second Commandment against images, etc.

(vii) "... a year, two years, and half a year" (Dan. 7:25; Rev. 12:6). This totals three and a half years, or 1,260 days, symbolizing the Papacy's 1,260 years of primary power from AD 538 to AD 1798, the latter year being the year in which Napoleon's armies marched into Rome and captured and deposed Pope Pius VI, who subsequently died in prison.

For the Adventists, these parallels are not coincidental and point clearly to the Papacy as the only possible candidate for the Antichrist. Consequently, the Antichrist is not a single individual who is to appear some time in the future, but a system of apostasy and persecution that would dominate the world for over twelve centuries.

'Hunting the Whore of Babylon'

Alongside the allegations that the Pope is the Antichrist is the claim that the Catholic Church is the "Whore of Babylon" mentioned in Rev. 17 and 18. The American Evangelical writer Dave Hunt advances nine arguments as to why the Catholic Church is the Whore:

(i) "... the seven heads are seven hills on which the woman (Whore) is seated" (Rev. 17:9). The city of Rome is built on seven hills. The Catholic Church is the church of Rome.

(ii) "... the woman ... is the great city which has dominion over the kings of the earth" (Rev. 17:18). Which city ever had dominion over kings? Only Vatican City when its ruler, the Pope, held sway over Christian kings.

(iii) "... with whom the kings of the earth have committed fornication" (Rev. 17:2). The "fornication" committed by kings are the 'unholy alliances' forged between the Vatican and other nations, e.g., Rome's concordats with Italy under Mussolini and Germany under Hitler.

(iv) "The woman was clothed in purple and scarlet" (Rev. 17:4). Catholic bishops and Cardinals wear purple and red vestments.

(v) "... adorned with gold and jewels and pearls" (Rev. 17:4). The Catholic Church possesses enormous treasures and wealth accumulated over centuries.

(vi) "... holding in her hand a golden cup full of abominations" (Rev. 17:4). The golden cup symbolizes the Mass, the center of the Catholic Church's alleged idolatrous and blasphemous worship.

(vii) "Babylon the Great" (Rev. 17:5). The name "Babylon" is a code word for Rome. Rome was the greatest city of the first century AD. The Catholic Church is the church of Rome.

(viii) "... mother of harlots and of earth's abominations" (Rev. 17:5). The Catholic Church gives birth to world-wide harlotry through the sexual sins of its clergy.

(ix) "... drunk with the blood of the saints and the blood of the martyrs of Jesus" (Rev. 17:6). The Catholic Church has the blood of millions of true Christians on its hands through the forced conversion of nations, inquisitions and the Nazi holocaust.

For Hunt, the Catholic Church is the only organization that fulfils the description of the Whore. The coincidences are just too great to be ignored. True Christians are obliged to warn innocent Catholics to "come out of her" (Rev. 18:4) before the final judgment of God throws down Babylon "with violence" (Rev. 18:21).

Vicarius Filii Dei

The *Vicarius Filii Dei* theory focuses on the Beast of Rev. 13 who speaks "haughty and blasphemous words ... and (is) allowed to exercise authority for forty-two months" (Rev. 13:5). This Beast also makes "war on the saints" (Rev. 13:7), has authority "over every tribe and people" (Rev. 13:7), is followed by the "whole earth" with wonder (Rev. 13:3) and is worshiped (Rev. 13:4). No one can buy or sell unless they have the mark of the Beast, that is, the name of the beast or the number of its name (Rev. 13:17). The number of the Beast is 666 (Rev. 13:18).

The *Vicarius Filii Dei* theory was first proposed by the Seventh-Day Adventist Uriah Smith in 1866. In his book, *The United States in the Light of Prophecy*, he wrote:

> The pope wears upon his pontifical crown in jeweled letters, this title: "Vicarius Filii Dei," "Viceregent of the Son of God"; the numerical value of which title is just six hundred and sixty-six. The most plausible supposition we have ever seen on this point is that here we find the number in question. It is the number of the beast, the papacy; it is the number of his name, for he adopts it as his distinctive title; it is the number of a man, for he who bears it is the "man of sin."[1]

In Latin, letters double up as numbers. Looking at *Vicarius Filii Dei* in capital letters - VICARIVS FILII DEI - the relevant letters add up as follows:

$V = 5; I = 1; C = 100; I = 1; V = 5$ (U is taken as V); $I = 1; L = 50; I = 1; I = 1; D = 500; I = 1$

$5+1+100+1+5+1+50+1+1+500+1 = 666$

The Catholic Response

Putting the above three theories together, we are confronted with the following propositions: (i) the institution of the Papacy is the Antichrist; (ii) the Catholic Church is the Whore of Babylon; and (iii) a future Pope is the Beast. For many Catholics, the arguments presented

---

[1] Seventh-day Adventist Publishing Association, Battle Creek, Michigan, 1884, 4th edition, p. 224.

by the proponents of these theories seem both compelling and frightening. But do they stand up to scholarly scrutiny? In each case the answer is an emphatic, "No!"

Firstly, the Antichrist cannot be an institution involving a long succession of Popes reigning nearly thirteen centuries. Scripture is clear that the Antichrist will be an individual, "*the man* of lawlessness" and "*the son* of perdition" (2 Thess. 2:3) who will perform "pretended signs and wonders" and will be destroyed by the Lord Jesus "with the breath of his mouth" (2 Thess. 2:8 & 9). These verses point to a single individual in the same way the Old Testament prophecies pointed to a single, individual Messiah. Being only one individual, it is not possible for the Antichrist to reign 1,260 years.

Next, the Antichrist will set himself up "in the temple of God" (2 Thess. 2:4). If the Papacy is the Antichrist, then the Adventists must admit that either St John Lateran or St Peter's Basilica in Rome, rather the Jewish temple in Jerusalem as they claim, is the "temple of God," for the Popes from AD 538 to AD 1798 never resided in Jerusalem. Yet, the Adventists would be unwilling to admit that any Catholic Church could be a "temple of God."

Furthermore, St Paul in the same letter to the Thessalonians states that the "man of lawlessness" will "exalt himself" ... "proclaiming himself to be God" (2 Thess. 2:4). Yet, no Pope from AD 538 to AD 1798 or since has ever done such; rather, the Pope's very title "Vicar of Christ" is an acknowledgement of a divine power above himself. Nor has any Pope ever denied "that Jesus is the Christ" (1 Jn 2:22-23) or refused to "acknowledge the coming of Jesus Christ in the flesh" (2 Jn 1:7), denials that, according to St John, are essential indicia of the Antichrist. Again, all the Popes before and since the Council of Nicaea (AD 325) have acted to the contrary, demanding of all the Catholic faithful a public confession of the divinity of Christ and his coming in the flesh.

Finally, the dates of AD 538 and AD 1798 are both arbitrary and irrelevant. The claim that the Emperor Justinian in AD 538 gave the Pope temporal authority over Rome and all the world's churches is a pure fiction. Rather, Justinian and his wife, Theodora, sought to exercise control over the Papacy to overthrow the decrees of Chalcedon condemning the Monophysite heresy. Pope Silverius was deposed, sent into exile and died in AD 538. Justinian and Theodora arranged a pawn, Vigilius, to be elected to the Papal office. Providentially, Vigilius remained firmly aligned with Chalcedon. Certainly, as the Emperor lived in Constantinople, the Papacy became by default responsible for the everyday running of Rome. However, it was only on 13 August 554 that Vigilius was given official sanction to run the civil affairs of Rome and Italy on behalf of the Emperor. Vigilius died on the way home from Constantinople in AD 555.

The years between AD 538 and AD 1798 witnessed no domination by the Papacy "over every tribe and people and tongue and nation" (Rev. 13:7). Most of the world during that time remained either in the darkness of paganism or subject to the conquering sword of Islam. Though the Age of Christendom witnessed the height of Papal power and influence, the Popes did not enjoy an unchallenged supremacy. They were often subject to imprisonment, exile, and death at the hands of unscrupulous temporal rulers. During the eighth and ninth centuries, Roman barons dominated the Papacy as their personal plaything. The tenth and eleventh centuries witnessed constant German interference in Italian and Papal affairs. The eleventh century also saw the Eastern Orthodox churches split from Rome. The fourteenth century saw the Papacy under the control of the French king. The Reformation would split Europe and take whole regions and nations away from Papal influence. These facts alone testify that the claim of Papal world domination from the sixth to eighteenth centuries is another pure fiction.

The capture and imprisonment of Pope Pius VI by the armies of Napoleon in 1798, dramatic and tragic as it was, was no worse than what befell other Popes from AD 538 to AD 1798 (for example, the murders of Martin I [649–653], John VIII [872–882], John XII [955–964], Benedict VI [973–974], and John XIV [983–984]) and certainly did not see the end of Papal power and authority. Pius VI, despite his imprisonment, remained Pope until his death on 29 August 1799. Pius VII succeeded him on 14 March 1800 and, though suffering arrest and imprisonment at the hands of Napoleon for six years from 1808 until 1814, reigned until 1823. Since 1823, there have been another fifteen Popes who, despite the loss of the Papal States in 1870, have continued to exercise the essential power of the Papal office, namely, the shepherding of the flock of Christ.

There are also many reasons why the Catholic Church cannot be the Whore of Rev. 17 and 18. Firstly, Rev. 17:9-10 tells us that the seven hills on which the Whore is seated are also seven kings, "five of whom have fallen, one is, the other has not yet come." If five of the seven kings had fallen before St John's day, and the sixth was currently reigning, then the Whore existed in St John's time. Yet, according to Protestants neither the Papacy nor the Vatican existed in the first century.

Secondly, the seven mountains on which the Whore is seated are said to be the "seven hills of Rome." These are well known and have the following names: Aventine, Caelian, Capitoline, Esquiline, Palatine, Quirinal and Viminal. They are all located on the east side of the Tiber. Yet, the Vatican is not built on any of these hills; rather, it is built on Vatican Hill, which is located on the west side of the Tiber.

Thirdly, despite the extent of Papal power in the Middle Ages, the Vatican currently has no dominion over present-day kings and governments. In fact, never since the days of official Roman persecution has the Church exercised less influence in society. Instead, wherever we currently look we witness the Church being ignored by Western governments, ridiculed and smeared by the media, or, as in the case of Islamic and Communist countries, outrightly persecuted.

Fourthly, neither is the Catholic Church responsible for the blood of tens of millions of saints and martyrs. Rev. 18:20 makes it clear that the Whore spilt the blood of "saints and apostles and prophets." Apostles existed only in the first century, so the Whore must have existed in the first century, again precluding the Vatican. Moreover, irrespective of what one thinks of the various inquisitions, their total number of victims was only between 3,000 and 4,000. Furthermore, as hard as historical revisionists try, the Catholic Church had no role or responsibility for the Nazi holocaust. Rather, historical records attest to the quiet resistance initiated by Pope Pius XII, which resulted in the saving of 800,000 Jewish lives. If there has been a consistent victim of persecution it has been the Catholic Church, which since the sixteenth century has endured persecution and repression in Elizabethan England, Lutheran Germany, the French

Revolution, the German Kulturkampf, the Mexican Revolution, the Spanish Civil War, Nazi Germany, the Russian Revolution, Maoist China, and so on. Modern day secularism has unleashed a new wave of repressions through media bias and 'politically correct' legislation.

Finally, Rev. 18 depicts the Whore as a major center of world commerce. When it is finally judged the world's merchants and shipmasters will wale and mourn (Rev. 18:19). Regardless of what wealth it possessed in the past, the Catholic Church was not the hub of world commerce in the first century. Neither is it currently the center of world commerce. In the first century it was Pagan Rome. Since the Reformation, the great economies have been Protestant England, Holland, followed by Germany and pagan Japan. Currently, it is the United States. In the future it may be Communist China.

The *Vicarius Filii Dei* theory can be easily dismissed by the simple fact that the Pope has never held any such title. The official titles of the Pope are: Bishop of Rome; Vicar of Jesus Christ; Successor of St Peter; Prince of the Apostles; Supreme Pontiff of the Universal Church; Primate of Italy; Archbishop and Metropolitan of the Roman Province; Sovereign of the Vatican State; Servant of the Servants of God. Nor has the title *Vicarius Filii Dei* ever been inscribed on any Papal tiara made before or since 1866.

Who are the Whore, Beast and Antichrist?

There are certainly more appropriate candidates for the Whore, the Beast and Antichrist than the Catholic Church. Most probably, we are dealing with three separate organizations/persons belonging to different ages.

One theory for what we read in Rev. 17 is that it is a symbolic depiction of the mid-first century alliance between pagan Rome (the Beast) with apostate Jerusalem (the Whore) to persecute early Christianity. It is a message of hope to encourage the early Christians to persevere, for God will ultimately destroy both for their evil ways.

Considering, firstly, the Beast. It has seven heads, which are both seven mountains (Rev. 17:9) and seven consecutive kings (Rev. 17:10). The Beast as an individual is one of these seven kings (Rev. 17:11). This man forces everyone to worship him under pain of death

(Rev. 13:12 & 15). The identifying number of this man is 666, which requires "wisdom" to understand (Rev. 13:18).

First century pagan Rome fits the above description of the Beast very well. It sat on seven hills, it was ruled by a succession of Caesars, these Caesars persecuted Christians who did not participate in the cult of emperor-worship, and the name of one of these Caesars, Nero Caesar, adds up to 666 in Hebrew and Aramaic (N = 50; R = 200; W = 6; N = 50; Q = 100; S = 60; R = 200). Nero was the first emperor to initiate a public persecution of Christians, resulting in the martyrdom of Sts Peter and Paul.

The Whore, meanwhile, sits on the Beast (Rev. 17:3). This symbolizes apostate Jerusalem's alliance with Rome to persecute Christians. Because of her apostasy, Jerusalem is that "great city ... called Sodom and Egypt, where their Lord was crucified" (Rev. 11:8). In apostate Jerusalem is "found the blood of prophets and of saints" (Rev. 18:24). This ensures that the Whore is Jerusalem and not Rome, for only the former was known for slaying Prophets (Mt 23:37). The vision of the Beast (with the "ten horns") eventually hating the Whore and desolating, devouring and burning her and forcing her to give over her royal power (Rev. 17:16-17) was fulfilled when the Romans and her allies destroyed Jerusalem in AD 70, as prophesied by Jesus (Lk 21:5-24).

As for the Antichrist, he is altogether another figure still to appear some time in the future. What can be safely said about him is limited, but would include the following:

- He is an individual who will appear before the second coming of Jesus (2 Thess. 2:3).
- He will perform pretended signs and wonders with the power of Satan (2 Thess. 2:9).
- He will deny that Jesus is the Christ (1 Jn 2:22-23) and has come in the flesh (2 Jn 1:7).
- He will exalt himself and proclaim himself to be God (2 Thess. 2:4).
- The price of accepting the Antichrist's solution to the world's problems will be apostasy and damnation (CCC 675).

- The Church will pass through a final trial that will shake the faith of many (CCC 675).
- The Church will be persecuted to the point of extinction, only to be saved by the second coming of Jesus (Rev. 13:7; CCC 677).
- The Lord Jesus will destroy the Antichrist with the breath of his mouth upon his appearing (2 Thess. 2:8).

What has been speculated by some of the Church Fathers about the Antichrist includes the following:

- He will be Jewish in origin, of the tribe of Dan;
- He will rebuild the Temple in Jerusalem;
- He will offer to fulfil the political aspirations held by many of the Jewish people for the Messiah.

Conclusion

The accusation that the Catholic Church is the Whore of Babylon and the Pope is the Antichrist should be regarded as no more than wild and discredited polemic belonging to a by-gone era. The evidence just does not stack up. Far from denying Jesus' coming in the flesh, the Catholic Church has proclaimed it for over twenty centuries, and continues to do so. Far from exalting himself above Jesus, the Pope continues to shepherd his people as servant of the servants of God. The Catholic Church is the Bride of Christ and the Pope the Vicar of Christ. It is not surprising, however, that the same old allegations continue to be repeated, for "If they have called the master of the house Beelzebul, how much more will they malign those of his household" (Mt 10:25).

The Fathers

The Didache 16, 3-4 (AD 90-150)
"For in the last days false prophets and corrupters shall be multiplied, and sheep shall be turned into wolves ... and then shall the deceiver of the world appear, pretending to be the Son of God, and [he] shall do signs and wonders, and the earth shall be delivered into his hands."

St Polycarp of Smyrna, *Letter to the Philadelphians* 7,1 (AD 135)
"Everyone who does not confess that Jesus Christ has come in the flesh is an antichrist; whoever does not confess the testimony of the cross is of the devil; and whoever perverts the sayings of the Lord for his own desires, and says that there is neither resurrection nor judgment, such a one is the firstborn of Satan."

St Irenaeus of Lyons, *Against Heresies* 5, 25, 1-2 (AD 180)
"(B)y means of the events which shall occur in the time of the Antichrist it is shown that he, being an apostate and a robber, is anxious to be adored as God, and that although a mere slave, he wishes to be proclaimed as king. For he, being endued with all the power of the devil, shall not come as a righteous king nor as a legitimate king in subjection to God, but as an impious, unjust, and lawless one ... setting aside idols to persuade [men] that he himself is God, raising himself up as the only idol. ... Moreover [Paul] has also pointed out this which I have shown in many ways: that the temple in Jerusalem was made by the direction of the true God. For the apostle himself, speaking in his own person, distinctly called it the temple of God (2 Thess. 2:4) ... in which the enemy shall sit, endeavoring to show himself as Christ."

St Hippolytus of Rome, *The Antichrist* 6 & 14 (AD 200)
"Now as our Lord Jesus Christ, who is also God, was prophesied of under the figure of a lion, on account of his royalty and glory, in the same way have the scriptures also beforehand spoken of Antichrist as a lion, on account of his tyranny and violence. For the deceiver seeks to liken himself in all things to the Son of God. Christ is a lion, so Antichrist is also a lion. Christ is a king, so Antichrist is also a king. The Savior was manifested as a lamb, so he too in like manner will

appear as a lamb without; within he is a wolf. The Savior came into the world in the circumcision (i.e., the Jewish race), and he will come in the same manner ... The Savior raised up and showed his holy flesh like a temple, and he will raise a temple of stone in Jerusalem ... For as Christ springs from the tribe of Judah, so Antichrist is to spring from the tribe of Dan. And that the case stands thus, we see also from the words of Jacob: 'Let Dan be a serpent, lying upon the ground, biting the horse's heel' (Gen. 49:17)."

St Hippolytus of Rome, *Discourse on the End of the World* 23-25 (AD 217)

"Above all, moreover, he will love the nation of the Jews. And with all these [Jews] he will work signs and terrible wonders, false wonders and not true, in order to deceive his impious equals ... And after that he will build the temple in Jerusalem and will restore it again speedily and give it over to the Jews."

St Cyprian of Carthage, *Letters* 69, 3 (AD 253)

"If they [the heretics] desire peace, let them lay aside their arms. If they make atonement, why do they threaten? Or if they threaten, let them know that they are not feared by God's priests. For even Antichrist, when he shall begin to come, will not enter into the Church (even though) he threatens; neither shall we yield to his arms and violence, (though) he declares that he will destroy us if we resist."

Lactantius, *Divine Institutes* 7, 17 (AD 307)

"(A) king shall arise out of Syria, born from an evil spirit, the overthrower and destroyer of the human race, who shall destroy that which is left by the former evil, together with himself. ... But that king will not only be most disgraceful in himself, but he will also be a prophet of lies, and he will constitute and call himself God, and will order himself to be worshiped as the Son of God, and power will be given to him to do signs and wonders, by the sight of which he may entice men to adore him. He will command fire to come down from heaven and the sun to stand and leave his course, and an image to speak, and these things shall be done at his word. ... Then he will attempt to destroy the temple of God and persecute the righteous people."

St Cyril of Jerusalem, *Catechetical Lectures* 15,12 (AD 350)

"This aforementioned Antichrist is to come when the times of the Roman Empire shall have been fulfilled, and the end of the world is drawing near. There shall rise up together ten kings of the Romans, reigning in different parts, perhaps, but all reigning at the same time. After these there shall be an eleventh, the Antichrist, who by the evil craft of his magic shall seize upon the Roman power. Of the kings who reigned before him, three shall he humble (Dan. 7:24), and the remaining seven he shall have as subjects under him. At first he shall feign mildness – as if he were a learned and discreet person – and sobriety and loving kindness ... Having beguiled the Jews by the lying signs and wonders of his magical deceit, until they believe he is the expected Christ, he shall afterwards be characterized by all manner of wicked deeds of inhumanity and lawlessness, as if to outdo all the unjust and impious men who have gone before him. He shall display against all men, and especially against us Christians, a spirit that is murderous and most cruel, merciless and wily. For three years and six months only shall he be the perpetrator of such things; and then he shall be destroyed by the glorious second coming from heaven of the only-begotten Son of God, our Lord and Savior Jesus, the true Christ, who shall destroy him with the breath of his mouth (2 Thess. 2:8), and deliver him over to the fire of Gehenna."

St Augustine of Hippo, *The City of God Against the Pagans* 20, 19 (AD 419)

"Daniel prophesies of the last judgment in such a way as to indicate that the Antichrist shall first come and carry on his destruction to the eternal reign of the saints. For when in prophetic vision he had seen four beasts, signifying four kingdoms, and the fourth conquered by a certain king, who is recognized as Antichrist, and after this the eternal kingdom of the Son of Man, that is to say, of Christ."

The Roman Catechism (1566)

The Roman Catechism made no reference to the Antichrist or his identity.

Catechism of the Catholic Church (1992)

No. 675: Before Christ's second coming the Church must pass through a final trial that will shake the faith of many believers. The persecution that accompanies her pilgrimage on earth will unveil the "mystery of iniquity" in the form of a religious deception offering men an apparent solution to their problems at the price of apostasy from the truth. The supreme religious deception is that of the Antichrist, a pseudo-messianism by which man glorifies himself in place of God and of his Messiah come in the flesh.

No. 676: The Antichrist's deception already begins to take shape in the world every time the claim is made to realise within history that messianic hope which can only be realised beyond history through the eschatalogical judgment. The Church has rejected even modified forms of this falsification of the kingdom to come under the name of millenarianism, especially the "intrinsically perverse" political form of a secular messianism.

No. 677: The Church will enter the glory of the kingdom only through this final Passover, when she will follow her Lord in his death and Resurrection. The kingdom will be fulfilled, then, not by a historic triumph of the Church through a progressive ascendancy, but only by God's victory over the final unleashing of evil, which will cause his Bride to come down from heaven. God's triumph over the revolt of evil will take the form of the Last Judgement after the final cosmic upheaval of this passing world.

Cruci*fiction*?

Objection: *"No sane person can believe the story of the crucifixion of Jesus. Jesus could not have died if he were God. Rather, he was only a Prophet of Allah. If the story of the Cross is disproved, then the very foundation on which Christianity is based is demolished!"*

Islam denies that Jesus was crucified and died on the Cross, as is recounted in the four Gospels of the New Testament. According to the Qur'an, it was not Jesus who died on the Cross but another man put in his place:

> They denied the truth and uttered a monstrous falsehood against Mary. They declared: "We have put to death the Messiah Jesus the son of Mary, the apostle of Allah." They did not kill him, nor did they crucify him, but they thought they did.
>
> Those that disagreed about him were in doubt concerning his death, for what they knew about it was sheer conjecture; they were not sure that they had slain him. Allah lifted him up to his presence; he is mighty and wise. There is none among the People of the Book but will believe in him before his death; and on the Day of Resurrection he will be a witness against them (*Sura* 4:157, 158).

Islamic scholars, however, are aware that Christians do not accept the Qu'ran to be the word of God and hence give no credence to any quotes from it. Consequently, to further their claims, Islamic apologists turn to the Gospels and attempt to highlight alleged contradictions and inconsistencies to discredit the crucifixion accounts as fabrications. The following objections taken from Islamic sources are examples of such attempts:

(i) *"The Bible testifies to the fact that Jesus was known among the Jews; he used to preach and deliver sermons in the Temple of Solomon in Jerusalem. It was therefore unnecessary to hire a Jew for thirty pieces of silver to direct them as related in Matthew."*

The betrayal of Jesus by Judas was neither unnecessary nor fictional; it was a tragic fulfilment of centuries-old prophecies made by Jeremiah and Zechariah (Jer. 32:7-9; Zech. 11:12-13). Jesus certainly was well known among the Jews for his public preaching, but it was not simply the ordinary Jews or Scribes and Pharisees who sought and ordered his arrest. This came at the counsel of the High Priest Caiaphas (Jn 11:49, 18:14). Caiaphas had not seen Jesus in the flesh; this came only after his arrest (Mt 26:3; Jn 18:28). Consequently, he needed to employ the services of a one-time intimate associate of Jesus to secure his capture. In any case, Caiaphas did not seek Judas' help. Judas *offered himself* to the Jews to betray Jesus (Mt 26:14-15). Judas' offer was an unexpected boost to the Jewish leadership who were perplexed as to how best to arrest Jesus and kill him without causing a tumult among the people (Mt 26:5). Judas knew of the secluded garden across the Kidron Valley where Jesus often met with his disciples – the Garden of Gethsemane – a meeting place unknown to any outside the Twelve (Jn 18:2). It was only here at night and through the help of Judas that the Jewish leaders could achieve their objective of arresting Jesus *quietly*.

(ii) *"There are numerous contradictions in the Gospel accounts of Jesus' arrest, trial and crucifixion. If Jesus wanted to die for the redemption of humanity then why did he ask that his Father turn away the cup of affliction from him? Furthermore, how could the disciples of Jesus be asleep when Jesus was suffering in the Garden of Gethsemane? Such a weakness could not be spoken of righteous pupils of a pious teacher, let alone disciples of Jesus the Prophet."*

There is no contradiction in Jesus' request that his Father take away the cup of suffering. Muslims find it incredible that such words could come from a believer in God, let alone a Prophet. Jesus was not simply true God, but also true man. As true God, Jesus could not suffer, yet in his humanity this was possible. Knowing the future even in his human intellect, Jesus' humanity naturally recoiled from the sight of the immense suffering he was about to endure. Yet, ultimately there was no disobedience towards his Father, for Jesus' human will triumphantly submitted to the divine: "... not as I will, but as Thou wilt" (Mt 26:39).

As for the disciples, they were not exempt from the deficiencies that afflicted all humans in general. According to the Scriptures, they suffered from pride, weakness, ignorance as well as cowardice: "And he said to them, 'Do you not understand this parable? How then will you understand all the parables?'" (Mk 4:13). These faults manifested themselves on several occasions long before Jesus' passion and persisted (as in the case of Judas' greed) despite having the benefit of Jesus' intimate teachings and personal example for three years. What transformed all of them after the death and resurrection of Jesus was the descent of the Holy Spirit at Pentecost: "And I will pray the Father, and he will give you another Counselor, to be with you for ever, even the Spirit of truth, whom the world cannot receive, because it neither sees him nor knows him; you know him, for he dwells with you, and will be in you" (Jn 14:16-17).

After Pentecost, the Apostles preached the resurrected Jesus with courage and conviction: "Let all the house of Israel therefore know assuredly that God has made him both Lord and Christ, this Jesus whom you crucified ... And fear came upon every soul; and many wonders and signs were done through the apostles" (Acts 2:36 & 43). But even if they were now men of courage, the Apostles had nothing to gain from foisting a huge deception upon the world. Why would the Apostles compile written Gospels all speaking of the crucifixion of Jesus that also showed themselves to be ignorant, cowardly, and denying; and why would they continue to preach the resurrected Jesus even unto death? These are facts that testify to their sincerity.

(iii) *"As a Prophet it was essential that Jesus always spoke up for truth and denied falsehood. How could he then have remained silent before Pilate when the truth was being challenged?"*

Everyone who heard Jesus speak and preach acknowledged his greatness with words: "And when Jesus finished these sayings, the crowds were astonished at his teaching, for he taught them as one who had authority, and not as their scribes" (Mt 7:28-29). Pilate already had doubts about Jesus' guilt and was sceptical of the charges brought against him (Mk 15:10). He was even anxious to be rid of the whole matter, for he feared political complications. If Jesus had spoken in his own defense, he undoubtedly would have answered all the charges brought against him and once more the Scribes and Pharisees might have "marvelled, and ... left him and went away" (Mt 22:22). Jesus would have been released, he would not have been crucified and raised from the dead and we would still be in our sins: "But how then should the Scriptures be fulfilled, that it must be so?" (Mt 26:54). Thoughts of Jesus avoiding crucifixion are not the thoughts of God but of men: "But he turned and said to Peter, 'Get behind me, Satan! You are a hindrance to me; for you are not on the side of God, but of men'" (Mt 16:23).

Furthermore, Jesus told his disciples, "Do not give dogs what is holy; and do not throw your pearls before swine, lest they trample them under foot and turn to attack you" (Mt 7:6). He may have judged that Caiaphas and Pilate could not be given a dignified and full answer because they lacked the necessary dispositions to hear him fruitfully.

(iv) *"To believe that Jesus could cry out from the Cross, 'My God, my God, why hast thou forsaken me,' is a blasphemous assertion that a Prophet lost faith in God!"*

These words of Jesus have indeed been a source of much speculation over the centuries. There is great significance in them but they are far from being blasphemous.

Whenever Jesus spoke or preached, he frequently quoted from the Old Testament Scriptures. This is not surprising, especially as the Old Testament contains dozens of prophecies relating to the coming of the Messiah. Perhaps the most prophetic messianic verses of the Old Testament are contained in Ps. 22. It is from this psalm that Jesus quoted the above words. Why did he do so? To prompt the Scribes and Pharisees before him into a certain realization. The Scribes and Pharisees generally knew the Scriptures by heart. Jesus wanted them to recall Ps. 22 in its entirety and realize that they were fulfilling it as they watched and mocked him on the Cross. However, the Jews failed to pick up the hint and thought that Jesus was just calling upon Elias.

Crucifiction?

Christians see the following verses in Ps. 22 as relating directly to Jesus' crucifixion:

"My God, my God, why hast thou forsaken me? Why art thou so far from helping me, from the words of my groaning?" (v. 1).

"But I am a worm, and no man; scorned by men, and despised by the people" (v. 6).

"All who see me mock at me, they make mouths at me, they wag their heads" (v. 7).

"He committed his cause to the Lord; let him deliver him, let him rescue him, for he delights in him!" (v. 8).

"They open wide their mouths at me, like a ravening and roaring lion" (v. 13).

"I am poured out like water, and all my bones are out of joint; my heart is like wax, it is melted within my breast" (v. 14).

"My strength is dried up like a potsherd, and my tongue cleaves to my jaws; thou dost lay me in the dust of death" (v. 15).

"Yea, dogs are round about me; a company of evildoers encircle me; they have pierced my hands and feet" (v. 16).

"I can count all my bones – they stare and gloat over me" (v. 17).

"They divide my garments among them, and for my raiment they cast lots" (v. 18).

Jesus' words from the Cross can also be understood in a mystical sense. For love of humanity, Jesus freely chose to place no limit on his sufferings, pouring out his Blood to the very last drop. It is legitimate to hypothesize that Jesus also endured and offered up a suffering that would have been greater than any other – the sense in his human intellect of being totally abandoned by God the Father. Of course, God never abandons any of his servants, let alone his only Son. Nevertheless, in the history of the Church a number of the most elevated saints endured such a sense of abandonment in the so-called 'dark night of the soul.' The purpose of such is to purify the soul of every vestige of self-love so that it loves God for God's sake alone, not for any consolation he may confer. For Jesus, his 'dark night' would have afforded him the opportunity to demonstrate perfect love for his Father at a time when all things seemed hopelessly lost. Hence, his final dying words, "Father, into your hands I commit my spirit" (Lk 23:46).

(v) *"To say that Allah redeemed humanity by sending his so-called Son down to earth to be humiliated and crucified is an extremely odd idea. Could not Allah have simply willed to forgive humanity without all that horrible bloodshed? And what about those sinners who lived before Jesus? How are they forgiven if they had no opportunity to know him and believe in the Crucifixion?"*

The very beginning chapters of the book of Genesis record the fall of humanity and the first promise of the Messiah: "I will put enmity between you and the woman, and between your seed and her seed; he shall bruise your head, and you shall bruise his heel" (Gen. 3:15). It was always the great expectation of the people of Israel, her Patriarchs and Prophets, that the Messiah would come: "Truly, I say to you, many prophets and righteous men longed to see what you see, and did not see it, and to hear what you hear, and did not hear it" (Mt 13:17). To many Jews, this Messiah would be a triumphant warrior king who would deliver Israel from the Romans and exalt her above all other nations. But to a more enlightened few, the Messiah would be of humble origin, the mysterious suffering servant and man of sorrows, as is made evident in the prophecies of Micah, Isaiah and Simeon:

"But you, O Bethlehem Ephrathah, who are little to be among the clans of Judah, from you shall come forth for me one who is to be ruler in Israel" (Mic. 5:2).

"He was despised and rejected by men; a man of sorrows, and acquainted with grief; and as one from whom men hide their faces he was despised, and we esteemed him not. Surely he has borne our griefs and carried our sorrows; yet we esteemed him stricken, smitten by God, and afflicted. But he was wounded for

our transgressions, he was bruised for our iniquities; upon him was the chastisement that made us whole, and with his stripes we are healed ... He was oppressed, and he was afflicted, yet he opened not his mouth; like a lamb that is led to the slaughter, and like a sheep that before its shearers is dumb, so he opened not his mouth" (Is. 53:3-7).

"Behold, this child is set for the fall and rising of many in Israel, and for a sign that is spoken against ..." (Lk 2:34).

Also, we have already noted how King David, writing hundreds of years before Isaiah and Micah, spoke specifically of the particular sufferings of the Messiah in Ps. 22.

If one asserts that Abraham and Moses were Prophets of God (or Allah), then one ought to hope what they hoped for, that is, the coming Messiah, and with later Prophets in the same line, expect that the Messiah be "wounded for our transgressions ... bruised for our iniquities." All these prophecies, and more, were comprehensively fulfilled in the person and life of Jesus as recorded in the Christian Gospels. Yet, Islam, while claiming that Abraham, Moses, etc., were authentic Prophets of Allah, denies any expectation of a suffering Messiah. This is because the Abraham, Moses and Jesus of Islam are not the traditional figures of Old and New Testament Judaism and Christianity, but rather revisionist versions of the early seventh century AD: *"For if some one comes and preaches another Jesus than the one we preached, or if you receive a different spirit from the one you received, or if you accept a different gospel from the one you accepted, you submit to it readily enough"* (2 Cor. 11:4).

Rather than being an extremely "odd idea," the sending of Jesus into the world to redeem humanity on the Cross was the manifestation of God's great love for us, a gesture utterly unmerited and undeserved: *"For God so loved the world that he gave his only Son, that whoever believes in him should not perish but have eternal life"* (Jn 3:16). This act on God's part restored us to his sonship, and therefore heirs to his kingdom: *"But when the time had fully come, God sent forth his Son, born of woman, born under the law, to redeem those who were under the law, so that we might receive adoption as sons"* (Gal. 4:4-5). By dying such a horrible death, Jesus also set a noble example of self-denial, sacrifice and discipleship: "Greater love has no man than this, that a man lay down his life for his friends" (Jn 15:13); "And he said to all, 'If any man would come after me, let him deny himself and take up his cross daily and follow me'" (Lk 9:23). Finally, the figure of a bloodied Messiah dying in agony on the Cross should develop within us a greater realization of the gravity of sin as well as a deeper appreciation of our redemption.

Certainly, God in his mercy could have redeemed us in any way he pleased, for example, by simply expressing his desire to forgive us, or by Jesus offering up the sufferings of just one insult or blow. Nevertheless, God ordained that in our redemption his mercy and justice would work together simultaneously. As the sin of Adam and Eve offended the infinite dignity of God, justice demanded that the atoning satisfaction due to God needed to be of infinite value, and that such satisfaction be made by man. However, no mere creature could make such a satisfaction since no creature, however holy or exalted, could offer more than finite reparation. It is here that God's infinite mercy comes into play, by sending a Messiah who was true God and true man – God, so that his atoning act would be infinitely meritorious; man, so that his sacrifice could be offered on our behalf: "For there is one God, and there is one mediator between God and men, the man Christ Jesus, who gave himself as a ransom for all" (1 Tim. 2:5).

The fact that there lived and died countless millions of people before the coming of Jesus presents no problem to Christianity. God judged all these people according to the law they knew, that is, according to their consciences. God searched their hearts and minds to see if they sincerely sought to do his will as they knew it, did good and avoided evil according to the precepts of the natural law imbedded in our nature (Rom. 2:11-14), and were sorry for their sins before death. Regarding the Jews specifically, they were judged according to their fidelity to the respective covenants made with Abraham and Moses and whether they were steadfast in their belief in the coming of the Messiah. God in his goodness bestowed divine grace on all the pre-Christian Jews (as well as all other ancient peoples) to assist them to fulfil faithfully their obligations under each covenant. This grace was given in view of Jesus' future death on the Cross. Those who were found unfaithful were condemned to damnation: "The rich man also died and was buried; and in Hades, being in torment, he lifted up his eyes, and saw Abraham far off and Lazarus in his bosom" (Lk 16:22-23); those who were found faithful were sent to the Limbo of the Patriarchs, or Abraham's Bosom, where they were visited by Jesus after his crucifixion and wherefrom he took them finally into heaven on the day of his ascension: "The poor man died and was carried by the angels to Abraham's bosom" (Lk 16:22); "... he went and preached to the spirits in prison" (1 Pet. 3:19).

The Fathers

St Ignatius of Antioch, *Letter to the Smyrnaeans* 1, 1 (c. AD 110)
"... you are confirmed in love by the Blood of Christ, firmly believing in regard to our Lord that he is truly of the family of David according to the flesh, and God's Son by the will and power of God, truly born of a Virgin, baptized by John so that all justice might be fulfilled by him, in the time of Pontius Pilate and Herod the Tetrarch truly nailed in the flesh on our behalf ..."

Letter of Barnabas 7, 2 (inter AD 117-132)
"If, then, the Son of God, being the Lord and destined to judge the living and the dead, suffered so that his being wounded might make us live, let us believe that the Son of God could not suffer, except for our sake. Furthermore, when he was crucified he was given gall and sour wine to drink ... The Lord commanded this because he himself was about to offer the vessel of his spirit as a sacrifice for our sins, so that the type established in Isaac, who was offered on the altar, might be fulfilled."

St Hippolytus of Rome, *The Antichrist* 4 (c. AD 200)
"Although he was without flesh, the Son of God took on flesh from the Holy Virgin, like a bridegroom putting on a robe, which he wove for himself in the sufferings of the cross, so that by uniting our mortal body to his own power, and mixing the corruptible with the incorruptible and the weak with the strong, he might save man who was perishing. The beam of the loom, therefore, is the suffering of the Lord which he endured on the cross."

St Hilary of Poitiers, *Commentaries on Psalm 54* (c. AD 365)
"We have declared repeatedly and without cease that it was the only-begotten Son of God who was crucified, and that he was condemned to death: he that is eternal by reason of the nature which is his by his birth from the eternal Father; and it must be understood that he underwent the passion not from any natural necessity, but for the sake of the mystery of man's salvation; and that his submitting to the passion was not from his being compelled thereto, but of his own will ... God suffered, therefore, because he voluntarily submitted himself to the passion."

St Gregory of Elvira, *Homilies on the Books of Sacred Scripture* 2 (inter AD 365-385)
"The tree of the cross, clearly represents an image which to some seems as hard and rough as wood, because on it the Lord was hung so that our sins, which came to us from the tree of transgression, might be punished by being affixed – again, it is through the same man – to the tree of the cross ... To others it stands for shade and refreshment, because believers are protected from the heat and rigor of persecution, and there refreshed."

Pope St Leo I the Great, *Letter to the Monks of Palestine* 124, 3 (AD 453)
"What hope, then, do they, who deny the truth of the human substance in the body of our Savior, leave for themselves in the efficacy of this sacrament? Let them tell by what sacrifice they have been reconciled; let them tell by what blood they have been redeemed. Who is he that gave himself up on our behalf, as an oblation and victim to God in an odor of sweetness? And what sacrifice was there ever that was more sacred than that which the true High Priest placed upon the altar of the cross by the immolation of his own flesh?"

The Roman Catechism (1566)

Pt. I, Ch. V: Many other reasons which the Fathers have discussed in detail might be adduced to show that it was fit that our Redeemer should suffer death on the cross rather than in any other way. But, as the pastor will show, it is enough for the faithful to believe that this kind of death was chosen by the Savior because it appeared better adapted and more appropriate to the redemption of the human race; for there certainly could be none more ignominious and humiliating. Not only among the Gentiles was the punishment of the cross held accursed and full of shame and infamy, but even in the Law of Moses the man is called accursed that hangeth on a tree.

Catechism of the Catholic Church (1992)

No. 601: The Scriptures had foretold this divine plan of salvation through the putting to death of "the righteous one, my Servant" as a mystery of universal redemption, that is, as the ransom that would free men from the slavery of sin. Citing a confession of faith that he himself had "received," St Paul professes that "Christ died for our sins in accordance with the scriptures." In particular Jesus' redemptive death fulfils Isaiah's prophecy of the suffering Servant. Indeed, Jesus himself explained the meaning of his life and death in the light of God's suffering Servant. After his Resurrection he gave this interpretation of the Scriptures to the disciples at Emmaus, and then to the apostles.

Answering Islam –
Basic Objections

Introduction

The fastest growing religion in the world today is Islam. Ever since the Iranian revolution in 1978, Islam has experienced a militant resurgence throughout the world. Due to high levels of immigration and above-average birth rates, Islamic communities now number millions of members in many Western countries. All this comes at a time when Christian populations and Christian practise in the West are both undergoing marked decline. Consequently, for the first time since the retreat of the Ottoman Empire from Europe, Islam constitutes a direct and major challenge to Western culture and Christianity. Meanwhile, Christian communities in the Middle East and elsewhere continue to endure discrimination and persecution with little material or moral aid coming from the West.

Part of the modern-day Muslim challenge is the explosion of Islamic apologetics against Christianity. Islamic apologists are producing vast amounts of material against the Christian Faith, particularly the teachings of the Catholic Church. These attacks are normally focussed against belief in the Blessed Trinity, the Divinity of Christ, and his crucifixion, death and resurrection. At the same time, history is rewritten portraying Islam as a peaceful religion, while Christianity is depicted as aggressive and expansionist through past events such as the Crusades, etc.

Young Christians are encountering these vibrant and aggressive Islamic apologists at university and college campuses, through pamphlet distribution, in youth gatherings, on street corners, social media, etc. Many young Christians come away from such encounters challenged and without answers. A number even abandon Christianity and embrace Islam. It is necessary to immediately respond to the Islamic challenge at all levels. The 'easy' part is to answer Islamic challenges in word and in writing; the more difficult part is to regain the practise of our Faith and to live it once again vibrantly and fruitfully in Western countries that were once Christian.

First objection: *"The greatest of Christian blasphemies are belief in the Trinity and the divinity of Christ. The Qu'ran (Koran) warns about the consequences of false worship when it says, 'Verily, whosoever sets up partners in worship with Allah, then Allah has forbidden Paradise for him, and the fire will be his abode ... Surely, the disbelievers are those who said, 'Allah is a third of the three (in a trinity)' (Al-Ma'idah 5:72-73) The Prophet Jesus neither taught the Trinity nor his own divinity!"*

The Blessed Trinity and the divinity of Christ are the two most contentious Christian beliefs for Muslims. Islam is a staunchly monotheistic religion and views the doctrine of the Trinity as a polytheistic absurdity that sets up three gods in the place of one (Allah). Furthermore, Allah is supremely transcendent, so the idea that God has a Son who became incarnate and lived among humans adds further insult to injury.

Muslims use both their Qu'ran and the Old and New Testaments to undermine belief in the Trinity and the divinity of Christ. For the record, some quotes from the Qu'ran include:

"Verily, the likeness of Jesus before Allah is the likeness of Adam. He created him from dust, then said unto him: 'Be' and he was" (3:59).

"People of the Book, do not transgress the bounds of your religion. Speak nothing but the truth about Allah. The Messiah, Jesus the son of Mary, was no more than Allah's apostle and his word which he cast to Mary: a spirit from him. So believe in Allah and his apostles and do not say 'Three.' Forbear, and it shall be better for you. Allah is but one God. Allah forbid that he should have a son!" (4:171).

"Surely in disbelief are they who say that Allah is the Messiah, son of Mary. Say: 'Who then has the least power against Allah, if he were to destroy the Messiah, son of Mary; his mother and all those who are on the earth together?'" (5:17).

"The Messiah, son of Mary is no more than a Messenger. Many were the Messengers that passed away before him" (5:73-74).

From the Old and New Testaments, Muslim apologists often quote the following:

"*God is not man, that he should lie, or a son of man, that he should repent ...*" (Num. 23:19).

"*And Jesus said to them, 'A prophet is not without honor, except in his own country, and among his own kind, and in his own house*" (Mk 6:4).

"*This people honors me with their lips, but their heart are far from me; in vain do they worship me ...*" (Mk 7:6).

"*Jesus answered, 'The first is, Hear, O Israel: The Lord our God, the Lord is one'*" (Mk 12:29-30).

"*So Jesus answered them, 'My teaching is not mine, but his who sent me'*" (Jn 7:16).

Regarding what the Old and New Testaments actually say in support of the Trinity and the divinity of Christ, it is best to refer readers back to chapters 1 and 2 of this book, namely *The Blessed Trinity* and *The Divinity of Christ*. For our present purposes, what did Jesus claim about himself in the New Testament?

Jesus' claims

Jesus claimed to pre-exist Abraham, identifying himself with the God of Moses:

"*Truly, truly, I say to you, before Abraham was, I am*" (Jn 8:58).

Jesus claimed equality with God the Father:

"*I and the Father are one*" (Jn 10:30).

Jesus claimed to be equal to God the Father in power:

"The Father loves the Son and has given all things into his hand" (Jn 3:35).

"... whatever he (the Father) does, that the Son does likewise" (Jn 5:19).

"All that the Father has is mine" (Jn 16:15).

Jesus claimed unity with God the Father:

"... know and understand that the Father is in me and I am in the Father" (Jn 10:37-38).

"Have I been with you so long, and yet you do not know me, Philip? He who has seen me has seen the Father ... Do you not believe that I am in the Father and the Father is in me?" (Jn 14:8-10).

Jesus claimed to be the supreme lawgiver:

"For the Son of man is lord of the sabbath" (Mt 12:8).

Jesus claimed to be the supreme judge:

"When the Son of man comes in his glory, and all the angels with him, then he will sit on his glorious throne. Before him will be gathered all the nations, and he will separate them one from another as a shepherd separates the sheep from the goats" (Mt 25:31-32).

Jesus claimed to forgive sins by his own authority:

"'Take heart my son; your sins are forgiven' ... 'This man is blaspheming' ... 'But that you may know that the Son of man has authority on earth to forgive sins ... Rise, take your bed and go to home'" (Mt 9:2-6).

Jesus performed miracles as Supreme Master:

"Little girl, I say to you, arise" (Mk 5:41).

"Young man, I say to you, arise" (Lk 7:14).

Jesus' claim to divinity was understood but rejected by his enemies:

"... *because you, being a man, make yourself God*" (Jn 10:33).

"*Then the high priest tore his robes, and said, 'He has uttered blasphemy. Why do we still need witnesses? You have now heard his blasphemy. What is your judgment?' They answered, 'He deserves death'*" (Mt 26:65-66).

Jesus' character

Jesus' claim to divinity needs to be examined in the light of his character. Firstly, was Jesus mad? The evidence suggests not. On the contrary, we read that the wise and common people universally acclaimed him:

"*... for he taught them as one having authority, and not as their scribes*" (Mt 7:29).

"*... and all who heard him were amazed at his understanding and his answers*" (Lk 2:47).

"*... and all the people rejoiced at all the glorious things that were done by him*" (Lk 13:17).

"*No man ever spoke like this man!*" (Jn 7:46).

In public debate, Jesus left his opponents humbled and confounded:

"*When they heard it, they marveled; and they left him and went away*" (Mt 22:22).

The Pharisees also hung off his every word "*to entangle him in his talk*" (Mt 22:15) but could not bring one true charge against him. Consequently, no one "*from that day ... dare to ask him any more questions*" (Mt 22:46).

Jesus gave us his teachings in private and public — are the following the teachings of a madman?

The Perfect Law:

"And he said to him, 'You shall love the Lord your God with all your heart, and with all your soul, and with all your mind. This is the great and first commandment. And a second is like it, You shall love your neighbor as yourself'" (Mt 22:37).

The Beatitudes:

"Blessed are the poor in spirit, for theirs is the kingdom of heaven. Blessed are those who mourn, for they shall be comforted. Blessed are the meek, for they shall inherit the earth. Blessed are those who hunger and thirst for righteousness, for they shall be satisfied. Blessed are the merciful, for they shall obtain mercy. Blessed are the pure in heart, for they shall see God. Blessed are the peacemakers, for they shall be called sons of God. Blessed are those who are persecuted for righteousness' sake, for theirs is the kingdom of heaven. Blessed are you when men revile you and persecute you and utter all kinds of evil against you falsely on my account" (Mt 5:2-11).

His teaching on the value of the soul as against all the treasures of the world:

"For what will it profit a man, if he gains the whole world and forfeits his soul? Or what shall a man give in return for his soul?" (Mt 16:26).

His teaching on turning the other cheek:

"To him who strikes you on the cheek, offer the other also; and from him who takes away your cloak do not withhold even your coat as well" (Lk 6:29).

His teaching on forgiving an enemy over and over:

"Jesus said to him, 'I do not say to you seven times, but seventy times seven" (Mt 18:22).

His teaching on the Prodigal Son:

"And he arose and came to his father. But while he was yet at a distance, his father saw him and had compassion, and ran and embraced him and kissed him" (Lk 15:20).

His teaching on the Good Shepherd:

"I am the good shepherd. The good shepherd lays down his life for the sheep" (Jn 10:11).

His teaching that power is to serve, not to lord it over others:

"And Jesus called them to him and said to them, 'You know that those who are supposed to rule over the Gentiles lord it over them, and their great men exercise authority over them. But it shall not be so among you; but whoever would be great among you must be your servant'" (Mk 10:42).

The Romans knew that Jesus was not mad – crucifixion was never given to the mad, only to the bad and Jesus was 'bad' because he was acclaimed as a king who might rival Caesar and because of his alleged blasphemy: "because you, being a man, make yourself God" (Jn 10:33).

Was Jesus a fraud? If so, would a fraud:

- Show mercy to the poor and repentant.
- Attack hypocrisy and overturn the moneychangers at his peril.
- Teach all to be pure of heart.
- Flee from the poor who tried to make him King.
- Engage himself in a business that left him penniless and with nowhere to lay his head.
- Keep continued company with the poor, powerless and sinners.
- Teach that power was to serve, not to lord it over others.
- Endure his passion with enormous courage, without uttering one cry in his defense or of anguish.
- Ask his Father to forgive those who put him to death.

Judas, who betrayed Jesus, realized (though too late) that he was innocent (Mt 27:4). Pilate could find "no crime" in him (Jn 18:38). The Roman centurion declared, "Certainly, this man was innocent!" (Lk 23:47).

Jesus' innocence and virtue are proof that he was not a deceiver, leading to the assumption that he was not lying when he claimed to be divine.

What about the Apostles and Evangelists who wrote the Gospels? Did they have anything to gain by writing books that portrayed Jesus as divine? The Apostles were not the type of men to foist a huge deception upon the world – they had run in terror in the Garden of Gethsemane! Even if they were men of courage they had nothing to gain from perpetuating a lie that resulted in them all being put to death.

Jesus' claim to divinity is contained in the Gospels the Apostles wrote. Yet, why would the Apostles write Gospels that showed themselves to be ignorant, cowardly, and denying? Again, this fact creates a presumption that their testimony on other matters is reliable also. Further, Jesus' resurrection is the greatest proof of his divinity – his mastery over death. The Apostles preached the resurrected Jesus in the face of ever-present persecution and threats of death. They all maintained this preaching even unto death – further proof of their sincerity.

Reliability of the Scriptures

However, are the Old and New Testaments possessed and relied upon by Christians authentic? Not according to Islam. They claim belief in the revealed Scriptures (Torah, Psalms, Gospels) *in their original form*. For them, the Scriptures that speak of the Trinity and the divinity of Christ have been fraudulently altered. However, is there any historical evidence to support such an accusation?

The oldest copies of parts of the Old Testament are contained in the Dead Sea Scrolls – five hundred manuscripts of the Essene community written between 250 BC and AD 70 – found in a Judean desert cave in 1947. In addition, the oldest manuscript copies of the Old and New Testaments in existence are:

Codex Vaticanus: in Rome; fifth century; Gen. 46:28 to Heb. 9:14; Greek; Egyptian origin.

Codex Sinaiticus: fourth century; complete copy of the Greek Septuagint; discovered in the monastery of St Catherine in Sinai.

Codex Alexandrinus: early fifth century; has a complete text of the Book of Revelation; discovered in Egypt.

Codex Bezae: fifth century; complete texts of all four Gospels plus Acts and a part of 3 John; Graeco-Roman.

Codex Ephraimi: fifth century; contains all books of the New Testament except for 2 Thess. and 2 John.

Codex Amiatinus: seventh century; earliest Latin copy of the Vulgate; produced in England as a gift for Pope Gregory II.

Experts who have examined all these ancient codices unanimously agree that there exist no contradictions in any of them vis á vis our modern-day versions of the Bible with respect to the person, mission and works of Jesus. This is so even though among the many thousands of different ancient manuscript copies textual variants exist in 6,176 verses out of a total of 7,948 in the New Testament alone. These variations range from simple letters that change a word or its tense, to whole sentences that are missing or significantly different.

Was there, however, a possibility of earlier alteration or forgery before the fourth century AD? Note the following manuscripts:

Q7 manuscript – pre-AD 70; a fragment of Mark's Gospel from the Dead Sea Scrolls.

John Wylands manuscript (P52) – c. AD 130; a fragment of John's Gospel chapter 18 discovered in Egypt in 1920.

Chester-Beatty Papyrii – found in Egypt in 1931; inter AD 155 to somewhere in the third century; manuscript of one hundred and eighty leaves of the Old Testament, thirty leaves from the Gospels and Acts and twenty leaves from Paul and Revelation.

Bodmar Codex – found in Egypt in 1955; a one hundred and fifty-four-page manuscript of John's Gospel written in Greek between AD 130-200; contains the first fourteen chapters and parts of the other seven.

There exist no discrepancies between any of the above ancient documents and modern versions of the Christian Scriptures either with respect to the person, mission or works of Jesus.

It should also be noted that if there were any systematic attempts to add, change or falsify the sacred texts at any time during the first three centuries of Christianity a storm would have been raised. The early Christians were particularly scrupulous in the copying and preservation of the original texts. To possess a copy of the Christian Scriptures was to invite martyrdom. Christians were not prepared to die for tampered texts.

As a final argument, it is worth noting that no one seriously questions the authenticity of ancient manuscripts of pagan works. This is so despite the existence of only a few manuscript copies of these works, most of which date back only to the Middle Ages. For example: Homer's Iliad – 643 copies; Sophocles – 193 copies; Aristotle – 49 copies; Tacitus – 20 copies (earliest ninth and tenth centuries AD); Caesar – 10 copies (earliest ninth century AD); Herodotus – 8 copies; Pliny – 7 copies. On the other hand, we possess over twenty-four thousand ancient copies of the New Testament in multiple languages. Different peoples in different languages and at different times copied the sacred writings and universally preserved the same texts – the only differences being copyist errors!

In summary, the evidence demonstrates the following concerning the Christian Scriptures:

1. That there is no historical proof of alteration or forgery over the centuries.
2. The Gospels, by academic standards applied to test all ancient works, are reliable historical documents.

3. Therefore, Jesus' teaching on the Trinity and his claim to be divine contained within the Gospels are historical.
4. All Scriptural accounts of Jesus' personal character preclude that he was mad or a fraud while teaching the Trinity or his own divinity.

Consequently, after more than two thousand years all Christians can still justifiably say of Jesus the same words St Thomas the Apostle spoke, "My Lord and my God!" (Jn 20:28).

Second objection: *"The Christian belief in original sin is manifestly unjust. Why should children and grandchildren bear the guilt for a sin committed by someone else? As the Qu'ran (Koran) says, 'And no bearer of burdens shall bear another's burden ...' (Faatir 35:18)." Further, 'Every son of Adam is bound to commit sins' (Al-Tirmidhi 24:23). Sin is part of human nature and Allah gives man a solution for it through repentance."*

The original sin itself was a primeval act committed by our first parents, Adam and Eve, who, succumbing to pride disobeyed God's command not to eat of the fruit of the Tree of Knowledge of Good and Evil located in the Garden of Eden (Gen. 3:6).

After committing the original sin, Adam and Eve were immediately punished. They lost the sonship of God by being stripped of sanctifying grace, and hence the right to enter heaven. Four wounds opened within them: malice in the will; ignorance in the intellect; inordinate desire for pleasure (concupiscence); and debility (or weakness in the doing of difficult things). They were driven out of Paradise, angels guarding the entrances with flaming swords to prevent their return and access to the Tree of Life. Toil and sickness were their lot henceforth, and with the forfeiture of the gifts of impassibility and immortality they became subject to pain, suffering, sickness and death: "In the sweat of your face you shall eat bread till you return to the ground, for out of it you were taken; you are dust, and to dust you shall return" (Gen. 3:19). The following passages in the Old and New Testaments testify to the doctrine of original sin: Ps. 51:5; Rom. 5:12; Rom. 15-19; 1 Cor. 15:21-22; Eph. 2:3.

Islam has no objection to the belief that Adam and Eve committed a sin for which they were punished. What Muslims object to is the belief that we, as children of Adam, suffer consequently as well. Mohammad tells his followers, "all people are born true Muslims, innocent and pure" (*Sura* 30:30). Whatever Adam and Eve did it was not a catastrophic event. Their sin, like ours, can be forgiven through repentance and obeying Allah's will.

The doctrine of original sin would certainly be an unjust one if it was as taught by the Christian heretic, John Calvin. He asserted that God not only held Adam and Eve to be personally guilty for their sin in the Garden, but that he also legally imputes their guilt to each and every one of us as their children. It is as if we ourselves had deliberately eaten the forbidden fruit. Common sense alone tells us that such a teaching is completely incompatible with justice (let alone divine justice), human free will and responsibility.

The Catholic Church's teaching on original sin, however, is altogether different from Calvin's. For the Church, only Adam and Eve are personally guilty for their sin. We, as their children, are 'guilty' in an analogical sense, that is, by being deprived of the supernatural and preternatural gifts that would have been passed onto us by Adam if he had not sinned. As the *Catechism of the Catholic Church* says:

> How did the sin of Adam become the sin of his descendants? It is a sin which will be transmitted by propagation to all mankind, that is, by the transmission of a human nature deprived of original holiness and justice. And that is why original sin is called "sin" only in an analogical sense: it is a sin "contracted" and not "committed" – a state and not an act.[1]

Far from being natural to humanity, sin is rather a consequence of our *fallen nature*. As stated above, God, in his goodness and generosity, created Adam and Eve in a state of innocence and happiness, free from sin and death. They were enriched with supernatural gifts to 'divinize' them, enabling them to participate in the life of God. This was to last until God transported them, body and

---

[1] CCC #404.

soul, into heaven for all eternity. It was through the deliberate rebellion of our original parents, and not God's own creative design, that sin became a part of human life.

Yet, despite sin's entrance, God mercifully deigned to deliver humanity from its predicament. God gave humanity time for repentance and promised a new Adam and Eve, namely Jesus and Mary, who would co-operate together to redeem our lost innocence and regain the kingdom of heaven (Gen. 3:15). It is this Jesus as the long-awaited Messiah of Israel who is the remedy for sin, as the Church has always taught:

> If anyone asserts that the sin of Adam ... is taken away either by the powers of human nature, or by any other remedy than the merit of one mediator, Our Lord Jesus Christ, who has reconciled us to God in his own blood, made unto us justice, sanctification, and redemption; or if he denies that the said merit of Jesus Christ is applied, both to adults and to infants, by the Sacrament of Baptism rightly administered in the form of the Church: let him be anathema.[2]

Third objection: *"Islam is closest to the truth because it believes in all the Prophets and Messengers (Noah, Abraham, Moses and Jesus) and whose founder, Mohammad, was foretold by both Moses and Jesus!"*

Islam can claim lineage to all the Prophets known in the Judeo-Christian tradition, yet it is a much more difficult task to prove such a claim. Abraham was the patriarchal founder of the Hebrew people, Moses the deliverer of the Hebrew peoples from the bondage of Egypt and their lawgiver, and Jesus the long-awaited Messiah of Israel and the Savior of the world. None of these three is recorded to have foretold or expected the coming of any post-Messianic prophet such as Mohammad before the writing of the Qu'ran. Rather, in the case of Abraham and Moses (not to mention King David and all the other Jewish Prophets) their missions and prophecies pointed to and were fulfilled completely in the person of Jesus of Nazareth.

---

[2] The Council of Trent, *Decree on Original Sin*, Session V, 1, 3, 17 June, 1546.

After Abraham proved his fidelity to God on Mt Moriah, God made the following promise to him: "And your descendants shall possess the gate of their enemies, and by your descendants shall all the nations of the earth bless themselves" (Gen. 22:17-18). From the Gospel of Matthew (1:1-17) we read the lineage from Abraham through David to Jesus – fourteen generations between Abraham and David, fourteen generations from David to the Babylonian exile, and fourteen generations from the Babylonian exile to Jesus. Matthew proved to the Jewish readers of his Gospel that Jesus was the expected descendant of Abraham who would be the cause of blessing to all the nations through his death and resurrection and his commissioning of the Apostles to preach the Gospel throughout the world. The followers of Mohammad cannot produce a complete or similar type of lineage that shows direct descent from Abraham to argue that he was the one promised in Gen. 22.

Islamic claims that Mohammad was foretold in the Bible stem from the following verse in the Qu'ran:

> Those who follow the Apostle, the unlettered Prophet, whom they find mentioned in their own – in the Law and the Gospel (*Sura* 7:157).

Deuteronomy 18: *"A prophet like you."*

Moses foretold that another would come after him like himself:

"The Lord your God will raise up for you a prophet like me from among you, from your brethren – him you shall heed ... I will raise up for them a prophet like you from among their brethren; and I will put my words in his mouth, and he shall speak to them all that I command him" (Deut. 18:15-18).

Muslims in general are very quick to seize on Deut.18 and claim that Moses was prophesying about the future coming of Mohammad. Volumes have been written highlighting the following as supposed similarities between Moses and Mohammad, for example:

(i) Both were married.
(ii) Both became prophets at the age of forty.

(iii) Both were initially rejected by their peoples, went into exile, and returned years later to lead their peoples.
(iv) Both were lawgivers, military leaders and spiritual guides to their peoples.
(v) Both were succeeded by leaders (Joshua and Omar) who conquered the land of Palestine.

The above parallels between Moses and Mohammad are interesting but pale into insignificance in comparison to the parallels between Moses and Jesus:

(i) Both Moses and Jesus were saved by God from slaughters of innocent children launched by jealous kings.
(ii) Both Moses and Jesus were "called out of Egypt."
(iii) Moses left the right-hand of Pharaoh and became a slave to rescue the Hebrews from slavery; Jesus came from the right-hand of the Father and became a slave to rescue the world from spiritual slavery.
(iv) Moses offered a Passover Lamb to save the Hebrews from slavery; Jesus was the Passover Lamb offered to save the world from spiritual slavery.
(v) Moses spent forty years in the desert before returning to rescue the Hebrews; Jesus spent forty days in the desert before returning to rescue humanity.
(vi) Moses gave the Hebrews in the desert bread from heaven; Jesus gives his followers new bread from heaven (the Eucharist).
(vii) Moses gave the Hebrews in the desert water from a rock; Jesus gives his followers water "that springs up for eternal life."
(viii) Aaron walked in front of Moses to prepare the way; John the Baptist prepared the way for the coming of Jesus.
(ix) The Hebrews were baptized into Moses in the Red Sea; Christians are baptized into Jesus Christ.
(x) Both Moses and Jesus were lawgivers.
(xi) Moses heralded the Covenant of Law; Jesus heralded the Covenant of Grace.
(xii) God spoke to Moses on Mount Sinai; the Father spoke to Jesus on Mount Tabor (the Transfiguration).

It is Matthew who relates the event of the Transfiguration to prove that Jesus was the one that we should listen to:

"And he was transfigured before them, and his face shone like the sun, and his garments became white as light ... lo, a bright cloud overshadowed them, and a voice from the cloud said, 'This is my beloved Son, with whom I am well pleased; listen to him'" (Mt 17:2-5).

The voice was obviously that of God the Father testifying to the divine Sonship of Jesus that was revealed by his transfiguration, and to directly link this event with Deut. 18 Moses (together with Elijah representing the Prophets) appears talking with Jesus (v. 3).

None of this escaped the attention of the early Church, who, through St Peter after the descent of the Holy Spirit on Pentecost Day, was told the following:

"But what God foretold by the mouth of all the prophets, that his Christ should suffer, he thus fulfilled ... Moses said, 'The Lord God will raise up for you a prophet from your brethren as he raised me up. You shall listen to him in whatever he tells you' ... And all the prophets who have spoken, from Samuel and those who came afterwards, also proclaimed these days. You are the sons of the prophets and of the covenant which God gave to your fathers, saying to Abraham, 'And in your posterity shall all the families of the earth be blessed'" (Acts 3:18-25).

The Jews, through the promises made to Abraham and Moses, expected the coming of the Messiah. The Christians are those who believe Jesus to be that Messiah. Both Jews and Christians see clearly that Mohammad, neither in his life nor mission, fulfils the prophetic requirements of that expected Messiah.

John 14: *"Another Counselor."*

Muslims claim that Jesus himself foretold Mohammad's mission. As evidence, they quote the following words of Jesus as recorded in the Gospel of John:

"And I will pray the Father, and he will give you another Counselor, to be with you for ever, even the Spirit of truth, whom the world cannot receive, because it neither sees him nor knows him; you know him, for he dwells with you, and will be in you" (14:16-17).

This "another Counselor" is allegedly Mohammad. The argument goes that the Greek word in John's Gospel for "advocate" (parakletos – παράκλητος) is a later corruption replacing the original *periklutos*, which means 'one worthy of praise.' The Arabic for *periklutos* is 'Ahmad,' one of Mohammad's adopted names, making Mohammad the Counselor.

Such an argument, however, fails for the following reasons:

(i) There is no evidence of any corruption ever having taken place. All the Greek manuscripts of John predating Mohammad say parakletos, not periklutos. In fact, the word periklutos appears nowhere in the Bible.

(ii) *"... to be with you forever"*: Mohammad died in AD 632. It is impossible to argue that he has been with the followers of Jesus "forever."

(iii) *"... the Spirit of truth"*: Being flesh and blood, Mohammad cannot fit the description of a spirit, let alone "the Spirit."

(iv) *"... neither sees him"*: The world cannot receive the Spirit because it cannot see him. Mohammad in his humanity was very visible.

(v) *"... he dwells with you ... will be in you"*: By no stretch of the imagination could Mohammad be considered to dwell within each and every believer.

(vi) Jesus promised that he would send this new Advocate to the disciples and told them to remain in Jerusalem for his coming (Acts 1:4). Nine days after his ascension into heaven the new Advocate arrived as promised in the form of fiery tongues: "They (the disciples) were all filled with the Holy Spirit" (Acts 2:3-4). So, the prophecy of Joel 2:28-32 was fulfilled according to the words of Jesus – in Jerusalem, upon the disciples, nine days after his ascension – not in Arabia, on the tribe of Quraish, six hundred years later!

Fourth objection: *"Of all these Prophets, including Jesus, Mohammad is the last and the greatest!"*

Of all the claims of Islam, perhaps the most audacious is that Jesus and Mohammad are both Prophets and that Mohammad is the greater of the two. We have already outlined above some of the greatest of Jesus' teachings. His teachings on the love of God, neighbor and enemy are unmatched by any other religious founder. He introduced revolutionary teachings on humility, purity of heart and sacrificial fraternal love. He warned against the love of money, adultery in the heart, and violence as a means to an end. He abolished divorce, restored the permanence of marriage and extolled virginity and poverty for the sake of the Kingdom. He taught that good could be done on the Sabbath, abolished the old dietary prohibitions and the over-emphasis on outward signs of justification (such as circumcision). His personal life was the embodiment of all these teachings, climaxing in the greatest act of love of God and neighbor in all of history – his crucifixion and death on Mt Calvary. None could justly accuse or convict Jesus of sin. The rationalist Rousseau, a great enemy of Christianity, had to declare that no hero in history was comparable to Jesus. Likewise, the Biblical critic Harnack, who denied the divinity of Jesus and his miracles, still felt compelled to state that no one else's teachings matched his. If the Gospels that record the life and teachings of Jesus are concoctions, then the man or men who forged them are nevertheless geniuses for having imagined them!

On the other hand, Mohammad's teachings either contradict Jesus' or fall far short of them. They amount to a partial return to Judaic teachings through the reintroduction of circumcision, dietary laws and the practice of divorce. Of more concern, Mohammad advocated and practised polygamy, thereby denying the equal dignity of women, and urged violence to spread Islam and destroy its enemies

None of the biographies of Mohammad were compiled in his lifetime and those between AD 800 and AD 1000 should not be read as reliable historical documents. In his early years, Mohammad was simple in his habits and careful in his external appearance. He was imaginative, affectionate and magnanimous towards personal and family friends. On the negative side, Mohammad had an acute aversion to pain, suffered apparently from epilepsy and was of a highly nervous temperament.

Unlike Jesus, Mohammad married at the age of twenty-five and to a wealthy widow named Khadeejah, fifteen years his senior. Promoting his wife's business interests, Mohammad grew in confidence and stature, developing commercial savvy and a flare for communication.

In the practice of his religion, Mohammad was zealous, pious and austere. He would often wander in the hills for weeks on end around Mecca, meditating in solitude. It was in the year AD 610, when Mohammad was forty that his life changed forever. One night, known subsequently as the *Night of Power*, Mohammad claimed to receive a visitation from the Angel Gabriel who said to him, *"You are the Messenger of God."* Mohammad would claim continuous revelations from the Angel Gabriel for the next twenty-two years.

Politically, Mohammad was courageous, a great general and patriotic. His charisma and leadership ability convinced his early followers to sever all ties with birthplace and clan. This enabled the early Muslims to survive ostracism, persecution and exile from the local Meccans.

While in exile Mohammad approved *razzias*, or armed raids against caravans travelling from Mecca to Syria. Soon enough, Mohammad would claim revelations making booty and ransom lawful and allotting one-fifth of all spoils to himself. Many innocent merchants were killed in these raids. At least twenty-seven people were killed at Mohammad's orders, mostly by assassination.

Mohammad's military victories began with the battle of *Badr* in AD 624. Mohammad rejoiced at the death of his enemies and officially declared himself to be the "enemy of infidels," fresh revelations describing them as the "worst of animals." Jews were special targets. On one occasion, nine hundred Jewish men of the tribe of Banu Qurayzah were decapitated in front of their women and children for refusing to convert to Islam. Soon enough, there was not a Jew in Arabia who did not fear for his life.

Throughout his life, Mohammad personally took part in the following military expeditions:

Defend the Faith!

Waddan; Buwat; Safwan; Dul Ashir; Badr; Kudr; Sawiq; Banu Qaynuqa; Ghatafan; Bahran; Uhud; Al-Asad; Banu Nadir; Nejd; Invasion of Badr; First Jandal; Trench; Banu Qurayza; Second Banu Lahyan; Banu Mustaliq; Hudabiyyah; Khaybar; Fidak; Third Qura; Dhat al-Riqa; Banu Baqra; Mecca; Hunayn; Autas; Taif; Tabouk.

Mohammad also ordered the following military expeditions: Nakhla; Nejd; First Banu Asad; First Banu Lahyan; Al Raji; Umayyah; Bir Maona; assassination of Abu Rafi; Maslamah; Second Banu Asad; First Banu Thalabah; Second Banu Thalabah; Dhu Qarad; Jumun; Al-Is; Third Banu Thalabah; Hisma; First Qura; Second Jandal; First Ali; Second Qura; Uraynah; Rawaha; Umar; Abu Bakr; Banu Murrah; Banu Uwal; Third Fadak; Yemen; Banu Sulaym; Kadid; Banu Amir; Dhat Atlah; Mu'tah; Amr; Abu Ubaidah; Abi Hadrad; Edam; Khadirah; First Khalid ibn Walid; Suwa; Manat; Second Khalid ibn Walid; Yaghuth; First Autas; Second Autas; Banu Tamim; Banu Khatham; Banu Kilab; Jeddah; Banu Udhrah; Third Khalid ibn Walid; Fourth Khalid ibn Walid; Abu Sufyan; Jurash; Fifth Khalid ibn Walid; Second Ali; Third Ali; Dhul Khalasa; Usama.

It was through military conquest, rather than miracles or preaching, that Mohammad brought Arabia under Islam.

After the death of his wife Khadeejah in AD 619, Mohammad claimed the rights of a prophet to take at least another twelve wives, including the seven-year-old Aisha, consummating the marriage when she was nine and he was fifty-three.

In AD 632, Mohammad completed a solemn pilgrimage to Mecca, together with forty thousand followers. His conquest of Arabia was complete. Soon after, he died of a violent fever at the age of sixty-three.

From this brief overview, it is quite clear that the claim that Mohammad is greater than Jesus Christ cannot be sustained.

The Crusades

Objection: *"The Crusades together amount to the most scandalous episode in the Catholic Church's history. The Crusaders were for the most part vicious, bloodthirsty and rapacious. They were responsible for countless deaths and atrocities and deserve to be roundly condemned!"*

A myriad of critics are ready to condemn the Crusades and the Catholic Church for promoting them. According to these critics, the Crusaders were obviously ruthless and greedy adventurers used by Popes and Kings to realize their worldly economic and territorial interests, under the pious motive of "recapturing the Holy Sepulcher." No justification can be had for a movement that so obviously illustrated how far the Catholic Church had strayed from Jesus' Gospel of love, peace and forgiveness.

To respond to such charges, it is necessary to examine the Crusades in the context of the ongoing struggle between Christianity and Islam. This struggle began immediately after the death of Mohammad in AD 632. After conquering most of Arabia, the successors to Mohammad rapidly expanded the Muslim realm throughout the Middle East, North Africa, southwest Asia and Western Europe. The various Caliphs and their respective conquests were as follows:

Abu Bakr (AD 632-634): conquered the remainder of the Arabian Peninsula and entered Palestine.

Omar (AD 634-644): fought and won the following battles – Ajnadain (634); Damascus (635); Yarmuk (636); Qadisiya (636); Ramla, Fihl and Jerusalem (638); Heliopolis (640); Mosul (641); Alexandria (642) and Nehavend (642). By the time of his death, Omar had spread Islam into the Tigris–Euphrates region, overrun Persia, conquered Syria, Lebanon and Palestine, entered Asia Minor, devoured Egypt, and advanced into Libya.

Othman (AD 644-656): conquered Tripoli in North Africa (644); attacked Cyprus (648); captured Persepolis (648); conquered

Nishapur, Herat and Balkh in Afghanistan (651); attacked the island of Rhodes (654); won at Basra (656).

Ali (AD 656-661): expansion stalled under his reign due to Berber resistance in North Africa.

The Umayyad Caliphate (AD 661-750): restored Islamic expansion with the conquest of Kabul in 664. With the construction of the naval base of Kairouan in North Africa in 670, Islam became a major naval power enabling the conquest of Carthage (698) and the invasion of Spain in 711. After victories at Rio Barbate, Lisbon and Cordoba (711) and Toledo (712) most of Spain was quickly subjugated. France was then invaded with Narbonne captured in 715 and Toulouse in 721. In the East, expansion continued with the conquest of Bukara and Samarkand (710), Multan (711) and the occupation of the Sind region in northwest India (712). The Umayyads also twice besieged Constantinople in the years 673-678 and 717-718.

In the one hundred years between AD 632 and 732 the Middle East, North Africa and Spain, regions that had known Christianity for up to six centuries, were now lost to the followers of Mohammad. At the same time, the Christian Byzantine Empire with its capital of Constantinople (the first city in history founded and dedicated as a Christian city by the Emperor Constantine) was under the constant threat of being overwhelmed. What had to be the response of Christendom in the face of this grave crisis?

Contrary to the opinions of certain schools of thought, Christianity has never advocated pacificism as an essential part of "Jesus' Gospel of love, peace and forgiveness." Rather, the Church has always advocated the concept of the 'just war.' The conditions for when a just war may be fought are outlined in the *Catechism of the Catholic Church*:

> The strict conditions for legitimate defense by military force require rigorous consideration. The gravity of such a decision makes it subject to rigorous conditions of moral legitimacy. At one and the same time:
> – the damage inflicted by the aggressor on the nation or community of nations must be lasting, grave and certain;

- all other means of putting an end to it must have been shown to be impractical or ineffective;
- there must be serious prospects of success;
- the use of arms must not produce evils and disorders graver than the evil to be eliminated. The power of modern means of destruction weighs very heavily in evaluating this condition.

These are the traditional elements enumerated in what is called the 'just war' doctrine.

The evaluation of these conditions for moral legitimacy belongs to the prudential judgment of those who have responsibility for the common good.[1]

The first great Christian victories against the tide of Islam were achieved at Constantinople (673-678 and 717-718), Covadonga in Spain (722) and Poitiers in France (732). The Christians fought these battles as defensive battles against an unjust aggressor. They had to fight, for Islam at the time was in no mood for peaceful co-existence and if left unopposed, the damage inflicted on the Christian world certainly would have been "lasting, grave and certain."

Despite suffering military setbacks in the early eighth century, Islam retained its appetite for military conquest. Crete was conquered in 823, Sardinia in 827 and Corsica in 850. Repeated raids were also launched into southern Italy and the Rhone River region of France. After a struggle of one hundred and fourteen years, Sicily finally capitulated to the Muslims in 941. The conquerors now were the Abbasid Dynasty, who displaced the Umayyads in 750. Unlike the Umayyads, the Abbasids were less tolerant of non-Islamic beliefs. Previously, subjugated Christians and Jews were generally left alone to practise their beliefs, subject only to the payment of a special tax. Now, conversion to Islam was more insisted upon and commonplace.

This change was most particularly evident after the defeat of the Byzantines at the battle of Manzikert in 1071. The Byzantine Emperor had raised a well-armed and highly disciplined force of over 60,000 men. Their opponents were over 100,000 Seljuk Turks,

---

[1] CCC #2309.

descendants of wild Mongolian horsemen from the Russian steppes. These nomads were easy converts to Islam as its looser morality and aggressive spirit coincided with their own. During the battle itself, the Christian army, exhausted by great heat, was outmanoeuvred and overwhelmed by repeated waves of swift horsemen firing showers of arrows. The Turkish warriors then moved in for the kill with their razor sharp curved swords.

The consequences of defeat at Manzikert for Christendom were far-reaching. The heartland of Anatolia, once the region where St Paul had planted the first seeds of Christianity, was now in the hands of a more fanatical strain of Islam. Constantinople was once again threatened, while pilgrimages to the Holy Land were now subject to an official policy of harassment. Word of deaths and oppression would soon be reaching the ears of a concerned Europe. Pope St Gregory VII first conceived the idea of a crusade to relieve the East in 1073, but he did not live to see it materialize. However, when Byzantine Emperor Alexius I Comnenus sent a plea for assistance to Pope Bl. Urban II in 1095, the West was now ready and willing to respond.

Western Christendom was already very familiar with and experienced in the crusading spirit. The Spanish Reconquista was nearing its four hundredth year and had achieved great successes under King Alfonso II in the ninth century and currently under the legendary Rodrigo del Bivar (El Cid). However, few could have foreseen the overwhelming response to Pope Bl. Urban II's speech delivered at the Council of Clermont on 10 November 1095 calling for a large expeditionary force to turn back the Muslim advance and liberate the Holy Land. In his speech, the Pope promised a plenary indulgence – a full remission of temporal punishment due to sin – to all those prepared to take up the cross and reclaim the Holy Sepulcher. Pope Urban then quoted from the Gospel of Matthew: "... every one who has left houses or brothers or sisters or father or mother or children or lands, for my name's sake, will receive a hundredfold, and inherit eternal life." The crowd of thousands then exclaimed with one voice, "*God wills it!*"

From that day forward, tens of thousands of commonfolk, soldiers, knights, nobles and even kings took up the standard of crusade. Admittedly, not everyone's motives were pure. Besides the spiritual values underpinning the crusade, some were lured by the prospect of territorial gain, rich treasure and financial opportunities, others by a simple thirst for adventure. Nevertheless, in its ideal the crusade was a true expression of faith based on the sacrifice of one's life for the sake of Christ.

All up, there were eight official crusades and two unofficial ones. The official crusades, their leaders and achievements were as follows:

First Crusade (1096-1099):

Godfrey de Bouillon, Raymond of Toulouse, Bohemund of Taranto. Captured Jerusalem and established the four Crusader states of Jerusalem, Tripoli, Antioch and Edessa. A total success.

Second Crusade (1147-1149):

Conrad III of Germany; Louis VII of France. Aimed at alleviating the threat to the Crusader states after the loss of Edessa in 1144. A major and demoralizing failure.

Third Crusade (1189-1192):

Frederick I of Germany; Richard I of England; Philip II of France. Aimed at recapturing Jerusalem lost to Saladin on 2 October 1187. Conquered Cyprus, recaptured Acre. Saladin also defeated at Arsuf and Jaffa. Lacking manpower, a treaty was negotiated with Saladin allowing pilgrims to enter Jerusalem. A partial success.

Fourth Crusade (1202-1204):

Thibaud of Champagne. Aimed at recapturing Jerusalem through Egypt; Crusaders diverted from their original objectives to capture the Hungarian dependency of Zara for Venice and sacked Constantinople on 13 April 1204 after failing to secure agreed transportation to the East. The Latin kingdom of Constantinople was established – a kingdom that would earn the hatred of the Greeks. A total disaster.

Fifth Crusade (1218-1221):
Papal Legate Cardinal Pelagius. Aimed to capture Egypt. Damietta captured in November 1219. Christian forces negotiated an eight-year truce and withdrew after the failure of Frederick II's forces to appear. A frustrating failure.

Sixth Crusade (1228-1229):
Frederick II of Germany. Despite being under the penalty of excommunication for delaying to fulfill his vow to go on crusade, the German Emperor secured control of Jerusalem, Bethlehem and Nazareth through negotiation. A surprising success.

Seventh Crusade (1248-1254):
St Louis IX of France. Aimed at recapturing Jerusalem lost to the Turks in 1244. The Crusaders won a major victory at Damietta in Egypt in June 1249 but were later defeated at Mansura on 8 February 1250. Captured by the Egyptians on 6 April 1250, St Louis was forced to pay a large ransom for his release. He returned to France four years later after failing to secure an alliance with the Mongols. Another frustrating failure.

Eighth Crusade (1270-1271):
St Louis IX of France and Edward I of England. Aimed at propping up the flagging fortunes of the Christians after the fall of Antioch to the Mamelukes in 1268. St Louis landed at Tunis and besieged the city before contracting the plague and perishing. His brother, Charles of Anjou, took control of the army, negotiated a treaty with the Muslims, and retreated to France. Edward I continued on to Acre where, after fighting a number of battles, he returned to England after concluding a treaty with the Mameluke Sultan, Baybars. Once again, another frustrating failure.

After 1271, Christian resolve weakened further, and in the following twenty years the Mamelukes systematically reduced the remaining Crusader strongholds. The last to fall was Acre, which was besieged by 120,000 men under the leader Malek–Aschraf. The 25,000 Christian defenders resisted heroically for three months, only fleeing in their ships to Cyprus when all was lost. The garrison of Knights Templars, however, remained and together with the Christian presence in the Middle East was completely annihilated.

Without a doubt, the Crusades for the Holy Land from the military point of view were ultimately a failure due in large part to the self-interest, contention, infidelity and avarice that racked and divided the Christian forces. The various massacres after the fall of Jerusalem in 1099 and at Constantinople in 1204 are without excuse and still leave their scars on East-West relations. In addition, the unofficial People's Crusade of 1096 and the Children's Crusade were tragic follies that led to the deaths of tens of thousands of enthusiastic but misled individuals. In his Easter Message of 2000, Pope St John Paul II showed that the Church was willing to admit responsibility for "sins committed in the service of truth." But those who continually raise these failings in order to denigrate the whole crusading movement and the Church *per se* overextend themselves. Excesses occur in any just war – for example, the bombing of Dresden by the Allies in February 1945. Nevertheless, the ideal of the crusade stands unchallenged; that is, wars fought in self-defense to recapture what was lost to an unjust aggressor whose actions over the previous four hundred and fifty years had showed an intention to devour the whole of Christendom.

Critics of the Crusades are also strangely silent about Islamic militarism and expansion. One never hears outrage over the Muslim conquests of Christian regions and the large-scale kidnappings of Christian children, discriminatory taxation policies and the forced conversions of whole populations to Islam. Apologies are never demanded of the Muslims for invading Western Europe in the eighth century or Eastern Europe in the fourteenth century. This silence also extends to present-day persecutions of Christians in most Islamic countries, including Algeria, Egypt, Pakistan, Saudi Arabia, Syria, Iraq, etc.

Nor does one hear from the critics anything about the positive aspects of the Crusades. The renewed communication with the East brought about a greater exchange of trade and culture; there was renewed contact with beleaguered Christians such as the Maronites in Lebanon; the West benefited from contact with Muslim mathematicians and philosophers versed in Aristotelian thought; the

Defend the Faith!

rise and flourishing of the religious military orders of the Knights Hospitallers and the Knights Templars brought about a renewal of lofty ideals and noble fighting spirit; and, most importantly, the Crusades delayed the desired Islamic invasion of Eastern Europe for nearly two hundred years.

Despite the final defeat of the Crusades, the authentic crusading spirit was to live on for another four centuries. Continued Islamic expansionism necessitated further Christian efforts at self-defense, particularly after the conquest of Constantinople by Mohammed II in 1453. The great battles and the heroes who fought them on behalf of Christendom were as follows:

Belgrade (1456): Prince John Hunyadi and St John Capistrano against the Turkish Sultan Mohammed II; 10,000 Christian troops against 150,000 Muslim; a flotilla of two hundred ships led by John Hunyadi and St John Capistrano sailed down the Danube River and broke the Turkish blockade; after a five hour battle the relieving Christians entered the besieged city; the Christian defenders then destroyed the counter-attacking Janissaries with a burning wall of sulphur, pitch and gunpowder; after losing their main battery of siege cannons to a Christian onslaught the Turks retreated; Hungary was saved for another sixty years.

Albania (1443-1467): George Castriota (Scanderberg) – destroyed sixteen successive Turkish invasions led by Sultans Murad II and Mohammed II; the Turks invaded with armies of 40,000 in 1443, 160,000 in 1450 and two of 200,000 in 1466 and 1467. While Scanderberg lived, the Turks could never capture Albania.

Malta (1565): The Knights of St John Hospitaller against the Turkish Sultan Suleiman the Magnificent; 65,000 Turks invaded Malta which was defended by only 7,000 knight monks led by Jean la Valette; the Turkish siege of three fortresses lasted for four months; Turkish losses during the campaign totalled 30,000; when Spanish reinforcements of 7,000 finally arrived only 600 of the original defenders were left; exhausted, the Turks abandoned the siege.

Lepanto (1571): Continued Ottoman aggression in the eastern Mediterranean led to the capture of Cyprus in 1570 and the massacre of all the Christian inhabitants of Nicosia and Famagusta; under the auspices of Pope St Pius V an alliance of Spain, Venice, Genoa, the Papal States and Knights of Malta was effected in May 1571; Don Juan of Austria was appointed commander-in-chief of the Christian forces; the Pope ordered all convents and monasteries in Rome to pray for the coming battle; St Pius V himself fasted three days a week and prayed hours every day; Mass and Holy Rosary were said on every ship each day; the battle was joined with the Turkish fleet under Ali Pasha in the Strait of Corinth; the din of noise on the Ottoman ships contrasted with the silence, prayer and absolutions on Christian ships; losses – 7,500 Christians killed, 12 ships lost; 30,000 Turks killed, 8,000 taken prisoner; 225 Turkish ships sunk or captured; 15,000 Christian galley slaves freed; Ali Pasha was captured and beheaded; St Pius V was told miraculously of the victory which was confirmed two weeks later by courier; the Pope attributed the victory to Our Lady Help of Christians and added this invocation to the Litany of Loreto and decreed 7 October the Feast of Our Lady of Victory.

Vienna (1683): 200,000 Turks were camped outside Vienna under the command of the Grand Mustapha; only 10,000 Christian troops remained in Vienna as defenders; Mustapha decided to starve out the city; meanwhile, two armies, one from Poland (under King Sobieski) and one from Lorraine were advancing towards Vienna to give added strength to the defenders; on 12 September 1683, these two armies, numbering 45,000 men, descended on the surprised Turks; the Catholic armies now possessed greater discipline and determination, and by the end of the day the Turks had fled; on hearing the news of victory, Bl. Pope Innocent XI declared 12 September the Feast of the Holy Name of Mary in thanksgiving for Our Lady's intercession.

Zenta (1697): As the years progressed the Turks suffered further defeats: Buda, Neuhausel, Gran, Mohacs, Athens, Belgrade; in 1697, the Turks reinvaded Transylvania at Zenta; a Catholic army led by Prince Eugene of Savoy met them on 11 September; the battle was engaged and ended with 20,000 Turks killed and only 300 Christians dead; on 26 January 1699, the Turks signed the Treaty of Carlowitz, restoring Transylvania and most of Hungary to the Holy Roman Empire; it was the first time that the Turks had negotiated with Christian forces; the Turks had made their last attack on Europe.

Defend the Faith!

Other Christian military campaigns possessing the Crusader spirit can also be mentioned, including the war against the Albigensians launched by Pope Innocent III in the thirteenth century and the final stages of the Spanish Reconquista under Queen Isabella in the late fifteenth century. All the above wars and battles were fought in ages when the character of European states was Christian, and so their armies were also. It is not illegitimate for a nation, Christian or otherwise, to possess an army and to employ it in self-defense.

The secularisation of the Western world in the past two centuries has only resulted in more frequent wars and greater atrocities. Modern attacks launched against the Crusades are generally one-sided affairs which fail to consider the history of Islamic aggression against Christianity, and which are more motivated not out of love of Jesus' message of "peace, love and forgiveness" but by a broader anti-Catholic secularist agenda. If Christendom existed today and it faced imperilment from an unjust external aggressor, the cry of *"Onward Christian soldiers!"* would still be a noble call to answer.

The Inquisition

Objection: *"Between fifty and ninety-five million people were killed by the Catholic Church through inquisitions because they believed in Jesus and the Bible. Therefore, it is anti-Christ!"*

When most people today hear the word "Inquisition" images of unjust trials, torture, persecution and burnings at the stake automatically come to mind. Not only is the Inquisition attacked for its inexcusable abuses, but also the very concept of inquisition is execrated as contrary to the modern, democratic and neutral attitude towards religion that characterizes our era. Any attempt to defend the Inquisition can only be a qualified one. In the following it is intended to provide a brief response to the most outlandish or exaggerated attacks against it.

Some have argued that Moses conducted the first religious inquisition after he descended from Mount Sinai and found that the Hebrews had made to themselves a golden calf to which they sacrificed and bowed in adoration. Moses, illuminated by God, shattered the tablets on which were written the Ten Commandments, destroyed the calf and beat it to powder, and then made the Hebrews drink water containing the dust of it. Afterwards, he assembled the sons of Levi and said to them, "Thus says the Lord God of Israel, 'Put every man his sword on his side, and go to and fro from gate to gate throughout the camp, and slay every man his brother, and every man his companion, and every man his neighbor.' And the sons of Levi did according to the word of Moses; and there fell of the people that day about three thousand men" (Exod. 32:27-28). In his zeal to preserve the true religion of God and prevent all the Hebrews falling into the degradation of idolatry, Moses had three thousand of his own people killed that day. Furthermore, God specifically authorized Moses to continue to act as an inquisitor among the Jewish people and punish severely offenses against the law of God:

"If there is found among you, within any of your towns which the Lord your God gives you, a man or woman who does what is evil in the sight of the Lord

your God, in transgressing his covenant, and has gone and served other gods and worshiped them, or the sun or the moon or any of the host of heaven, which I have forbidden, and it is told you and you hear of it; then you shall inquire diligently, and if it is true and certain that such an abominable thing has been done in Israel, then you shall bring forth to your gates that man or woman who has done this evil thing, and you shall stone that man or woman to death with stones. On the evidence of two witnesses or of three witnesses he that is to die shall be put to death; a person shall not be put to death on the evidence of one witness" (Deut. 17:2-6).

To understand the various Catholic inquisitions properly, it is necessary to place them in their historic contexts. It is still universally recognized that the State has the right to protect itself and its citizens from external and internal enemies that seek either to undermine or destroy it. Therefore, no reasonable person questions the need for any State to maintain an appropriate army, police force, or civil emergency force. Nor is it questioned when a State erects and maintains a just court system to enforce the law of the land to secure public order and protect the common good. Parliaments often erect special tribunals, Royal Commissions or committees of investigation. All these are forms of inquisition.

Medieval European societies were Christian societies. They were, despite their known deficiencies, wonderful fruits of the redemption of Jesus Christ. To quote Pope Leo XIII, *Immortale Dei*, the medieval age was "a time when the philosophy of the Gospel governed the states ... The influence of Christian wisdom and its divine virtue penetrated the laws, institutions and the customs of the people. Then the religion instituted by Jesus Christ ... flourished everywhere, thanks to the favor of princes ... Then the Priesthood and the Empire were united by a happy concord."[1]

Therefore, unlike today, Medieval European states were not neutral towards religion, but, like individuals, possessed a religion themselves. They saw it as their duty to promote the common good by supporting the religion of God both within and without their borders. In such societies, to promote a religion contrary to the State religion

---

[1] 1 November, 1885, #21.

The Inquisition

was considered not only an offense against God but also treason against the State. The creeds of certain heretical groups, if put into practice, would have undone the whole structure and fabric of society. Laws were put into place prohibiting proselytism and propaganda in favor of such sects and these laws were enforced and offenders punished. Thus, came about the establishment of either religious or secular courts of inquiry, or inquisitions.

Second objection: *"The Medieval Inquisition targeted innocent Bible-believing Christians who questioned the tyranny of Rome!"*

During the twelfth and thirteenth centuries, violent Gnostic sects appeared in southern Europe, attacking the Church and encouraging revolt against civil authorities. These sectarians claimed to possess a secret source of religious knowledge, considered the material world to have been created by an 'Evil Principle' and so believed all matter to be evil, scorned marriage, encouraged suicide, and forbade the taking of oaths which bound the fabric of feudal society.

Some moderns claim an affinity with these Gnostics simply because they possessed a vernacular translation of the Scriptures. They conclude from this fact that the Catholic Church was persecuting them because they were 'Bible-Believers.' One such person is the Evangelical Dave Hunt, who in recent years has written, "It is quite clear that the Vaudois, Albigenses, Waldenses, and other similar groups were heretics to Rome only. In fact, their beliefs were much like those of the Reformers, of whom they were, in a sense, the forerunners."[2] Yet, even Henry C. Lea, the most anti-Catholic writer on the Inquisition had to admit, "the cause of orthodoxy was the cause of progress and civilization. Had Catharism become dominant, or even had it been allowed to exist on equal terms, its influence would have been disastrous."

The Church, together with secular governments, established the Medieval Inquisition in 1184. Its object was to try charges of heresy. If the person charged was prepared to recant his/her errors, a public penance was imposed; if he/she remained obdurate, he/she was

---

[2] Dave Hunt, *A Woman Rides the Beast*, Harvest House, 1994, p. 257.

declared guilty of heresy and handed over to the State for punishment. Its punishments were severe and ranged from loss of property, to imprisonment or death. The Church at the time approved the severe repression of heresy and believed that, considering the overall threat at hand, it was proportionate in the circumstances.

In 1232, Pope Gregory IX appointed the newly formed Dominicans and Franciscans as specialist and permanent inquisitors. These religious were dispassionate, unselfish, highly popular, fearless, beyond corruption, and desired solely to serve the interests of the Church and the salvation of souls. In appointing such men, Pope Gregory was motivated by various factors, including stemming the encroachment of secular courts into religious affairs. However, his chief desire was to protect the people of God from error while insisting that the accused be brought back into the grace of God. Court procedures and rules were also improved and unjust inquisitors removed and punished.[3]

It was deemed a failure for an inquisitor if he could not convert the accused and had to hand him/her over to the secular arm to be executed. One popular myth is that the vast majority of those who appeared before the Inquisition were sentenced to death. In fact, extant records indicate otherwise. For example, out of the nine hundred and thirty cases that appeared before the tribunal in Toulouse, France, only forty-two were abandoned to the secular arm to be executed, three hundred and seven imprisoned, while two hundred and seventy one were released from punishments.[4] Other penalties included the confiscation or destruction of property, to hear Mass and religious services, to abstain from manual labor, to receive Communion, to forsake soothsaying and usury, to give alms, or to go on pilgrimage or crusade.

Unfortunately, Popes Innocent IV, Alexander IV and Clement IV sanctioned the use of torture. It was intended to be employed only once for the purpose of eliciting the truth and with the consent of the local Bishop. It was not to cause "loss of limb or imperil life." However,

---

[3] William Thomas Walsh, *Characters of the Inquisition*, TAN Books and Publishers Inc., Rockford, Illinois, 1987, pp. 47-48.
[4] *Ibid.* p. 55.

these restrictions were not always heeded and its application was in many cases extreme. In hindsight, the Church acknowledges that torture and capital punishment should not have been employed. As the *Catechism of the Catholic Church* says, "Torture which uses physical or moral violence to extract confessions ... frighten opponents, or satisfy hatred is contrary to respect for the person and for human dignity ... In recent times it has become evident that these cruel practices were neither necessary for public order, nor in conformity with the legitimate rights of the human person" (CCC #2297-8).

Third objection: *"The Spanish Inquisition is proof that the Catholic Church more than any other institution is guilty of intolerance and persecution."*

The Spanish Inquisition was established in 1478 and is the most famous, or infamous, of all inquisitions, depending on which version of history one prefers.

In 1492, Spain was finally united as a single country after nearly eight centuries of struggle against the Moors. Queen Isabella knew that Spain's unity depended upon a strong Church. She set about halting many abuses, and reforming the Church by raising educational and moral standards.

One of the more serious problems faced by Isabella was the number of Jews and Moors who had *pretended* to convert to the Catholic religion without really believing in it. These dubious converts had risen to high positions in government and Church, and many were secretly plotting the downfall of Isabella, Spain and the Church.

The method chosen by Isabella to find these agents was the Inquisition. What is often overlooked is that the Spanish Inquisition was instituted for persons who professed to be Catholics and not for practising Jews or Moslems. It also aimed to unearth and bring to penance bigamists, adulterers, heretics, blasphemers and other baptized men and women who violated the teachings of the Church.

At first there were abuses, with many people being falsely accused, tortured and imprisoned. Popes Leo X, Paul III, Paul IV and Sixtus IV condemned these abuses. Pope Leo X, for example, excommunicated the Catholic tribunal at Toledo and ordered the arrest of the witnesses who appeared before it for perjury. New judges were appointed, headed by the Dominican friar Thomas de Torquemada. Contrary to the popular opinion, Torquemada reformed procedures, making them more lenient, improved prison conditions and personally heard appeals.

The sixteenth century was a brutal period. The use of torture and execution by burning at the stake was common in Catholic and Protestant Europe. In the Elizabethan courts of Protestant England, priests were hung, drawn and quartered for hearing Mass in private homes. Contemporary English opinion would have us believe that Elizabeth I was "good Queen Bess" and that Mary Tudor was "Bloody Mary" for executing Protestant leaders after she became Queen. In fact, Elizabeth's reign of forty-four years and four months was one of repression and persecution. The Protestant historian Hallam asserts, "the rack seldom stood idle in the Tower for all the latter part of Elizabeth's reign" (*Constitutional History*; Elizabeth, Chap. III).

Furthermore, not only was the Mass illegal in Elizabethan England but anyone who did not attend Anglican services was fined. Anyone who refused to take the Oath of Supremacy after two refusals was executed. Bringing Catholic religious items into the country was punished by confiscation of property. To convert to Catholicism was high treason. Priests could be executed if caught. Informers roamed the country reporting on priests and Catholic activity.

In fact, the Spanish Inquisition was more just than its contemporary secular counterparts. Only around 3,000 of the 100,000 put on trial were executed in the Inquisition's 356-year history. By keeping Spain Catholic, that country avoided the religious wars that racked the rest of Europe and saw the loss of countless lives. In addition, the witchcraft hysteria that swept through Protestant Germany, England, Scotland and America (which saw tens of thousands of women executed on little or no evidence) was found to be baseless by the Inquisition, saving many innocent lives.

Fourth objection: *"What more evidence do we need for the Catholic Church's hostility towards science than the Roman Inquisition's treatment of Galileo?"*

The Inquisition

The Roman Inquisition was established in 1542 and was the least active of the three Inquisitions, yet this fact has not spared it from criticism – mainly for the celebrated case of Galileo Galilei. Since this case, the Church has had to suffer the accusation of being anti-scientific and bent on keeping humanity in the darkness of superstition.

Galileo was born in 1564 and was an Italian Catholic working in physics, mathematics and astronomy. In 1610, Galileo published his book *Siderius Nuncius* in which he attempted to defend the 'Copernican System.' Copernicus had decades earlier proposed a heliocentric solar system with the sun rather than the earth at its center. When still a student in Rome, Copernicus defended his thesis with the approval of ecclesiastical authorities. He even had permission to dedicate his book to Pope Paul III. Copernicus later became a highly-respected canon.

In 1616, Galileo drew attention from the Roman Inquisition. The opinion of theological experts working for the Holy Office was that the heliocentric view of the Solar System was dangerous and that the assertion of the immobility of the sun was formally heretical, being at least apparently inconsistent with Josh. 10:12-13, which infers the motion of the sun: "'Sun, stand thou still at Gibeon, and thou Moon in the valley of Aijalon.' And the sun stood still, and the moon stayed, until the nation took vengeance on their enemies." There were also Psalms 93 and 104, as well as Ecclesiastes 1:5, which all infer earthly stability and solar mobility.

Galileo asserted that it was "a fatal and very common mistake to stop always at the literal sense." In this he was correct, but where he erred was in his scientific proofs in support of the Copernican system, which were demonstrably wrong and inadequate. Despite his own stated opinion that "To me and to me alone it has been given to make all the discoveries in astronomy," Galileo was not the outstanding astronomer of his day. Contrary to popular mythology, he did not invent the first telescope; rather, he built his own only after first hearing of its creation in Holland. Galileo continued to assert in opposition to Tycho Brahe that comets were mere atmospheric phenomena, stubbornly rejected Johannes Kepler's concept of planetary elliptical orbits in favor of Copernicus' cumbersome theory of epicycles, and also rejected Kepler's suggestion that the moon was the cause of the tides. In fact, Galileo's pride and arrogance prevented him from engaging in any form of collaboration with Kepler, a pride and arrogance that revelled in ridiculing others and later led to his troubles with the Church.

Neither could Galileo produce any evidence of 'stellar parallax', that is, shifts in the position of a star as the earth moved from one side of the sun to the other (a valid scientific objection not answered until 1838 when Friedrich Bessel determined the parallax of the star 61 Cygni). Added to this, the writings of other scientists such as Francis Bacon and Christopher Clavius still provided unanswerable arguments in favor of geocentrism. Considering all this and the opinion of consulting theologians, the Pope directed Cardinal Bellarmine to convince Galileo to cease holding and supporting the heliocentric system.

In 1632, Galileo published his *Dialogue on the Two Great World Systems*. Though Galileo initially had the permission of Pope Urban VIII to publish this work, Galileo deliberately violated his promise to present the competing Ptolemaic and Copernican theories without any personal endorsement of the latter and allow the dialogue to conclude in a draw. Instead, Galileo's Copernican spokesman completely demolished the Ptolemaic advocate (named Simplicius) using as proof for the Earth's motion Galileo's theory of the tides.

Pope Urban was furious at learning that Galileo had broken his promise of impartiality. After being informed by Jesuit scientists from the University of Rome that Galileo's tidal theory was poor physics, Pope Urban ordered Galileo to be tried by the Inquisition. The 1616 theological opinions were reiterated and Galileo was condemned as a heretic. Galileo again renounced his views, the sale of his book was stopped and he was placed under house arrest. It is patently untrue that he was ever tortured or placed in prison. He was confined with a valet to a luxurious apartment overlooking the Vatican gardens, one of the better residences in Europe! The Pope at the time remained friendly towards him and granted him a lifetime pension from 1632 and his blessing on his deathbed in 1642.

Even though both Pope Paul V and Pope Urban VIII were convinced anti-Copernicans, Papal infallibility cannot be impugned. Neither Pope condemned the Copernican system *ex cathedra*. As for the decree of 1616, it was issued by the Congregation of the Index, which possessed no competence to issue a dogmatic decree. Admittedly, the Pope approved this decree but only for the purpose of prohibiting the publication of writings considered harmful. Such approval does not of itself change the nature of the pronouncement into an *ex cathedra* decree. As for the 1633 trial, the sentence issued against Galileo implied a condemnation of Copernicanism but the court issued no formal decree on the subject, nor did the sentence receive the Pope's signature. Neither should the Catholic Church be attacked for being unscientific, especially by anti-Catholic Fundamentalists, for their forefathers were even more radically opposed to the Copernican System:

> Martin Luther:
>
> People gave ear to an upstart astrologer who strove to show that the earth revolves, not the heavens or the firmament, the sun and the moon ... This fool wishes to reverse the entire science of astronomy, but sacred Scripture tells us (Josh. 10:13) that Joshua commanded the sun to stand still, and not the earth.[5]
>
> Philip Melanchthon:
>
> Certain men, either from the love of novelty, or to make a display of ingenuity, have concluded that the earth moves ... Now, it is a want of honesty and decency to assert such notions publicly and the example is pernicious ... It is the part of a good mind to accept the truth as revealed by God and to acquiesce in it ... The earth can be nowhere if not in the center of the universe.[6]
>
> John Calvin answered Copernicus with a line from Ps. 93:1:
>
> "The world also is stabilized, that it cannot be moved" – and asked, "who will venture to place the authority of Copernicus above that of the Holy Spirit?"[7]

---

[5] Table Talk, 4 June 1539, quoted in Thomas Kuhn, *The Copernican Revolution*, NY: Vintage Books, 1959, p. 191.
[6] Melanchthon, *Initia Doctrinae Physicae*, 1549, quoted in Kuhn, *ibid.*, p. 191.

As a final point, it is noteworthy that supporting arguments for the Copernican system were developed by Jesuit scientists such as Frs Francesco Grimaldi (1618-1663) and Adam Kochansky (1631-1700), free from any form of harassment or discouragement from the Church. Their research remotely prepared the way for Pope Benedict XIV to order the Holy Office to grant an imprimatur to the first edition of Galileo's complete works in 1741. Galileo's works were also eventually removed from the Index of Forbidden Books and in 1822, at the request of Pope Pius VII, the Holy Office granted an imprimatur to the work of Canon Settele, which presented Copernicanism as an astronomical fact.

Fifth objection: *"If the Catholic Church had its way it would bring back the Inquisition overnight!"*

God forbid! One can only repeat here in full paragraph 2298 of the *Catechism of the Catholic Church* cited earlier:

> In times past, cruel practices were commonly used by legitimate governments to maintain law and order, often without protest from the Pastors of the Church, who themselves adopted in their own tribunals the prescriptions of Roman law concerning torture. Regrettable as these facts are, the Church always taught the duty of clemency and mercy. She forbade clerics to shed blood. In recent times it has become evident that these cruel practices were neither necessary for public order, nor in conformity with the legitimate rights of the human person. On the contrary, these practices led to ones even more degrading. It is necessary to work for their abolition. We must pray for the victims and their tormentors.

Conversion to the fullness of Catholic truth can only ever occur in the context of love and freedom.

---

[7] Will Durant, *The Reformation*, vol. 6, *The Story of Civilization*, NY: Simon & Schuster, 1967, p. 849.

Persecution

Objection: *"Persecution is a hallmark of the Catholic Church. The Inquisition, Bloody Mary and the St Bartholomew's Day Massacre typify Rome's intolerance and bigotry!"*

Introduction

Many modern religious and secular history books tend to portray the Catholic Church as an institution characterized by persecution, repression and intolerance. Furthermore, these same histories rarely, if ever, mention the persecution of Catholics (or even of Protestants by other Protestants), leaving the impression that the Catholic Church possesses a monopoly on persecution. The purpose of this chapter is not to justify the persecution of non-Catholics by Catholics but to provide a basic reminder to students of history that persecution was advocated and perpetrated by all major religious leaders and movements of the sixteenth and seventeenth centuries and that Catholics were victims of persecution as much as, and in some cases even more than, any one else.

Protestant persecution of Catholics and others

Martin Luther:

In his words ...

"Even unbelievers should be forced to obey the Ten Commandments, attend church, and outwardly conform ..." (Letter to Joseph Metsch, 26 August, 1529).

"There are others who teach in opposition to some recognized article of faith which is manifestly grounded in Scripture and is believed by all good Christians all over the world ... Heretics of this sort must not be tolerated, but punished as open blasphemers" (Commentary on Psalm 82, 1530).

"It is our custom to affright those who ... fail to attend the preaching; and to threaten them with banishment and the law ... In the event of their still proving contumacious, to excommunicate them ... as if they were heathen" (Letter to Leonard Beyer, 1533).

"Secular authorities are also bound to restrain and punish avowedly false doctrine ... secular authorities are bound ... to inflict corporal punishment on the offenders ... the stubborn sectaries must be put to death" (Pamphlet of 1536).

"If I had all the Franciscan friars in one house, I would set fire to it" (Table Talk 180:1540).

In his actions ...

Martin Luther supported the expulsion of Catholics, as did his right-hand man, Melanchthon. In Luther's home territory of Saxony all Catholics were banished in 1527. On 10 March, 1528, the Catholic Faith was interdicted in Constance. Altars, organs, statues were smashed, Church treasures confiscated in scenes similar to destruction wrought in Wittenberg in 1522 and Rotenberg in 1525. Luther personally encouraged the Peasant's Revolt of 1525 only to later turn against it and order its repression, leading to the deaths of up to one hundred thousand people. Luther later remarked:

> I, Martin Luther, slew all the peasants in the rebellion, for I said that they should be slain; all their blood is upon my head. But I cast it on the Lord God, who commanded me to speak this way (Werke, Erl. Edition, lix, p. 284, 'Table Talk').

Lutheran Strasbourg acted to suppress all Catholic writings in 1524. Luther denied the right and power of Catholic authorities to ban his books but when he learned in 1529 that an opponent named Emser was about to publish a Catholic version of the Bible in Rostock he appealed to the Duke of Mecklenburg and the councillors of the Elector of Saxony to prevent it from happening. All writings that opposed Luther were formally placed on his own Index at Wittenburg. In 1534 under the leader Martin Bucer all Anabaptists were driven out of the city of Augsburg with only eight days' notice. Those who attempted to return faced mutilation, branding or drowning. Likewise, Osiander persecuted and threatened death to Anabaptists in Nuremburg. In April 1535, the Lutheran cities of Lubeck, Bremen, Hamburg, Stralsund, Rostock and Wismar all voted to hang Anabaptists and lash Catholics and Zwinglians before sending them into exile. Contempt for the Bible as interpreted by Luther was now regarded as "rank blasphemy" and punishable even with death. So did the vaunted freedom of the Gospel disappear.

Luther also encouraged the looting of Church property. He declared all monasteries and abbeys to be the property of the German princes. In Lutheran Sweden, for example, King Gustavus Vasa stripped the Church of all its landed properties and raised the percentage of land held by the Crown from 5.5% to 28%. Greedy Princes would replicate such behavior elsewhere in Europe while caring little for religion.

Ulrich Zwingli

In his words ...

"The bishops will not desist from their fraud ... until a second Elijah appears to rain swords upon them ... It is better to pluck out a blind eye than to let the whole body suffer corruption" (Zwingli's Works, VII, 174-184).

In his actions ...

In his sixty-seven theses against the Catholic Church Zwingli declared, "No compulsion should be employed in the case of such as do not acknowledge their error, unless by their seditious conduct they disturb the peace of others." Yet in Zurich, Switzerland, Zwingli abolished the Mass in 1525, followed by the destruction of churches and the burning of monasteries. The bishops of Constance, Basle, Lausanne and Geneva were compelled to flee from their sees. The presence at sermons was enjoined under pain of punishment. Deviations from 'official' teaching and worship were punishable. Religious pictures and images were forbidden even in private homes under pain of severe punishment. Concerning Anabaptists and those who rejected infant baptism, Zwingli enjoined their drowning, burning, or beheading for "tearing the fabric of a seamless Christian society." At the instigation of Zwingli, the St Gall city council decreed on 26 March 1530 that,

> All who adhere to or favor the false sect of the Baptists, and who attend hedge-meetings, shall suffer the most severe punishments. Baptist leaders, their followers, and protectors shall be drowned without mercy.

Zwingli died while fighting the Swiss Catholic cantons during the battle of Kappel on 11 October 1531, bringing great joy to his religious adversaries, especially Luther.

John Calvin

In his words ...

(In defense of stoning false preachers) *"The father should not spare his son ... nor the husband his own wife. If he has some friend who is as dear to him as his own life, let him put him to death"* (Sermon on Deuteronomy, 13:6-11).

(On repressing Anabaptists) *"These altogether deserve to be well punished by the sword, seeing that they do conspire against God, who had set him in his royal seat"* (Letter to the Duke of Somerset, 22 October, 1548).

"Persons who persist in the superstitions of the Roman Antichrist ... deserve to be repressed by the sword" (Ibid.).

"Many people have accused me of such ferocious cruelty that they allege I would like to kill again the man I have destroyed. Not only am I indifferent to their comments, but I rejoice in the fact that they spit in my face" (Against the Errors of Servetus, 1554).

In his actions ...

Calvin's predecessor in Geneva, William Farel, had the Mass abolished in August 1535, seized all the churches, and closed all the monasteries and convents. His sermons were usually followed by riots wherein statues were smashed, pictures destroyed and treasures disappeared. Another disciple of Calvin, John Knox, passed legislation in Scotland forbidding anyone to say or attend Mass. Those found guilty of violating this prohibition forfeited all goods and received a flogging for the first offense, banishment for a second offense, and a death sentence for a third offense. Every heretic in his view deserved death and cities predominantly heretical deserved to be destroyed by the sword.

Calvin himself was true to his own beliefs that governments should put heretics to death. While reigning in Geneva between 1542 and 1546, fifty-eight individuals were executed for heresy. Some of Calvin's more famous victims included James Cruet (beheaded in 1547 for blasphemy), Michael Servetus (burned alive in 1553 for heresy) and the Comparet brothers (tortured, beheaded and dismembered in 1555 for their part in a drunken riot). Calvin had seen the fragmentation of Protestantism into a hundred sects and would have none of them in Geneva. Geneva became an autocratic state wherein the individual was obliged to conform completely to the established power. The task of passing on Calvin's harsh doctrine of religious compulsion was achieved by his successor, Theodore Beza, in his notorious book, *On the Duty of Civil Magistrates to Punish Heretics.*

In France, much is made of the terrible St Bartholomew Day's massacre of 1572 that saw the slaughter of over five thousand Huguenots. In the minds of many Protestants, it was the worst of the sixteenth century's religious massacres and reinforced the conviction that Catholicism was a bloody and treacherous religion. Yet, nothing today is heard of the atrocities perpetrated by the same Huguenots during the years 1561 and 1562 that resulted in the deaths of four thousand Catholic priests, nuns and monks, the ransacking of twenty thousand churches, and the destruction of two thousand monasteries, all in the name of restoring 'primitive Christianity.'

The Dutch Calvinists were no more tolerant in protecting their status as the official religion. The Arminian Barneveldt was beheaded as a traitor in 1619, while the prominent Grotius was condemned to life imprisonment. Though the victims of persecution in Scotland, Calvinists were the persecutors of Anabaptists, Unitarians and Arminians elsewhere.

The same can be said of the English Puritans. They fled England due to the persecutions of Elizabeth I, James I and Charles I only to impose their own form of religious oppression upon Catholics and Quakers in New England. Religious 'deviants' were either mutilated or hanged. In October 1654, the ascendant Puritan faction in Maryland repealed the Act of Toleration and outlawed Catholicism, executing four Catholics and leaving all others marginalized and excluded from any participation in public life until the American Revolution. The Puritans were also responsible for the witch burning frenzy that swept through Salem in Massachusetts in 1692.

Henry VIII

After Henry's formal break with Rome with the passing of the Act of Supremacy in 1534, his henchmen seized control of every ecclesial function, from the building of chapels to the wording of the liturgy. Church revenues were diverted from Rome into the royal treasury. In 1539, Parliament completed its seizure of all monastic lands, selling some for instant revenue and dispersing others to Henry's supporters. Meanwhile, many dispossessed religious, especially nuns, were reduced to destitution and despair. One, the famous 'holy maid of Kent,' rebuked the king publicly and was executed for her troubles. In May and June 1535, six Carthusian monks, a Bridgettine monk, St Thomas More and St John Fisher (Bishop of Rochester) were all executed for refusing to swear to Henry VIII's new title of "Supreme Head of the Church of England." There were approximately one thousand Dominicans in Ireland before Henry's schism; by the time Elizabeth I ascended the throne their number had been reduced to four.

The new English Church, however, in its "Six Articles" of 1539 reaffirmed most Catholic theology, except Papal supremacy. In his later years, Henry also grew suspicious of popular Protestantism, which was spreading into England and Scotland from the Continent. Dozens of Anabaptists were put to death from 1535 onwards. The most notable among them was Anne Askew, a woman of Lincolnshire, who was tried for heresy and burned in 1546, a year before Henry's death.

Elizabeth I

In 1559, Elizabeth reintroduced the Act of Supremacy and issued an injunction against the preaching of any doctrine contrary to the Church of England. These imposed fines, forfeiture of goods and lands, imprisonment and execution for maintaining the spiritual or ecclesiastical authority "of any foreign prelate" (i.e., the Pope). All who refused to take the Oath of Supremacy were subject to like penalties. This was followed by the Act for the Uniformity of Religion, which made the doctrine and practice of the Church of England the law of the land. Anyone who refused to attend an Anglican service was fined twelve pence for each offense. 'Heretical' books were banned and 'royal visitations' set up to travel throughout the country and search out heretics.

The legal situation for Catholics worsened after Elizabeth's excommunication by Pope St Pius V in 1570. Two Acts were directed against the Bull of Excommunication making it high treason to deny the Queen's right to the Crown, to declare her a heretic or schismatic, to reconcile anyone or be reconciled to the Catholic Church, or to publish any Papal writing whatsoever. The anti-Catholic laws were strengthened in 1581, 1585 and 1593, prohibiting Masses and attendance at Mass, prohibiting the importation of Catholic items into the country, restricting the movement of suspected Catholics, prohibiting Catholics from taking refuge abroad, outlawing the presence, harboring or support of priests, and allowing for the imprisonment of any person suspected of being a priest. Priests, especially Jesuits, were the main victims during and following Elizabeth's reign, with over one hundred and sixty martyrs recorded between 1570 and 1660. The English executed Irish bishops in 1578, 1585 and 1611.

Besides Catholics, Puritans, Anabaptists and Unitarians also suffered imprisonment, banishment, mutilation and burning to death for non-conformity. The number of overall executions in England for religious reasons steadily increased until they numbered about eight hundred a year. The situation for Catholics received no relief with the accession of James I in 1603. During his first year on the throne all Elizabeth's anti-Catholic statutes were confirmed with aggravated penalties. It was not until 1679 that capital punishment for heresy was abolished in Protestant England and 1778 before the slow repeal of anti-Catholic laws began, culminating in the Catholic Emancipation Act of 1829.

Oliver Cromwell

During the English Civil War (1642–1649) the Catholics sided with the King, and Oliver Cromwell punished them, along with royalist Anglicans, by confiscations and executions. After the Republican victory, the Cromwellian Parliament sought to exterminate the entire Irish Catholic priesthood. It was decreed that every Catholic priest should be hanged, beheaded and quartered and his head fixed to a pole in a public place.

Cromwell led a military expedition to Ireland in 1649 to repress Irish rebels. At Drogheda (11 September) Cromwell's troops massacred every soldier and priest they could capture and slaughtered thousands of civilians. Exactly one month later (11 October) Wexford received similar treatment, with a further one thousand five hundred civilians put to death. In his usual style, Cromwell viewed these massacres as "a righteous judgment of God upon ... barbarous wretches."

Altogether, Cromwell's army slaughtered over forty percent of the native Irishmen, who clung uncompromisingly to Catholicism and loyalist sentiments; the remaining Irishmen were forcibly transported to County Connaught under the Act of Settlement of 1653.

Conclusion

It is quite clear from the brief outline above that persecution on religious grounds is not just "a Catholic thing." Yet the myth remains that Catholicism was and remains oppressive while Protestantism is inherently tolerant and favors intellectual and spiritual freedom. The exact contrary was the truth during the sixteenth, seventeen and eighteen centuries. Lutherans, Zwinglians, Anglicans and Calvinists never thought of extending religious liberty to others while they held the upper hand. While they had the power to persecute they did. What makes Protestant persecutions even more scandalous is the fact that they contradicted one of the primary pillars of Protestantism – the right of private judgment and interpretation. It is illogical to assert the right to privately interpret the Bible and then torture and kill others for doing so!

The final word on this subject should go to one of the more balanced Protestant writers on the Reformation, Owen Chadwick:

> The Protestant states did not question that teachers of disapproved doctrines should be prevented from preaching. Nor did they question that the state should use laws to encourage churchgoing. In Anglican England and Lutheran Germany, Reformed Holland and Catholic Spain the citizens were alike liable to penalties if they failed for no good reason to attend the worship of their parish churches (*The Reformation*, Pelican Books, 1982, p. 398).

The argument that persecution is one reason why Catholicism should be rejected no longer has any credibility. Both sides employed compulsion, both sides practised torture and the shedding of blood, both sides are deserving of criticism and blame.

Jesuits!

Objection: *"The Jesuits are the Gestapo of the Pope. They were founded to oppose the light of the Reformation and are known for their cunning, their advocacy of dubious moral principles, and their deceptiveness!"*

On 15 August, 1534, in the crypt of the church of Montmartre in Paris, seven men renounced the world. They were Ignatius de Loyola, Francis Xavier, James Laynez, Alphonsus Salmeron, Nicolas Bobadilla, Peter Faber and Simon Rodriguez. Of these seven, all were Spanish except the latter two, who were from Savoy and Portugal respectively. Little did any one suspect at the time that a movement had begun that would profoundly shape world history for the next five centuries.

While Martin Luther was raising the banner of revolt against the Papacy and the Catholic Church, God was raising another individual to combat his divisiveness and impiety. That man was St Ignatius de Loyola. Born into the noble Loyola family, Ignatius in his youthful manhood was caught up in the sentimental chivalrous spirit of the Renaissance, desirous of fighting heroic wars and charming the ladies at Court. It was while taking part in a siege of a local castle in Pamplona, Navarre, that a cannon ball fired in the battle exploded close enough to him to shatter one of his legs. From this physical injury that befell Ignatius, God was to draw many spiritual blessings.

In the months of recuperation that followed, Ignatius was principally concerned about whether he would ever walk normally again, and whether his damaged leg would end up shorter than the other. Boredom set in, so he commanded one of his servants to get books for him to read to pass the time more easily. When the servant returned, he told Ignatius that all he could find was a book on the life of Jesus and some others on the lives of the saints. At first indignant, Ignatius soon resigned himself and began reading them.

Before long, the action of God's grace began to enlighten Ignatius. Overcoming an initial sense of insipidness, Ignatius saw in the lives of Jesus and the saints a collection of heroic deeds that far outdid the greatest deeds of any swordsman or chevalier. Before long, Ignatius declared, *"If they could do it, so can I!"* (1520).

There followed for Ignatius years of study, spiritual purgation and voluntary deprivation. Choosing to forego his family's wealth, Ignatius begged to pay for his studies at Paris University. It was there that he met St Francis Xavier and Bl. Peter Faber. The three eventually shared the same dormitory while living at university.

By 1534, these three had been joined by four others. Ignatius now had in mind to form a new company living under formal vows. Besides the three normal vows of poverty, chastity and obedience, Ignatius proposed a fourth – a vow to place themselves at the disposal of the Pope. Ignatius saw a need to re-emphasize obedience to the Papacy at a time when Protestantism was sweeping northern Europe and taking millions away from such obedience. For Ignatius, the root cause of this new disobedience was the same old enemy – pride – the same pride that caused the highest angel and the first man to fall.

By 1540, Ignatius' new company numbered sixty. An initial plan to go to the Holy Land was thwarted by war with the Ottomans. Instead, they worked in Rome serving the sick and poor. Ignatius himself was also studiously drawing up the company's constitutions. This he did with great prayer and deliberation. In the private notes of Ignatius we find that he listed eight arguments in favor of one article's inclusion and eighteen arguments in favor of an alternative. With respect to another article, Ignatius spent forty days praying for light on whether to include it or not.

On 27 September, 1540, Pope Paul III approved the constitutions of Ignatius' company in the bull *Regimini Militantis Ecclesiae*. After carefully reading its provisions the Holy Father exclaimed, "The finger of God is here!" The formal name of Ignatius' group was now the *Company of Jesus*. Later it would be changed to the *Society of Jesus*. Individual members were informally known as *Jesuits*. The constitutions were devoid of articles that required long vigils, fasts, corporal penances and the recitation of the Divine Office in common. Rather, practices were designed to enable members to be involved in active and varied tasks – shock troops available for any mission the Pope and Holy Mother Church would ask of them.

The constitutions required total obedience towards the General of the Company, who was elected for life. In his turn, the General promised entire submission to the Pope. In the words of Ignatius, "Those who live under obedience are to allow themselves to be moved and directed by Divine Providence through their superiors just as though they were a dead body." Though the Company possessed a strict hierarchy, any member could communicate directly with the General.

If the constitutions were the governing laws of the Company, the *Spiritual Exercises* were its soul. Composed by Ignatius in the wild solitude of Manresa, it is a manual of precepts and maxims to be used on retreats to aid the soul in its choice of vocation and along the road of sanctification. The *Exercises* were to be practised, not simply read through. In sanctioning their use, Pope Paul III described the *Exercises* as "full of piety and holiness, very useful and salutary, tending to the edification and spiritual progress of the faithful."

Ignatius had no wish for his spiritual sons in the Company to be raised to episcopal honors. Rather, he desired for them another glory: that persecution and suffering might be their lot. On one occasion Ignatius was radiant after a long meditation. Asked why this was so he replied, "Our Lord has deigned to assure me that, in consequence of my earnest prayer to this intention, the Society will never cease to enjoy the heritage of his passion in the midst of contradictions and persecutions."

Being founded during the first decades of the Reformation, it was inevitable that the Company of Jesus should have a major role in combating Protestantism. The Jesuits were intent upon reunifying a Christendom now shattered by the various heresies of the innovators. Heresy had spread rapidly, due to the weakening of knowledge and practise of the Catholic Faith among western Europeans, a weakening caused by the humanism of the Renaissance. Education was seen as a principal means towards redressing this crisis.

Within the Company, members undertook up to thirteen years of study and formation before entering upon their life's apostolic work. Once his formation was complete, the Jesuit possessed the armoury that a thorough knowledge of the natural and spiritual sciences offered. Then, he was able to be the master educator of others.

The Jesuits aimed at reinvigorating education in the Faith at all levels of society. For those called to be rulers of either Church or State, the Jesuits founded the Roman and German Colleges in Rome. By the mid-1580's the Roman College alone had over two thousand one hundred students. Between the years 1552 and 1750, one Pope, twenty-four Cardinals, twenty-one Archbishops, two hundred and twenty-one bishops, six Electors of the Holy Roman Empire and nineteen princes were former graduates of the German College.

For the education of all youth who entered Jesuit schools, the fifth General of the Order, Father Claudius Aquaviva, devised the *Ratio Studiorum* (Plan of Studies). In its day, the *Ratio* was considered the greatest system of study ever devised. According to Francis Bacon, "Never has anything more perfect been invented." The *Ratio* produced countless celebrated men in the fields of science, history, antiquity, mathematics and literature. The following all studied under this method: Popes Gregory XIII, Benedict XIV, Pius VII, St Francis de Sales, the preacher Bossuet, the philosopher Descartes, generals Don Juan of Austria, Tilly, Wallenstein and Conde, and Emperors Ferdinand and Maximilian of Austria.

Within the Company of Jesus itself, a plethora of men of academic distinction was produced. Two of the original Jesuits, Fathers Laynez and Salmeron, were theologians of such high calibre that they were both appointed official theologians representing the Holy See at the Council of Trent. They were allowed to address the Council Fathers for three hours at a time when the customary limit was one hour. The entire Council was even suspended on one occasion after Father Laynez became ill. Other eminent Jesuit scholars and men of outstanding achievement included:

- Fr Christopher Clavius (1538-1612) was the most renowned astronomer of his time and assisted in the formulation of the Gregorian calendar.
- Fr Francisco Suarez (1548-1617), the 'Jesuit Aquinas' (called the *Doctor Eximius* by Pope Paul V).
- Fr Cornelius á Lapide (1567-1637), the great Scripture commentator.

- Fr Emmanuel Sa (1530-1596), who revised St Jerome's Latin Vulgate.
- Fr Louis Bourdeloue (1632-1704), the highly eloquent and popular preacher in the Court of King Louis XIV of France.
- Fr Benedict Goës (1562-1607) discovered and traversed the overland trade route from India to China c. 1594.
- Fr Francesco Grimaldi (1618-1663) discovered and named the phenomenon still known today as the "*diffraction of light.*"
- Fr Jacques Marquette (1637-1675) discovered the mouth of the Missouri River in North America in 1673.
- Fr Claude-Jean Allouez (1622-1689) was the first European to sight the shores of Lake Superior in North America in 1667.
- Fr Athanasius Kircher (1602-1680) was considered the "master of a hundred arts" and numbered among his achievements the hypothesis that the plague was spread by infectious micro-organisms.
- Fr Francesco Lana de Terzi (1631-1687) was the first person to conceive how a 'lighter than air' aircraft might be constructed. Fr Terzi also anticipated by more than a century methods of lip reading and Braille writing and reading for the blind.
- Jesuit educated Fr Bartholomew Gusmao (1685-1724) was the first to demonstrate a lighter than air ship in 1709.
- Fr Samuel Fritz (1654-1728) published the first map of the Amazon River in 1707.
- Jesuits in Peru discovered the medicinal qualities of quinine.
- Jesuits discovered the use of India-rubber.
- Jesuits imported the rhubarb plant from Turkey.
- Jesuits imported turkeys from China.

Not only were the Jesuits outstanding educators and men of great achievement, they were also missionaries of the highest zeal and courage. Due to their preaching and apostolic works, whole regions and countries were restored to the Catholic Church. These included parts of Germany, Austria and Bohemia. Protestant influence in Poland and Hungary was significantly reduced, while the valiant efforts of the graduates of the Douai College in Belgium kept the underground Church in England alive.

Campion, Parsons, Southwell, Garnet and Ireland became household names to English Catholics during the era when Catholicism in England was terribly repressed. These Jesuits preached the Faith in a land where spies abounded watching for Catholic activity, and would continue to witness for Jesus in prison, under torture, and on the Tyburn gibbet. Anti-Jesuit hysteria was whipped up from time to time to justify and maintain severe anti-Catholic laws. Father Henry Garnet was executed for the alleged Gunpowder Plot of 1605, and six other Jesuits were executed for the fabricated Titus Oates Plot of 1678.

Even more impressive was Jesuit missionary activity outside of Europe. The greatest of the overseas missionaries was the intrepid St Francis Xavier. He single-handedly introduced the Catholic Faith to India, Indonesia and Japan, enduring incredible hardships from hostile locals, language barriers, disease and poor climates. Only a premature death prevented him entering the mysterious land of China. That mission was achieved by another brilliant innovative missionary, Matteo Ricci. The work of St Francis in India was carried on by Fathers Barzeus, Mesquita, de Torres and Robert de Nobili. Adopting the dress and manners of the Brahmin, the saintly Father de Nobili, early in the 1600's, penetrated into this hitherto inaccessible caste and began to convert and baptize them. By the end of the century, the mission numbered one hundred and fifty thousand.

In South America, Father Emmanuel de Nobrega, Bl. Ignatius Azevedo, and St Joseph Anchieta labored for the conversion of the natives in Brazil. The latter, gifted with the charisms of tongues and miracles, wrote a rule of life for the *Reductions*, communities of native Indian converts. The most famous of the Reductions were those of Paraguay. Together, they formed a virtual empire based on virtue. Even one of the greatest enemies of Christianity, Voltaire, said of the Reductions, "they appear to be in some respects the triumph of humanity."

North America was no less a missionary field of activity for the Jesuits. French Jesuits such as Fathers Lejeune, Bressani, Jogues, Lalemant and Brebeuf worked tirelessly among the Iroquois and Huron tribes in northeast America. Epic heroism was not lacking in the horrific torture of Father Bressani and the martyrdom of Saint Isaac Jogues in the 1640's.

Nor was heroism lacking elsewhere. Returning by ship to Brazil in 1570, Bl. Ignatius Azevedo, together with thirty-nine other Jesuits were intercepted by a Dutch pirate. All of them were offered their lives and freedom if they apostatized to Calvinism. All of them, to the youngest novice, refused and were subsequently butchered. As he fell, mortally wounded, Bl. Ignatius Azevedo declared, "Angels and men are witness that I die on behalf of the holy Church, Roman, Catholic, and Apostolic."

This heroism was surpassed by the Jesuit missionaries of Japan. By 1597, the members of the infant church founded by St Francis Xavier numbered two hundred thousand. The Emperor (Taicosama), stirred into believing that the Jesuits were a threat to his rule, launched a massive persecution of the Church that lasted for decades. Among the hundreds of thousands that suffered for the Faith were numerous Jesuits. Three were martyred in Nagasaki in 1597. Father Charles Spinola was martyred in 1622 after being confined to a cage for four years. In the same year, Father Constanzo was burnt alive and Father Carvalho froze to death after being thrown into an ice pond with some of his converts. In 1626, the Jesuit Provincial, Father de Couros, expired after spending many months hiding and suffering in a pit. His successor, Father Sebastian Vieyra, was arrested and put to death in 1632. Father Mastrilli was beheaded in 1637; and Father Anthony Rubino and four other Jesuits were executed after seven months' torture in 1643.

Only one Jesuit apostatized in the midst of all this – Father Christopher Ferreyra. After five hours of torture, he surrendered and became a turncoat, assisting the Japanese authorities over the next nineteen years to hunt down and arrest his former brothers. In 1652, however, he confessed himself a traitor and announced his desire to return to his Order and God. Sixty-eight hours of torture failed to break him, and Father Christopher died purified by his repentance and suffering.

In addition to these great missionaries and martyrs, there have been many other outstanding Jesuit saints:

- *St Francis Borgia*: the princely Spaniard who renounced a life of worldly honors to become the third General of the Order.
- *St Stanislaw Kostka*: the holy Polish youth who spent just ten months in the Order before his death at the age of eighteen. Even though his profound humility shrouded many of his gifts, his reputation had spread far and wide, as evidenced by the throngs that came to venerate his remains.
- *St Aloysius Gonzaga*: another youth of Italian background and angelic innocence who died at the early age of twenty-one while nursing the sick in Roman hospitals.
- *St Peter Canisius*: the great apologist and missionary of Germany where, for fifty years, he labored through preaching and writing for the salvation of souls. His catechism, a masterpiece of brevity and clarity, was translated into every European language.
- *St John Berchmans*: a native of Belgium, he was known never to have committed an act or utter a word the least imperfect.
- *St Robert Bellarmine*: the great theologian and Doctor of the Church whose apologetical works against Protestantism were unchallenged in his day.
- *St Francis Regis*: the French missionary who tirelessly evangelized the villages of southern France, hearing up to two thousand confessions a month.
- *St Peter Claver*: another Spaniard who gave himself heart and soul to the physical and spiritual service of many thousands of Negro slaves, particularly those cursed by leprosy. He called himself, "the slave of the Slaves."

All the above missionaries, martyrs and saints are but a sample of the great men who belonged to the Society of Jesus. However, where there exists such radical good it is not surprising that an equally radical opposing hatred would simultaneously arise. By the middle of the eighteenth century, powerful secular forces were combining to destroy the Jesuits. Their real target was the Church in general, but to destroy the Church it was felt necessary to first destroy her vanguard.

The alliance against the Jesuits comprised the following: de Pombal in Portugal, Choiseul, Madame de Pompadour and the French

Parliament in France; d'Aranda and Charles III in Spain; Joseph II in Austria, Tanucci in Naples, Jansenists, and free-thinkers such as Voltaire. In carefully planned stages, the Jesuits were expelled from the Portuguese, French and Spanish Empires, then Naples and Parma. All the protests of Pope Clement XIII were ignored. After Spain threatened to leave the Church altogether, Pope Clement XIV signed the decree *Dominus ac Redemptor Noster* suppressing the Jesuits (21 July, 1773). The General Superior Lorenzo Ricci was then imprisoned.

Ironically, the Order survived in Protestant Prussia and Orthodox Russia, for the leaders of these two nations were not bound to obey the Papal decree. Subsequent Popes Pius VI and Pius VII wanted to restore the Order. By now, Europe was being torn by the French Revolution and the Napoleonic Wars. This chaos led to the destruction of the Bourbon monarchies that campaigned against the Jesuits. Happily, after the downfall of Napoleon and the release of Pius VII from captivity, the Jesuits were restored by Papal decree on 7 August, 1814.

Numerous other attacks have also been made against the Jesuits over the centuries. Protestants have repeated claims that the Jesuits taught dubious and immoral doctrines, including regicide and the saying "the end justifies the means." Cries have also been raised about the alleged *"Jesuit Oath"* and the *"Monita Secreta."*

The charge of regicide is traced to a work published in Spain in 1599 by the Jesuit, Mariana. He laid down the principle that a king who violates the rights of his subjects and his coronation oath may lawfully be deposed and even put to death. General Aquaviva, on being made aware of the contents of this work, immediately condemned it and ordered the work to be suppressed until the objectionable parts were purged. The original has only been preserved by Protestant controversialists seeking to make capital out of it.

The maxim "the end justifies the means," rightly understood, is correct. It means that there is always a right way of achieving a right thing. So, if it is permissible to eat beef it is right to kill and cook oxen; if it is permissible to have children, it is right to marry; if it is permissible to kill in self-defense, it is right to make and bear arms, etc. If it means that one may do evil for a good intention, or that a good end or purpose justifies *any* (immoral) means, then this doctrine is condemned by the Catholic Church, as it was by St Paul (Rom. 3:8).

The *"Monita Secreta"* was said to be secret instructions given to all Jesuits to pursue every crooked and unprincipled tactic to advance the interests of the Society, even at the expense of other Catholic religious orders. In reality, the *Monita* is an elaborate fraud emanating originally from Cracow, Poland, in 1614. All reasonable Protestant historians hold the *Monita* to be simply a spurious lampoon of the Order. Likewise, the *"Jesuit Oath"* is nothing more than the hysterical fabrication of one Robert Ware in his work, *Foxes and Firebrands*, produced in the late seventeenth century. Among other things, the oath swears all Jesuits to assume the outward form of any religion in order to deceive unwitting Protestants back into the arms of Rome. Of course, no such oath was ever taken by any Jesuit. It reminds one of the fabricated plots of the same period implicating Catholics in alleged attempts to overthrow the English Monarchy aimed at re-igniting anti-Catholic sentiment throughout Britain.

The above illustrates in part the contribution of the Society of Jesus to the cause of Christ and the Church in the world since her foundation. Today, the Society of Jesus continues with a different collection of triumphs and crosses. Those members who strive to uphold faithfully the original spirit of St Ignatius maintain the struggle for orthodoxy and fidelity to the Pope. In all things, these Jesuits forge on, keeping in mind St Ignatius' original motto for the Society, *Ad Majorem Dei Gloriam!* (For the Greater Glory of God!).

The Index of Forbidden Books

Objection: *"The Index of Forbidden Books proves that Rome has always sought to repress religious truth and scientific knowledge. At least the rest of the world has managed to free itself from ignorance and superstition!"*

In all places and at all times the Catholic Church has used and promoted books as a means of fulfilling her mission to spread the Gospel of Christ. Always cautious of propagating and preserving the truth, the Church has certainly and properly exercised a firm hand in ensuring that various books are submitted for her examination before publication, and/or banning the publication, sale, reading, retaining of prohibited books.

In a world today swamped by all sorts of literature and new forms of visual and electronic communications and where meaningful censorship has been suppressed by the ideologues of unrestrained liberty, the Catholic Church has now become an easy target for her past and present policies concerning the control of information. Even to suggest censorship of any form these days is to invite howls of protests from all quarters allegedly claiming to uphold rights of free speech, expression and access to information. In fact, the Catholic Church is not only the victim of attacks for supporting censorship, but is herself constantly ridiculed, mocked and vilified for any or all of her beliefs and practices by a media taking advantage of the present climate of license.

Unfortunately, discussion of such issues as the *Index* or censorship is hampered not only by religious and historical bias against Catholicism but also by an equally appalling ignorance of the intention and operation of the Church's regulations. One of the worst offenders is the professional anti-Catholic Loraine Boettner who, in his work *Roman Catholicism* published in 1962, reduces the *Index* to nothing more than an anti-Protestant mind-controlling tool:

The Index of Forbidden Books, still in effect as rigidly as ever, proscribes all the controversial books, magazines, and other publications of Protestants and others who oppose Romanism, and so makes it impossible for Roman Catholics to know both sides of a question ... Roman Catholic students, therefore, in a real sense are forbidden to think. They let the priests think for them. But the fallacy of that system is that the priests too are forbidden to think. They too are limited by the Imprimatur and the Index (pp. 363-364).

Basic assumptions underlie the Church's control of reading. The Church is the divinely instituted custodian of revelation and, therefore, it is her solemn duty to interpret and protect the teachings of Jesus for the welfare of her members. The Gospel of Jesus has been "once and for all delivered to the saints" (Jude 1:3), and the Scriptures certainly warn Christians to be wary of false doctrines and instructs the Church to be intolerant of them:

"For the time is coming when people will not endure sound teaching, but having itching ears they will accumulate for themselves teachers to suit their own likings, and will turn away from listening to the truth and wander into myths" (2 Tim. 4:3-4).

"But I have this against you, that you tolerate the woman Jezebel, who calls herself a prophetess and is teaching and beguiling my servants to practice immorality and to eat food sacrificed to idols" (Rev. 2:20).

The earliest example of Christianity's attitude towards profane or perverted literature is found in the Acts of the Apostles, where citizens in Ephesus, after their conversion to Christianity by St Paul, burnt superstitious books valued at fifty thousand pieces of silver (Acts 19:19). In subsequent early Church writings, we find the beginnings of a more formalized approach to censorship. The *Muratorian Canon* (c. AD 170) gives a list of those books that belong to the New Testament and a group that should be excluded from liturgical use. In AD 405, Pope Innocent I wrote to the Bishop of Toulouse outlining the total number of books which belonged to the Old and New Testament canons and several apocryphal books that were condemned. More importantly, in AD 496, Pope Gelasius I published a decree which was divided into three sections: a list of authentic books of the Scriptures; a list of recommended readings from the Church Fathers and the Acts of the Martyrs; and a list of apocryphal and heretical books that had been banned by the Councils and the Popes.

During the Middle Ages control over literature by the Church could be exercised to a high degree owing to her temporal power and the relatively small number of books. The laborious nature of hand copying meant that only small numbers of books could be produced and only over a long period of time. During these centuries, the Church was particularly vigilant over reproductions of the Scriptures. Heretical groups such as the Albigensians, Waldensians, and the Lollards (Wycliffites) produced their own vernacular versions of the Scriptures in order to support their novel teachings. The Church, out of zeal for the authentic word of God, through local and universal laws prohibited the reading of the Scriptures *without the appropriate safeguards* (e.g., Toulouse 1229, Tarragona 1233, Oxford 1408).

However, with the invention of the printing press in Gutenberg in 1456 a deluge of printed books began to flood Europe. This made the examination of each new book quite impractical. Nevertheless, in 1467 Pope Innocent VIII decreed that all books treating on Christian doctrine be submitted to the local Church authorities for examination and permission before publication for general reading. The license to publish and the name of the local Ordinary were to be printed at the beginning of each book. A similar decree was issued by Pope Leo X at the Fifth Lateran Council on 4 May 1515 and was addressed to the whole world. With the outbreak of the Protestant Reformation, the Council of Trent (1545-1563) commissioned a group of Fathers to draw up rules regarding prohibited books. These *Tridentine* regulations remained in force for the next three hundred years and served as a guide to the average reader for any publications not condemned.

The first general list of forbidden books entitled *Index* was issued by Pope Paul IV in 1557 and was soon followed by a new *Index* issued in 1564. In 1571, Pope St Pius V established the *Congregation of the Index* to handle all matters concerning Church evaluation of literature. It was responsible for publishing updated editions of the

Index and judging works referred to it for final decision. In 1753, Pope Benedict XIV published new detailed regulations governing the examination of suspected books: the examination was to be carried out by two revisors, independent of each other, who were well versed in the particular language of the book and the branch of learning in question, and who would pass judgment free from all partisanship and in accordance with general Catholic dogma. Only when both revisors believed a book should be prohibited was the matter forwarded to the Cardinals of the Congregation for a final decision.

By the pontificate of Pope Leo XIII (1878-1903) there were over three thousand books on the *Index*. Some of the more famous individuals whose works were listed included Francis Bacon, Rene Descartes, Blaise Pascal, Thomas Hobbs, John Locke, David Hume, John Milton, Francois Voltaire, Jean-Jacques Rousseau, Emile Zola, Honore de Balzac, Alexander Dumas, Victor Hugo, Jeremy Bentham, Lord Acton, and Edward Gibbon. These writers generally wrote in the fields of philosophy, history or fiction and many were baptized Catholics. In 1897, Pope Leo XIII, considering the changed social and literary conditions of the nineteenth century, again revised the general rules of the Church's book legislation and incorporated them into the new *Index of Forbidden Books* published in 1900.

In 1904, Pope St Pius X proposed a complete codification of canon law. This was completed and approved by Pope Benedict XV on 27 May 1917. Canons 1384-1405 related to book legislation. They were divided into three classifications: prior censorship before publication; the prohibition of books and the general classes of books prohibited; and the penalties assessed against violator of the regulations. These canons remained in force until the promulgation of the new *Code of Canon Law* in 1983. After the Second Vatican Council, Pope St Paul VI in 1966 abolished the *Congregation of the Index* and the *Index of Forbidden Books*, replacing them with a set of norms on the reading of books dangerous to Catholic faith and morality.

The present canons in the 1983 *Code of Canon Law* governing the Church's mission as censor include the following:

Can. 823 §1: In order to safeguard the integrity of faith and morals, pastors of the Church have the duty and the right to ensure that in the writings or in the use of the means of social communication there should be no ill effect on the faith and morals of Christ's faithful. They also have the duty and the right to demand that where writings of the faithful touch upon matters of faith and morals, these be submitted to their judgment. Moreover, they have the duty and the right to condemn writings which harm true faith or good morals.

Can. 825 §1: Books of the sacred Scriptures may not be published unless they are approved by the Apostolic See or the Episcopal Conference. The publication of translations of the sacred Scriptures requires the approval of the same authority, and they must have necessary and sufficient explanatory notes.

Can. 826 §3: Prayer books, for either the public or the private use of the faithful, are not to be published except by permission of the local Ordinary.

Can. 827 §1: ... the publication of catechisms and other writings pertaining to catechetical formation, as well as their translations, requires the approval of the local Ordinary.

Can. 827 §2: Books dealing with matters concerning sacred Scripture, theology, canon law, church history, or religious or moral subjects may not be used as textbooks on which the instruction is based, in elementary, intermediate or higher schools, unless they were published with the approbation of the competent ecclesiastical authority or were subsequently approved by that authority.

Can. 830 §2: In carrying out this task, a censor must put aside all preference of persons and look only to the teaching of the Church concerning faith and morals, as declared by its *Magisterium*.

Can. 831 §1: Unless there is a just and reasonable cause, no member of Christ's faithful may write in newspapers, pamphlets or periodicals which clearly are accustomed to attack the Catholic religion or good morals. Clerics and members of religious institutes may write in them only with the permission of the local Ordinary.

Far from being a tool for repressing "religious truth and scientific knowledge," the *Index* historically was a significant instrument in ensuring that the Catholic faithful were fed the pure milk of true doctrine, science and morality. Nor was it a weapon aimed solely at Protestantism. The Church sought to protect her children by screening books relating to all the following areas: The Bible, theology, Church history, canon law, natural theology, ethics, religious and moral sciences, ascetic or mystical doctrine, sacred pictures with or without prayers and all writings having a special bearing on religion or morality. The term "books" included booklets, pamphlets, magazines, periodicals, newspapers, etc.

Book dealers were also prohibited from selling, loaning or keeping books treating of "obscene matters." Considering the current avalanche of pornography in the written and electronic medias, which reasonable Christian could object to such a prohibition? Nor could any Christian object to the Church's provisions against books that promoted Freemasonry, superstition, fortune telling, magic, spiritism, séances, suicide, or divorce.

If fact, the Church's book legislation always was and is still simply designed to assist Christians in their pre-existing personal obligation to practise censorship. Due to our fallen nature, Christians cannot deliberately expose themselves unnecessarily to proximate occasions of sin. For example, we are obliged to avoid prostitution houses, nude beaches, pornographic magazines or any other situation that could arouse our sexual passions. That being the case, how can any self-professed Christian find it objectionable if the Church seeks to guide her children to fulfil this obligation, an obligation imposed upon all Christians by Jesus himself?

"And if your hand or your foot causes you to sin, cut it off and throw from you; it is better for you to enter life maimed or lame than with two hands or two feet to be thrown into the eternal fire. And if your eye causes you to sin, pluck it out and throw it from you; it is better for you to enter life with one eye than with two eyes to be thrown into the hell of fire" (Mt 18:8-9).

In this context, Loraine Boettner's attacks against the *Index* fall completely flat. In addition to his above-mentioned quote, he rails against the *Index* as follows:

> The Bible was first officially forbidden to the people by the Church of Rome and placed on the Index of Forbidden Books by the Council of Valencia in the year 1229 (p. 99).

The Index of Forbidden Books

... even the Bible as such remains on the Index of Forbidden Books! ... What St Paul wrote, if it stands by itself, is on the Index. What was written by St Peter himself, who according to Roman Catholic tradition was the first pope, is on the Index unless some Roman Catholic annotates his writing (p. 101).

One of the most flagrant denials of freedom in the Roman Church is the Index of Forbidden Books, a device which deprives the people of freedom of judgment as to what they may read. This restriction is imposed on the pretense of shielding them from error; its real purpose is to isolate them from liberal and Protestant ideas, to maintain control over them, and so to hold them in the Roman Church (p. 417).

In response to these paragraphs Catholics should point out the following:

- The Bible was never officially forbidden to the people, only doctored versions produced by heretical sects as stated above.
- There was no *Index* in 1229 to place the Bible on in any case.
- If Catholics should be free to read Protestant versions of the Bible indiscriminately, just which version should they ultimately follow? And why not read the *New World Version* of the Jehovah's Witnesses or even the *Book of Mormon*?
- What is inherently wrong with producing Bibles with explanatory notes? The Presbyterian *Schofield-Darby* version of the Bible was the first of now many Protestant Bibles to include explanatory notes. Explanatory notes are a safeguard against the "ignorant and unstable" who "twist" the Scriptures "to their own destruction" (2 Pet. 3:16).
- Would Loraine Boettner or any other anti-Catholic Protestant indiscriminately recommend Catholic literature? Would they hand out Bibles produced by Catholic editors and commentators without warning?
- Do not Protestant churches warn their members against pornography, immorality or other forms of obscene material? And if they do what would be the problem if they listed objectionable material in writing for their members?

- Does Boettner advocate freedom for freedom's sake? Freedom is a gift given by God to use in the service of truth and goodness. Freedom used to vainly read heretical or immoral material is freedom abused, not used.
- What proof is there that the Catholic Church employed the *Index* only "on the *pretense* of shielding them from error"? This unsubstantiated claim by Boettner is another example of his presumptive thinking.
- What "liberal and Protestant ideas" would Boettner like Catholics to be exposed to? Would Boettner encourage Protestant views opposed to his own? And when did Jesus advocate so-called "liberal" views?
- Many of the "liberal" views condemned in the *Index* are expounded by authors unfriendly not only to the Catholic Church but also to Christianity *per se*. Would Boettner promote the atheistic views of Rousseau, Voltaire or Zola to his congregation simply in the name of liberalism?

The current degenerate moral condition of the world is due in part to the abolition of censorship laws by the governments of the Western world. No person in good faith can contest in principle the need for a return to laws restricting the levels of violence and vulgarity, the blasphemy and erotica that have flooded society and which are aimed particularly at the young. Should it be any surprise that while censorship has virtually vanished, the levels of sexual promiscuity, marriage and family breakdowns, drug use, violence and rebellion have simultaneously skyrocketed, while religious practise has plummeted? Nor is the publication of hundreds of millions of items of literature by tens of thousands of conflicting and contradictory Protestant churches objectively a good thing. The Church in her wisdom knew that steps were necessary centuries ago to stem the tide of dangerous literature. Far from being free from "ignorance and superstition," the Western world has collectively extinguished its own light of reason and is now hurtling down a revolutionary process of self-destruction. If the Church's policy concerning censorship overall and the *Index* in particular were successful, the world would not be in the sorry state it is in today.

Dawkins' Delusions

Introduction

Richard Dawkins is currently the most famous atheist in the world. He is the 'leader' of a quartet of Anglo-American atheists nick-named the 'Four Horsemen' – the other three being Sam Harris, Christopher Hitchens and Daniel Dennett. The aim of this chapter is to provide an introductory exposé of the weaknesses in Dawkins' atheism – weaknesses that expose his poor understanding of religion, philosophy, morality, and history, not to mention his brazen prejudice and contempt for all persons and things religious.

Dawkins describes himself as a *de facto* atheist who declares that "God is very improbable, and I live my life on the assumption that he is not there" (*The God Delusion*, p. 51). For Dawkins, the implications of his worldview are stark. In his words, the world has "no design, no purpose, no evil and no good, nothing but blind, pitiless indifference" (*River out of Eden*, p. 133).

Dawkins readily admits that his case against religion is primarily a case against Christianity (*The God Delusion*, p. 37), though he does not hesitate to attack all religions. His style is usually direct and caustic, declaring that God is not only "a delusion" but also "a pernicious delusion" (*The God Delusion*, p. 31). His most famous quote against God is found at the beginning of Chapter Two of *The God Delusion*:

> The God of the Old Testament is arguably the most unpleasant character in all fiction: jealous and proud of it; a petty, unjust, unforgiving control-freak; a vindictive, bloodthirsty ethnic cleanser; a misogynistic, homophobic, racist, infanticidal, genocidal, filicidal, pestilential, megalomaniacal, sadomasochistic, capriciously malevolent bully.

Dawkins approvingly quotes on page 113 of *The God Delusion* Sam Harris' *The End of Faith*: "while religious people are not generally mad, their core beliefs absolutely are." Why? Because he believes there is no evidence for religious beliefs according to the system of inquiry and verification employed by the natural sciences. For Dawkins, "Faith is the great cop-out, the great excuse to evade the need to think and evaluate evidence. Faith is belief in spite of, even perhaps because of, the lack of evidence" (Untitled Lecture, Edinburgh Science Festival [1992]).

However, whatever Dawkins might think, the question of whether God exists or not is not a scientific but a philosophical one. This is because science is incapable of discovering and understanding the non-material, while philosophy is prepared to admit the possibility of the non-material in its quest to discover and understand the ultimate cause. Dawkins is not a philosopher and in *The God Delusion* "is operating mostly outside the range of his scientific expertise" (Nagel, *The Fear of Religion*, 2006). He also too often ties together the idea of God with the phenomenon of religion and critiques them as if they were one and the same thing. We, therefore, should not be so surprised that for the well-read individual *The God Delusion* is both unpersuasive and an embarrassment, even for many atheists.

Prejudice and offensiveness

Dawkins might consider himself to be a scholar, but he is certainly no gentleman. In all scholarly endeavors one would expect a certain level of manners, impartiality and balanced observations. Not so with Dawkins. In the words of one reviewer, "one shouldn't look to this book (*The God Delusion*) for even-handed and thoughtful commentary. In fact, the proportion of insult, ridicule, mockery, spleen, and vitriol is astounding" (Plantinga, *The Dawkins Confusion*, 2007). The atheist Thomas Nagle notes that Dawkins deliberately violates "the etiquette of modern civilization" in order to be "as offensive as possible" (*The Fear of Religion*, 2006). Theistic opponents are brushed off with contempt as simpletons with nothing to say. Furthermore, such is Dawkins' partiality that "he can scarcely bring himself to concede that a single human benefit has flowed from religious faith, a view which is as *a priori* improbable as it is false" (Eagleton, *Lunging, Flailing, Mispunching*, 2006).

More worrying is Dawkins' vulgar caricature of religion as a "mind virus" that is passed on from generation to generation of "faith sufferers" through "memes" (a word Dawkins invented), or units of cultural ideas. Being a virus, religion can only be 'cured' by atheism. For Dawkins, belief in God is as credible as belief in "fairies at the bottom of the garden" (*The God Delusion*, p. 51). His demand, "If God has a more solid basis than fairies, then let us hear it" (*Reply to Poole*, p. 47), implies that no one over the past two thousand years has ever thought or written about proofs for the existence of God, though they all exist under his very nose in the theological collection in the University of Oxford.

Dawkins' disdain for religion equally applies to theology: "What has 'theology' ever said that is of the smallest use to anybody? When has 'theology' ever said anything that is demonstrably true and is not obvious? What makes you think that 'theology' is a subject at all?" (RichardDawkins.net). However, Dawkins' caricatures of theology would "make a first-year theology student wince" and have been described as "shoddy" and a "travesty" (Eagleton, *Lunging, Flailing, Mispunching*, 2006). An example of this is his title for Christ as the "fatherless man" (*The God Delusion*, pp. 207-208). Dawkins illustrates a misunderstanding of theology that even a casual reading of easily accessible source documents could have avoided. Is it any wonder that one critic felt compelled to declare that, "The most disappointing feature of *The God Delusion* is Dawkins' failure to engage religious thought in any serious way" (Orr, *A Mission to Convert*, 2007).

One thing ominous about Dawkins' proposed cure for religion is the suggestion that the state should actively intervene to prevent the religious 'indoctrination' of children. His reasoning is simple. If all religion is false, then parents are guilty of child abuse by imposing beliefs that cannot be questioned. In fact, children have a 'right' to be protected from the harmful nonsense that is religion as much as they have a right to be protected from sexual abuse. For Dawkins, worse than sexual abuse is "the long-term psychological damage inflicted by bringing up the child Catholic in the first place" (*The God Delusion*, p. 317).

There is much in Dawkins' mindset that resembles the angry and unrestrained persecutions conducted by totalitarian regimes and endured by many Christians during the twentieth century. Indeed, Christians would be dangerously complacent, if not foolish, simply to ignore Dawkins' comments as the ravings of a harmless ivory tower academic.

Ignoring contingency

Contingency is a philosophical term for what lay people commonly recognize as dependence. In classical Catholic understanding, all creatures are contingent, meaning they depend on God for their existence; only God is self-existent, or necessary being. Contingency needs to be considered whenever one asks why anything exists at all.

Dawkins ignores the notion of contingency. In *The God Delusion* he asserts that that the origins of life are chemical and takes for granted the physical-chemical material that is the precondition for evolutionary theory. Nowhere, however, does Dawkins ask how matter and energy came into existence in the first place. So, while Dawkins is willing to provide a proximate cause for the emergence of life over long periods of time through natural selection he does not bother to proffer any ultimate cause. As for consciousness, thought, will, sensations, value and purpose, they are just "lucky events" produced by a purely physical causal process outside of natural selection (*The God Delusion*, pp. 168-169). Evolutionary theory cannot explain its own existence; neither does Dawkins provide an answer. One has to ask whether Dawkins believes matter and energy to be eternal, an eternity he is unwilling to grant to God.

Dawkins' endeavors to exclude God as the ultimate cause for life on earth has led him at times into ridiculous conclusions. Take, for example, the following quote from an interview with Ben Stein in *Expelled: No Intelligence Allowed*:

> Well, it could come about in the following way. It could be that at some earlier time, somewhere in the universe, a civilization evolved, probably by some kind of Darwinian means, probably to a very, very high level of technology, and designed a form of life that they seeded onto perhaps this planet. Um, now that is a possibility, and an intriguing possibility. And I suppose it's

possible that you might find evidence for that if you look at the details of biochemistry, molecular biology, you might find a signature of some sort of designer.

So, it was aliens who caused life on earth? Who, dare we ask, caused the aliens? Sadly, for Dawkins any designer will do so long as it is not God.

Dawkins is not much better when speaking on the origins of the universe. The following quote comes from his classic, *The Ancestor's Tale*:

> The universe could so easily have remained lifeless and simple - just physics and chemistry, just the scattered dust of the cosmic explosion that gave birth to time and space. The fact that it did not – the fact that life evolved out of nearly nothing, some 10 billion years after *the universe evolved literally out of nothing* – is a fact so staggering that I would be mad to attempt words to do it justice.

So, according to Dawkins the universe evolved "literally out of nothing." What ever happened to *nihilo ex nihilo* (nothing comes from nothing)? It seems Dawkins even prefers nothingness to God as creator.

Dawkins becomes worse, if possible, when speaking on God. He ponders that if God were to exist he must be "some complex physical inhabitant of the natural world." However, as the philosophical atheist Nagel points out, for those who believe in God he is not an "intramundane phenomenon" subject to the question, "*Who made God?*", rather:

> God, whatever he may be, is not a complex physical inhabitant of the natural world. The explanation of his existence as a chance concatenation of atoms is not a possibility to which we must find an alternative, because that is not what anybody means by God. If the God hypothesis makes sense at all, it offers a different kind of explanation from those of physical science (Nagel, *Dawkins and Atheism*, 2009).

Dawkins critiques and rejects a 'God' who is a secondary cause contingent on evolutionary theory. However, this is a straw-man God of his own invention, not the Christian God. God is not a secondary cause alongside other secondary causes. Rather, for Christians he is the primary cause who actualizes the cosmos and creates true secondary causes that have their own nature and act according to verifiable laws to give real explanations for events and occurrences in the universe.

God — complex or simple?

God's supposed 'complexity' is one of Dawkin's chief arguments against his existence. In fact, he claims it is his "central argument" and "main conclusion" (*The God Delusion*, pp. 187 & 189). At the end of Chapter 3 he succinctly presents his argument as follows:

> A designer God cannot be used to explain organized complexity because any God capable of designing anything would have to be complex enough to demand the same kind of explanation in his own right. God presents an infinite regress from which he cannot help us escape. This argument ... demonstrates that God, though not technically disprovable, is very, very improbable indeed.

Dawkins' God is, therefore, merely a finite scientific cause who for two reasons most probably does not exist: (i) because he needs to be more complex than anything in the sequence he has caused; (ii) any superhuman intelligence who is the author of evolution would in turn need to be the product of an evolutionary process authored by another superhuman intelligence, and so on *ad infinitum, ad absurdum*.

However, in saying the above Dawkins is guilty of contradicting his own promotion of Darwinism as the explanation for all living things. Dawkins states, "The theory of natural selection is genuinely simple" (*The God Delusion*, pp. 180). If natural selection can be simple, why not an intelligent creator God?

Dawkins' other mistake is to imagine that divine and human intelligence are modally the same, namely, that they are both purely material in function and evolutionary in origin, the only difference being that God's intelligence is much, much more powerful. Dawkins' argument would only be plausible if God was just like humans, except with a super body and super brain. What does Dawkins ultimately prove here? Nothing at all. As Hahn and Wiker (2008) conclude:

> It is only in Dawkins' treating God as having an evolved, material intelligence that allowed him the dubious luxury of discounting his existence as very, very improbable ... since God is by definition purely spiritual, then the contingency of material atom-shuffling is inapplicable, and therefore, the very idea of treating God as improbable is entirely misconstrued.

God is simple, meaning he is spiritual and made of no parts. He is eternal, self-existent (the uncaused Cause) and infinitely powerful and intelligent, knowing himself and all created things and the infinite array of possibilities in one divine idea, known in Christian theology as the Word. This is the God Dawkins should critique, not his own straw-man.

The argument from design

Dawkins categorically rejects design as an argument for the existence of God. As he states in *The God Delusion* (p. 79):

> The argument from design ... still sounds to many like the ultimate knockdown argument ... the mature Darwin blew it out of the water. There has probably never been a more devastating rout of popular belief by clever reasoning than Charles Darwin's destruction of the argument from design.

In the place of design Dawkins substitutes chance. His assumption is that the existence of chance variation and natural selection utterly excludes the possibility of design. But is such really the case? Can intelligence use chance events to achieve planned outcomes?

From the perspective of faith, the universe is as large and as old as it is so that both necessity and chance can operate to achieve the outcomes God wills. If the universe were simply deterministic there would be no room for human freedom. A universe that allows real chance is a universe where real freedom is possible. St Thomas Aquinas noted the tension between determinism and chance in the thirteenth century by posing the following dilemma:

If all things that are done here below, even chance events, are subject to divine providence (read: divine design), then, seemingly, either providence cannot be certain (read: there is no real design), or else all things happen by necessity (read: there is no real chance) (*Summa Contra Gentiles* 3:94).

This apparent dilemma is solved by distinguishing between two levels of causation, primary and secondary. God is the primary cause that causes all other being to be, including all secondary causes. Secondary causes correspond to what are usually called "laws of nature" and these include classical and statistical laws. Through the latter, God can achieve a desired outcome or design using chance events as a secondary cause.

Returning to the stated dilemma, St Thomas provides the following resolution:

> If God foresees that this event will be, it will happen ... But it will occur in the way that God foresaw that it would be. Now, he foresaw that it would occur contingently. So, it follows that, without fail, it will occur contingently and not necessarily (*Summa Contra Gentiles* 3:94).

Design and chance are, therefore, not mutually exclusive. In summary:

- God is primary cause, the cause of being.
- God creates secondary causes.
- Secondary causes include classical and statistical laws that can be understood and explained by science.
- Contingent events are random and are encompassed within verifiable statistical laws.
- God can and does use contingent events to arrive at foreseen determinate outcomes.
- Dawkin's rejection of design based on the existence of contingency, hence, has no foundation.

The deification of chance

Dawkin's intense desire to eradicate belief in God has led him to irrational conclusions concerning the powers of chance. For Dawkins, life and miracles are not the products of an all-powerful God but rather simply the chance outcomes of extremely improbable molecular events. Concerning miracles, Dawkins asserts:

> ... events that we commonly call miracles are not supernatural, but are part of a spectrum of more-or-less improbable natural events. A miracle, in other words, if it occurs at all, is a tremendous stroke of luck (*The Blind Watchmaker*, pp. 139).

Dawkins believes that extremely rare molecular events can lead to all sorts of natural 'miracles.' One example is the case of the waving marble statue:

> In the case of the marble statue, molecules in solid marble are continuously jostling against one another in random directions ... if, by sheer coincidence, all the molecules just happened to move in the same direction at the same moment, the hand would move ... In this way it is possible for a marble statue to wave at us (*The Blind Watchmaker*, pp. 159-160).

Another natural 'miracle' is the case of the jumping cow:

> It is theoretically possible for a cow to jump over the moon with something like the same probability (*Ibid.*).

In fact, according to Dawkins "Given infinite time, or infinite opportunities, anything is possible" (*The Blind Watchmaker*, p. 139). However, all Dawkins achieves by such an argument is to lead his readers into the absurdity of treating the impossible as possible in order to eliminate any possibility of the supernatural.

To believe that extremely improbable molecular events by themselves can also create life, one must believe that chance is as powerful as the idea of a creator God. But God can create instantaneously or over any length of time; chance requires extremely long periods of time to produce only meagre results against incredible odds. Despite such odds, Dawkins feels that he has got nothing to prove: "however improbable the origin of life might be, we know it happened on Earth because we are here" (*The God Delusion*, p. 137). This is lazy thinking on the part of Dawkins. One does not prove the creative power of chance simply by asserting the existence of life.

The reality, in fact, is quite the opposite. The very existence of life disproves the creative power of chance. For example, the odds of forming just one simple protein structure by chance are 12×10^{129} (or 12,000,000,000,000,000,000,000,000,000,000,000,000,000,000,000,000,000,000,000,000,000,000,000,000,000,000,000,000,000,000,000,000,000,000,000,000,000,000,000,000,000,000,000) to one against. The incredible odds against even the simplest life form being created by chance indicate that the chance production of higher life forms is *impossible* rather than improbable. This realization has led two other world-renowned atheists, Antony Flew (philosophical atheist) and Francis Crick (co-discoverer of DNA), eventually to despair in the creative power of chance in favor of an intelligent cause for life. Flew renounced atheism in favor of belief in God (albeit a deistic version who does not care to involve himself in human affairs), while Crick (similarly to Dawkins) has felt compelled to hypothesize about the possibility of 'panspermia,' or the seeding of life on earth by intelligent aliens.

In the final analysis, Dawkins' version of chance fails both as creator and miracle worker. The odds against chance having such powers are just too great. To believe in the improbable is one thing; to believe in the impossible by disguising it as improbable is another.

Overall, Dawkins' arguments relating to contingency, design and chance, among others, have led various scholars to dismiss his philosophy as "amateurish" and "weak" (Nagle, *The Fear of Religion*, 2006). According to the philosopher Alvin Plantinga:

> (Dawkins') forays into philosophy are at best sophomoric, but that would be unfair to sophomores; the fact is (grade inflation aside), many of his arguments would receive a failing grade in a sophomore philosophy class (*The Dawkins Confusion*, 2007).

Macabre moral philosophy

Dawkins' forays into moral philosophy are no better than his arguments against the proofs for the existence of God. As a fundamental starting point, Dawkins wishes "to build a society in which individuals cooperate generously and unselfishly towards a common good ... let us try to teach generosity and altruism, because we are born selfish" (*The Selfish Gene*, pp. 2-3). This sounds all well and good, however, the arch-evolutionist Dawkins admits that for such to occur we cannot rely on evolution because a "Darwinian society would be a Fascist state" (interview with *Die Presse*, 30 July, 2005). What other source, then, can there be for morality? Obviously, for the atheist Dawkins that source cannot be Christianity for there is no God and in any case Christianity is immoral. Such conclusions, though, raise multiple dilemmas. What basis is there for morality if both nature and the supernatural are discounted? Furthermore, without either a natural or supernatural basis for morality how can Dawkins declare Christianity or any other belief or thing to be moral or immoral?

Of further concern is Dawkins' praise of the Australian philosopher-ethicist Peter Singer (*The God Delusion*, p. 271). In his various writings, we find Singer, among other things, advocating:

- That all animals with "brain power" should be treated as moral equals with humans (i.e., the elimination of all species distinction, or "specism").
- Voluntary euthanasia on demand ("We cannot condemn euthanasia just because the Nazis did it").
- The termination of the lives of retarded, feeble-minded and handicapped persons without their consent.
- Abortion on demand.
- Infanticide up to twenty-eight days after the child's birth (regardless of the child's state of health).
- Bestiality ("Sex with animals does not always involve cruelty").

The list goes on and on. For Singer and Dawkins, all is permitted so long as pain is minimalized or eliminated. What is ultimately frightening for all people of faith and goodwill is the modern political tendency that has seen what was once prohibited become permitted and then soon afterwards mandated. We face having imposed an amoral universe where good and evil are arbitrarily determined by the will of the majority (read: dictatorship of relativism) or by the most powerful (read: fascism). We have much to fear about the future from Dawkins' atheism.

Misrepresentation of history

Dawkins often makes historical comments and judgments that are so filled with errors of fact that most honest High School teachers of history would be embarrassed. Why would an Oxford scholar, though, be such a poor historian? Dawkins' error-filled history is not due simply to an ignorance of facts; it is the product of his endeavor to build a case for atheism's supposed moral superiority over Christianity and religion in general. The following are just some examples of Dawkins' 'historical-moral' argument:

> I do not believe that there is an atheist in the world who would bulldoze Mecca – or Chartres, York Minster or Notre Dame, the Shwe Dagon, the temples of Kyoto or, of course, the Buddhas of Bamiyan (*The God Delusion*, p. 249).

> ... the mature Stalin was scathing about the Russian Orthodox Church, and about religion in general. But there is no evidence that his atheism motivated his brutality (*The God Delusion*, p. 309).

> I cannot think of any war that has been fought in the name of atheism. Why should it? ... Why should anyone go to war for the sake of an absence of belief? (*The God Delusion*, p. 316).

Contrary to Dawkins' assertions, there are numerous and mammoth examples in the twentieth century of atheist regimes and states going to war in order to eradicate belief and destroy places of worship. The widespread destruction of Orthodox and Catholic Churches in Russia and the Ukraine during the Soviet era is profusely attested. Furthermore, according to Time Magazine, 24 June, 2001:

In the Bolsheviks' first five years in power, 28 bishops and 1,200 priests were cut down by the red sickle. Stalin greatly accelerated the terror, and by the end of Khrushchev's rule, liquidations of clergy reached an estimated 50,000. After World War II, fierce but generally less bloody persecution spread into the Ukraine and the new Soviet bloc, affecting millions of Roman Catholics and Protestants as well as Orthodox.

On top of this, Lenin and Stalin ordered mass executions, induced widespread famines, initiated wars and practised enforced labor that collectively resulted in the deaths of nearly thirty million people. Countless tens of millions of others were victims of similar policies carried out in Maoist China, Cambodia, North Korea, Vietnam, Cuba and regimes in Eastern Europe. Such carnage was unknown before the advent of atheist regimes. At the same time, it cannot be argued that Marxism, more than atheism, was responsible for such misery as Marxism claims to be the fulfilment of atheist principles. The most famous Soviet dissident, Alexander Solzhenitsyn, who suffered many years' imprisonment in the infamous Siberian Gulag, concluded:

> I have spent well-nigh fifty years working on the history of our Revolution. In the process, I have read hundreds of books, collected hundreds of personal testimonies, and have already contributed eight volumes of my own towards the effort of clearing away the rubble left by that upheaval. But if I were asked today the main cause of the ruinous Revolution that has swallowed up some sixty million of our people, I could not put it more accurately than to repeat: "Men have forgotten God; that's why all this has happened" (Templeton Address, 1983).

So, while Dawkins rejects God and religion because religious people have tended to start wars and engage in destructive behavior, we find that the same repugnant behavior characterizes regimes led and controlled exclusively by atheists, the only difference being that atheist regimes have been guilty of war and destruction on a much greater scale. Sadly, Dawkins' version of history is an insult to historians, the countless victims of atheist ideology, and, ultimately, an insult to human intelligence.

Conclusion

Dawkins' stated mission on his website (RichardDawkins.net) "is to support scientific education, critical thinking and evidence-based understanding of the natural world in the quest to overcome religious fundamentalism, superstition, intolerance and human suffering." As it stands, however, Dawkins needs to be reminded of Nietzsche's warning, *"Be careful when you fight the monsters, lest you become one."* Dawkins' vitriol, mockery, smugness, misrepresentation of Christianity, deification of chance, poor philosophy, macabre morality, inaccurate history, etc., all collectively disqualify him from being ranked among true gentlemen and scholars. Instead, he comes across as no more than an ignorant and intolerant secular fundamentalist. Together, Christians and atheists, scientists and philosophers have critiqued and panned his works. Nevertheless, no personal animosity should be intended or directed towards Dawkins. He is deserving of our patience, prayers and charity no less than anyone else, so that one day he, like his former atheist contemporary Antony Flew, can declare ... *"I must say, there is a God!"*

Appendices

A. ECUMENICAL COUNCILS

Nicaea I	325
Constantinople I	381
Ephesus	431
Chalcedon	451
Constantinople II	553
Constantinople III	680
Nicaea II	787
Constantinople IV	869–70
Lateran I	1123
Lateran II	1139
Lateran III	1179
Lateran IV	1215
Lyons I	1245
Lyons II	1274
Vienne	1311–12
Constance	1414–18
Florence-Basel-Ferrara	1431–45
Lateran V	1512–17
Trent	1545–63
Vatican I	1869–70
Vatican II	1962–65

B. DOCTORS OF THE CHURCH

St Irenaeus of Lyons	+c.202
St Hilary of Poitiers	+368
St Ephrem of Edessa	+373
St Athanasius	+373
St Basil the Great	+379
St Cyril of Jerusalem	+386
St Gregory of Nazianzus	+c.390
St Ambrose of Milan	+397
St John Chrysostom	+407
St Jerome	+420
St Augustine of Hippo	+430
St Cyril of Alexandria	+444
St Peter Chrysologus	+450
St Leo I the Great	+461
St Gregory I the Great	+604
St Isidore of Seville	+636
St Bede the Venerable	+735
St John Damascene	+c.749
St Gregory of Narek	+1003
St Peter Damian	+1072
St Anselm	+1109
St Bernard of Clairvaux	+1153
St Hildegard of Bingen	+1179
St Anthony of Padua	+1231
St Thomas Aquinas	+1274
St Bonaventure	+1274
St Albert the Great	+1280
St Catherine of Siena	+1380
St Teresa of Avila	+1582
St John of the Cross	+1591
St John of Avila	+1591
St Peter Canisius	+1597
St Lawrence of Brindisi	+1619
St Robert Bellarmine	+1621
St Francis de Sales	+1622
St Alphonsus de Liguori	+1787
St Therese of the Infant Jesus	+1897

C. FATHERS OF THE CHURCH

Greek

St Anastasius Sinaita +700
St Andrew of Crete +740
St Archelaus +282
St Athanasius +373
Athenagoras +2nd c.
St Basil the Great +379
St Caesarius of Nazianzus +369
Clement of Alexandria +217
St Clement I of Rome +97
St Cyril of Alexandria +444
St Cyril of Jerusalem +386
Didymus the Blind +c.398
Diodore of Tarsus +392
St Dionysius the Great +264
St Epiphanius of Salamis +403
Eusebius of Caesarea +340
St Eustathius of Antioch +4th c.
St Firmilian +268
Gennadius I of Constantinople +5th c.
St Germanus +732
St Gregory of Nazianzus +390
St Gregory of Nyssa +395
St Gregory Thaumaturgus +268
Hermas +2nd Century
St Hippolytus of Rome +236
St Ignatius of Antioch +c.110
St Isidore of Pelusium +c.450
St John Chrysostom +407
St John Climacus +649
St John Damascene +749
St Julius I +352
St Justin Martyr +165
St Leontius of Byzantium +6th c.
St Macarius +c.390
St Maximus the Confessor +662
St Melito of Sardes +c.180
St Methodius of Olympus +311
St Nilus the Elder +c.430
Origen +254

St Polycarp +c.155
St Proclus +c.446
Pseudo-Dionysius Areopagite +6th c.
St Serapion +c.370
St Sophronius +638
Tatian the Syrian +2nd c.
Theodore of Mopsuestia +428
Theodoret of Cyrrhus +c.458
St Theophilus of Antioch +2nd

Latin

St Ambrose of Milan +397
Arnobius +330
St Augustine of Hippo +430
St Benedict of Nursia +550
St Caesarius of Arles +542
St John Cassian +435
St Celestine I +432
St Cornelius +253
St Cyprian of Carthage +258
St Damasus I +384
St Dionysius +268
St Ennodius +521
St Eucherius of Lyons +450
St Fulgentius +533
St Gregory of Elvira +c.392
St Gregory the Great +604
St Hilary of Poitiers +367
St Innocent I +417
St Irenaeus of Lyons +c.202
St Isidore of Seville +636
St Jerome +420
Lactantius +323
St Leo I the Great +461
Marius Mercator +451
Marius Victorinus +4th c.
Minucius Felix +2nd c.
Novatian +257

St Optatus Milevis +4th c.
St Pacian of Barcelona +390
St Pamphilus +309
St Paulinus of Nola +431
St Peter Chrysologus +450
St Phoebadius Agen +4th c.
St Rufinus of Aquileia +410
Salvian +5th c.
St Siricius +399
Tertullian +c.220
St Vincent of Lerins +c.450
St Nilus the Elder +c.430

Syriac

Aphraates +4th c.
St Ephrem of Edessa +373

D. POPES

St Peter (+c. 67)
St Linus (67–76)
St Anacletus (76–88)
St Clement (88–97)
St Evaristus (97–105)
St Alexander I (105–115)
St Sixtus I (115–125)
St Telesphorus (125–136)
St Hyginus (136–140)
St Pius I (140–155)
St Anicetus (155–166)
St Soter (166–175)
St Eleutherius (175–189)
St Victor I (189–199)
St Zephyrinus (199–217)
St Callistus (217–222)
St Urban I (222–230)
St Pontian (230–235)
St Anterus (235–236)
St Fabian (236–250)
St Cornelius (251–253)
St Lucius I (253–254)
St Stephen I (254–257)
St Sixtus II (257–258)
St Dionysius (259–268)
St Felix I (269–274)
St Eutychian (275–283)
St Caius (283–296)
St Marcellinus (296–304)
St Marcellus I (308–309)
St Eusebius (309)
St Melchiades (311–314)
St Sylvester I (314–335)
St Marcus (336)
St Julius I (337–352)
Liberius (352–366)
St Damasus I (366–384)
St Siricius (384–399)
St Anastasius I (399–401)
St Innocent I (401–417)
St Zozimus (417–418)
St Boniface I (418–422)
St Celestine (422–432)

St Sixtus III (432–440)
St Leo I the Great (440–461)
St Hilary (461–468)
St Simplicius (468–483)
St Felix III (II) (483–492)
St Gelasius I (492–496)
St Anastasius II (496–498)
St Symmachus (498–514)
St Hormisdas (514–523)
St John I (523–526)
St Felix IV (III) (526–530)
Boniface II (530–532)
John II (533–535)
St Agapetus I (535–536)
St Silverius (536–537)
Vigilius (537–555)
Pelagius I (556–561)
John III (561–574)
Benedict I (575–579)
Pelagius II (579–590)
St Gregory the Great (590–604)
Sabinian (604–606)
Boniface III (607)
St Boniface IV (608–615)
St Adeodatus I (615–618)
Boniface V (619–625)
Honorius I (625–638)
Severinus (640)
John IV (640–642)
Theodore I (642–649)
St Martin I (649–655)
St Eugenius I (654–657)
St Vitalian (657–672)
Adeodatus II (672–676)
Donus (676–678)
St Agatho (678–681)
St Leo II (682–683)
St Benedict II (684–685)
John V (685–686)
Conon (686–687)
St Sergius I (687–701)
John VI (701–705)

Defend the Faith!

John VII (705–707)
Sisinnius (708)
Constantine (708–715)
St Gregory II (715–731)
St Gregory III (731–741)
St Zachary (741–752)
Stephen II (III) (752–757)
St Paul I (757–767)
Stephen III (IV) (768–772)
Adrian I (772–795)
St Leo III (795–816)
Stephen IV (V) (816–817)
St Paschal I (817–824)
Eugene II (824–827)
Valentine (827)
Gregory IV (827–844)
Sergius II (844–847)
St Leo IV (847–855)
Benedict III (855–858)
St Nicholas I (858–867)
Adrian II (867–872)
John VIII (872–882)
Marinus I (882–884)
St Adrian III (884–885)
Stephen V (VI) (885–891)
Formosus (891–896)
Stephen VI (VII) (896–897)
Boniface VI (896)
Romanus (897)
Theodore II (897)
John IX (898–900)
Benedict IV (900–903)
Leo V (903)
Sergius III (904–911)
Anastasius III (911–913)
Landus (913–914)
John X (914–928)
Leo VI (928)
Stephen VII (VIII) (928–931)
John XI (931–935)
Leo VII (936–939)
Stephen VIII (IX) (939–942)
Marinus II (942–946)
Agapetus II (946–955)
John XII (955–964)
Leo VIII (963–965)

Benedict V (964–966)
John XIII (965–972)
Benedict VI (973–974)
Benedict VII (974–983)
John XIV (983–984)
John XV (985–996)
Gregory V (996–999)
Sylvester II (999–1003)
John XVII (1003)
John XVIII (1004–1009)
Sergius IV (1009–1012)
Benedict VIII (1012–1024)
John XIX (1024–1032)
Benedict IX (1032–1044)
Sylvester III (1045)
Benedict IX (1045)
Gregory VI (1045–1046)
Clement II (1046–1047)
Benedict IX (1047–1048)
Damasus II (1048)
St Leo IX (1049–1054)
Victor II (1055–1057)
Stephen IX (X) (1057–1058)
Nicholas II (1059–1061)
Alexander II (1061–1073)
St Gregory VII (1073–1085)
Bl. Victor III (1086–1087)
Bl. Urban II (1088–1099)
Paschal II (1099–1118)
Gelasius II (1118–1119)
Callistus II (1119–1124)
Honorius II (1124–1130)
Innocent II (1130–1143)
Celestine II (1143–1144)
Lucius II (1144–1145)
Bl. Eugene III (1145–1153)
Anastasius IV (1153–1154)
Adrian IV (1154–1159)
Alexander III (1159–1181)
Lucius III (1181–1185)
Urban III (1185–1187)
Gregory VIII (1187)
Clement III (1187–1191)
Celestine III (1191–1198)
Innocent III (1198–1216)
Honorius III (1216–1227)

Popes

Gregory IX (1227–1241)
Celestine IV (1241)
Innocent IV (1243–1254)
Alexander IV (1254–1261)
Urban IV (1261–1264)
Clement IV (1265–1268)
Bl. Gregory X (1271–1276)
Bl. Innocent V (1276)
Adrian V (1276)
John XXI (1276–1277)
Nicholas III (1277–1280)
Martin IV (1281–1285)
Honorius IV (1285–1287)
Nicholas IV (1288–1292)
St Celestine V (1294)
Boniface VIII (1294–1303)
Bl. Benedict XI (1303–1304)
Clement V (1305–1314)
John XXII (1316–1334)
Benedict XII (1334–1342)
Clement VI (1342–1352)
Innocent VI (1352–1362)
Bl. Urban V (1362–1370)
Gregory XI (1370–1378)
Urban VI (1378–1379)
Boniface IX (1389–1404)
Innocent VII (1404–1406)
Gregory XII (1406–1415)
Martin V (1417–1431)
Eugene IV (1431–1447)
Nicholas V (1447–1455)
Callistus III (1455–1458)
Pius II (1458–1464)
Paul II (1464–1471)
Sixtus IV (1471–1484)
Innocent VIII (1484–1492)
Alexander VI (1492–1503)
Pius III (1503)
Julius II (1503–1513)
Leo X (1513–1521)
Adrian VI (1522–1523)
Clement VII (1523–1534)
Paul III (1534–1549)
Julius III (1550–1555)
Marcellus II (1555)
Paul IV (1555–1559)

Pius IV (1559–1565)
St Pius V (1566–1572)
Gregory XIII (1572–1585)
Sixtus V (1585–1590)
Urban VII (1590)
Gregory XIV (1590–1591)
Innocent IX (1591)
Clement VIII (1592–1605)
Leo XI (1605)
Paul V (1605–1621)
Gregory XV (1621–1623)
Urban VIII (1623–1644)
Innocent X (1644–1655)
Alexander VII (1655–1667)
Clement IX (1667–1669)
Clement X (1670–1676)
Bl. Innocent XI (1676–1689)
Alexander VIII (1689–1691)
Innocent XII (1691–1700)
Clement XI (1700–1721)
Innocent XIII (1721–1724)
Benedict XIII (1724–1730)
Clement XII (1730–1740)
Benedict XIV (1740–1758)
Clement XIII (1758–1769)
Clement XIV (1769–1774)
Pius VI (1775–1799)
Pius VII (1800–1823)
Leo XII (1823–1829)
Pius VIII (1829–1830)
Gregory XVI (1831–1846)
Bl. Pius IX (1846–1878)
Leo XIII (1878–1903)
St Pius X (1903–1914)
Benedict XV (1914–1922)
Pius XI (1922–1939)
Pius XII (1939–1958)
St John XXIII (1958–1963)
St Paul VI (1963–1978)
John Paul I (1978)
St John Paul II (1978–2005)
Benedict XVI (2005–2013)
Francis (2013–present)

Further Reading

Archbishop. M. Sheehan, *Apologetics and Catholic Doctrine* (The Saint Austin Press, London, revised by Father Peter Joseph, 2010).

Carl E. Olson, *Will Catholics be "Left Behind"* (Ignatius Press, 2003).

Dave Armstrong, *A Biblical Defense of Catholicism* (Sophia Institute Press, 2003).

Father Frank Chacon and Jim Burnham, *Beginning Apologetics — How to Explain and Defend the Catholic Faith*; *Beginning Apologetics II: Answering Jehovah's Witnesses and Mormons* (San Juan Catholic Seminars 1996).

Father Jacques Jomier, *The Bible and the Qur'an* (Ignatius Press, 2002).

Father John O'Brien, *The Faith of Millions* (W. H. Allen, 1952).

Father Luigi Gambero, *Mary and the Fathers of the Church* (Ignatius Press, 1999).

Father Stenhouse MSC, *Catholic Answers to Bible Christians* (Chevalier Press, 1988).

Francis J. Beckwith, *Return to Rome* (Brazos Press, 2009).

Mgr Paul Glenn, *Apologetics* (Herder Book Co., 1931).

Mike Aquilina, *The Fathers of the Church* (Our Sunday Visitor, 1999).

Mike Aquilina, *The Mass of the Early Christians* (Our Sunday Visitor, 2001).

Henry Bettenson, *Documents of the Christian Church* (Oxford University Press, 1967).

Henry Bettenson, *The Later Christian Fathers* (Oxford University Press, 1970).

John Francis Coffey, *The Gospel According to Jehovah's Witnesses* (The Polding Press, Melbourne, 1979).

Karl Keating, *Catholicism and Fundamentalism* (Ignatius Press, 1988).

Karl Keating, *What Catholics Really Believe* (Ignatius Press, 1995).

Karl Keating, *The Usual Suspects* (Ignatius Press, 2000).

Ludwig Ott, *Fundamentals of Catholic Dogma* (The Mercier Press, Ltd., 1958).

Mark Shea, *Making Senses Out of Scripture* (Basilica Press, 1999).

Mark Shea, *Mother of the Son Vols. 1-2-3* (Catholic Answers, 2009).

Patrick Madrid, *Surprised by Truth* (Basilica Press, 1994).

Patrick Madrid, *Surprised by Truth 2* (Basilica Press, 2000).

Patrick Madrid, *Any Friend of God is a Friend of Mine* (Basilica Press, 1996).

Patrick Madrid, *Pope Fiction* (Basilica Press, 1999).

Patrick Madrid, *Where is that in the Bible?* (Our Sunday Visitor, 2001).

Rev. Henry G. Graham, *Where We Got the Bible* (TAN Books and Publishers Inc. 1977).

Rev. John Laux, *Church History* (TAN Books and Publishers Inc., 1989).

Robert Sungenis, *Not by Scripture Alone* (Queenship Publishing, 1997).

Further Reading

Robert Sungenis, *Not by Faith Alone* (Queenship Publishing, 1998).

Robert Sungenis, *Not by Bread Alone* (Queenship Publishing, 2000).

Rod Bennett, *Four Witnesses – The Early Church in Her Own Words* (Ignatius Press, 2002).

Rumble and Carty, *Radio Replies* (TAN Books and Publishers Inc., 1979).

Scott Butler, Norman Dahlgren, David Hess, *Jesus, Peter & the Keys* (Queenship Publishing, 1996).

Scott Hahn, *Rome Sweet Home* (co-written with Kimberly Hahn), (Ignatius Press, 1993).

Scott Hahn, *The Lamb's Supper: The Mass as Heaven on Earth*, (Doubleday, 1999).

Scott Hahn (and Benjamin Wiker), *Answering the New Atheism: Dismantling Dawkins's Case Against God*, (Emmaus Road Publishing, 2008).

Scott Hahn, *Reasons to Believe: How to Understand, Explain, and Defend the Catholic Faith*, (Doubleday, 2007).

Stephen K. Ray, *Crossing the Tiber* (Ignatius Press, 1997).

Tim Staples, *Nuts & Bolts: A Practical, How-To Guide for Explaining & Defending the Catholic Faith* (Catholic Word, 1999).

William A. Jurgens, *The Faith of the Early Fathers* (Liturgical Press, 1970).

William Thomas Walsh, *Characters of the Inquisition* (TAN Books and Publishers Inc., 1987).

About the Author

Dr Robert M. Haddad holds qualifications in law, theology, philosophy and religious education, namely, a LL.B (USyd.), Grad. Cert. in RE (Charles Sturt Uni.), Grad. Dip. Ed. (ACU), Grad. Dip. in Teacher Ed. (College of Teachers, London), AMLP (Oxford), MA Theo. Studies (UNDA – University Medalist), MRelEd (UNDA), M. Phil (ACU) and a Ph.D. (UNDA). For his Ph.D Robert researched the 'new apologetics' and constructed an apologetics curriculum for Catholic secondary students.

In addition to his studies, Robert has authored various books, including *Lord of History Series*, *The Apostles' Creed*, *Law and Life*, *The Family and Human Life*, *The Case for Christianity – St Justin Martyr's Arguments for Religious Liberty and Judicial Justice*, *Answering the Anti-Catholic Challenge*, *1001 Reasons Why It's Great to be Catholic!*, *Always Be Prepared*, and *Jesus Played Marbles*.

From 1990-2005 Robert worked at St Charbel's College, Sydney, teaching Religion and History. He held the positions of Year Coordinator and Religious Education Coordinator concurrently for ten years and was Assistant Principal (Welfare) for a total of six years.

From 2006-2008 Robert worked as the Convener of the Catholic Chaplaincy at Sydney University. He was also lecturer at the Centre for Thomistic Studies from 1996-2008, teaching Apologetics, Church Fathers and Church History, a lecturer at the Adult Catholic Education Centre from 2010-2013, and assisted part-time with *Lumen Verum Apologetics* from 1996 to 2020. In addition, from 2007 to 2019 Robert worked as a sessional lecturer at the University of Notre Dame (Sydney) in Theology and Religious Education.

From 2009-2012, Robert was the Director of the Confraternity of Christian Doctrine (Sydney) and in that capacity was the chief editor of the revised *Christ our Light and Life* (3rd Edition) religious education K-12 curriculum used by Catholic students in state schools as well as the *Gratia Series* sacramental programs for children preparing for Reconciliation, First Holy Communion, and Confirmation in the Archdiocese of Sydney. In 2014 Robert edited a new RCIA resource for use in Catholic schools in the same Archdiocese entitled *Initiate!*

In 2014, Robert was awarded an Australia Day Award by the Australia Day Council of New South Wales for his overall contribution to education and in 2020 the Dempsey Medal by Archbishop Anthony Fisher OP for his work in evangelisation. Currently, he is the Manager, Network Catholic Identity for Sydney Catholic Schools with responsibility for staff faith formation, family evangelisation and youth ministry in 152 primary and secondary schools.

Other Works by the Author

Introduction to the Greatest Fathers of the Church (Parousia Media, 1999)

A Seat at the Supper (General Editor, self-published, 2001)

Introduction to Early Church History (Parousia Media, 2002)

The Apostles' Creed (Parousia Media, 2004)

Law and Life (Parousia Media, 2004)

The Case for Christianity – On St Justin Martyr's Arguments for Religious Liberty and Judicial Justice (Connor Court Publishing, 2009)

The Family and Human Life (2nd Ed. co-authored with Bernard Toutounji, Parousia Media, 2011)

Answering the Anti-Catholic Challenge (General Editor and author of ch. 3, Modotti Press, 2012)

1001 Reasons Why It's Great to be Catholic! (Dynamic Catholic, 2015)

Christ our Light and Life (General Editor 3rd Edition, 2012) religious education curriculum K-12 used by Catholic students in government schools throughout the state of New South Wales.

Gratia Series (General Editor, 2012) sacramental programs for children preparing for Reconciliation, First Holy Communion, and Confirmation in the Archdiocese of Sydney.

Initiate! (General Editor, CEO Sydney Publications, 2014), a RCIA resource for use in Catholic schools in the Archdiocese of Sydney.

Jesus Played Marbles (CEO Sydney Publications, 2015)

Always Be Prepared (Parousia Media, 2021)

www.ingramcontent.com/pod-product-compliance
Lightning Source LLC
Chambersburg PA
CBHW071850290426
44110CB00013B/1090